DATE DUE

June 25, 2015	
April 19, 2016	

BRODART, CO.   Cat. No. 23-221

FOLLOW THE MONEY

How George W. Bush
and the Texas Republicans
Hog-Tied America

JOHN ANDERSON

SCRIBNER
NEW YORK   LONDON   TORONTO   SYDNEY

SCRIBNER
A Division of Simon & Schuster
1230 Avenue of the Americas
New York, NY 10020

First Scribner hardcover edition September 2007

SCRIBNER and design are trademarks of
Macmillan Library Reference USA, Inc., used under license
by Simon & Schuster, the publisher of this work.

For information about special discounts for bulk purchases,
please contact Simon & Schuster Special Sales:
1-800-456-6798 or business@simonandschuster.com.

DESIGNED BY KYOKO WATANABE
Text set in Stempel Garamond

Manufactured in the United States of America

1   3   5   7   9   10   8   6   4   2

Library of Congress Cataloging-in-Publication Data is available.

ISBN-13: 978-0-7432-8643-5
ISBN-10: 0-7432-8643-X

To the memory of my father
Charles Wyatt Anderson,
fifth-generation Texan
And for Hilary, Charlie, and my mother

CONTENTS

Contents

The committee did not need a Deep Throat to tell us to follow the money.

—*Senator Byron Dorgan of North Dakota, vice chairman of the 2006 Senate Indian Affairs Committee, investigating the scandal involving Republican lobbyist Jack Abramoff*

The government is us. . . . You and me!

—*President Theodore Roosevelt, 1902*

✳

Third World Capital

The thing you have to remember about Texas, a lawyer there remarked to me recently, "is that it's a Third World country, the capital city of which is Houston."

The nominal capital of Texas is, in fact, Austin, located some 163 miles to the west of Houston. But Austin, as my friend said, is "too little"—a mere 718,912 in population—"too liberal and too educated" to mirror properly the state it purports to represent. Not only is the state's government located there but also the flagship branch of the University of Texas, with some fifty thousand students and sixteen thousand faculty. Austin is compact, startlingly beautiful, and infused with a sweet, laid-back character.

Houston is none of these things.

The vast sprawl that is Houston grew up around what is today a twenty-five-mile-long complex of docks, warehouses, and industrial parks. With more than 200 million tons of cargo moving through it annually, the Port of Houston is the nation's second largest. Running west to east, the Houston Ship Channel carries petrochemical products past belching refineries and into the warm waters of the Gulf of Mexico.

More than six hundred square miles in area, much of it barely above sea level, and occupying a fetid, mosquito-infested plain, Houston lacks only malaria to be a torrid Latin American coastal city like

Guayaquil in Ecuador. Today, more than half the population is non-white: 37 percent of Houstonians are Hispanic in origin, 25 percent are African-American. The city they inhabit is one of the most ozone-polluted areas in the country. Contributing to their distress is the fact that Houston is the largest city in the United States without zoning regulations. Here, a massive billboard; there a strip club; and over there, a residential neighborhood. In all likelihood, a rather poor, black residential neighborhood.

This is Houston, a city of incredible riches and incredible poverty, the squalid housing of the historically black Fifth Ward seemingly as far from the palatial spreads of the famed River Oaks section as is Mars from Earth.

As the capital of a Third World state within the United States, Houston looms large. Which is also a way of saying that if you want to understand America today—the scandals rippling through Washington, the moral collapse of the Bush administration—you have to understand Texas, and to understand Texas, you have to understand Houston.

Houston is big. The city's population has edged to just over 2 million people, which makes it our nation's fourth largest, behind only New York, Los Angeles, and Chicago. Meanwhile, Houston is second only to New York as a headquarters for Fortune 500 companies. The amount of wealth held by Houston's leading citizens, many of whom own those palatial spreads in River Oaks, is correspondingly staggering. Find yourself stuck in traffic during rush hour on one of Houston's ten-lane freeways, and you'll notice the many luxury cars, most of them foreign, not just Cadillacs and Lexuses, but BMWs and Benzes, Volvos and Saabs, and what seems to be a endless supply of Mercedes SUVs. There is money aplenty in this town, its leading citizens truly the masters of Houston's universe.

Their world, the world of power and privilege, lies at the very heart of downtown Houston. Anchored by a fifteen-block section of Louisiana Street, this area of skyscrapers, many designed by the late Philip Johnson or I. M. Pei, is dense with corporate and legal power.

On the eastern edge rises the baseball stadium, Minute Maid Park (the former Enron Field), where the Astros play and where former president and Mrs. George H. W. Bush attend as guests of the owners. The Bushes, of course, sit behind home plate.

In the midst of downtown, at 1111 Louisiana Street, stands One Reliant Plaza, home of Reliant Energy. Reliant is the nexus, where the energy business, the downtown law firms, and the Republican Party come together. Executives at Reliant—which sprang from a rich dinosaur, the former Houston Lighting & Power, a traditional electric company—prospered wildly from the 2000 California "energy crisis." Eventually, Reliant came close to failing, but, unlike Enron, never went into bankruptcy. Across the parking lot from Reliant Energy is One Shell Plaza. Its occupants: the powerful Baker Botts law firm and Shell Oil (the American refining subsidiary of Royal Dutch Shell), a company that recorded a record $5.28 billion in profits in 2006 alone. Four blocks to the south stands what remains of Enron, the corrupt heart of the downtown. Dynegy Corp., Enron's great and hated rival in the energy-trading business, is just across the street.

It was here, in downtown Houston, a world inscribed by the energy companies and the law firms that service them, in the social whirl of Rice University just a few dozen blocks away on Main Street, and in the schools, clubs, churches, banks, real estate agencies, and restaurants, that the operatives of the Texas Republican Party went hunting for money and power in the 1990s, both of which they found in unprecedented amounts. Once they leveraged Houston, they could get the whole state. It was here, and in the Texas State House in Austin, that the representatives of George W. Bush—not the least of whom was Karl Rove, the younger Bush's "brain"—worked out in Texas the outline for what they intended to do to the country as a whole if only they could first make George W. Bush governor and then president.

Yet for a complete accounting of Houston's symbols and institutions of power, one would have to take a short cab ride from downtown to a quieter corner of the Rice campus, where, astride a marshy plain, sits a perfect little jewel box of a building: the James A. Baker III Institute for Public Policy.

Much of the work of the so-called Baker Commission, the ten-member bipartisan Iraq Study Group (ISG) quietly took place over many months last year. Here too that recommendations in the ISG's report, *The Way Forward,* were put to paper. For much of 2006, the little-known but highly influential Baker Institute was a beehive of activity, where policymakers met to contemplate not so much "the way forward" but "the way out" of Iraq.

The Baker Institute is, after all, not an "institute for policy studies," but an "institute for policy," which suggests something rather different: a center for affirmative, hands-on, policy-engendering work, the Texas-style antithesis to an East Coast–Ivy League approach. Consider the Baker Institute's advisory board. The membership includes a former secretary of energy (Charles Duncan, who served in the Carter administration) and no less than three former secretaries of state (James A. Baker III, Madeleine Albright, and Colin Powell). The director, Edward Djerejian, is a former ambassador to two of the world's leading tinderboxes, Israel and Syria. While plenty of academics teach at the Baker Institute, teaching is only one focus. Policymaking—American foreign-policy making—is another.

The jewel box—some have called it the Taj Ma Jim, though in reality its architecture seems to be imbued with a more or less Mideastern or Near Eastern character—faces another impressively regal new building on the Rice University campus: the sprawling Jesse H. Jones Graduate School of Management.

The placement of the two buildings could not be more appropriate—or more symbolic. For while Jesse Jones was the representative Houston man of affairs of his generation—roughly the first half of the twentieth century—James A. Baker III has played a similar role for the past quarter century or more. Where Jones had been an entrepreneur, newspaper publisher, and New Dealer, Baker is a lawyer, behind-the-scenes politico, and diplomat. It matters little that Jones was a Democrat and Baker is a Republican, for, at heart, both became conservatives of the downtown business-establishment variety.

Sculptured bulls and bears guard the doors to the Jones School, a not very subtle reminder that Houston has always been about "bidness," having begun life as a coastal railroad terminus, the Southwestern outpost of Wall Street interests. The exhibits lining the hallways of the

Jones School tell another story: of the rise of an indigenous class of mostly self-made Texas millionaires, big ranchers and timber barons, oil-field wildcatters, and entrepreneurs of all sorts—and the professional class, the doctors and lawyers and accountants who serviced them.

Jesse Jones was the big man of his day, owner of the dominant newspaper, the *Houston Chronicle*, head of the Reconstruction Finance Corporation (the New Deal's celebrated RFC)—a role that made "Uncle Jesse" the nation's banker of last resort during some of the worst years of the Depression—and secretary of commerce under Franklin D. Roosevelt. Even among the other big men in town—such as the construction magnates Herman and George Brown of Brown & Root (part of today's Halliburton), who were the sugar daddies of Lyndon B. Johnson—Jones was the towering figure.* At a time when a new car cost $420, a new house $7,109, a gallon of gas 11¢, and a loaf of bread 10¢, Jones was a millionaire many times over. Until Roosevelt fired him in 1945, Jones thought he might even one day succeed "the Boss." He was right about much, but wrong about that.

James Addison Baker III, scion of the city's first family of lawyers, briefly toyed with the idea of running for president. In the end, he passed. Baker's genius—whether as White House chief of staff, treasury secretary, Republican presidential campaign manager, secretary of state, and 2000 Florida presidential vote-recount manager—has been of another sort, lying in closed-door maneuverings and artful compromises, flying beneath—far beneath—the radar as often as possible.

Jim Baker has long been noted for being diplomatic and composed, but also proud—and not destitute of vanity. The foyer to the Baker Institute is meant to impress, and it does. Here are to be found a few of Baker's worldwide honors, many of them in the form of beribboned medals: the commemorative medal struck in gold and bronze by the U.S. Mint in honor of Baker's service as the sixty-seventh secretary of the treasury; the Gold Cross of Merit of the Holy Sepulchre of

---

*One of Jones's properties was the Lamar Hotel, whose Suite 8F was occupied by George Brown. The "8F Crowd" included Brown, Jones, their closest associates—and Lyndon B. Johnson. The Lamar Hotel was torn down in July 1983. On its site today sits the headquarters of Reliant Energy.

Jerusalem Award for Mideast Peace; the Grand Cross First Class of the
Order of Merit of the Federal Republic of Germany (awarded by Ger-
man president Richard von Weizsäcker); the Decoration of the Special
Class by the State of Kuwait; the Zayed the First Order of the United
Arab Emirates (1998); all the way down to the Order of Liberty, given
in honor of the tenth anniversary of democracy in Mongolia.

There are photographs of Jim Baker with the presidents he has
served, most notably his fellow Houstonian and longtime tennis partner, George H. W. Bush. Photographs too of Baker with Colin Powell and UN secretary-general Kofi Annan.

Also to be found, carved in bronze, is a list of the donors who contributed to the building of the Taj Ma Jim, some of them anonymous,
but for the most part a who's who of Houston, circa 2000. Powerful
as these figures are in the behind-the-scenes world of business and
politics, few have names that would ring bells with the American
public.

The corporate donors are another matter entirely: the Coca-Cola
Foundation, the Shell Oil Company Foundation, Conoco, Coopers &
Lybrand, the Annenberg Foundation, the Brown Foundation, Ford
Motor Company, the Archer Daniels Midland Foundation, Penzoil
Co., AT&T, Southwestern Bell Telephone Company, Dresser Indus-
tries, and McKinsey & Co., among them. What exactly James A. Baker
III did to earn the financial gratitude of the likes of these is unanswered
by the tombstone.

Buried among the many other corporate names is one of particular
interest: the Carlyle Group, the multibillion-dollar international
investment fund whose investors include Arab princes and potentates
and whose principal advisers have included former president George
H. W. Bush, former British prime minister John Major—and former
secretary of state James A. Baker III.

A few of the corporate donors, of course, are no longer in business:
Enron Corp. and its accountants, Arthur Andersen LLP, for example.
Other givers are still very much in business, among them the govern-
ment of Kuwait—saved from Saddam Hussein during the first Persian
Gulf War by a military coalition led by President George H. W. Bush
and his secretary of state, James A. Baker III. The Kuwait Foundation

for the Advancement of Science has its name prominently inscribed on the list of donors.

Still, on a bone-chilling, early-December day in 2005, the most revealing item on display at the Baker Institute is neither a photograph nor a medal, nor the names on the bronze plaque, but is instead page after page displayed in a glass case, each page marked TOP SECRET, the word-for-word transcription of a meeting held prior to the first Gulf War between Secretary of State Baker and his Iraqi counterpart, Foreign Minister Tariq Aziz.

It was there that Baker warned Saddam Hussein via Aziz that, should the Iraqi army resort to the use of weapons of mass destruction, the coalition forces were prepared to reply in a kind unspecified, but starkly threatening. The warning worked. Diplomacy worked.

By December 2005, the message in the glass case seemed obvious. With its chaotic aftermath fast spiraling into civil war, the second Iraq war—the neocon-dreamed-up Iraq adventure—had failed miserably. The thing was a fiasco. And this was Jim Baker's way of saying so.

The fact that the institute displays official U.S. government documents was telling. Like it or not, Houston, once a mere outpost of Wall Street and of the old-fashioned "Eastern interests," was now vying with New York and Washington to be the nation's political center of gravity.

And, as with the 2000 election of President George W. Bush, you could thank Baker—and those little-known, but vastly well heeled Texas Republicans whose names are inscribed on the gleaming bronze plaque in his palace—for it.

As I left the Baker Institute behind me that day in December 2005 and turned onto Rice Boulevard—a neighborhood of graceful Tudor and Georgian mansions, at least one sporting a huge Texas flag—I found myself reflecting on the state of the state. Clearly, no one was hurting among these well-heeled Houston Republicans this Christmas. Santa, one could say, was full of good cheer. Both houses of the Texas state legislature were in the Republicans' pockets. The governor was a pen stroke waiting to be added to whatever legislation was put in front of him. The lieutenant governor, the attorney general, the speaker of the state house of representatives, the land commissioner, and even the agriculture commissioner were all Republicans. The state courts were also solidly Republican, unanimously so in the case of the state supreme court. The federal courts, at both the district and appellate levels, were largely presided over by Republican judges, appointed for life. Both U.S. senators were Republican. The Texas delegation to the U.S. House of Representatives stood at twenty-one Republicans and only thirteen Democrats. No one seemed to believe that one of those Texas representatives, House majority leader Tom DeLay, was in any kind of real trouble, even after he'd been indicted on felony charges by a grand jury in Austin. And indicted Washington lobbyist Jack Abramoff might just as well not have existed. No one even seemed to know or care that Abramoff and DeLay had once been connected at the hips.

It was Christmastime, and the Texas Republicans were in hog heaven. Texas was theirs, and the good old USA seemed next in line.

Follow the money trail, and you'll see what they did—and how they almost got away with it.

FOLLOW THE MONEY

CHAPTER ONE

✮

The Changing of the Guard

Flash back to the spring of 1994. Between then and now, a vast chasm yawns across the political surface of Texas. It's hard to believe, but what seems like an aeon of political change took place in little more than a decade. But change it did.

Back then, Texas was a different place.

This was the political landscape of Texas as the 1994 election cycle loomed: The state house of representatives was Democratic; the state senate was Democratic. The state supreme court and most of the lesser state courts were Democratic. All these too were Democrats: Governor Ann Richards; Lieutenant Governor Bob Bullock; Attorney General Dan Morales; and Land Commissioner Garry Mauro. It was a deep bench the Democrats fielded—and an ambitious one. Some among them dreamed of being governor themselves; others dreamed of the Senate; one, at least, might have had higher ambitions still. None of their dreams were to be fulfilled.

The Texas congressional delegation stood at twenty-one Democrats and nine Republicans in the U.S. House of Representatives. Among these were some of the most powerful and senior members of Congress, led by the veteran Judiciary Committee chairman Jack Brooks of Beaumont.

Only in the U.S. Senate were the Texas Republicans dominant. And the two serving senators from the Lone Star State were widely accorded to be among the least impressive of its members: the thin-lipped, whiny-voiced Phil Gramm, his native, nasal Georgia accent never having left him, and Kay Bailey Hutchison, elected only the year before in a special election to replace the long-serving mandarin Democrat Lloyd Bentsen. Gramm, with his delusions of grandeur unabated, yet with his presidential aspirations fast going up in smoke, was among the least liked by his fellow senators, while Hutchison, for all her personal charm, was a very junior senator. Neither had more than limited influence. Neither was ever going to be a major presence in the U.S. Senate.

How then is it possible that such cataclysmic change came to Texas—and in such a short time?

True, Texas had had a Republican governor in its recent past—the first since the post–Civil War age of Reconstruction, millionaire oilman William P. Clements of Dallas. Clements served two nonconsecutive terms as governor (1979–83 and 1987–91) and was widely judged a fail-ure both times. Arrogant to the point of abrasiveness, Clements made few friends in Austin and proved a poor public face to put on the rise of Texas Republicanism, but he was colorful.

The football-loving Clements had also served as chairman of the Southern Methodist University trustees. There, he helped preside over one of the worst scandals in NCAA history. Players on the SMU Mus-tangs football team—52-19-1 between 1980 and 1986—had, it turned out, been paid thousands of dollars from a slush fund run by boosters. The NCAA responded by handing SMU the so-called death penalty, barring the team from bowl games and television appearances for two years and reducing football scholarships by fifty-five over four years—and mandating an entire year's absence (1987) from the play-ing field.

Ironically, Clements's political comeback could be traced to foot-ball. His pallid successor as governor, Democrat Mark White, follow-ing the advice of Dallas billionaire Ross Perot, had rammed a "no-pass, no-play" law through the state legislature—and had lived to pay for it with his political hide. Football-loving Texans of the Clements variety were horrified to learn that high school athletes would be barred from playing when the only sin they had committed was earning a failing grade or two in class. Largely on the basis of public resentment over no-pass, no-play, Mark White found himself bounced from office.

After his second term, Clements called it a day. His handpicked successor, multimillionaire Texas oilman Clayton Williams, running a well-financed, "good ole boy" campaign, was expected to cruise to victory. At times, Williams held as much as a twenty-point lead over his Democratic opponent, State Treasurer Ann Richards. But then "Claytie" Williams self-destructed, first by refusing to shake hands with Richards, then by equating a sudden Texas thunderstorm to rape, joking with reporters that "as long as it's inevitable, you might as well lie back and enjoy it." That was the day that the bumptious Williams lost the emerging "soccer mom" generation of middle-class, suburban Texas women—and with it the 1990 gubernatorial election as well.

Even so, Richards squeaked to victory, with less than 50 percent of the vote. The argument could be made—and has been made—that Ann Richards's 1990 electoral win was a fluke, merely putting off by four years Republican rule in Texas. That argument, however, fails to consider the widespread popular support enjoyed by Richards for most of her governorship. In truth, the state had never had a politician quite like her. She was neither overbearing (like Clements) nor bland (like Mark White). Richards, the former wife of a legendary Texas labor and civil rights lawyer, was, instead, spunky and outspoken, humorous and energetic.

Richards's keynote address to the 1988 Democratic National Convention had been a sensation. Referring to Republican presidential candidate George H. W. Bush, Richards had uttered the memorable line "Poor George, he can't help it. . . . He was born with a silver foot in his mouth." She had also earned a lifetime of enmity from the Bush family and their followers.

The Richards governorship was notable for more than mere acerbic wit. The long-stagnant Texas economy, stimulated by the new governor's economic revitalization programs, began to grow again. Aggressive audits were said to have saved the state some $6 billion in the same period. As governor, Richards took on problems that other

Texas governors had passed on, beginning with an attempt to reform the state's notoriously overcrowded prison system; a very un-Texas-like attempt to reduce the sale of semiautomatic weapons; and, most problematic of all, an effort to reform the way in which public schools were funded. The so-called Robin Hood plan sought to channel money from the state's richest school districts into its poorest districts, most of them black and Latino in population.

Ann Richards was liberal, without being too liberal—her pragmatic progressivism masked by the thick and distinctly Texan accent in which she set forth her latest program. Richards always had a narrow pathway to walk politically. Many of her programs were controversial—none more so than the Robin Hood plan—and Richards made many friends and many enemies along the way. It did not help that Richards was a tough taskmaster, known for driving her staff hard, nor that she refused to make kindly with some in the local media. In the words of the spouse of a high-ranking *Texas Monthly* editor, "Ann was never very inviting." Richards's attitude was, the spouse added, in studied contrast with that of her successor, who made a point of having the panjan-drums of the press "over to the mansion."

But govern Ann Richards did—and in a state where the governor's powers are derived as much from personal persuasion as from statute. She was surely bigger than life.

Her Republican opponent in the 1994 election was anything but. Indeed, apart from bearing a famous name and a reputation for having helped rescue the Texas Rangers baseball team from its notoriously cheap (and wildly right-wing) owner, Eddie Chiles—and making him-self a multimillionaire in the process—George W. Bush was a virtual unknown.

At the time, Eddie Chiles, though never a candidate for office, was a bigger presence on the Texas political scene than Bush. Chiles, in the great right-wing tradition of H. L. Hunt, had paid good money to espouse his reactionary views on spot radio ads. The ads, remembered by a generation of Texans, began with the exhortation "I'm Eddie Chiles, and I'm mad!" Usually it was taxes that Eddie Chiles was mad about, taxes written up there in Washington, D.C., by a bunch of tax-and-spend Democrats, not a few of them *Texas* Democrats.

George W. Bush inherited the message—but not the style—of an Eddie Chiles. At first glance, he seemed, if anything, to be a mild-mannered fellow. A listener too, if for no other reason than he sure didn't want to be seen to be a talker.

The story has been told before—often and well, in, for example, *Bush's Brain,* by Wayne Slater and James Moore—but the gist of it is that the brilliant Austin-based Republican strategist Karl Rove found in the young Bush the perfect candidate, virtually a political tabula rasa. Governor Richards and her strategists expected—not entirely without reason—that the younger Bush would, like Claytie Williams, self-destruct in the campaign. Rove, however, kept the candidate "on message," and, as much as possible, away from the media.

Bush ran on only four issues—among these, school financing reform and tort reform—and the same themes, encapsulated in easy-to-remember sound bites, were repeated constantly whenever he spoke. Rove saw to it that the candidate received a series of tutorials designed to teach him the rudiments of Texas state government. Moore and Slater call it "a crash course on Texas civics." The veteran legislator Bill Ratliff, the chairman of the Senate Education Committee and an expert on school finance, was flown in twice for daylong sessions with Bush in a small conference room in Dallas. The candidate, Ratliff discovered, "didn't know much." Nor did he take notes, preferring to try to absorb the "stream" of information Ratliff poured out. If an aide is to be believed, the candidate didn't even know the difference between Medicaid and Medicare. "Now, I hear these two," Bush explained. "They're different. What's the difference between the two?"

Probably the most important of Bush's briefers was Mike Toomey, a former Republican state legislator who was by now one of the leading business lobbyists in Austin.

Toomey had belonged to the celebrated "Class of 1983" in the Texas state house, along with fellow Republican Tom DeLay. Now he was tutor-in-chief to the presumptive Republican candidate for governor. Besides trying to guide Bush through the ins and outs of the state's $70 billion budget, Toomey was also expected to give him political advice. About one issue, Toomey was emphatic. The next governor, Toomey told Bush, would need to reform the state's antiquated, pro-plaintiff tort laws. That would be Job One.

Needless to say, Toomey found Bush a receptive listener. He was already preaching to the converted.

And on election day 1994, George W. Bush prevailed over Ann Richards in an upset, garnering 53 percent of the vote.

Current Houston mayor Bill White, widely regarded as the standard-bearer of his state's party these days, was chairman of the Texas Democratic Party in 1994. In retrospect, he says, it's clear that 1994 was "the watershed election."

Tall, slightly awkward in manner, his bald pate shining under the lights of his art deco City Hall office, White would seem a most unlikely savior for the state's Democrats. But he also exudes an air of confidence, considerable intelligence, and, above all, competence. A University of Texas–trained lawyer, White is a self-made millionaire, an entrepreneur and investor, and, in the words of one of the city's top lawyers, "truly the smartest guy in town." White is also, says a female Democratic lawyer, "the absolute un-W."

What you have to understand about 1994, White explains, "is that it was the first election in which talk radio turned the tide." Traveling around Texas, putting countless miles onto the odometer of his car, raising money, and speaking on behalf of local and statewide candidates, White was amazed to find that "whether it was in the Panhandle or in West Texas, Dallas or Houston, Rush Limbaugh was the most listened-to guy on the airwaves."

With the sole exception of the twelve counties of far South Texas ("the Borderland") and in largely Hispanic Bexar County (San Antonio), says White, the election was "all about guns and gays—the social issues." (Other observers add a third g to the litany: they say the election was "all about guns, gays, and God.")

Party chairman White had assured his fellow Democrats that "we'd keep the base in East Texas," but there too he was wrong. There too "it was all Rush, all the time."

It hadn't helped that Richards, rather than her inexperienced oppo-

nent, had made the most important verbal slip of the campaign—
referring in public to the younger Bush as a "jerk." It also hadn't
helped that an old-fashioned, anonymous campaign of innuendo had
been run against Richards in rural, Baptist East Texas. The governor,
the whisper campaign went, was a lesbian. That East Texas had traditionally been a populist stronghold—well suited, one might have
thought, to Richards's message and her I'm-just-a-good-old-girl
persona—mattered greatly. Yet, come election day, Ann Richards lost
East Texas—and with it, some would argue, the state.

It also hadn't helped that other, equally strong currents were at
work in the election of 1994. These were powerful, national currents
that carried with them a host of seemingly lesser Republicans in
Austin—and in Washington.

Among these was one Thomas D. DeLay.

The story of the man named Tom has been told often and in detail,
never better than in the words of the talented Texas reporters Lou
Dubose and Jan Reid, in their books *The Hammer* and *The Hammer
Comes Down*. The short version of it goes like this: The son of an itin-
erant roustabout named Charlie DeLay, young Tom had grown up in
many places, the Borderland brush country of South Texas, for one;
the oil fields of Venezuela, for another. Aged twelve, Tom along with
his family returned to Texas, making their new home in the Gulf Coast
city of Corpus Christi.

Suffice it to say that DeLay married young (to Christine); had a
daughter, Danielle (known as Dani); graduated from the University of
Houston; and went to work in the pest-control business—hence his
subsequent political nicknames (the Exterminator and the Bug Man)—
and settled in suburban Sugar Land near Houston. DeLay's career
enjoyed a strange and unexpected trajectory: from that of a distinctly
small, semisuccessful businessman to ardent conservative of the most
virulently right-wing variety, to obscure Republican state legislator. In
Austin, as a junior minority member of a Democratic-controlled legislature, DeLay was little more than "furniture" on the floor of the
house.

While in Austin, DeLay had earned a well-deserved reputation—practically the only reputation he developed there—for being one of the legislature's most active "party animals," drinking, carousing, and, in general, enjoying life's favors. Along the way, though, DeLay had found Jesus. And, in doing so, the suddenly abstemious DeLay found himself with an entirely new constituency: the religious right, with which he would for three decades closely be identified.

Elected to the U.S. House of Representatives from a suburban Houston district in 1984, DeLay continued to toil in obscurity as a minority backbencher. For much of his first ten years in Congress (1984–94), DeLay occupied a lonely place in the House, the object of Democratic scorn, and an outsider within his own Republican ranks.

In this, DeLay was following in the footsteps of the recently retired Dallas congressman Jim Collins and fellow Houston congressman Bill Archer.

Collins's mere presence before a microphone in the well of the House had been enough to set off a wave of hoots and jeers, so outrageously right-wing was he. The gawky, supremely inarticulate Collins, his voice rising to a high pitch, his face flushed crimson, had long been a favorite of Democratic derision.

Archer, the congressman from Houston's silk-stocking district (once represented by George H. W. Bush), was a more serious character, if only because of his seniority. Eventually ascending to the position of ranking minority member on the powerful tax-writing Ways and Means Committee, Bill Archer was the House's leading opponent of the federal income tax, both personal and corporate.

Less wacky than Collins, less serious than Archer, "Bug Man" DeLay completed the Texas trio. House Democrats laughed on, knowing they had nothing to fear from such as these.

How wrong they were.

By 1994, Collins had long since left the House; but Archer and DeLay had remained—and risen to power. The congressional Democrats in Washington were about to discover what it was like to be on the losing side of the aisle.

The Republican Revolution—fueled by new Speaker Newt Gingrich's cleverly publicized Contract with America, conservative anger over gays in the military ("don't ask, don't tell"), and widespread dissatisfaction with the Clintons' failed effort to reform national health care—had led to an unexpected GOP sweep in the 1994 midterm elections.

With the House Republicans newly resurgent, Tom DeLay—by defeating the conservative Pennsylvania firebrand Robert Walker, the close friend and candidate of new Speaker Gingrich—was elected majority whip of the House of Representatives in January 1995. Winning the post made DeLay the third highest-ranking Republican in the House, behind only Speaker Gingrich and Majority Leader Armey. From then on, it was all blue sky for congressional right-wingers. The much maligned Tom DeLay was now, suddenly, a very big cheese indeed.

If Gingrich was the architect of Republican House ascendancy, DeLay was soon to emerge as its financier, and therein lay his claim to power. The day before Republicans were to organize the 104th Congress—the first time in forty years that they were the majority party in both houses—DeLay opened the doors of the majority whip's office for the purpose of setting in motion the innocently named Project Relief. The not-so-innocent goal of Project Relief was to cut corporate taxes and loosen government regulation over big business. The name given the project was a pure piece of advertising (like Contract with America)—but full of irony, foretelling an ominous future. The "victims" awaiting relief turned out not to be the country's many millions of poor and indigent, but were instead a handful of America's richest citizens and biggest corporations.

While Tom DeLay cracked the whip in public, his chief of staff, Ed Buckham, lurked, ever present, in the shadows. That no one outside Capitol Hill knew his name mattered little. For Buckham, elected to nothing, exercised the power that his boss had seized—exercised it ruthlessly too.

Buckham was, like most of DeLay's senior staffers, an experienced hand on Capitol Hill, a Republican operative who had spent years toiling in the political vineyard on behalf of conservative GOP House members, most recently as executive director of the Republican Study Group (RSG).

John Feehery was for a time DeLay's communications director, working closely with Buckham. Feehery would later write that he thus "experienced the Republican revolution firsthand"—and watched as Tom DeLay began to consolidate his power over the House. DeLay was notably assertive—"ruthless" and "obnoxious" were the words Democrats often used to describe the majority whip—but Buckham went well beyond even his boss in this regard.

From behind the arras, Feehery watched as Buckham pushed DeLay to be more radical in the tactics he used against his Democratic foes. In this, Buckham exemplified the men and women who made up DeLay's inner circle. Tony C. Rudy, press secretary and later deputy chief of staff, was a Brooklyn native and amateur ice hockey player. Rudy, a graduate of the George Mason Law School, affected a taste for expensive cigars, but he exhibited all the sensibility of a punishing winger in a brutal contact sport—an elbow in the ribs here, a stick in the chops there—as he stalked the halls of Congress. A GOP lobbyist once described Rudy as DeLay's "harder edge," adding, "It was always push, push, push, pressure, pressure, pressure." Rudy, the same person said, "was someone who was very aggressive and on the edge, [yet] who had Tom's complete trust." Capitol Hill reporters soon learned that Rudy was not someone you wanted to cross. Rudy was, in the words of his former boss Feehery, "DeLay's enforcer."

Another of Rudy's tasks—one that might at first glance have seemed menial to outsiders, but which actually brought with it significant power—was to oversee the whip's "member maintenance" operation. This amounted to running a concierge service that provided Republican House members with private town cars and expensive meals—at no charge—during late-night votes. "The whole purpose of this," Rudy boasted, was "to treat members of Congress as kings and queens."

Buckham, however, wasn't content to be a concierge or even a gatekeeper. His boss, DeLay, had already shown the way. Where Gingrich was obsessed with ideology and with his personal place in history, for Buckham, as for DeLay, it was—24/7/365—all about the benjamins.

☆　☆　☆

Among the host of Republican hangers-on who showed up in January 1995 to reap the rewards wrought by the Gingrich Revolution was a former College Republican leader and sometime lawyer, Hollywood B-picture producer and full-time schemer named Jack Abramoff.

Born in Atlantic City, New Jersey, Abramoff, aged ten, had moved with his family to Beverly Hills. There, the teenaged Jack played football and became a high school weight-lifting champion. He would later tell the story of how his life turned around when, as a boy of twelve, he sat in the audience of *Fiddler on the Roof.* As a consequence, said Abramoff, "I made the decision that I would become religious in order to preserve the faith in our family."

By the time he had finished college, Abramoff was well on his way to being one of the best-connected young Republicans of his day. Among the friends of Jack Abramoff in those days were Grover Norquist, Karl Rove, and Ralph Reed. Each would, in time, play a key role in his rise.

Abramoff first met Norquist in 1980 when Abramoff was an undergraduate at Brandeis University (class of 1981) and Norquist was a student at the Harvard Business School. Both were active in the College Republican National Committee, and both worked that year in the Massachusetts campaign of Republican presidential candidate Ronald Reagan.

Reed's and Abramoff's paths first crossed in 1982, when the then chairman of the College Republican National Committee (1981–85), Abramoff, hired Reed to be his executive director (1983–85). Reed, who arrived in Washington as a nineteen-year-old Senate intern, soon became close to Abramoff, so much so that he could sometimes be found sleeping on the boss's couch. It was close pal Reed who introduced Abramoff to his future wife, Pamela.

Abramoff, Norquist, and Reed would eventually prove a formidable trio in Republican Party politics, but in 1982–83, they were just a bunch of young politicos on the make. The trio broke the College Republicans budget with a 1982 national direct-mail fund-raising campaign that ended up a "colossal flop," in the words of the then

Republican National Committee (RNC) deputy director, Rich Bond. It fell to Bond to banish the trio from GOP headquarters. "You can't be trusted," he told Abramoff.*

In Hollywood, Abramoff achieved minor renown as the producer and coauthor of *Red Scorpion,* a 1989 "Cold War classic" starring Dolph Lundgren. The *Los Angeles Times* called *Red Scorpion* "a numbskull live-action comic book," while Frank Rich of the *New York Times* tersely dismissed it as "seriously God-awful."

Columnist Peter Carlson of the *Washington Post* later satirized Abramoff's Hollywood career thusly: "He Was No Run of De Mille Movie Mogul." Not with the kind of chillingly right-wing baggage the movie and its producer carried. *Red Scorpion* had been filmed not on a Hollywood sound set but in South Africa using soldiers and military equipment lent by the white, apartheid government. Which did not make *Red Scorpion* or its sequel, *Red Scorpion 2* (1994), popular with American liberals. Imagine, Carlson wrote, if those same liberals had "known that the International Freedom Foundation, a right-wing group founded by Abramoff, was secretly bankrolled by the South African army."

Or imagine if Jack Abramoff's new colleagues at the Preston Gates law firm had known as much in early 1995. But they didn't. As the freshly minted director of governmental affairs in the Washington, D.C., office of Preston Gates Ellis & Rouvelas Meeds, Abramoff worked for the Seattle law firm whose longtime leader and name partner was William H. Gates Sr., the father of the world's richest man, Microsoft cofounder Bill Gates.

---

*After that, Abramoff briefly ran something called Citizens for America, a right-wing advocacy group funded by drugstore multimillionaire Lewis E. Lehrman. There, Abramoff had frequent contact with marine lieutenant colonel Oliver North, the Reagan White House national security staffer who would later be implicated in the Iran-contra scandal.

Abramoff's undoing at Citizens for America came when he organized a "convention" of anticommunist guerrillas from Laos, Nicaragua, and Afghanistan. The meeting was held in a remote part of Angola, under the auspices of Angolan renegade leader Jonas Savimbi. Shortly afterward, Lehrman fired Abramoff in a dispute over how the budget of Citizens for America had been spent.

★ ★ ★

What Jack Abramoff brought with him, to begin with, were a bunch of somewhat dubious IOUs, based on his close ties to Norquist, Reed, and Rove. Eventually, the IOUs would come due, but in early 1995, the old friendships counted for little more than introductions. Still, one such introduction did prove pivotal, when Norquist began opening doors on Capitol Hill for Abramoff. Norquist was by then already an important figure among the Contract with America crowd. His Americans for Tax Reform (ATR), founded in 1985, had gradually evolved into a right-wing strategy shop during the early Clinton years.

One door, in particular, that Norquist helped open—the door to a suite of rooms occupied by the House majority whip and, later, the House majority leader—would remain open for Jack Abramoff for much of the next ten years. Thanks to Norquist, Jack Abramoff was soon able to expand the orbit of his right-wing fellowship to include the powerful inner circle of House majority whip Tom DeLay, beginning with his chief of staff, Ed Buckham.

It was Buckham who became Jack Abramoff's lasting entrée into the majority whip's office. According to John Feehery, "In those early days . . . we knew [Abramoff] mainly as a friend of Buckham's." Buckham, speaking of Abramoff, told reporters, "He is someone on our side. He has access to DeLay."

But back in January 1995, Abramoff was still basically a D.C. wannabe. DeLay and Buckham were already in the political promised land. And, by implementing Project Relief and, later, what was called the K Street Project, Tom DeLay was about to make himself the most powerful House majority whip ever. More powerful, in time, than the majority leader, more powerful even than the Speaker.

But, first, DeLay would have to suffer Gingrich—while attempting to sidetrack him. The best way to do that, DeLay realized, would be to transform the office of the majority whip and make it into a separate power center. For this, the Texan congressman had a plan.

CHAPTER TWO

✫

A Pig Roast on the Island

Tom DeLay had never been close to the extended Bush family. The rough-hewn former exterminator didn't travel in the same circles as the patrician, Episcopalian, Yale-educated former president. Nor was DeLay particularly enamored of newly elected Texas governor George W. Bush, despite the latter's oft-proclaimed evangelical Christian beliefs.

The old man was too Eastern WASPy, while the younger Bush, despite the boots and the Stetson, the contrived accent and the chaw, was—by DeLay's high standards—not sufficiently tough enough. The new governor's right-hand man, Karl Rove, didn't meet the test either. Despite his take-no-prisoners air, Rove projected just the sort of smarty-pants-intellectual-with-an-attitude style that DeLay despised. Nor did Rove enjoy the trust of the big-name Christian evangelical pastors who increasingly formed the base of DeLay's power bloc.

DeLay did, however, have something in common with Rove: Big Tobacco. During the "Tobacco Wars" of the early 1990s, Rove had been the chief political operative in Texas for the Philip Morris Company. Rove's job back then had been to try to keep the Texas attorney general from joining with other state attorneys general in bringing suit against the tobacco companies over the alleged cancer-causing effects of nicotine found in cigarettes. Rove lost that battle—the state's Democratic attorney general at the time, Dan Morales, joined in the war against tobacco—but gained the undying goodwill of the tobacco industry.

In the process, Rove learned firsthand to hate tort lawyers, the mostly Democratic plaintiffs' lawyers known now as "the tobacco lawyers," who first instigated the multibillion-dollar class actions over smoking. The Texas tobacco lawyers, who themselves eventually reaped millions from the defeated industry, in turn, learned to hate Karl Rove, for Rove brought Big Tobacco's money to the Republican table.

It wasn't the Bushes' Yale and Harvard degrees or their Eastern ways that Tom DeLay appeared to envy. It was their easy access to money—Big Money, Old Money, Wall Street Money, and, thanks in part to Rove, Tobacco Money.

If he wanted to be a player and ultimately challenge Newt Gingrich, Tom DeLay would have to have access to his own hoard of cash. Thus was born DeLay's personal political action committee, or PAC, officially known as Americans for a Republican Majority, but better known by its acronym, ARMPAC. Wielding the millions of dollars contributed to ARMPAC by right-wing millionaires and big corporations, the whip could ensure not merely his own reelection, but the election of individual Republican congressmen, indebted above all to himself.

The man DeLay chose to run ARMPAC was Karl Gallant, a former tobacco industry lobbyist with ties to R.J. Reynolds and Philip Morris. Gallant's background also included work with the National Right to Work Committee and the Ramhurst Corporation (which has been described as "a stealth group created by the tobacco industry to lobby and organize 'grassroots' pro smoking campaigns"). Joining Gallant at ARMPAC was another former R.J. Reynolds operative, Jim Ellis, along with DeLay's 1996 campaign manager, Bob Mills.

DeLay having hired Big Tobacco's men, Big Tobacco returned the favor. The seed money for ARMPAC came from R.J. Reynolds ($17,000) and Philip Morris ($10,000).

Gallant's first big coup came at a 1995 Houston fund-raiser—ostensibly in honor of newly crowned Speaker Gingrich—sponsored by Enron and its CEO, Kenneth Lay. (The Enron executives alone wound up contributing $280,000 to the event.) Before that Houston fund-raiser, Gingrich's personal PAC (GOPAC) had raised $1.5 million as opposed to ARMPAC's $780,000. After the fund-raiser, the numbers flipped. Gingrich might have had the big title, but DeLay now had the big bucks.

Like future vice president Dick Cheney, DeLay well understood the nature of power. Willpower and tenacity, a well-known disposition not merely to defeat but to destroy one's enemies, coupled with a stockpile of readily disbursable cash, would always, or nearly always, trump those who were merely dressed in the accoutrements of power. The glue was the money. And in the city of Washington in the District of Columbia, there was no better place to go looking for money than K Street, the traditional home to the city's lobbyists.

Men like Karl Gallant and Jack Abramoff worked the gray area of politics known as the Lobby. Lobbyists were neither congressmen nor senators—though many had previously served in one or both houses of Congress. Instead, they were the unelected, if better paid, representatives of corporations, trade associations, labor unions, and nonprofit organizations with strong ideological platforms—men and women who prowled the corridors of power in search of votes and influence. By the time Abramoff arrived on the scene in late 1994, the ranks of Washington lobbyists numbered in the thousands.

So-called for the lobbies lying just outside the House and Senate chambers, the Lobby and those who work it have long figured in American political history. Congressional approval for the funding of the transcontinental railroads, for example, was largely the result of early-day lobbying. Railroad bonds and cash were showered on the powerful and the waffling, and many a congressman emerged from the experience a wealthier man. No wonder: the cost of building the railroads was staggering, well into the billions, as measured in today's dollars.

Nor were even the great and the good exempt from the enticements of the Lobby. In 1864, in the midst of the Civil War, a bill was introduced by Senator John Sherman to give capitalists more incentives to invest in the transcontinental railroad project. The bill's Indiana Republican sponsor was Union general William Tecumseh Sherman's brother, the author many years later of the famed Sherman Antitrust Act, and a future secretary of state.

Illinois congressman E. B. Washburne called Sherman's bill "a most monstrous and flagrant attempt to overreach the government" and warned of "Wall Street stock jobbers who are using this great engine for their own private means."

Washburne knew whereof he spoke. The Washington of 1864 was filled not only with Union soldiers but with lobbyists working the corridors of Congress on behalf of the transcontinental railroad bill. The lead investor behind the Union Pacific, Thomas "Doc" Durant, was but one of many railroad promoters in town handing out money and stock in return for votes. Just how much Durant of the UP and Collis P. Huntington of the rival Central Pacific spent to get the 1864 act passed has never been found out. One thing, though, was for sure. As the late historian Stephen Ambrose has noted, "A lobbyist hired by Durant . . . distributed $250,000 in UP bonds, with $20,000 of them going to Charles T. Sherman, eldest brother of the senator and the general." Durant, Ambose wrote, "was a genial paymaster." Ambrose might have added that Durant was a model Washington lobbyist—of the mid-nineteenth-century variety.

With so much money at stake, the building of the transcontinental railroad continued to be a source of congressional graft—and a boon to the Lobby—for years to come.

Less than a decade after the passage of the 1864 funding act, the *New York Sun* dropped a bombshell in the middle of the otherwise torpid 1872 presidential race between Republican incumbent Ulysses S. Grant, the Civil War hero, and the quixotic newspaper editor Horace Greeley. The paper's exclusive occupied the whole of page one, with headlines that blared: "THE KING OF FRAUDS. How the Crédit Mobilier Bought Its Way Through Congress. COLOSSAL BRIBERY. Congressmen who Have Robbed the People, and who now Support the National Robber. HOW SOME MEN GET FORTUNES. Princely gifts to the Chairmen of Committees in Congress."

As the result of a bidding scam, the Crédit Mobilier had been awarded some 675 miles of Union Pacific transcontinental railroad tracks to build, the hefty fees due Crédit Mobilier to be paid by the federal government. Pliant congressmen—those who had voted funding for the project—were given stock at face value rather than market value. And while the Union Pacific ultimately teetered on bankruptcy, investors in the Crédit Mobilier were said to have walked off with a profit of $21 million—perhaps as much as a half-billion dollars in today's money.

The Crédit Mobilier scandal having broken during a presidential election, congressmen, senators, cabinet members, railroaders, investors—and lobbyists—were sent scurrying for cover. A congressional investigation of thirteen of its own members—not the first or last investigation focusing on the Lobby and Congress—eventually implicated more than thirty officials in the scandal. Among those fingered were a former vice president (Republican Schuyler Colfax), a future Republican presidential candidate (House Speaker James G. Blaine), and a future president (Republican James Garfield). The *Sun* wrote that Speaker Blaine "was a poor man when he became a member of Congress in 1864. He is now a millionaire."

The pattern had been set. Every decade or so, a major scandal involving the Lobby would surface. Page-one headlines would ensue. The predictable congressional investigation would follow. Reforms would then be enacted. Not infrequently someone would go to jail.

And then the cycle would begin anew.

Today's lobbyists are less apt to be found handing out money and stock to congressmen—it is illegal to do so—and far more likely to be found making contributions to their political action committees or PACs.

The reason: they, like the lobbyists of old, want to influence the language of the law and the passage of new legislation. Sometimes they endeavor for something positive, such as the search for votes for the funding of the transcontinental railroad; or sometimes, negative, as when the client fears the burden of some new tax and is determined to stop its passage into law.

Influence, however, comes in many forms and fashions. Outright corporate gift-giving to political campaigns and PACs is merely the most obvious manifestation. There are a host of other, subtler ways to gain influence: sponsored trips to faraway places; the use of corporate private jets; a night or two at a Four Seasons or Ritz-Carlton hotel; a hearty meal and a bottle of fine wine at a fancy restaurant; drinks and cigars — preferably illicit Cuban cigars — at one of Washington's grander private clubs; a day on the links at a fabled golf course. There are, needless to say, congressional rules governing these things, but the rules, as young Congressman DeLay soon discovered, are fungible in the extreme; while the so-called House Ethics Committee has long been the joke of Capitol Hill.

On the other side of the table, if you were a successful lobbyist, working either at a major lobby shop (a company devoted solely to the business of lobbying) or at one of Washington's premier law firms with a governmental affairs department doing the same sort of work, you could expect to make hundreds of thousands of dollars a year — maybe, if you were both good at it and well connected, millions even.

Not for nothing were the lobby shops of K Street housed in gleaming steel and glass. The very nature of the street bespoke power and money.

The magic words — *the Lobby* — if you liked them, sang a siren song.

There was nothing subtle about Tom Delay's K Street Project. It aimed to force the rich and powerful Capitol Hill lobby shops to hire a slew of newly enfranchised Republican lobbyists — many of them personally beholden to Tom DeLay.

Together with a brash, ambitious, newly elected Republican senator — and former fellow House member — from Pennsylvania named Rick Santorum, Majority Whip DeLay put out the word on K Street that Democratic lobbyists need no longer apply. After November 1994, only dyed-in-the-wool Republican lobbyists would be welcome on Capitol Hill.

Change came quickly to K Street — and to the halls of Congress.

The Lobby was now everywhere. No longer limited to K Street or to prowling the Capitol Hill hallways, lobbyists were to be found in congressional committee rooms—themselves writing the legislation. DeLay, Santorum, and their crowd had gone beyond something anyone was previously familiar with. The pressure was on firms to hire Republicans—and to fire Democrats. When reporter Elizabeth Drew suggested to Grover Norquist that many Democratic lobbyists were essentially nonideological, Norquist replied, "We don't want nonideological people on K Street, we want conservative activist Republicans on K Street." Norquist, Drew concluded, was "the leading enforcer of the K Street Project outside Congress."

Among the supplicants come to dine at the feast was the newly named head of governmental affairs at the Preston Gates law firm, Norquist's old buddy, Jack Abramoff.

There was a hitch though. The K Street Project could open doors on the Hill, but it couldn't necessarily guarantee a client base. The main problem, of course, was that the White House was still in the hands of Democrats. For the next six years, big business—Wall Street, in particular—remained, in large part, supplicant to the party of William Jefferson Clinton. During the eight years of the Clinton presidency, corporate America had at least to pay token obeisance to the Democrats. On occasion, there was palpable love, as in the Clinton administration's support for NAFTA. The implementation of the North American Free Trade Agreement—enacted over the howls of labor union leaders and other traditional party sponsors—was a prime example of this new moderate-Democrat liaison with Wall Street, a liaison symbolized by the central policy position occupied within the Clinton administration by Treasury Secretary and former Goldman Sachs chair Robert Rubin. NAFTA too was exemplary of the Clinton administration's forward-thrusting, consensus-building, get-it-done side. A side of the administration that was anything but ideological.

In such a world of compromise in which Republicans and Democrats, legislators and lobbyists and Wall Street movers and shakers alike, did deals with one another daily, if not minute by minute, there wasn't going to be much business for an uncompromising, outspoken right-wing ideologue such as Jack Abramoff—no matter how well connected he was on one side of the table. But if the goal was not measured by *positive* achievement, if it was instead measured in *negative* terms, with the power of the House majority whip and his team aligned to *defeat* legislation, that was another matter. For to stop a bill from reaching the president's desk, you merely had to defeat it in one house. And if your friend controlled that one house . . . and if your name was Jack Abramoff and your friend was Tom DeLay . . .

This then would be the genius of Jack Abramoff during his first six years in Washington. And it all lay in the power to stop legislation from happening.

Abramoff's first important client—and for a long time his biggest client—was the Commonwealth of the Northern Mariana Islands (CNMI). Located two hundred miles from Guam and some eight thousand miles and fourteen time zones ahead of Washington, D.C.—sixty-six hundred miles and thirteen time zones ahead of Houston—the CNMI was famous as the setting for a June 20, 1944, air-sea battle between the U.S. Navy and the Imperial Japanese Navy. The Battle of the Philippine Sea had been a disaster for the Japanese, resulting in the near total destruction of their carrier-based air forces. To this day, it is referred to as the Great Marianas Turkey Shoot.

In more recent times, the Commonwealth became home to garment factories doing approximately $1 billion a year in business. While residents of the Marianas (population 53,552) were U.S. citizens, the bulk of the population (58 percent) was nonresident, mostly Chinese. And where U.S. workers earned a minimum wage of $5.15, workers in the Marianas received a mere $3.05.

As things stood, the textile owners were allowed to have "Made in the USA" labels sewn onto clothing destined for middle-class American favorites such as Tommy Hilfiger and The Gap. The garments, in turn, were made in factories that were notorious sweatshops employing mostly female, mostly illegal laborers. Here, women from the Philippines, Thailand, Bangladesh, Sri Lanka, and, above all, China worked eighty-four-hour weeks in fenced-in industrial parks.

The textile owners of the Marianas and Majority Whip DeLay shared a common enemy in President Bill Clinton, whose administration proposed to extend U.S. labor, immigration, and minimum-wage laws to the Marianas. The Department of Labor had committed itself to rooting out the sweatshops, destroying the islands' infamous system of brothels, and instituting fair-labor laws. The textile owners were just as determined to stop them from doing so.

Prodded by the Clinton administration, the Senate in 1995 passed legislation that would have stripped the Commonwealth of the Northern Mariana Islands from its exemptions from U.S. labor and immigration laws.

From the point of view of the all-powerful sweatshop lords, something had to be done to stop the bill from ending up on President Clinton's desk. The answer to the textile owners' prayers: Tom DeLay, Ed Buckham, and Jack Abramoff.

No longer a K Street neophyte, Abramoff had swiftly risen among the ranks of D.C. lobbyists. The chief reason for his success was Abramoff's perceived closeness to DeLay and Buckham. Speaking of his longtime friend Abramoff, Grover Norquist told David Rosenbaum of the *New York Times*, "He walks in to see DeLay, and DeLay knows that he is representing clients whose views are in sync with DeLay's views."

Commonwealth governor Froilan Tenorio, a former garment-industry executive, first contracted with Preston Gates in 1994, one year into the Clinton presidency. Over the next seven and a half years, the Commonwealth would pay Abramoff and the firms that employed him some $7.2 million in lobbying fees. During this period, Abramoff billed the Marianas for 187 contacts with DeLay's office in 1996 and 1997—among them, 104 discussions with Buckham and 16 direct meetings with DeLay.

It wasn't just Abramoff who benefited from the relationship. Governor Tenorio also awarded a $1.2 million contract in 1996 to Seattle-based, but South African–born-and-raised Rabbi David Lapin—the brother of the man who had first introduced Jack Abramoff to Tom DeLay in 1994—to promote "ethics in government." Rabbi Lapin's original contract called for him to provide Commonwealth officials with eight days of ethics training. Clearly, ethics training was in order. Within a year, the value of the contract awarded David Lapin had swollen to $1.2 million. Pam Brown, the attorney general for the Marianas, would later admit that the government there still hadn't been able to determine what work Lapin had actually performed. "We haven't been able to figure out what the deliverables were," Brown reportedly said.

The Marianas had no such problem with the work Jack Abramoff performed. In his case, the deliverable had a name: Thomas D. DeLay, who liked nothing so much as a fact-finding trip, especially if the location was exotic, the lodgings swank, the fare first-class, and an inviting golf course beckoned.

And what better time to visit someplace far away and warm than Christmastime? That's how it was that DeLay, wife Christine, and daughter Dani DeLay Ferro, a political organizer for her father, found themselves journeying to Saipan, the largest island in the Commonwealth. Joining them were Chief of Staff Ed Buckham and Communications Director John Feehery. The sponsors of the trip: the Commonwealth of the Northern Mariana Islands and the Saipan Garment Manufacturers' Association, both of them Abramoff clients.

Waiting to greet them at the airport, Feehery recalls, was "a throng of well-wishers, musicians, elected officials—and Jack Abramoff." Capping off the first day's events, remembers Feehery, was the luau held for the DeLay party that night, "complete with dancers and a roasted pig." Their host was Willie Tan, the most important man on the islands as well as its biggest garment manufacturer (through his Tan Holdings).

When DeLay arrived for his triumphal tour of the Marianas in December 1997, the textile owners pulled out all the stops. The event was one big pig roast—and a great place to raise more money for DeLay. Making sure that this happened was the job of fellow participant Ed Buckham. As for the boss, reporter Rosenbaum noted in the *Times,* "Mr. DeLay came back enthralled."

During the visit, the close-knit DeLay family, Ed Buckham

included, brunched with the obliging Willie Tan, played golf, and were wined and dined—courtesy of Tan—at the Pacific Islands Club. At a sumptuous New Year's Eve dinner, a glowing majority whip referred to a beaming Jack Abramoff as "one of my closest and dearest friends." DeLay closed his speech with the exhortation "Stand firm. Resist evil. Remember that all truth and blessings emanate from our Creator." As John Feehery recalls, DeLay "told the assembled revelers to resist evil, referring to a minimum wage hike." After which, in the words of a *Washington Post* account, "He then departed with Tan to see a cockfight."

Congressman George Miller, a liberal Democrat from California, has long been one of the most vocal advocates for reform in the Marianas. Abramoff, said Miller, the ranking Democrat on the House Education and the Workforce Committee—and the former ranking member on the House Resources Committee (with oversight of America's far-flung territories)—"spent a lot of time, effort and money to protect a system that was a growth industry for sex shops, prostitution, abuse of women, slavery, illegal immigration, worker exploitation and narcotics, and he did it all in the name of freedom."

While Tom DeLay's New Year's visit to Saipan had officially been arranged by the National Security Caucus Foundation (on whose board Jack Abramoff would later serve), which claims to "promote a strong national defense, democracy and human rights," the tab itself was paid for by Preston Gates, from monies paid by its Marianas clients.

Returning from Saipan, Majority Whip DeLay extolled the virtues of the Marianas in remarks before the U.S. House of Representatives. The Commonwealth of the Marianas, DeLay now asserted, was the "model of reform."

The Christmas visit was but one of a number of fact-finding missions dispatched by DeLay to the Marianas. Another would feature campaign manager Bob Mills accompanied by Chief of Staff Ed Buckham. In Saipan, Mills and Buckham met with Marianas kingpin Tan, the island's largest employer. A month later, Marianas politician

Benigno "Ben" Fitial, a longtime Tan associate, returned the favor, traveling to Capitol Hill, where he sang "Happy Birthday" to a delighted Tom DeLay in the whip's office.*

In servicing the interests of the powerful textile owners of the Marianas, Jack Abramoff dealt with officials in the U.S. Department of the Interior and the congressional oversight committees involved with America's overseas possessions. Not that Abramoff expected favors from the Clinton administration, but it paid to become familiar with the inner workings of Interior. The *Washington Post* would, for example, later report that the Marianas desk officer at Interior, Roger Stillwell, accepted dinners at Abramoff's restaurant, Signatures, as well as tickets to Redskins games. But Abramoff became most adept with the inner workings of the congressional committees, thanks in no small measure to his friendship with DeLay.

During the long years of Democratic stewardship, the House and Senate Committees on the Interior had regularly been led by conservation-minded Westerners, such as the late Morris Udall of Arizona. Under House Republican management, the names of the committees were changed to reflect a not-so-subtle shift from conservation to exploitation: in the Senate, it was now the Energy and Natural Resources Committee; in the House, the Committee on Resources (which, strange to say, also had oversight of America's Indian tribes and overseas territories and commonwealths) and the Committee on Energy and Commerce. The new stewards tended to be extreme conservatives from oil-rich states—men who were apt as not to be in sync with Jack Abramoff—and who, in the House at least, were sure to be in sync with Tom DeLay. Men such as Energy and Commerce chairman Billy Tauzin of Louisiana and his successor, Joe Barton of Texas, and Resources chairman Richard Pombo, a rancher from California,

---

*Shortly afterward, DeLay shouted a holler back to Saipan. That's when he and his fellow Texan, Republican majority leader Dick Armey, wrote Governor Tenorio, promising to block the Clinton administration's Marianas legislative package. (Three years later, a similar bill that would have barred use of the "Made in the USA" label on Marianas-made garments failed to come to a vote in the House—despite having 234 cosponsors in the lower chamber.)

whose strident antienvironmentalism and willingness to let them drill anywhere anytime made him a favorite of energy companies.

Tucked within the same, overlapping bodies of officialdom (Interior and the congressional appropriations and oversight committees) lay control over the wealth of America's national parks and wilderness lands, its overseas commonwealths and territories (such as the Marianas, Puerto Rico, the Virgin Islands, and Guam), and a host of semi-autonomous and, in some cases, fabulously rich Indian tribes.

At some point, surely, Jack Abramoff realized what lay before him, the vast treasure trove waiting to be looted.

To the world, of course, Abramoff presented a different face. In an April 2002 interview with David Rosenbaum of the *New York Times,* Abramoff asserted, "All of my political work is driven by philosophical interests, not by a desire to gain wealth." Indian reservations and island territories were, Abramoff added, "just what conservatives have always wanted, which is enterprise zones—tax free, regulation free zones where with the right motivation, great industry could take place and spill out into the general communities."

And into the wallet of Jack Abramoff.

CHAPTER THREE

✴

The Fabulous Rise of Casino Jack and DeLay Inc.

There was a time, not so long ago, when almost all of this country's Native Americans were have-nots. In less than three decades, that picture has radically changed. Today, America's Indian tribes are divided between the haves—possessors of vast fortunes—and the have-nots, those that have, if anything, sunk even deeper into poverty and despair. The reason for this chasm is, in a word, gambling.

The picture of tribal life at the bottom of the heap is as bleak as ever. A 2002 study by the University of Maryland found that the median household income among Indians was 60 percent lower than that of other Americans. Poverty rates, meanwhile, were five times higher than national averages, the high school dropout rate twice the national average. A fifth of Indian households lacked indoor plumbing. A sixth did not even have kitchens. More than half lacked telephones.

Among other tribes, the scene could not be more different. For example, the Pequots, whose land is in Connecticut, are among the tribal rich. To visit the tribal home in Uncasville is truly to step into the luxury of twenty-first-century life. Why this should be so, and why there is such a disparity between these tribes and their humble fellow tribes, is easy enough to explain.

In 1987, the U.S. Supreme Court ruled that state gambling laws did not apply on Indian land. Responding to the ensuing rush to open casinos on Indian reservation land, Congress passed the Indian Gaming Regulatory Act of 1988 (IGRA), which provided that the proceeds from Indian gaming could only be used for governmental or charitable purposes—among these, health, education, human services, law enforcement, roads, water and sewer projects, and tribal courts—in effect making Indian gaming revenue analogous to state revenue used to fund state programs.

As a result, more than 200 of the roughly 340 Indian tribes in the lower forty-eight states today have gaming operations, which, in 2003, generated some $16 billion in revenues. Research shows that tribal gaming has fueled economic relief not only on tribal lands, but also in surrounding communities. Non-Indians hold about 75 percent of the half million jobs connected with tribal gaming. That, in turn, generates over $4 billion in annual revenue for the federal government, over $1 billion for the states, and more than $50 million for local governments. In addition, tribes donate some $68 million annually to charity.

That the casinos generate that much revenue for the states, however, is an unintentional result of the IGRA. That legislation required compacts between the tribes and the states. A subsequent 1996 Supreme Court decision held that the states could demand long-term payments for agreeing to compacts with the tribes. Due to that decision, the states have in the years since been able to hold the tribes up for ransom.

Connecticut politicians, for example, facing a budget crisis but anxious to avoid instituting a state income tax, forced the Pequots to agree to pay 25 percent of their slot revenues in return for a compact that allowed slot-machine gambling at the tribe's Mohegan Sun and Foxwoods Resort. Between January 1993 and November 2006, the State of Connecticut thus collected $2.379 billion in revenue. Similarly, in a 1999 deal, the State of California and some forty tribes signed compacts allowing up to two casinos and two thousand slots on any reservation. In return, the tribes agreed to pay a total of $100 million a year into a state fund.

An abundant new source of wealth available for the taking, a complicated pattern of applicable federal and state laws, and layers of overlapping governmental oversight put a bull's-eye on America's tribes. With his connection to Tom DeLay's apparatus and his insights into the workings of the Interior Department, Jack Abramoff was the very man to take advantage of a situation waiting to be plundered.

Within a year of his arrival in Washington in 1994, Preston Gates lobbyist Abramoff had secured the first of his Indian tribal clients: the Mississippi Band of Choctaw Indians, whose profitable casino complex had made it into one of the haves.

The Choctaws were a proud and numerous tribe with close to ten thousand members—residing in eight reservation communities located in five counties in east-central Mississippi. They were, moreover, the descendants of the Choctaw people who, for a decade (1830–40) valiantly resisted attempts of the U.S. government to uproot and move them to the Indian Territory (today's Oklahoma). The tribe was, in other words, used to fighting back when it had to do so.

Still, by the early 1960s many tribal members were in an abject state. According to a report of the Senate Indian Affairs Committee, "By 1964, ninety percent of the Tribe's population lived in poverty."

All that changed beginning in 1994 when the Choctaws opened the Silver Star Hotel and Casino. So successful was the Silver Star that a mere six years later the tribe was able to open a second hotel-casino, the Golden Moon. Today the tribe is the third-largest employer in Mississippi, operating not only the two hotel-casinos, but also a shopping center as well as the Dancing Rabbit golf course.

But the tribe's luck changed in other ways as well beginning in 1994. That's when legislation was introduced in the newly Republican Congress designed to apply the federal Unrelated Business Income Tax (UBIT) to the proceeds of Indian gaming operations.

In the words of the Senate report, "Confronted with this legislation and a sea of unknown"—mostly Republican—"faces in Congress, the Choctaw decided to hire outside lobbyists." The search, run by Nell Rogers, the tribe's planner for legislative affairs, led them to Jack Abramoff—and thence to his buddy, tax reformer and DeLay K Street Project overlord Grover Norquist.

In 1996 and again in 1997, Abramoff teamed with Norquist to lobby on behalf of the Choctaws against the proposed federal tax on Indian casino profits. The bill's sponsor was the curmudgeonly chairman of the House Ways and Means Committee, Bill Archer of Houston, Texas—a man senior in tenure to Tom DeLay among House Republicans. Curiously, after Abramoff and Norquist "helped persuade key members of Congress to kill the idea," the bill died in the bosom of Archer's own committee. It is a fair surmise that only one "key member" of Congress had that kind of clout—and cared enough about protecting Indian casino gambling to deep-six a bill proposed by so important a figure as the chairman of the House Ways and Means Committee. That man could only have been Tom DeLay.

Two years into DeLay's tenure as majority whip—and in anticipation of the fall 1996 congressional and presidential elections—Chief of Staff Ed Buckham set about organizing a nonprofit "public advocacy" group that came to be known as the U.S. Family Network (USFN). The purported goal of this "grassroots" group would be to turn out tens of thousands of right-wing fundamentalist voters at election time.

In a fund-raising letter sent to potential donors, Tom DeLay would later describe USFN as "a powerful nationwide organization dedicated to restoring our government to citizen control." In correspondence with the Internal Revenue Service, USFN's first director—DeLay's 1996 campaign manager Robert Mills—described the group's goal as one of advocating "economic growth and prosperity, social improvement, moral fitness, and the general well-being of the United States." In contrast to the worldly Clintons and their liberal Democratic followers, USFN would help restore "moral fitness" to American political life.

All was not, however, as it seemed. Dressed up in this highfalutin language, USFN had some big goals for an otherwise obscure outfit that opened its doors with seed money of only $15,000. The donor, known only to a few within the DeLay political network, was the Mississippi Band of Choctaw Indians. The contribution, small as it was, would have seemed strange indeed but for one thing: the Mississippi Choctaws were, as we have seen, Republican lobbyist Jack Abramoff's clients.

From those microscopic beginnings sprang something big. Over its five-year existence (1996–2001), USFN brought in more than $3.02 million in donations, its donor list perpetually shrouded in secrecy. Curiously, when the donor list was at last revealed, it turned out that this "powerful nationwide organization" had essentially been sustained by just four separate groups of givers, each with a great deal to gain from the relationship.

The *Washington Post* laid bare the sources of the cash: $650,000 alone came from the owners of textile companies headquartered in the Northern Marianas.

The USFN did well by the Marianas. In early 1997, companies controlled by textile magnate Willie Tan wrote three checks for $10,000 each to USFN. Ed Buckham's wife, Wendy, received a fourth check for $10,000, as her "commission" for bringing in the $30,000. Eventually, a total of twenty-three such checks would be made out to USFN, totaling $650,000.

Textile owners in the Marianas, an Indian tribe, the National Republican Congressional Committee, and some Russian energy executives. These were the sources of more than $2.6 million in contributions to a nonprofit "grassroots" Christian organization that never had more than one full-time staff member, spent next to nothing on public advocacy, and didn't even bother to try to turn out voters. Judged by these standards, USFN had a sorry record indeed of delivering on its stated promises.

But like so many of the entities that constituted what might reasonably be called DeLay Inc., USFN was, in fact, very good at doing something for which it never claimed any public credit: acting as a money-laundering machine.

The Russians, the Choctaws, and the textile owners all had problems—very different problems, mind you—but problems, nevertheless, that might well be solved with help from the House majority whip. All three had something else in common: they were Abramoff clients. As for the NRCC, well, its stated purpose was to keep Congress Republican—

and thus sustain Tom DeLay in power where he could do much good for those that needed his help and could pay for it.

The Mississippi Band of Choctaw Indians were among those that could.

In little more than a decade, the once impoverished tribal members had become rich off a gambling casino located on reservation land near Meridian, Mississippi. By 1996, they were the owners not only of a prosperous 990,000-square-foot casino, but also a five-hundred-room hotel. Business was booming, but trouble lay close at hand, in the form of the rival Poarch Creek Indians of Alabama, who also wanted to get into the gaming business. Choctaw leadership was determined that this should not happen.

The Choctaws knew where to turn, too. In late March 1997, Chief of Staff Buckham and Deputy Chief of Staff Tony Rudy became the first staffers from the Office of the Majority Whip to inspect the Choctaw Reservation. The visit had been arranged by Abramoff.

DeLay; his wife, Christine; and Susan Hirschmann—another high-ranking staffer who would later go on to find greener pastures as a K Street lobbyist—were the next to visit Meridian, Mississippi. Their trip, taken four months later (July 31–August 2), would be described in House disclosure forms as a "site review and reservation tour." The trip, arranged for by none other than Ed Buckham, included the by now obligatory time-out for golf.

One day after the DeLay party departed for Washington, USFN received an initial $150,000 payment from the Choctaws. Separately, the Choctaws paid Abramoff $4.5 million during 1998 and 1999; and, in turn, Abramoff and his wife, Pamela, contributed $22,000 to DeLay's campaigns from 1997 to 2000.

Coincidentally, a letter on USFN stationery was soon sent to Alabama residents announcing a petition drive to block the Poarch Creek Indians from building their rival casino. "The American family is under attack from all sides: crime, drugs, pornography, and one of the least talked about but equally as destructive—gambling," read the letter, signed by DeLay crony Congressman Bob Riley. "We need your help today," the future Republican governor pleaded, "to prevent the Poarch Creek Indians from building casinos in Alabama."

Rich as the Mississippi Band of Choctaw Indians was, the Coushatta tribe of Louisiana was richer still. Why this should be so can easily be seen by looking at a map. The Choctaw casino is located near Meridian (population 39,968, in a state, Mississippi, with a population of 2,844,000). Conveniently, the casino is also a mere twenty-five miles from the Alabama border and can draw on that state's larger population (4,447,100).

The Coushatta tribe, on the other hand, is based in Elton, Louisiana, with its Coushatta Casino Resort located about fifteen minutes away in nearby Kinder, just north of and midway between Lake Charles (population 71,757) and Lafayette (population 110,257), the capital of Cajun Country. Lake Charles and Lafayette both lie on Interstate 10 and in a direct line with Houston, as noted earlier, a wealthy city of 2 million located in the nation's second-largest state (population 20,851,820). Much, if not most, of the Coushattas' gaming business is derived from Texas, a mere three-hour drive to Kinder, 185 miles away.

The Louisiana Coushatta casino soon began to generate some $300 million annually. For the 837 tribal members, suddenly and spectacularly affluent after 1995, that amounted to a whopping lot of dough.

For most of a decade, it was Ralph Reed rather than Abramoff who got the headlines. Reed's career took off in 1988 when television evangelist Pat Robertson hired him to run his campaign for the Republican presidential nomination against George H. W. Bush.*

---

*The suave Robertson was not your typical TV evangelist, being as corporate as he was evangelical. No one ever confused him with the disgraced "tele-evangelist" Jim Bakker, for example. A Phi Beta Kappa in history from Washington and Lee University and a graduate of the Yale University Law School, Robertson was, in fact, a notably sophisticated fellow.

Reed, like his boss Robertson, was positively sartorial in his dress—some might say too much so—and extremely well-spoken. He cut a sharp image. But he also had sharp elbows; and he was, at least in the opinion of some, a regular sharper. Reed took the remnants of the Robertson for President campaign and turned it into the Christian Coalition, with himself as executive director, in 1989.

Over the next decade, Reed learned a lot about politics, organizing phone banks, direct-mail campaigns, and, in general, running, under cover of darkness, down-and-dirty "grassroots" political campaigns for right-wing evangelical Republican candidates.

As Reed famously explained it, "I want to be invisible. I do guerrilla warfare. I paint my face and travel at night. You don't know it's over until you're in a body bag. You don't know until election night." This was the man who appeared on the cover of *Time* on May 15, 1995, under the cover line "The Right Hand of God."

In 1997, Reed left the organization, which two years later lost its tax-exempt status as a nonpartisan group.

Freed of his responsibilities at the Christian Coalition, Reed set himself up in business as Century Strategies, a political consulting and communications firm with headquarters in Atlanta and offices in Washington. Reed's client list would eventually embrace such corporate giants as Verizon, Enron, and Microsoft.

As he put it to Abramoff at the time (1999), "Hey, now that I'm done with the electoral politics, I need to start humping in corporate accounts. I'm counting on you to help me with some contacts." Still, it was in backdoor political black-box work that Reed excelled—just the sort of down-and-dirty work that matched perfectly with Abramoff's needs.

Among Reed's clients were the Mississippi Choctaws and the Louisiana Coushattas. (The money he was paid for his time and efforts was, conveniently, passed through Abramoff's law firm, Preston Gates, and thence through mutual friend Grover Norquist's Americans for Tax Reform—though at no small cost to Abramoff and Reed.) Reed's job: to drum up support among Christian evangelicals in opposition to Indian gambling in Texas and Alabama.

With Reed preparing to go all out in his "grassroots" campaign against the Poarch Indians of Alabama, Norquist e-mailed Abramoff, "What is the status of the Choctaw stuff? I have a $75k hole in my budget from last year. Ouch." On another occasion, Abramoff e-mailed Reed to let him know that a payment of $300,000 was on its way, adding that it would, unfortunately, prove "a bit lighter" than that because he had had to "give Grover something for helping." That something amounted to $25,000, Grover Norquist's standard fee for acting as a "pass through" for Indian gambling money. Following yet another money transfer to Reed via ATR, Abramoff had cause to complain, "Grover took another $25K!" And so it went.

Norquist's appetite for money was insatiable—as was Reed's (whose "management fee" could run as high as $45,000 per month)—as was Abramoff's. No wonder these three proved such good friends. They no doubt saw more than a little something of themselves in each other.

It was a busy summer for Tom DeLay, who in July 1997 failed to oust Speaker Gingrich, his once bright glow dimmed by a series of ethical lapses, in a botched coup attempt. The failure of the coup badly tarnished the careers of a number of fellow plotters, among them DeLay's chief rival, House majority leader Dick Armey, and New York congressman Bill Paxon. It was when Paxon, backed by DeLay, laid claim to the speakership that Armey suddenly got cold feet and spilled the beans to Gingrich.

DeLay, somewhat miraculously, emerged from the event stronger vis-à-vis Armey. But then, fellow Texan Armey, a former college professor, wasn't a fund-raiser or a money-mover. Tom DeLay was. Much like Gingrich, Armey fancied himself "a big thinker." DeLay, rooted in more physical realities, had nothing but scorn for "big thinkers."

Late that summer, on August 5–11, DeLay had a chance to move even more money. The traveling whip, heretofore little known for his interest in international affairs (save for denouncing the late godless communist Soviet Union), made his first visit to Moscow, accompanied by Chief of Staff Ed Buckham. DeLay told reporters that the trip had been arranged and paid for by a conservative nonprofit organization, the National Center for Public Policy Research (NCPPR).* (For this same August 1997 trip, Jack Abramoff billed the Commonwealth of the Northern Marianas twenty hours for his "interactions" with the majority whip.) What DeLay didn't tell reporters was that the NCPPR was run by Jack Abramoff's close friend and fellow former College Republican Amy Moritz Ridenour, who had been sent to the Marianas gratis, courtesy of his clients there, by Abramoff in November 1996.

Records would later show that the real sponsor of DeLay's six-day August 1997 Moscow trip was a Bahamian shell company controlled by Russian oil oligarchs.† When this fine-wining-and-dining experience was over, Buckham headed home—via the Concorde, at a cost of $5,500. A DeLay spokesman explained to reporters that the purpose of the Moscow trip was so that the majority whip could "meet with religious leaders there."‡

Two months later, in October, DeLay and Buckham were back in

---

*The National Center for Public Policy Research was founded in 1982. Tax returns show that the NCPPR had an annual revenue of more than $6 million in 2003. Tax returns also show that President Amy Ridenour and her husband, David, the center's vice president, were paid a combined $275,000 that year. Amy Ridenour, a frequent newspaper op-ed contributor, has championed Social Security "reform" while calling for reduced governmental regulation, particularly on the environment. A report issued by the center described environmentalists as having engaged in "a jihad . . . against corporate America." Abramoff was on the NCPPR board from 1995 to 2004. Later it would be discovered by Senate investigators that the NCPPR had paid $1.275 million in 2003 to KayGold, a limited liability corporation whose sole director and officer was one Jack Abramoff.

†The expense-paid trip for DeLay and four staffers cost $57,238. According to an account in the *Washington Post*, DeLay and his team "played golf, met with Russian church leaders and talked to Prime Minister Viktor Chernomyrdin, a friend of Russian oil and gas executives associated with the lobbying effort."

‡The globe-trotting DeLay traveled handsomely, whether it was to Moscow or to London. The *National Journal* reported that DeLay's trip to the United Kingdom resulted in $4,285.35 in London hotel bills (at the Four Seasons, no less) for Tom and Christine DeLay. The majority whip's new chief of staff, Susan Hirschmann, and her husband, David, also along for the ride, toted up an additional $5,174.64 in hotel bills, including $3,109 for a "superior" room at the Four Seasons, $129 at the lounge, $75 at room bar, and $422 for chauffeured cars.

The trip, which, of course, included rounds of golf at St. Andrews in Scotland, had as its stated goal "significant policy meetings," including one with former British prime minister Margaret Thatcher.

the heart of the formerly godless communist Soviet Union, as dinner guests of the oil and gas oligarchs Marina Nevskaya and Alexander Koulakovsky of Naftasib, whose principal clients were the Russian ministries of interior and defense.

The common denominator behind both Moscow trips was Abramoff, who had been working on behalf of the Russian energy executives. The Russians had long since, by now, become frequent guests at Abramoff's skyboxes at the MCI Center basketball and hockey complex in suburban Washington.

What exactly the Russian oligarchs were seeking from DeLay has never fully been ascertained. The *Washington Post* has reported that federal prosecutors believed that Nevskaya and Koulakovsky were seeking congressional earmarks for a modular home construction firm headquartered in Russia and for the construction of a fossil-fuel plant in Israel. Other sources claim that the two Russians, who traveled in the company of bodyguards armed with machine guns, wanted in part to be seen in the company of the powerful American legislator to give them credibility with the Russian government and with Gazprom, the giant government-owned energy company.

According to an account in the *Post,* a former Abramoff associate said the two executives had "wanted to contribute to DeLay," at one point actually asking over dinner in Moscow, "What would happen if the DeLays woke up one morning" and found a luxury car in the front of their driveway?

Christopher Geeslin, a Frederick, Maryland–based pastor who served as USFN's director or president from 1998 to 2001, says that Buckham told him that the Russians were seeking DeLay's help with legislation that would have made it possible for the International Monetary Fund (IMF) to bail out the faltering Russian economy. Buckham explained to Geeslin, "This is the way things work in Washington."

The IMF funding issue continued to be a hot-button topic through-out 1998, the Russian stock market having fallen steeply in April and May and the government there having announced on June 18 that it needed $10–$15 billion in new international loans. Not quite one year after DeLay's first visit to Moscow, the Russian government devalued the ruble and defaulted on its treasury bills on August 18, 1998. The Russian stock market virtually crashed in response.

At first, DeLay criticized the Russians, then, turning on a dime, voted for a foreign-aid bill that contained new funds for the IMF account. DeLay, his spokesperson said, "makes decisions and sets legislative priorities based on good policy and what is best for his constituents and the country." He added, "Mr. DeLay has very firm beliefs, and he fights very hard for them."

Coincidentally, the same Bahamian company that paid for DeLay and Buckham's journeys to Moscow in 1997 also cut a check to USFN for $1 million in 1998. According to Geeslin, the Russians had offered to pay in cash, via a delivery to be picked up at a Washington-area airport.*

The money just kept pouring into the coffers of USFN. In 1998, R.J. Reynolds gave the group $100,000 to lobby against new regulations on cigarettes contained in legislation before Congress. Some of the money was used for "grassroots" purposes, among them a series of 1998 radio ads calling on President Clinton to resign his office, others attacking Democratic congressmen.

The largest contribution—apart from the $1 million from the Russians—came from the National Republican Congressional Committee (NRCC), which donated $500,000 to the USFN in a single pop. Authors Lou Dubose and Jan Reid, in their book *The Hammer,* write, "The huge cash transfer was never approved by the NCRR executive committee. Tom Davis, the Virginia Congressman DeLay had made NRCC chair, cut the check because he knew Ed Buckham would use the money to support Republican House candidates."

None of this went unnoticed at the time, though the public had little awareness. Among professional politicians, however, many a curi-

---

*The check for $1 million arrived on June 25, 1998. Tax forms show that the signatory was "Nations Corp, James & Sarch co." This was an English law firm whose clients included the Bahamian company Chelsea Enterprises, which was controlled by the Russian oligarchs. The Russian oligarchs subsequently funneled an additional $2.12 million to Abramoff via a Dutch shell company called Voor Huisen.

ous glance was cast the way of USFN. The Democratic Congressional Committee filed suit in federal court in 1998 alleging that DeLay's funding operations amounted to "racketeering" as defined by the federal RICO Act. The suit was heard by U.S. district judge Thomas Penfield Jackson—the same judge who heard the Microsoft antitrust suit. The DCC suit alleged that three "associated organizations"—the U.S. Family Network, the Republican Majority Issues Committee, and Americans for Economic Growth—were little more than shells used to launder money.

The men running the three organizations named in the suit were among Tom DeLay's closest cronies and most trusted political operatives: Bob Mills (USFN), ARMPAC's Karl Gallant (RMIC), and Jim Ellis (AEG). While the DCC eventually dropped its RICO suit, the NRCC was forced to acknowledge that it had violated federal election law as a result of its $500,000 donation to USFN. The NRCC settled with the Federal Election Commission (FEC) by agreeing to pay $280,000 in civil penalties.

But not before USFN had transferred $300,000 of the NRCC's $500,000 to another nonprofit, and also not before Ed Buckham had taken a cut, by way of commission. Unabashed, Buckham boasted, "If I raise money, I get a portion."

In the world of DeLay Inc., Ed Buckham was unique. For besides being chief of staff to the majority whip, he was also Tom DeLay's personal minister. DeLay liked to tell visiting coreligionists that his day began with morning prayers—in company of the balding, bespectacled Tennessean Ed Buckham. A licensed nondenominational minister, Buckham was not only DeLay's closest political confidant, but also, as it were, his private confessor.

As we have seen, others in the close-knit DeLay political family included wife Christine and fund-raiser daughter Dani, but also deputy chiefs of staff Tony Rudy and Susan Hirschmann.

Another key figure was Michael Scanlon, who joined the team as press secretary in 1997, when Rudy was promoted. Scanlon had worked on and off for Republican congressmen on Capitol Hill since the mid-1990s. His big break, though, came when he joined the office of the majority whip and teamed up with Tony Rudy.

Like Rudy, Scanlon was a competitive athlete, a runner who could do five miles in less than thirty minutes. Rudy and Scanlon had, however, more in common than just athleticism. In the words of the *Wall Street Journal*, "The two shared a pit-bull political style." The problem, as his immediate boss, Communications Director John Feehery discovered, was that Mike Scanlon "was the spinner who was always spinning for himself." That wasn't the half of it though. Eventually, Feehery says, he came to regard Scanlon as "a first-class rogue and a master of deception." Eventually Scanlon and Rudy would focus their pit-bull energies on unseating the president of the United States.

The convoluted tale leading up to the impeachment and trial of President William Jefferson Clinton has been told many times. Only the merest outline of the events will be sufficient for our needs.

Following the suicide of White House counsel Vincent Foster in January 1994, Attorney General Janet Reno appointed a prominent Republican trial lawyer, Robert B. Fiske, as "special counsel" to investigate his death as well as the Clintons' Arkansas financial dealings, known to the public as Whitewater.

But when Congress abolished the office of special counsel in passing the Independent Counsel Reauthorization Act of 1994, a three-judge special panel led by conservative D.C. court of appeals judge David B. Sentelle—a protégé of right-wing Republican North Carolina senators Jesse Helms and Lauch Faircloth—removed the non-partisan Fiske and replaced him with the zealous former federal judge and Bush I solicitor general Kenneth Starr.

President Clinton soon compounded his problems, first by famously saying, in a January 1998 press conference, "I did not have sexual relations with that woman, Miss Lewinsky," then by making misleading statements under oath to Starr's team of prosecutors.

By late 1998, with Tom DeLay driving his party onward, House Republicans, joined by a handful of Democrats, voted 228–206 to impeach Clinton on grounds of perjury and 221–212 to impeach him on grounds of obstruction of justice.* Rudy and Scanlon would, in particular, prove a formidable team during the impeachment.

As Communications Director John Feehery later observed, "Bill Clinton was impeached for three reasons: DeLay, Rudy, and Scanlon." While the rest of the Republican House leadership—Speaker Gingrich, Majority Leader Dick Armey, and Judiciary Committee chairman Henry Hyde—quickly went soft on the idea of impeachment, Whip DeLay not only held out for the plan, but pushed aggressively forward with it.

The two DeLay operatives, Feehery recalls, were, meanwhile, "everywhere, doing the briefing books, leaking to reporters, doing the legal research, and whipping the members." There was nothing they wouldn't stop at either. According to Feehery, Rudy and Scanlon even went so far as "to spread rumors that there was evidence that Clinton had raped a woman."

By the fall of 1998, Feehery was an unhappy camper, thanks largely to DeLay's unrequited bloodlust for William Jefferson Clinton. "My stomach wasn't in this effort," Feehery says today, speaking of the impeachment.†

Rudy and Scanlon obviously felt otherwise. Writing in *The Breach*, his account of the impeachment and trial of President Clinton, *Washington Post* reporter Peter Baker quoted Rudy and Scanlon impatiently e-mailing one another while waiting to find out how Clinton

---

*Lest it be forgotten: With polls showing that 65–70 percent of the American people were opposed to impeachment and removal, the new Senate in January 1999 voted 55–45 against removal on the grounds of perjury and 50–50 against removal on the grounds of obstruction of justice. The Starr investigation—having cost taxpayers at least $40 million—ended in a whimper. Bill Clinton went on to enjoy some of the highest favorable presidential opinion-poll ratings in history.

†It was all too much for Feehery—he left DeLay's office and went to work for Speaker of the House Dennis Hastert, a close ally who had once served as DeLay's chief deputy whip. Still later, Feehery wound up as a high-ranking executive in the Washington office of the Motion Picture Association of America (MPAA), thanks in no small part to DeLay's K Street Project.
    When the MPAA hired former Democratic congressman and Clinton administration secretary of agriculture Dan Glickman as its head, House Republicans removed some $1.5 billion in tax relief for the industry from a pending bill. Grover Norquist told *Roll Call*, "[Pennsylvania Republican senator Rick] Santorum has begun discussing what the consequences are for the movie industry." The appointment of Glickman, he added, was "a studied insult." Glickman—and the industry—got the message.
    They hired Feehery.

had fared with Kenneth Starr and the grand jury. "The waiting," Baker wrote, "was killing them."

"Still no word?" asked Rudy.

"He's going to admit it," Scanlon replied. "The big q is on what level—I still say we need to attack!"

Rudy wrote back, "We need to force dems to distance themselves from theliar [*sic*]. He looked into [A]merica's eyes and lied."

For his part, Mike Scanlon knew an American hero when he saw one, and he saw one in Tony Rudy—and another in himself: "God bless you Tony Rudy—Are we the only ones with political instincts— This whole thing about not kicking someone when they are down is BS—Not only do you kick him—you kick him until he passes out— then beat him over the head with a baseball bat—then roll him up in an old rug—and throw him off a cliff into the pound [*sic*] surf below!!!!!"

Tom DeLay and his henchmen had plotted their impeachment strategy from the second-floor master suite of a Capitol Hill town house located a mere three blocks from DeLay's congressional office. Members of DeLay Inc. had a name for it: the Safe House. The house, which DeLay made the scene of his fund-raising pitches, was owned by the USFN. Other rooms in the house were occupied by ARMPAC and, beginning in late 1998, Buckham's new lobby shop, the Alexander Strategy Group (ASG).

Having helped shepherd the impeachment of Bill Clinton through the House of Representatives in 1998, Buckham resigned from DeLay's staff. It was time to cash in.

Time to cash in, yes; but not time to leave the fold. A former aide explained, "If an individual called DeLay's appointment secretary saying they wanted to talk to DeLay about overregulation, the appointment secretary would say go speak to Buckham." Whatever his title, Ed Buckham, it was clear to just about everyone, was still DeLay's chief political adviser.

House majority leader Dick Armey was no fan of his fellow Texan Tom DeLay, but he had a well-earned reputation as an observer of the

Washington scene. When a reporter from the *New York Times* asked Armey what he made of Ed Buckham's entrance into the world of Washington lobbying, the former majority leader, as usual, was not at a loss for words.

Tom DeLay, Armey said, had sent his man Buckham downtown "to set up shop and start a branch office on K Street. The whole idea was 'What's in it for us?' That's what I thought at the time, and I've seen nothing in the way they've conducted themselves since then to dissuade me from that point of view."

A senior policy adviser—read lobbyist—at Washington's DLA Piper law firm, Armey "invoked Charles Dickens, likening Mr. DeLay to Fagin and Mr. Buckham to the Artful Dodger in *Oliver Twist.*"

Buckham hadn't forgotten his old friends in the Marianas either, despite leaving Congressman DeLay's employ in January 1999. The previous winter, DeLay had met with Enron lobbyists at his Sugar Land home. The object of the meeting had been to secure a $750,000 consulting contract for ARMPAC's Karl Gallant, the former Big Tobacco lobbyist, and his soon-to-be partner in the lobbying business—none other than Ed Buckham. At the time of the Sugar Land sit-down, Buckham was still DeLay's chief of staff, and under the circumstances, the meeting would seem to have violated House ethics rules. Not that that deterred DeLay—or Minister Buckham.

As a newly launched lobbyist, Buckham represented the Houston-based Enron in its bid to build an energy plant in the western Pacific, or to be more specific, an energy plant in the Commonwealth of the Northern Mariana Islands.

When Enron lost out to a Japanese company in the Marianas bidding war, an enraged Tom DeLay demanded that the bidding process be reopened. The unelected boss of the Marianas, textile king Willie Tan—who had been allied with the Japanese—now found himself up against a man mightier even than himself. The "congressman from Enron" prevailed. The local utility board reversed itself, and lobbyist Buckham had a happy client.

For the citizens of Saipan it was another matter, for with Enron

increasingly bogged down in its own internal financial miseries, the
once seemingly insignificant cost of a mere eighty-megawatt power
plant ($120 million) was too much for Enron to bear. In March 2001,
the company announced plans to scale down to a sixty-megawatt
plant. A month later, the Enron bosses backed out of the deal entirely.
The plant was dead in the water. And the citizens of the Marianas were
bereft of a new source of power—and jobs.

In his day, Buckham wore many hats in the DeLay constellation, not
least as gatekeeper, job-placement officer, and money-mover for
DeLay Inc. Just how this worked can be inferred from the relationship
between the nonprofit but rich USFN and the start-up for-profit
ASG, both of them controlled by Ed Buckham.

While ASG paid USFN a token payment for use of its quarters,
USFN paid ASG a monthly retainer of $10,000 to $12,000, beginning
in October 1997 (at a time when Buckham was still on DeLay's congressional staff), for "general consulting." DeLay's wife, Christine,
drew a monthly salary of $3,200 from ASG during three of the years
in which USFN was in business. (Christine DeLay eventually took
home a total of $115,000 from ASG. Her job: supplying Buckham
with the names of lawmakers' favorite charities.)

Investigators would eventually determine that over seven years the
DeLay family had collected some $490,300 from entities controlled
by Buckham. This included Christine DeLay's personal retirement
account, opened by Ed Buckham.

Between 2001 and 2006, DeLay's political action committee ARM-
PAC paid daughter Dani DeLay Ferro $350,304 in political consulting
fees. (During this same period, Tom DeLay's House salary ranged
from $136,700 to $180,100.) When you add ARMPAC payments to
wife Christine together with daughter Dani's payments, the total
surges to over a half million dollars for the same period. Disclosure
forms describe Dani DeLay Ferro's payments as "fund-raising fees,"
"campaign management," and "payroll," with her political consulting
firm Coastal Consulting of Sugar Land, Texas, having received
$222,000 of the $350,000-plus total. When the *New York Times*

reported these payments to daughter Dani, father Tom went ballistic, criticizing the *Times* for "just another seedy attempt by the liberal media to embarrass me." Why, said DeLay, "My wife and daughter have any right, just like any other American, to be employed and be compensated for their employment."*

The DeLays weren't the only ones cashing in. Within four weeks of resigning from his position in the whip's office, Buckham and ASG began receiving commissions from USFN, among them two $75,000 payments in 1998 and one for $104,500 in 1999. The total eventually reached $364,500. All told, during the five-year existence of USFN (1996–2001), Ed Buckham and his wife, Wendy, received $1,022,729 from the purported nonprofit.

And why not? Money was, after all, flying out the windows at USFN. Other payments went for the rental of a skybox at the Washington hockey and basketball arena, the MCI Center ($149,000 beginning in summer 1998); Salvador Dalí and Peter Max prints ($62,375); a Royal Doulton vase ($20,100, listed as "office equipment"); airfare and meals for Jack Abramoff ($11,548); and for travel and entertainment expenses that appear mostly to have benefited the Buckhams ($267,202). "They were using donor funds for interior decorating," the abashed Pastor Geeslin told the *Washington Post*.

So who was signing off on all these expenditures? The USFN board consisted of three evangelical Christians from the town of Republic, Washington (population 954). Associates say that Ed Buckham met the men at a religious retreat. Board minutes from March 1997 show that the group considered appointing Abramoff—though he was an Orthodox Jew—to an expanded board, but never did.

---

*DeLay Ferro's handiwork helped lead to one of her father's three admonishments by the House Ethics Committee. In April 2002, after serving as DeLay's legislative director, Federalist Group lobbyist Drew Maloney and DeLay Ferro organized a two-day fund-raiser for energy companies at the Homestead golf resort in Hot Springs, Virginia. The timing couldn't have been better for all concerned: major energy legislation was heading for conference committee. Needless to say, the fund-raiser was replete with energy company attendees: Reliant Energy; Williams Companies of Tulsa; the El Paso Corp. of Houston; and Westar Energy of Topeka, Kansas, among them. In return for meals and a round of golf with the whip, attendees forked over $152,500 for various DeLay-connected political committees. Dani DeLay Ferro was herself the recipient of K Street love when, in May 2002, Maloney threw a baby shower for her in the Washington offices of his most important client, Houston's Reliant Energy.

In any case, all the real power lay in the hands of Buckham—and his wife, Wendy.

Wendy Buckham, though she served officially as USFN's treasurer for a mere five months in 1996 and 1997, continued to keep the books and sign checks until the outfit folded in 2001. In 1997, she was paid $43,000 in commissions by USFN on $524,975 in raised donations—all of them coming from Abramoff-connected entities.

As USFN began to unwind in 2001, its board awarded $200,000 to staff—and to themselves. The Safe House was sold at a loss of $19,000. And at its final January 2001 meeting, the board agreed to pay $150,000 to the Dorothy Joan Morris Foundation.

What is that? The Dorothy Joan Morris Foundation proved to be a front with headquarters located in an insurance-company office sitting in a Frederick, Maryland, strip mall. State papers show that the Dorothy Joan Morris Foundation was, in turn, owned by Foundation Ministries Inc., which had its offices in a Frederick, Maryland, private residence—the house belonging to Ed and Wendy Buckham.

This kind of corruption would soon seem like chicken feed, when compared to the tens of millions of dollars Buckham's pal Abramoff stole.

CHAPTER FOUR

✯

Who's Your Daddy? Part I

As fascinating as the stories of Jack Abramoff and Tom DeLay are—and there is a lot more story to go, including the aforementioned Indian reservations, a cruise-ship company, and a brain-dead woman in Florida who did not know she was being discussed in the halls of Congress—we must drop back in time to pick up the other more well-known strand of the complex weave that was Houston Republicanism, one that would in time braid itself with DeLay and his ardent enthusiasms.

In 1991, George W. Bush, three years away from being elected governor of Texas, found himself the subject of a Securities and Exchange Commission investigation. At issue was Bush's June 22, 1990, sale of 212,140 shares of Harken Energy—a company in which he was a director—for $848,560.

The younger Bush's now infamous relationship with Harken had from the beginning raised eyebrows. In September 1986, Harken had in effect rescued Bush from his ownership position in a failing oil venture known as Spectrum 7.

Spectrum 7 was the successor company to an earlier exploratory oil venture known as Arbusto Energy. *Arbusto,* its founder liked to point out, means "bush" in Spanish; but the more accepted translation is "shrub," hence the nickname that the late Molly Ivins gifted to George W. Bush—also the title for her best-selling book *Shrub.*

As he would so often in days to come, George W. Bush called on old family connections to raise the start-up money for Arbusto. The principal fund-raiser was George H. W. Bush's brother Jonathan, a Connecticut-based venture capitalist. Uncle Jon would eventually raise $4.7 million on behalf of his nephew, by tapping such well-heeled Eastern investors as Russell Reynolds, the head of one of America's premier executive-search firms. "Being a great friend of the Bushes," Reynolds told the right-wing *American Spectator*, he didn't hesitate to "put in a small amount of money." Another investor was multimillionaire Lewis Lehrman, an archconservative who spent $7 million of his own money in a losing race for New York governor and who would later, briefly, employ the young Jack Abramoff to direct another of his right-wing causes. Russ Reynolds, who would raise $4 million for George H. W. Bush's 1988 presidential campaign, explained to the *Dallas Morning News*, "These were all the Bushes' [*sic*] pals. This is the A-team."

Arbusto, thinly capitalized despite its deep-pocketed investors, proved little more than a tax shelter for most. The $1.55 million in profit distributions from Arbusto were dwarfed by the $3.9 million in tax write-offs that investors received for their $4.67 million investment. "A company balance sheet can be misleading," the Harvard-trained MBA CEO Bush would later say of Arbusto, adding, "There was momentum."

Arbusto received a temporary respite from its financial woes in 1982 — at a time when the elder George Bush was already vice president of the United States. The white knight was a wealthy Panamanian investor, Philip Uzielli, a Princeton classmate of Bush family consigliere James A. Baker III. Molly Ivins and Lou Dubose write that, with Arbusto "in a terminal cash crunch," Uzielli paid $1 million for 10 percent "of a failing company valued at $382,376, according to the company's financial statements." In other words, say Ivins and Dubose in their book *Bushwhacked*, "Uzielli paid $1 million for $38,200 in equity." Ultimately, Uzielli seems to have lost his entire $1 million investment, describing it to reporters as having been "a losing wicket," but also "great fun." For his part, George W. Bush was undeterred. "What Uzi was betting on, he's betting on me," the younger Bush told the *Dallas Morning News*.

Renamed Bush Exploration, the successor company to Arbusto once again had to be bailed out in 1984. This time the money came from Mercer Reynolds III and William O. DeWitt. DeWitt, in particular, shared much in common with the younger Bush: both came from old money and had gone to Yale (AB) and to Harvard (MBA). Better still, DeWitt's father had once owned the Cincinnati Reds; and this connection too would play a role in the making of George W. Bush. But that was still to come.

Renamed yet again, this time as Spectrum 7, the oil exploration venture did little better than its predecessors. Yet another white knight was clearly called for. The white knight this time was named Harken.

In exchange for Spectrum 7's dubious assets, Harken granted Bush $500,000 in stock, stock options valued at $131,250, and a consultancy paying $50,000 to $120,000 a year. He was also given a place on the Harken board—and a series of loans. The company awarded the struggling Bush sweetheart loans totaling $180,375—at 5 percent interest. That Harken should have taken such an interest in the welfare of an obscure young oilman stretches credulity. Until you look at the political equation, that is. Then, the murky picture clears. David Corn of the *Nation* quotes billionaire George Soros, a Harken investor at the time, as saying of Bush, "We were buying political influence. That was it. He was not much of a businessman."

The timing was surely right, for President George H. W. Bush had taken America and its coalition partners, including the Saudis, to war against Iraq on August 2, 1990, little more than a month and a half after George W. Bush sold his Harken stock.

Harken had problems of its own, though, including a failed deal in 1988 that had left the company with precious little cash-flow flexibility. Harken, in turn, masked those losses by selling 80 percent of a subsidiary, Aloha Petroleum, to an insider partnership for $12 million—$11 million of which came in the form of a loan from Harken. The sideshow that was Aloha suggests that what happened at Harken in those days presaged—albeit on a much smaller scale—the financial shenanigans that would later occur at Enron.

Fortunately, like so many of the companies associated with the young George W. Bush, Harken had its own white knight, in this case the Harvard Management Company, the investment management arm of the multibillion-dollar Harvard University endowment. In late 1990, Harken and Harvard Management—at this point Harken's largest shareholder—created something called the Harken Anadarko Partnership (HAP), which allowed parent Harken to move as much as $20 million in losses off its balance sheets and over to HAP. The effect was to reduce significantly the losses and liabilities shown by Harken over the next two years.

It was a good deal—if you could get it. Most companies, it's safe to say, wouldn't have gotten it.

Almost exactly two months from the time Bush sold his stock in late June of 1990, Harken announced a $23.2 million loss for the previous quarter, causing its shares to plummet over 20 percent, from $3 to $2.375, in a single day's trading session. Bush, however, had gotten out at $4 a share—a difference of almost $350,000 between what he sold for and what his shares would have been worth at the end of the trading day.

Inevitably, fingers were pointed at Bush, the politically active son of the sitting president of the United States. How, after all, could the younger Bush, a member of the Harken board's audit committee, not have known about the impending losses?

The circumstances were, at the least, suspicious. A May 20, 1990, internal memo had warned that Harken might not be able to meet its June payroll obligations. Less than a month later, lawyers from the company's outside counsel, the Dallas firm of Haynes & Boone, had specifically warned officers and directors about inside selling. The subject matter of the lawyers' memo read, "Liability for insider trading and short swing profits."

Undeterred, Bush sold his shares to an anonymous institutional investor one week later. The money was then used to repay an $800,000 loan Bush had taken out in April 1989. That loan—and the friendship of fellow investors, led by Bush's longtime best buddy, New York multimillionaire Roland Betts (a 1968 Yale classmate and DKE fraternity brother), and Bush Exploration investor Bill DeWitt—had made possible that same month Bush's purchase of a minority stake in the

Texas Rangers baseball team. And, eventually, it made him a million-aire, many times over. For when the team was sold in 1998, former managing partner Bush walked off with over $15 million, a return of 1,775 percent on his borrowed investment.

As managing partner of the Rangers—perhaps the only job that the future "CEO president" ever succeeded in—Bush served as the pub-lic face of the team, glad-handing politicians, sports agents, ballplay-ers, fans, and the local media. At this, he excelled. Not surprisingly, the sports media was quick to credit Bush with the building of The Ball-park at Arlington, the Rangers' popular retro-style playing field. In fact, most of the heavy lifting was done by a fellow Rangers executive named Tom Schieffer. Schieffer, whose $1.4 million investment in the team was roughly double that of Bush, had been a successful corporate lawyer in his native Fort Worth.*

Bush's Harken dealings eventually became the subject of a Securi-ties and Exchange Commission investigation. Representing the future president of the United States was a Baker Botts partner named Robert Jordan.†

The general counsel of the Securities and Exchange Commission at the time was one James Robert Doty, also a Baker Botts partner, on leave of absence while in service to the government. The formidably learned Doty (Rice BA in history summa cum laude; Phi Beta Kappa; Rhodes Scholar at Oxford; Harvard MA; and Yale Law School gradu-ate with honors) might have been expected to quiz the callow Bush. But Doty, who had earlier represented Bush in the deal that made him a 2 percent partner in the Texas Rangers, recused himself from the inquiry.

Doty's boss at the SEC, however, was yet another Baker Botts part-ner, Richard C. Breeden. And Breeden's background was even more interesting, for he had served as deputy counsel to the vice president of the United States from 1982 to 1985. The vice president under whom

---

*The brother of CBS News chief Washington correspondent Bob Schieffer, Tom Schieffer was a conservative Democrat turned Republican—and would later be appointed ambassador to Australia by President George W. Bush.

†Jordan would eventually be appointed U.S. ambassador to Saudi Arabia by Bush.

Breeden served was George H. W. Bush, who, as president, appointed the then Baker Botts partner as chairman of the SEC in 1989.

Curiously, no one, it seems, was much bothered by any of this at the time.

On August 21, 1991, an SEC staff report concluded that there was insufficient evidence to determine whether Bush had profited from insider information or advance knowledge of Harken's losses.

Score another quiet victory for Bush family connections and Baker Botts.

It didn't hurt that the Houston law firm had for generations been plugged into the nation's power grid, including a connection to the Bush family that predated George H. W. Bush's friendship with James A. Baker III by almost a half century. The formula had made Baker Botts the preeminent law firm in the state and one of the most powerful law firms in the nation. With a history that stretched back well before the Civil War, the firm enjoyed personal and institutional connections that were often many decades old—relationships that were carefully maintained, strategically leveraged, and intelligently linked forward as one generation of the powerful firm's lawyers gave way to the next.

A precursor firm to Baker Botts had opened its doors in the swampy little Gulf Coast town of Houston in 1840—at a time when Texas was still a republic. Statehood came five years later, the Civil War twenty-one years later, and war's end in 1865. The firm known as Gray & Botts was founded the very next year. Even in the midst of Reconstruction, the young firm's lawyers did not hesitate to ally themselves with the Yankee robber barons.

As the *Handbook of Texas* notes, "For the first thirty-four years of the firm's history, its partners were primarily trial lawyers, railroad lawyers, or both." By the late 1880s, lawyers at the firm were general counsel to both the Missouri Pacific and Southern Pacific railroads, companies that were to the late-nineteenth-century Southwestern economy what Dell and Compaq would be to the regional economy a century later.

One of the prize possessions of the firm today is a handwritten

$10,000 retainer dated 1872 from a corporate predecessor to the Southern Pacific Railroad. Over the years, the retainer passed from partner to partner, always hanging in the offices of the man who represented the railroad.

Baker & Botts was par excellence Wall Street's legal team in the Southwest. The law firm's clientele was a who's who of old Yankee money—and nouveaux robber-baron industry—not only the railroads but Northern brokerage houses, lumber companies, utilities—and, following the discovery of oil at a salt dome called Spindletop south of Beaumont on January 10, 1901, the captains of Big Oil.

Lawyer-writer Griffin Smith, as keen an observer of the Houston legal scene as there has ever been, put it this way: "From the 1870s to the 1930s, when the Southwest was just another province in the economic system that was centralized in the East, these interests required trustworthy lawyers to tend their gardens, and they found them." They found them in one firm, at one address: Baker & Botts, Houston.

The man who most embodied the power of Wall Street in those years—the man who was its de facto ambassador to the Southwest—was a cunning railroad lawyer from East Texas named Robert S. Lovett (1860–1932). Having joined Baker & Botts in 1882, Bob Lovett was hired as general counsel of the Union Pacific Railroad in 1892. "Mister Bob," as he was known, soon became the right-hand man of the Bill Gates of his day, the enormously wealthy robber baron E. H. Harriman, controlling owner of both the UP and Southern Pacific railroads. And all the while, the sly Texan Lovett remained a senior partner at Baker & Botts.

It was Lovett, along with his partner, James Addison Baker (1857–1941), who set the bar for Baker & Botts. Born in the East Texas hamlet of Huntsville, Baker was admitted to the practice of law in 1880. Two years later, aged twenty-five, Baker joined Gray & Botts. (His father, also named James and also a lawyer, had joined the firm not long after Lee's surrender at Appomattox.)

Setting a pattern that would be emulated in the twentieth century by James Elkins of rival law firm Vinson & Elkins, Baker went on to found a captive bank and, in effect, attach it to his law firm. The Commercial National Bank, which he organized, merged with the South

Texas National Bank, and Baker became chairman. He was also a founder and board member of the Houston Gas Company—the precursor of Houston Lighting & Power (known in its time as HL&P and today organized as two separate entities, Reliant Energy and CenterPoint Energy), a Baker Botts client from day one—and an organizer of the Galveston, Houston and Henderson Railway and the Southwestern Drug Company. President of the Houston Bar Association and a member of the Texas Philosophical Society, Baker was a Houston luminary in every sense.

His greatest public fame, however, derived from a murder mystery. As the personal lawyer for one of Houston's richest men, the cotton factor William Marsh Rice, Baker was instrumental in proving that his client had been murdered—by a shifty New York attorney in cahoots with Rice's valet. The two men, it turned out, had poisoned the old gentleman and substituted a second will leaving his $5.6 million estate (the equivalent of $100 million or more in today's dollars) to them.

"Captain" Baker—as he was known—ordered an autopsy that proved that Rice had indeed been murdered. The valet turned state's evidence, and the crooked lawyer wound up in Sing Sing. The inheritance went, as the transplanted Yankee Rice had intended, for the establishment of a college, the William Marsh Rice Institute (today's Rice University), which opened its doors in 1912 to "the white inhabitants of the City of Houston and State of Texas." The Rice Institute's first and longest-serving chairman of the board: Captain James Addison Baker, from 1891 until his death in 1941.

While Captain Baker looked after the daily affairs of the firm, "Mister Bob" Lovett held a series of ever more important jobs within the far-flung Harriman empire. Between 1898 and his death in 1932, Lovett served as president, executive committee chairman, and chairman of the board of the Union Pacific Railroad.

Lovett's hand could be found (if not seen) in every corner of Harriman's empire, from the prosperous Illinois Central to the grande dame of American railroads, old Commodore Vanderbilt's New York Central, just two of the many railroads on whose boards Lovett served (1913–32).

In 1919, at the conclusion of World War I, E. H. Harriman's son

Averell set off on his own, founding the investment bank of W. A. Harriman & Co. While Harriman served as chairman, the president, in charge of daily operations, was George Herbert Walker, who soon saw to it that his son-in-law, Prescott Bush, was made a vice president in 1926. Five years later, when W. A. Harriman & Co. merged with the London firm Brown Brothers, there was another new partner: Robert A. Lovett.

"Young Bob," though born in Huntsville, Texas, had been educated as a privileged Easterner. Yale class of 1918, Lovett was tapped for membership in the exclusive and even then notoriously secretive Skull & Bones by none other than Prescott Bush (Yale '17). By the early 1930s, they were both partners at Brown Brothers Harriman.

Robert A. Lovett would go on to serve Franklin D. Roosevelt as assistant secretary of war for air during the Second World War. Under Harry Truman, he would successively be undersecretary of state, deputy secretary of defense, and secretary of defense. In time, the younger Lovett, like Dean Acheson, would be known as one of "The Wise Men," the famous "Counselors to Presidents."

For his part, Young Bob Lovett's Yale pal Prescott Bush would go on to serve as Republican U.S. senator from Connecticut—and to found an American political dynasty.

As the latest political scion of the dynasty founded by Prescott Bush, George W. Bush inherited a name with a magic ring and seemingly limitless connections. (Among his first summer jobs as a teenager: working as a messenger at Baker Botts.) But, once elected governor of Texas, Bush also inherited from Ann Richards a job that was inherently weak. Being governor did not of itself bring with it power—nor did it necessarily lead to the White House. The reasons for this lay deep within the history and psychology of post–Civil War Texas.

Following the Civil War, Texas, like the other former Confederate states, fell under marshal law enforced by the might of the occupying Union Army. With most white Southern males temporarily disenfranchised, the vote—and thus public office—fell to newly liberated African-Americans and the rare Unionists left in the state. Among these was a lawyer named Edmund J. Davis.

Davis, a former judge, had served as a general in the Union Army, commanding the First Texas Cavalry Regiment. In the eyes of most white Texans that made the tall, gaunt Davis the state's leading home-grown scalawag, worse even than a carpetbagger come from up North.

After the war, Davis acted as chair of a state constitutional convention, later winning election in 1870 as governor. The constitution that the Radical Republican Davis had helped write made him the most powerful governor in Texas history—and, as the commander of a newly created state militia, the head of his own little army.

Not surprisingly, Davis was also the most despised governor in Texas history. When Texans next drew up a state constitution, in 1876, the state militia was abolished and the expansive powers of the governor ground into the dirt. The overwhelmingly white, conservative Democrats—most of them former Confederates—bequeathed Texas a diminished constitution. One hundred thirty-one years and more than four hundred amendments later, it is still the constitution of Texas.

The state political landscape wrought by the constitution of 1876 is littered with competing power bases, none inherently dominant over the next. To non-Texans—and not a few Texans—it can seem bewildering.

The governor's powers, having been vastly circumscribed in 1876, lie largely in the always dicey ability to persuade and "lead." The governor's appointive powers, for example, are extremely limited. There is no formal cabinet for the simple reason that most of the state's executive offices are elected. The elected officials include the lieutenant governor, attorney general, comptroller, land commissioner, agriculture commissioner, and the state's judges, from lowest to highest.

That leaves the governor with the power to appoint a secretary of state—a sinecure that would be held for a time under George W. Bush by an obscure Vinson & Elkins corporate lawyer from Houston named Alberto Gonzales (to whom we will return later)—and the members of various boards. Ironically, the most powerful of these boards are those that run the state's two major systems of higher education, the University of Texas and Texas A&M University. This is so not merely because of the fervent attachment of Texans to collegiate football—nowhere more so than in the heated rivalry between the

Longhorns and Aggies—but because the boards control how multi-billion-dollar endowments are invested. They also decide where the interest from those investments go, whether into faculty salaries, facilities maintenance, or construction. Hundreds of millions of dollars go into construction.

Counseled by his inner circle—"the Iron Triangle," consisting of chief of staff and future FEMA director Joe Allbaugh, political strategist Karl Rove, and communications director Karen Hughes—Governor George Bush moved to fill as many slots on as many boards and commissions as he could, beginning with the powerful state university system boards.

To these traditional venues was now added a new state commission whose board any governor would be interested in controlling. It was called the Texas Lottery Commission. What the commission, like the university boards, had to offer was control over money, contracts, and jobs. Bush's choice to head the Lottery Commission was prominent Dallas attorney Harriet Miers. If you were George W. Bush, there was much to like about the earnest Harriet Miers. Aged fifty at the time of her appointment, Miers was a graduate of Dallas's Southern Methodist University and of its law school. An evangelical Christian, Miers had spent most of her legal career at a politically connected Dallas law firm, Locke Liddell & Sapp. Having served as the first female president of the Dallas Bar Association, Miers was in 1992 elected as the first female president of the Texas Bar Association.

Described by *Newsweek* as "a hard-nosed Dallas lawyer," Miers was certainly that. But she was also a George W. Bush loyalist. One of Miers's jobs as head of the Lottery Commission had been to fire its executive director, a Democrat named Nora Linares, who promptly sued the lottery. But getting rid of Linares was merely prelude to the main act: a battle over the lottery operations contract.

With the lottery generating revenue by the bushel-load, the contract to operate it was obviously worth millions. The winner of that lucrative contract had been the Rhode Island–based G-TECH, the nation's leading lottery operator. Its Austin lobbyist: the onetime golden boy of Texas politics, Ben Barnes, a man many astute observers once believed would be "the next LBJ." In helping G-TECH win the state's contract, Barnes had helped himself to a fortune, garnering a lifetime deal with G-TECH that paid him a percentage of the company's Texas earnings.

All of this made G-TECH and Barnes likely targets for the Bush administration and its lottery chairwoman, Miers. As recounted by *Bush's Brain* coauthor James Moore, Miers wrote to the commission's in-house counsel, "The time has come. I am convinced the Texas Lottery Commission and the State of Texas will be best served by the rebid of the Lottery Operator contract as soon as possible."

Miers's choice to replace Nora Linares as commission executive director, Lawrence Littwin, had come in with promises to "clean-up the lottery." Yet six months later, in October 1997, Littwin too was gone, fired by Harriet Miers. Littwin brought suit, claiming that he had been dismissed after opening an investigation into the financial ties between the lottery, G-TECH—and Ben Barnes.

All this made lottery reformer Littwin a dangerous man: dangerous to G-TECH, dangerous to Barnes, dangerous too to George W. Bush. The reason: in a sworn deposition (since sealed), Barnes told how, when he was speaker of the Texas House of Representatives, he had helped get a politically connected young man named George W. Bush into the Texas Air National Guard.

With the threat of the draft hanging over the young Bush's head—his draft deferment having ended with his graduation from Yale in 1968—Barnes had gotten him into a Texas Air National Guard unit whose ranks were swollen with the sons of the state's privileged and a handful of Dallas Cowboys football players.

The story, as told by Barnes, was that he had been approached by an intermediary, millionaire Houston oilman Sidney Adger, on behalf of Congressman George H. W. Bush. That way neither Barnes nor the elder Bush would have to testify that he had talked to the other about the matter. Neatly done, so long as Ben Barnes kept his mouth shut. Until 1995, he had no reason to do otherwise.

But with pressure from Littwin on G-TECH to amend its multi-million-dollar contract with the former lieutenant governor, Barnes had plenty of reasons to threaten to talk. Millions of reasons, in fact.

In his lawsuit, Littwin claimed that G-TECH had taken Barnes off the company's books by settling with him to the tune of $23 million. The company, Littwin charged, had then pressured Miers and the lottery into firing him by threatening to reveal all, beginning with the story of George W. Bush's involvement with the Texas Air National Guard.

After a federal judge ruled that Miers did not have to testify in the lawsuit, Littwin settled with G-TECH for $300,000. As part of the settlement, Barnes's testimony was put under seal.

That did not, however, end Harriet Miers's involvement in efforts to protect the good name of the Bush family. In 1998, with Governor George W. Bush up for reelection, Miers, in her role as a law firm partner, was paid $19,000 by his campaign to vet the relevant Texas Air National Guard documents in the case. Miers's sidekick in the quest to vet and purge: future White House communications director and senior counselor Dan Bartlett. As author Jim Moore, among others, has noted, Miers, with her newly gotten Lottery Commission insights into the history of George W. Bush, the Texas Air National Guard, and Ben Barnes,* was uniquely suited for the job.

---

*No one understood better the complicated lay of the Texas political landscape than its former golden boy Ben Barnes. By the time CBS News's Dan Rather and his producer Mary Mapes rediscovered Barnes late in the summer of 2004, the former speaker of the House and lieutenant governor was sixty-five years old—and though a multimillionaire Austin lobbyist, largely forgotten by Texas voters.

Appearing with Rather on a September 8, 2004, segment of *60 Minutes Wednesday,* Barnes—a major fund-raiser that year for Democratic candidate John Kerry—finally, publicly confessed his role in getting the young George W. Bush into the Texas Air National Guard. Barnes's belated revelations were, however, as nothing compared to the hotly disputed revelations concerning Bush's service in the Air National Guard. Based on documents obtained by Mapes from retired Texas National Guard lieutenant colonel Bill Burkett, the *60 Minutes Wednesday* report claimed that these had previously been among the papers of Bush's former commanding officer Lieutenant Colonel Jerry Killian. During the ensuing controversy, flamed by right-wing bloggers, it was claimed that the censorious documents had been forged. The documents—they appeared to have been copies of copies—have never been authenticated. Nor have they definitely been identified as forgeries.

In early January of 2005, a two-man Independent Review Panel selected by CBS to investigate the investigation returned a scathing report, excoriating Rather and Mapes. Of the two "independent" investigators, one was a retired head of the Associated Press. The other was former attorney general Dick Thornburgh, a onetime member of President George H. W. Bush's cabinet, Republican governor of Pennsylvania, and Nixon appointee as U.S. attorney for western Pennsylvania. As a result of the controversy, Rather found himself shunted out of his longtime anchor's role, Mapes and other senior executives at CBS News were fired early the following year, and CBS News was forced to issue an abject apology. Not a few Texas observers thought they could intuit the fine hand of Karl Rove behind the whole affair.

☆   ☆   ☆

Governor George W. Bush's luck, recurrently good, continued with
the man who was his first lieutenant governor, Bob Bullock. A
stranger pair could hardly be imagined. Wily, vituperative, vindictive,
and just plain mean, Bullock had gone through five wives and countless bottles of bourbon in his lifetime. He'd also developed a reputation as the toughest guy in a tough sport, having earlier served as a
state representative, head of the Texas Democratic Party, secretary of
state, and comptroller.

After a lifetime in politics, the veteran Bullock knew where the
bones were hidden—and wasn't afraid to dig them up when necessary.
He was known to carry a six-shooter, "cussed up a storm," thought
nothing of using profanities when it suited him (frequently), and finished off every speech with his trademark "God bless Texas!" It did
not pay to cross Bob Bullock.

Like Tom Schieffer, Bullock was comfortable working behind the
scenes; and, like Schieffer, he was extremely competent at what he did.
The master of a largely Democratic state senate, Bullock was the man
newly elected Governor Bush would mainly have to reckon with.

That Bush's governorship disappointed many of the state's most
ardent right-wingers—and led many moderates and liberals to believe,
incorrectly, that Bush was himself a moderate conservative—had
everything to do with Bob Bullock and his counterpart, Democratic
house speaker Pete Laney.

Temperamentally, Laney was the opposite of Bullock, but was like
him in being a highly effective legislative leader. A soft-spoken cotton
farmer from West Texas, first elected to the state house in 1973 and
chosen speaker in 1993, Laney was widely considered to be the most
principled speaker in living memory. Texas Monthly, for example,
described him as having run "the fairest, cleanest, most open, most
democratic house in memory."

For four years, the tandem of Laney and Bullock, as much as
George Bush, ran Texas, driving the state's legislative agenda. And if
that agenda was, in fact, decidedly moderate and humane, then the
state—and Bush—had Bob Bullock and Pete Laney to thank for it.

☆ ☆ ☆

If there was one issue that Governor Bush and the people behind him were, in fact, devoted to, it was tort reform. Legions of high-powered lawyers, such as Harriet Miers, working at big firms, such as Locke Liddell, have spent a lot of time over the past few decades defending rich corporate clients in what seemed like a never-ending war with plaintiff's lawyers fought over a battleground strewn with mass tort actions.

The war began in 1994. That's when former Baker Botts partner Hugh Rice Kelly and a band of millionaire tort reformers, the Texans for Lawsuit Reform—multimillionaire homebuilder Dick Weekley, construction magnate Leo Linbeck, and wine retailer Richard Trabulsi—began putting their money where their mouths were, by investing in legislators. Convinced by their Austin lobbyist that the way to victory led through the Texas legislature, the TLR millionaires pumped $600,000 into the 1994 legislative elections, including $300,000 in three races being run by novice Republican candidates. All three won. The lesson stuck. By the time Governor George W. Bush was elected to a second term, his campaigns had been the recipient of more than $4 million thanks to the generosity of TLR.*

According to its Web site, TLR "seeks to create a civil justice system that discourages non-meritorious lawsuits or outrageous claims for damages." It seeks to create such a civil justice system, in large measure, by putting like-minded lawyers on the state's bench. "To meet our goals," the Web site declares, "TLR is active in political campaigns (through the TLR Political Action Committee), in legislative advocacy, in public relations, in judicial selection, and in the development of case law."

Back in 1994, recalls one of TLR's founders, "There were just too damn many Democratic plaintiff's lawyers in the legislature." He pauses. "We set out to do something about that."

---

*What "tort reform" meant for the average victim of bad medicine and cheap building practices is amply demonstrated in Mimi Swartz's excellent "Hurt? Injured? Need a Lawyer? Too Bad!" (*Texas Monthly*, November 2005). Needless to say, the millionaire founders of Texans for Lawsuit Reform were displeased when the article appeared.

George W. Bush's instincts were always to do what it took to preserve capital, the capital markets, and those who invested in the capital markets. And there was no finer word in his dictionary than
corporate. It therefore took not so much as a push to land George W.
Bush in the tort reform camp. He was born there.

But, in Mike Toomey and Karl Rove, Bush had two of the most
aggressive tort reform operatives in the state as his chief political counselors going into the 1994 election.

As we have seen, Governor George Bush had inherited a state government that was almost entirely composed of Democratic officehold-
ers. One of the most ambitious of these was the Harvard-educated
attorney general Dan Morales.

As ably recounted in *Boy Genius*—Carl M. Cannon, Lou Dubose,
and Jan Reid's book about Karl Rove—Morales had in 1996 joined
with other state attorneys general in filing suit against the tobacco
industry. Faced with billions of dollars of bills for health care for indigent patients with tobacco-related illnesses, Governor George Bush
was in a political quandary. Having promised tort reform, he now
found himself forced to support, if only tacitly, the biggest class-action
lawsuit of all time.

The multistate tobacco suit proved the summit for the tort lawyers.
After decades of fruitlessly—and at great expense—trying to convince
jurors and judges that America's tobacco companies had knowingly
marketed a product they knew caused cancer, the plaintiff's bar now
had the subpoena power, shiny respectability, and deep pockets of the
state attorneys general on their side. This was no longer about Big
Tobacco crushing the little guy and his two-bit lawyer. This was now
Big Tobacco versus Big Government, and Big Government was going
to win.

The endgame was, by the mid-1990s, playing itself out. Eventually,
Big Tobacco would settle with the State of Texas for $17 billion in dam-
ages. Separately, the tobacco companies agreed to pay $3 billion in legal
fees to the tort lawyers. As the authors of *Boy Genius* put it so neatly,
"The five trial lawyers"—and their partners and associates—"were
going to collect paychecks that would put them in a tax bracket with
Halliburton's [then CEO] Dick Cheney [and] Enron's Ken Lay."

Karl Rove's genius was to take the focus away from the whopping $17 billion the state and its citizens got from the settlement—take away too the focus on the tobacco companies' admitted marketing of a cancer-causing product. The focus, thanks to Rove, would be on the five "tobacco lawyers" and their $3 billion.

Rove's cat's-paw in this was to be the unctuous John Cornyn. Never mind that Cornyn had earlier been a San Antonio–based lawyer for large insurance companies—and a faithful supporter of the same big companies against the little man in his rulings from the bench of the state supreme court.

Thus it was that John Cornyn, wrapped in his service as a former supreme court justice, showed up on the steps of the federal courthouse in Texarkana, Texas, to denounce the greedy tobacco lawyers and their ill-gotten billions. Never mind that the legal fees had been set by an arbitration panel acceptable to all parties—and that the $3 billion was separate from the $17 billion and would revert to the tobacco companies if overturned.

John Cornyn had become the high-priced water boy for tort reform; and with the gust from $1.5 million in financing from the Texans for Lawsuit Reform behind his sails, he was soon to be attorney general of the Great State of Texas, not to mention one step closer to his ultimate goal, the United States Senate—making him yet another powerful Texan in the halls of Congress.

CHAPTER FIVE

✯

Casino Jack

Back in the nation's capital, Ed Buckham wasn't the only member of DeLay Inc. to decide that, with the impeachment and trial of William Jefferson Clinton come to its inglorious end, the time was right to move on—and cash in. Like Buckham before him, communications director Michael Scanlon looked longingly at the bright lights of K Street.

Scanlon had, moreover, already made some significant changes in his life. With his marriage on the rocks, Scanlon had begun having an affair with an attractive blond coworker, newly hired DeLay press secretary Emily Miller. Miller and Scanlon had much in common, for not only were they attracted to politics—and each other—they also were attracted to the game. Miller, who would later serve Secretary of State Colin Powell as press spokesperson, was a Georgetown University graduate and former ABC News producer. She was also known to have a temper.

In late 1999, Scanlon left his wife and young son and took a higher-paying public relations job. The following March, Jack Abramoff hired the former DeLay communications director at his law firm, Preston Gates. Mike Scanlon was now, officially, a member of Team Abramoff.

It was to be the start of a beautiful friendship—and one that would ultimately lead to federal criminal convictions for both Abramoff and Scanlon.

But it wasn't the only friendship that would end in jail time for Jack Abramoff. The thirty-six-year-old Adam Kidan and Abramoff, five years his senior, had known each other since their days working together as College Republican organizers.*

While Abramoff affected the tough-guy look and language—the F-word slipped easily and often from his tongue—and had made a modest name for himself producing action movies in Hollywood, Kidan bordered on being the real thing.

A 1989 Brooklyn Law School graduate, Kidan had worked in George H. W. Bush's presidential campaign. Later, he'd taken a job at the New York–based Four Freedoms Foundation, described by Matthew Continetti in the *Weekly Standard* as "a tax shelter disguised as an exercise in conservative benevolence." After that came a run as a fast-food-chain entrepreneur on Long Island. Kidan's partner in the bagel business was the late Michael Cavallo, said by authorities to be an associate of known gangsters.

What brought Adam Kidan and his old friend Jack Abramoff back together again was gambling—and the desire to make some easy money. By now, Abramoff was known to be one of the top gaming lawyers in America. And if his primary interest lay in Indian gaming, that didn't mean that Abramoff wasn't on top of other developments in the high-stakes, high-return industry. There was, for example, another, somewhat more obscure subset of the industry that was of interest to Abramoff, one that combined gambling and "cruises to nowhere."

SunCruz Casinos operated a fleet of eleven midsize cruise ships out of Florida ports. Each of the vessels also served as a floating casino, the idea being to take gamblers into international waters, beyond the reach of state and federal laws. The owner of this "cruise to nowhere"

---

*Kidan had been an undergraduate at George Washington University at a time when Abramoff, the group's chairman, was attending law school at nearby Georgetown University.

business, headquartered at Dania Beach near Fort Lauderdale, was one Konstantinos Boulis.* In 1994, Boulis sold his Florida-based Miami Subs chain, which had grown to over 150 franchises, to Nathan's. Boulis used some of his payoff as seed money for the SunCruz operation. Within five years, the cruise line was turning tens of millions in profits—while employing more than a thousand workers—and its owner, Boulis, was on the road to becoming a multimillionaire many times over.

But on August 3, 1998, federal authorities charged Boulis with violating U.S. shipping laws. The owner of an American flag vessel was required to be a U.S. citizen, which Boulis, a Greek immigrant, was not. As part of his settlement with the U.S. government, Boulis agreed to pay a $1 million fine—and sell the SunCruz line.

Boulis turned to his attorney, Art Dimopoulos, a partner in the Washington office of Preston Gates Ellis & Rouvelas Meeds, for advice. Dimopoulos then brought the matter to the attention of his firm's star lobbyist—and fixer—Jack Abramoff. From his long experience with Indian gaming, Abramoff was well aware that ownership of a casino was a license to print money. It wasn't often that such a profit-making machine went on the market—especially as the result of a fire sale.

Now that the opportunity arose, Abramoff, Kidan, and a third partner, former Reagan administration official Ben Waldman, pounced.† The original plan, Kidan would later tell a *Newsday* reporter, was to use SunCruz "to run casinos for Indian tribes." It sounded like a surefire way to make money—easy money, at that. The problem was that Abramoff and his partners didn't have the $150 million that it would take to buy SunCruz.

---

*Born in 1949 in the northeastern Greek prefecture of Kavala—his father was an Aegean fisherman—Boulis joined the merchant marine as a young man. In 1968, aged nineteen, Boulis jumped ship in Nova Scotia. Eventually, he landed in Toronto, where he took a job as a dishwasher in a Mr. Submarine sandwich shop. Five years later, he was the company's CEO. When the chain of some two hundred stores was sold, Gus Boulis walked away a multimillionaire at the age of twenty-five and moved to Florida.

†Like Kidan, Waldman had met Abramoff in College Republicans and had gone on to work in the Reagan-Bush Jewish Coalition. Like Abramoff's buddy Ralph Reed, he had also worked in the 1988 Republican primaries for Pat Robertson.

Only days after returning from a golfing trip to Scotland with Tom DeLay, Abramoff, on June 9, 2000, persuaded deputy chief of staff Tony Rudy to have the majority whip's office send the embattled SunCruz millionaire a flag that had flown over the Capitol. It was a nice touch and one full of irony: an American flag for the Greek immigrant who had been forced by an unforgiving U.S. government to sell his profitable, American-flagged fleet—and a vivid reminder, if Boulis needed it, of just how plugged into power Jack Abramoff really was.

If gentle persuasion didn't work, there was always the other kind. Abramoff now assigned Mike Scanlon the task of persuading Ohio congressman Robert Ney to help put the squeeze on Boulis. Ney, known as "the Mayor of Capitol Hill," was the chairman of the House Administration Committee and one of DeLay's deputy whips.*

Encouraged by Abramoff and Scanlon, Ney's chief of staff, Neil Volz, arranged for his boss to put critical comments regarding Boulis into the *Congressional Record.* In his March 30 remarks, Chairman Ney pronounced the Greek-born shipping magnate—even citing him by name—one of the "few bad apples" in the gaming industry. Ney went on to accuse dealers on SunCruz ships of "cheating passengers by using incomplete decks of cards." That kind of thing, Ney declared, "is just plain wrong," the "type of conduct [that] gives the gaming industry a black eye and should not be tolerated." Ney concluded his remarks in the *Record* with a stirring call on "the appropriate authorities to weed out the bad apples"—such as Gus Boulis—"so that we can protect consumers across the country."

The onslaught continued. In October, Ney praised Adam Kidan in

---

*His Web site boasted, "First sworn into the US Congress in 1995, Congressman Bob Ney is currently ranked the 11th Most Powerful Member of Congress by an independent, nonpartisan poll."

In the past, a fellow like Ney with such limited seniority would never have become chairman of a standing committee of Congress. Under the Democrats, with an exception here or there for the odd, hopelessly reactionary Southern Boll Weevil, seniority prevailed in the handing out of chairmanships. DeLay changed all that. Prospective chairmen were expected to appear before a Republican leadership committee (run by DeLay) and prove their mettle, largely based on absolute loyalty to the whip combined with evidence of their fund-raising abilities. For most, that meant becoming even more beholden to the largesse of K Street lobbyists.

the *Congressional Record,* improbably citing his "renowned reputation for honesty and integrity" and his "track record as a businessman." Kidan's actual track record included lawsuits, judgments, liens,
bankruptcies, and failed businesses.

Yet this was the same Adam Kidan who, Congressman Ney
claimed, "will easily transform SunCruz from a questionable enterprise to an upstanding establishment." Ney's reward: thousands of
dollars in Indian tribal contributions from Jack Abramoff's clients—
and an all-expenses-paid golfing trip to Scotland.

Busy as he was with trying to acquire SunCruz, not to mention funding antigambling crusades in Texas and Alabama, Jack Abramoff still
had time for other well-paying customers. Among these was an
obscure Internet gambling company called eLottery, which had found
itself on the congressional endangered species list.

The Internet Gambling Prohibition Act had passed the Senate and
was awaiting action in the House in the spring of 2000. Panicked executives at eLottery turned in May to Abramoff, to the tune of $100,000
a month in fees to Preston Gates. It was time to get out the golf
clubs—again. That same month, eLottery cut a check for $25,000 to
the National Center for Public Policy Research (NCPPR), a nonprofit
right-wing "think tank" run by another of Abramoff's College
Republican pals, Amy Ridenour. (Abramoff was on the board of the
NCPPR at the time.) The same $25,000 then went to pay for Tom
DeLay's now famous golfing trip to Scotland.*

On July 17, 2000, the Internet Gambling Prohibition Act went
down in flames in the House—to the astonishment of politicians and
the press.

The story of eLottery and the downfall of the Internet Gambling
Prohibition Act might well count as the most Machiavellian of all of
Jack Abramoff's triumphs. For, in the service of a company whose sole

---

*Among the other dedicated golfers on the journey were Jack Abramoff and DeLay's deputy
chief of staff, Tony Rudy. Weeks later, on June 15, Abramoff, Kidan, and Rudy would travel
together to the U.S. Open in Pebble Beach, California. Their mode of transportation this
time: a private jet belonging to SunCruz Casinos.

business was gambling, Abramoff channeled millions of dollars earned from Internet gambling, via tax reformer Grover Norquist's ATR organization, to antigambling forces led by the likes of Ralph Reed and the Reverend Louis P. Sheldon. The goal: to put "grassroots" pressure on antigambling representatives to vote to kill the Internet Gambling Prohibition Act.

As the *Washington Post* was later to report, Abramoff turned to Sheldon—whom the lobbyist liked to refer to as Lucky Louie—and to Ralph Reed to drum up opposition to the bill from a most unusual source—evangelical ministers. Sheldon, as the leader of the Orange County, California–based Traditional Values Coalition (TVC), was publicly opposed to gambling and claimed to represent some forty-three thousand churches. Reed, of course, was by now running his own "grassroots" organizing firm, Century Strategies.

Both were well paid for their efforts, using Norquist's Americans for Tax Reform as one laundering agent and the Faith and Family Alliance of Virginia Beach, Virginia, as another. On June 22, 2000, Abramoff's assistant Susan Ralston e-mailed the boss, "I have 3 checks from elot: (1) 2 checks for $80K payable to ATR and (2) 1 check to TVC for $25K. Let me know exactly what to do next. Send to Grover? Send to Rev. Lou?"

Abramoff responded: "Call Grover, tell him I am in Michigan"—where Abramoff was representing the Saginaw-Chippewa tribal gambling interests—"and that I have two checks for him totaling 160 and need a check back for Faith and Family for $150K."

Faith and Family Alliance had been founded by two Reed protégés. The man running the show in 2000, though, was Robin Vanderwall, a former Republican operative who was later to be convicted of soliciting sex with minors via the Internet and given a seven-year sentence in Virginia state prison.

From prison, Vanderwall explained that in July 2000 he was alerted by Century Strategies that he would be receiving a package. When the package arrived, it contained a check payable to Faith and Family for $150,000. The check was drawn on ATR and signed by Grover Norquist. Vanderwall did as he was instructed by Reed's people: he deposited the money and wrote out a check for $150,000, payable to

Century Strategies. As Vanderwall so succinctly put it in retrospect, "I was operating as a shell."

Tony Rudy was also working in the eLottery cause. As of June 2000, Rudy's boss, DeLay, still hadn't taken a stand on the bill. Rudy had—at least in private. Just five days after Rudy and DeLay returned from their golfing trip to Scotland, the DeLay deputy chief of staff e-mailed Abramoff on June 8, "911 gaming." There were a lot of squishy Republicans, Rudy warned Abramoff. The bill still clearly enjoyed majority support. Rudy's advice: push for a meeting with Speaker Dennis Hastert and Majority Leader Armey. Meanwhile, Rudy and Abramoff continued to hold backstage strategy sessions. One idea was to get Lou Sheldon in the same room with Tom DeLay. Eventually, they succeeded. On July 13, Lucky Louie met with the majority whip and told him, "I strongly opposed the bill."

In the meantime, a letter purportedly signed by Florida governor Jeb Bush began making the Republican congressional rounds. "While I am no fan of gambling," the letter read, "I see this bill as a violation of states' rights." (The letter turned out to be a forgery.)

Now, in the midst of much brouhaha, the bill's House sponsor, conservative Virginia Republican Robert W. Goodlatte, made a serious tactical error. Fearing that his bill would be amended to death on the floor during debate, Goodlatte chose to put it on the so-called suspension calendar, which, while banning amendments and limiting debate, would also require a two-thirds majority for passage.

The roll call—245 in favor, 159 opposed—was twenty-five votes short. The Internet Gambling Prohibition Act was dead. Otherwise fervid DeLay fans among the Christian evangelical crowd went apoplectic. Pastor James Dobson announced that he was "just sick about what the Republican leadership is doing with regard to gambling." The pressure soon built. The bill appeared likely to be resuscitated.

Abramoff's response was to send Lucky Louie out on a grassroots campaign against social conservatives who had voted in favor of the bill. His tactic would be to accuse these antigambling Republicans of being "soft on gambling." With their feet to the fire, the congressmen would, it was hoped, change their votes. Lest, of course, the wrath of God and a passel of right-wing voters righteously oust them in the next election. The move was, even by Abramoff standards, stunning in its utter cynicism: a dozen or so antigambling Republican social conservatives were about to be threatened with the loss of their seats—if they didn't vote in favor of Internet gambling.

Rudy and Abramoff, meanwhile, set about convincing the Republican leadership that, sans those dozen or so members, they would lose control of the House in November. DeLay and the impeachers had previously been punished in the 1998 midterm elections with the loss of Republican seats. Their House majority had been shaved to a razor-thin thirteen votes, and now, of course, the 2000 election was looming larger by the day.

On August 18, Abramoff wrote his clients at eLottery, asking for "a check as soon as possible for $150,000."

The check was cut a few days later. In an e-mail to Abramoff, Reed noted, "All systems go." And so they were. Mailboxes in the affected congressional districts were soon flooded with flyers. Among the targeted were prominent social conservatives such as J. C. Watts, the African-American Republican congressman from Oklahoma who was also one of Tom DeLay's deputy whips; Alabama congressman Robert Aderholt, as vigorous a champion of public displays of the Ten Commandments as there was; and California's Jim Rogan, one of the House managers in the impeachment and trial of President Bill Clinton. Despite impeccable conservative bona fides, all were now being accused of being "soft on gambling."

By late October, Abramoff and Reed's cynical ploy had succeeded to perfection: no one—and especially not a bunch of antigambling conservative Republicans scared to death that they might lose their seats—wanted to be accused of being "soft on gambling" in an election year.

At a preelection strategy session in late October, the House Republican leadership was confronted with a fait accompli. Once more—if anyone still needed a reminder that this was how business worked in a Republican House dominated by Tom DeLay—the meeting was attended not only by the Speaker, the majority leader, and the whip—but also by lobbyists, among them David H. Safavian.

Safavian would later gain infamy as yet another "victim" of the Abramoff scandals, but for now he was just a young Michigan-bred lobbyist on the make. A graduate of the Detroit College of Law, Safavian had made his bones at Preston Gates, where his boss was Jack Abramoff. Safavian had moved up the ladder in 1997 when he joined with Grover Norquist and Republican lobbyists Bethany Noble and Scott Hoffman at their newly opened Merritt Group.*

The client this day was Internet gambling interests. In the presence now of the House Republican high command, Dave Safavian took particular note of Tom DeLay's role in managing the affair. The majority whip, Safavian remembered, "spoke up and noted that the bill could cost as many as four House [Republican] seats. At that point, there was silence. Not even Rep. Dick Armey (R-Texas)—our previous opponent—said a word."

When the *Washington Post,* in October 2005, interviewed Lou Sheldon about his role in killing the Internet Gambling Prohibition Act, Lucky Louie professed not to know that Jack Abramoff was lobbying against the bill or that Abramoff's services—and thus Sheldon's own services—were being paid for by eLottery. "This is all tied to Jack?" Sheldon mused, adding, "I'm shocked out of my socks."

Jack Abramoff, it would seem, was all over the place that summer and fall of 2000. Abramoff and Kidan had still to convince their bankers to lend them the millions they needed to buy SunCruz. In his attempt to obtain a loan, Abramoff stretched the truth a bit, claiming that he was worth $13 million and that he was a partner—he wasn't—at Preston Gates. At a September 18 meeting in the midtown Manhattan offices of Foothill Capital's lawyers, the bankers agreed to a $60 million loan on the condition that Abramoff, Kidan, and Waldman put up $23 million of their own money.

That night, Abramoff, Kidan, and one of the bankers, Greg C. Walker, flew back to Washington to celebrate. The venue was familiar: Abramoff's luxury box—a box paid for by Indian gaming interests—

---

*As a lobbyist, Safavian had represented the Republic of Gabon (infamous for its human rights record) and former Congolese president Pascal Lissouba (who had been tried in absentia for treason and embezzlement), not to mention Muslim activist and Hezbollah and Hamas supporter Abdurahman Alamoudi.

at FedEx Field in Washington. The occasion was a *Monday Night Football* game between the Redskins and the Cowboys. The banker would later recall having met another guest in Abramoff's box that night: Majority Whip Tom DeLay.

Abramoff's courtship of the bankers having proved successful, Foothill Capital Corp. and Citadel Equity Fund formally agreed to lend Abramoff, Kidan, and Waldman $60 million toward the $147.5 million purchase of SunCruz on September 27, 2000.

There was just one last hitch: a key document faxed to the bankers by borrowers Kidan and Waldman turned out to be fraudulent. The fax indicated that a $23 million wire transfer had been made from Kidan's account at the Chevy Chase Bank to Boulis's bank. Records at the Chevy Chase Bank would, however, show that Kidan's account was closed at the time. Unbeknownst to the bankers, Abramoff and Kidan had gotten Boulis to agree to accept their IOUs to the tune of $20 million in exchange for a 10 percent interest in SunCruz.

R. Alexander Acosta, the U.S. attorney in Miami, would later explain that the "document was counterfeit; the defendants [Kidan and Abramoff—Waldman was not charged] never transferred these funds and never made a cash equity contribution toward the purchase of SunCruz." The FBI agent in charge of the case put it rather more succinctly: "Abramoff and Kidan did not put any of their own money into this deal."

Among Jack Abramoff's references for the $60 million loan were DeLay deputy chief of staff Tony C. Rudy and right-wing Republican congressman Dana Rohrabacher of California, a member in good standing of DeLay Inc.* Rohrabacher would later say of his college friend Abramoff, "Washington can be intoxicating at times." His pal Jack, Rohrabacher added, had "obviously made some very bad decisions."

As did the bankers, who went on to approve the $60 million loan. If he wanted to, the powerful D.C. lobbyist could now truly style himself "Casino Jack."

---

*Rohrabacher represents California's Forty-sixth District (the wealthy Long Beach and Huntington Beach areas) and is a ranking member of both the Science and Foreign Affairs committees (and under DeLay, served as chair of the latter's Investigations and Oversight Subcommittee).

CHAPTER SIX

✶

Who's Your Daddy? Part II

Theodore Roosevelt, it was said, was Rove's "favorite president." Like George W. Bush, he was a "strong president," a "cowboy president," and, of course, TR famously believed in carrying "a big stick." Never mind that the Republican Roosevelt was also the first great trustbuster, a conservationist keen on protecting America's natural resources, and a font of progressive legislation.

No, indeed.

Thus it was that, in the run-up to the 2000 elections, Rove's thoughts turned instead to a very different turn-of-the-century Republican president, William McKinley.

It was, of course, McKinley's death by assassination that had thrust Roosevelt into the presidency in 1901. "Now that damn cowboy is president," cried the anguished Republican strategist Mark Hanna, the Rove of his day and one of the few men in or out of politics who seemed genuinely to have felt affection for the cold and calculating McKinley.

McKinley was of a different generation and a different ideological persuasion from his exuberant vice president, the reform-minded former governor of New York. The last Civil War veteran to become president, McKinley was a party boss, backed by party bosses, for whom "reform" was anathema.

McKinley appealed to the pasty-faced amateur historian and full-time political operative for many reasons. Not least among these was McKinley's close, almost symbiotic relationship with Hanna, a wealthy industrialist, sometime Ohio senator, and brilliant electoral strategist.

The veteran journalists James Moore and Wayne Slater, writing in *The Architect*, their study of Rove and his "master plan for absolute power," recount how the modern Republican electoral genius first discovered William McKinley while taking a history class at the University of Texas.

Rove, they note, "wanted a fundamental partisan realignment of American politics" and, in Professor Lewis Gould's meditations on McKinley, found the template for the Ascendant Republican Majority, as he imagined it: a generation of Republican dominance that would condemn the Democrats to a minority status.

McKinley had served two consecutive two-year terms as the Republican governor of a big Midwestern state. He proudly wore the ribbon of the GAR (the Grand Army of the Republic), having mustered out as a captain. He looked solid and prosperous, dignified even; despised Democrats and labor unions; loathed populists and cheap-money men; revered Main Street, Wall Street, and Big Business; and had the good sense to share Hanna's admiration for the plutocracy. The rich were rich because they deserved to be rich. The poor were poor because they deserved to be poor. Well-to-do himself, McKinley had no doubt of his own deserts. He was, in short, a representative man of the Gilded Age.

In McKinley, Hanna believed he had found the ideal candidate for president—so long as he didn't have to campaign in public.

Former congressman McKinley had twice been turned out of office by the voters in his Ohio district, the last time even though he was chairman of the powerful House Ways and Means Committee. He was not a natural campaigner.

McKinley—portrayed by the lackeys of the press as supremely confident of victory—ran a "front-porch campaign" for president, hardly bestirring himself and only then to welcome the rich and famous come to play supplicant. Going out on the hustings, McKinley seemed to say, was beneath him. Meanwhile, his campaign manager, Hanna, feverishly went about the real business of politics, raising money—and spending it—garnering endorsements too, making his man "the front-runner."

Quietly, efficiently, Hanna raised a record $4 million from Wall Street and the trusts with which to devastate the Democratic candidate, William Jennings Bryan. And devastate the Republicans did.

Hanna's strategy worked to perfection, ushering in a span of thirty-six years of Republican ascendancy, broken only by Woodrow Wilson's victories in 1912 and 1916 (the latter, truly razor-thin).

McKinley proved no more charismatic as president than he had as governor or congressman. But in taking the United States to war with Spain over the "mining" of the battleship *Maine* in Havana Harbor, he reminded the country that he had himself once been a warrior. The "splendid little war" McKinley led America into proved nasty, brutish, quick—and successful.

No wonder Karl Rove loved William McKinley.

If Hanna could usher in such a golden age, beginning with the cold, dry McKinley, well, think what Rove could do with the warm, if callow George W. Bush.

Just over a hundred years after McKinley's 1896 presidential victory, Rove, "the Boy Genius" now become "the Architect," was poised to usher in a second golden age. Or was it actually a second Gilded Age?

In the years since 1896, Theodore Roosevelt's compact with America, the Square Deal, had given way to Franklin D. Roosevelt's New Deal, Harry S. Truman's Fair Deal, John F. Kennedy's New Frontier, and Lyndon B. Johnson's Great Society. In the process, the trusts had been busted; food and drugs regulated; great swathes of national land set aside for public use; African-Americans afforded their civil rights; the environment protected; and a vast social welfare net spun. It had taken almost a quarter century between the time Harry Truman proposed it and Lyndon Johnson saw it enacted, but Medicare was now among the laws of the land, yet another of the "entitlement programs," such as Social Security, that Karl Rove so despised.

Unknown to all but a few of his fellow Americans, the "kinder, gentler" Republican whom Rove now proposed to make president of the United States was hostile to almost every one of the great twentieth-century reforms. The born-again governor of Texas was, moreover, captive to a religious right that saw in liberal Jeffersonian democracy only atheism and moral laxity.

But these sides of George Walker Bush were seldom to be seen in the spring, summer, and fall of 2000. Instead, in a replay of his gubernatorial campaigns, Bush went forth scripted, always "on message," the messages few and crisp, carefully crafted by Rove and Karen Hughes. He would be "the education president," "the CEO president," kinder and gentler than his kind and gentle father, stronger and more warriorlike than the Vietnam veteran Al Gore. It mattered not that he could not recall the names of capitals or prime ministers, nor even find the places on the maps where their countries lie. He had advisers to advise him on these arcane matters. He was strong and upbeat, humorous and self-effacing. He was Good Neighbor George.

And to a surprising extent, Karl Rove did, in fact, model the campaign of 2000 after that of 1896. Unlike McKinley, George W. Bush at least possessed a famous name. But unlike the long-serving politician McKinley, Bush was inexperienced, unworldly even.

What better way then to hide the candidate's lack of experience— lack of judgment perhaps as well—and shield him from the terrors of the media than to run the twenty-first-century equivalent of the front-porch campaign?

Taking his cue from Professor Gould's study of McKinley, Karl Rove ran the first such campaign since the time of Warren G. Harding in 1920—and for many of the same reasons. Harding was dim and dull, a hearty, affable, essentially well-meaning man, but weak, waffling, and unquestioning. He'd rather play golf or a hand or two of poker than have to think about the business of governing. Best not to ask him too many questions.

George W. Bush, who was far less experienced than the lifelong politician Harding, thus ensconced himself in the stately Governor's Mansion in Austin throughout the vital preprimary season. There, he received important guests, among them former Swedish prime minister Carl Bildt and former U.S. secretary of state George Shultz. And, as he had in the run-up to his race against Ann Richards, he received tutoring, this time at the hands of the likes of Condoleezza Rice on foreign affairs and former Nixon administration official Herb Stein on economics. As befitted "the front-runner," Bush acted as though the election was a done deal.

Meanwhile, Karl Rove played the Mark Hanna role to the tee, lining up endorsements and money. With the Bush name and the Bush network it was not hard to do. As Carl M. Cannon, Lou Dubose, and Jan Reid note in their book *Boy Genius* (the other excellent study of Rove), "Bush would win [Rove told reporters] because the Haley Barbours of the party"—the national and state chairs—"and 114 U.S. House members, and fourteen U.S. senators, and a substantial majority of Republican governors had endorsed him. He was the candidate of the establishment, and he was ahead by more than ten points in the polls." Bush, Rove predicted, would carry every state between the Sierra Nevada and the Missouri River, and he would take all but three states in the South. It would be a lock.

Meanwhile, the money kept pouring in, from Enron and Ken Lay, from Rove's old employers in Big Tobacco, from corporate PACs and Republican Party PACs, from energy companies and mining companies, from just about every corporate entity in America that wanted less federal regulation and taxation and more access to plunder public lands and waters. The Texas oil billionaires, the state's landed grandees, the big Texas law firms and their partners and PACs—Rove was everywhere tapping the old, deep wells of money and privilege. And all the while, the Architect kept telling everyone who would listen, it was a lock.

But, then, of course, John McCain won the New Hampshire primary. Irreverent, funny, unpredictable, shooting from the hip at every angle, McCain was, above all, what George W. Bush was not: both warrior and war hero.

When McCain threatened to make toast of Bush in South Carolina, someone within the campaign—someone experienced and crafty, someone used to playing down and dirty—resorted to lies to stop him. As the authors of *Boy Genius* recall, "This time, instead of one rumor about McCain, there were scores. McCain was gay. McCain had fathered an illegitimate child with a North Vietnamese woman, which was why he had gotten special treatment from the Viet Cong. McCain had a black daughter. (McCain and his wife, Cindy, have an adopted daughter from Bangladesh.) McCain voted for the largest tax increase ever. McCain's wife stole prescription drugs from a charity and abused them while she was purportedly caring for their four children. McCain was pro-abortion. McCain left his crippled first wife. McCain was a liar, a cheat, and a fraud."

Well, someone surely was a liar, a cheat, and a fraud, but that someone was surely not John McCain.

It was, as all the old Bush watchers from Texas knew, a virtual repeat of the 1994 gubernatorial phenomenon: Ann Richards is a lesbian. Ann Richards is a drunk. Ann Richards sleeps with black men. Ann Richards is pro-abortion. Ann Richards. Ann Richards. Ann Richards.

And, like Ann Richards, John McCain learned the hard way that it would not do to underestimate George W. Bush—and the men and women around him.

After South Carolina, the candidate who was toast was McCain.

The professional politicians all knew that the presidential debates would be problematic for George W. Bush. The Gore people assumed, as had the Richards people in 1994, that Bush would blow himself up in the debates. Instead, and again as he had in 1994, Bush stuck to message. Rove and Hughes—not to mention the Democrats—had so lowered expectations that for Bush to survive a debate was tantamount to his winning the debate. Gore helped himself not a whit by occasionally acting "the Bad Gore," as his staff sometimes called him behind his back. Hard and arrogant, Gore bullied and badgered Bush, who remained affable throughout. A good neighbor, Al was not. It cost him.

By October the polls were indicating a Republican victory; but, late in the game, Gore began to surge. Then the Architect nearly made a fatal mistake. Rove too had stayed on message: His man was the front-runner. Bush was a lock. And, to prove it, to edge the winning margin of electoral votes skyward, Rove sent his man out West in the remaining days of the campaign. George W. Bush was never going to carry California, but there he went nevertheless, wasting time, energy, and money, to the possible detriment of carrying Florida. With but seconds left in regulation, Bush was shooting a hopeless jumper from midcourt, instead of going for the surefire layup.

It made for a brave face but a dumb move.

The game went into overtime.

The story of the troubled Florida 2000 election recount has often been retold, in press accounts and books. The *New Yorker*'s Jeffrey Toobin, in particular, has left us with a vivid recounting of that truly dense saga in his book *Too Close to Call*. For our purposes, only the most salient events will suffice, though more recent developments since the publication of these accounts add a deeper historical perspective to what was one of the darkest days in the history of American democracy.

Begin in Texas on election night 2000. The news of the day had not been good for Bush. The California strategy had clearly not worked, and exit polls suggested that "the front-runner" was in serious trouble in Florida. The Bush camp was well aware of the danger too. Throughout the day, the head of conservative Fox News' election-night team—none other than Bush's first cousin John Ellis—kept the campaign apprised of the latest exit polls.

Democrats had had buttons made that read THE TRIFECTA: MICHIGAN, PENNSYLVANIA AND FLORIDA. Here, in these three big swing states, the election would be determined. The earliest exit polls showed Michigan close, with Bush leading in Pennsylvania and Gore leading in Florida. The polls showed that Gore had a narrow lead. By midafternoon, the Gore camp was in a celebratory mood.

Thus it was at 7:49:40 p.m. Eastern time that NBC called Florida for Gore. Thirty-one seconds later, CBS called it for Gore; and ABC came on board at 7:52. Not quite two hours later, ABC and NBC called the election for Gore. It was, one of the Gore people would later say, "our seven-minute presidency."

By ten o'clock, the tide had begun to turn. The networks' statistical models were not holding. The Florida vote was narrowing. Over the next few minutes, the networks—led by Fox—began terming the Florida vote too close to call. By midnight, it was clear to all that Florida's twenty-five electoral votes would decide the election.

Two hours later, Florida's Republican secretary of state, Katherine Harris, announced the complete returns from Volusia County (Daytona Beach). Bush now led by 51,433 votes, with 97 percent of the total vote in and counted. Based on the Volusia votes, Fox—once again, the right-wing cable news network was calling the shots—gave the election to Bush. The time was 2:16 a.m. CBS and NBC quickly followed suit, with ABC piling on at the end. It was now 2:20 a.m. Al Gore, who had rehearsed his victory speech that afternoon, picked up the phone and conceded. The call took two minutes. For Gore, it must have seemed an eternity.

An eternity too when the call came from a Democratic operative in the Florida capital of Tallahassee. The numbers trotted out by the networks, he informed the Gore team, had been off, badly off. The networks—and Katherine Harris—had been wrong about Volusia County. Bush's lead was not fifty thousand plus. It was a tenth of that, about six thousand. Under Florida law, even a thirty-thousand-vote margin would be enough to set off a mandatory recount.

Over the next few minutes, the numbers closed. The margin was now less than two thousand. Gore campaign chairman Bill Daley—the son and brother of fabled Chicago mayors—again picked up the phone.

"We've got a situation here," Daley told Bush's close friend and campaign manager, Don Evans. "You've got to give us a few more minutes."

Gore himself now wanted to talk to Bush. The candidate picked up the phone. "The state of Florida is too close to call," Gore told him.

"Are you saying what I think you're saying?" Bush asked incredulously. "Let me make sure that I understand. You're calling back to retract that concession?"

What followed was a short, angry exchange between two tired, frustrated men. Two very different men of almost bitterly opposed stripes.

Gore snapped back, "You don't have to be snippy about it."

Bush replied that his "little brother," Governor Jeb Bush of Florida had assured him of his victory. The numbers showed that he had won the state. It was all over.

"Let me explain something," replied Gore. "Your little brother is not the ultimate authority on this."

The conversation ended on a frosty note, with George W. Bush telling Al Gore to "do what you have to do."

In Austin, Bush campaign manager Evans knew what he had to do. He picked up the phone and called James Addison Baker III.

Baker had begun Election Day in Washington at a meeting of the board of directors of the Howard Hughes Medical Institute. Afterward, he had flown to Austin to await the election results. That evening, he waited and watched in the hotel room of Dick and Lynne Cheney as the returns poured in.

They were old friends, the Cheneys and the Bakers. Cheney had been a White House chief of staff (under President Ford). Baker had been a White House chief of staff (under President Reagan). Later Cheney had been secretary of defense in the first Bush administration when Baker had been secretary of state. They were both conservative Republicans. They were both big businessmen. Cheney had been CEO of the Dallas-based energy-services giant Halliburton. Baker was not only a senior partner at Baker Botts, he was also a stakeholder in the Carlyle Group. Cheney had made millions at Halliburton. Baker's stake in the Carlyle investment group was said to be worth close to $200 million. The one man, in his late fifties, the other in his seventies, were now both of them Big Rich.

The similarities faded after that. Cheney and Baker were both courtiers, but with very different styles. On the surface, Baker was a charmer, a genteel, privileged Princeton gentleman, but, underneath, cold and calculating. Cheney was quieter, reserved even, keeping his innermost thoughts to himself. He had been a high school football player in Wyoming and had flunked out of Yale. He had then married Lynne and gotten serious. He'd worked hard to get where he was. He was serious, tough, and shrewd. Along the way, he'd learned how to rig the process, stack the deck, and put his own people in every possible cubbyhole. Like his close friend Donald Rumsfeld, Cheney was machiavellian.

Baker, long the elder Bush's closest confidant, had lost luster within the extended Bush "family" as a result of George H. W. Bush's failed 1992 presidential campaign. Baker, a grandee in the grand Baker family tradition, had chaffed at going from secretary of state to campaign manager that year. A return to the grubbier, nitty-gritty aspect of politics was beneath a man who had been both secretary of treasury and state. It did not help when George H. W. Bush then lost the election to Bill Clinton. George W. Bush never forgot Baker's failure to deliver—or his haughty attitude in the run-up. "Jimbo" was no real friend, as far he was concerned.

Just why George W. Bush thought Dick Cheney was his real friend is another matter. What we do know is that Cheney had started out in late April 2000 as the man charged with leading Bush's vice-presidential search team only to emerge three months later as the vice-presidential candidate himself. Cheney had put a number of potential rivals through an unprecedented vetting process, eliminating, among others, the perceived favorite, Oklahoma governor Frank Keating, as well as Pennsylvania governor Tom Ridge, Nebraska senator Chuck Hagel, Tennessee senator Bill Frist—a Rove favorite—and former Tennessee governor Lamar Alexander, among others. None was deemed sufficiently worthy to be number two to George W. Bush.

Dick Cheney, who, alone among the candidates, was spared a grueling vetting, was, however, found worthy. Three heart attacks, quadruple bypass surgery, high cholesterol, gout, and skin cancer did nothing to disqualify the Halliburton CEO from becoming the chief operating officer for "America's CEO."

Cheney, it was.

Now, as the evening faded on election night 2000, everything was on the line, Bush's fate, Cheney's fate, the Republican Party's fate—the nation's fate as well. Baker just wanted to go to bed.

Still suffering from a cold, badly in need of sleep, and expected to receive the Mexican foreign minister in Houston the next day, James Addison Baker III bade the Cheneys good night and took his leave. A plane awaited him.

Back in Houston, on his way home from the airport along with his wife, Susan, Baker relaxed in the car. Though he did not know it, these would be among the few restful moments he would have for more than a month.

The cell phone rang, and Baker answered it. On the other end of the line was Don Evans, and he wanted Jim Baker—now. The Gore campaign had named former Democratic secretary of state Warren Christopher to represent them in the Florida recount. Evans wanted Baker to represent Bush.

Evans got his man.

Joe Allbaugh flew in from Austin aboard a private plane later in the day. After the plane took off for Florida, with Baker aboard, Allbaugh turned to the former secretary of state and asked him how it would all end. Baker replied without hesitation, "It's going to be decided by the Supreme Court."

The Gore campaign well understood that everything had to fall right for them to win in Florida. Everything.

The vote, as it then stood, favored Bush but just barely. The count, for the moment, stood at 1,784 in favor of George W. Bush.

But it wasn't just the slim lead that favored the Texan. Florida's governor was both Bush's fellow Republican and his younger sibling; the Florida secretary of state, in charge of overseeing the voting, was the multimillionaire Republican heiress Katherine Harris; and both houses of the state legislature were Republican. When befuddled local election boards and supervisors turned to Tallahassee for help in understanding the law, they were, knowingly or unknowingly, putting themselves—and the vote—in the hands of Jeb Bush, Katherine Harris, and a host of Florida Republican Party apparatchiks.

Should the case find its way into the federal courts, the Eleventh Circuit Court of Appeals in Atlanta was famously conservative, overwhelmingly Republican. Only the Florida Supreme Court was Democratic.

Of the three most important law firms in the state, Miami-based Greenberg Traurig and Steel Hector & Davis had already signed up to represent, respectively, the Bush campaign and Secretary of State Harris. The state's biggest law firm, Holland & Knight, had signed on and then, mysteriously, signed off on representing Gore. "The brushoff from Holland & Knight," writes Toobin, "was a sign that Tallahassee would not be friendly territory for Gore's team. Implicitly, or explicitly, the big [law] firms did not want to offend Governor Jeb Bush."

Even with the deck stacked, Gore's strategists had a chance. Still, they didn't help themselves with their attitude. Gore was a creature of Washington Beltway culture. His father, Albert Gore Sr., had been a longtime Democratic congressman and senator from Tennessee, while the younger Gore had attended the exclusive St. Albans School.

Now, Gore worried about how his actions would play in the *New York Times* and *Washington Post* and among the capital's chattering classes. When the *Post*'s longtime political columnist David Broder or the *Times*' veteran Washington correspondent R. W. "Johnny" Apple, for example, worried about the effects to the country of a long, drawn-out recount, Gore worried with them.

Bush, as the Texan liked to say, decided. Gore dithered. Bush was all about results—good or bad. Gore was about process. Life, for him, was just one big question mark with no obvious answer in sight—and was all the more interesting because of it.

Gore's two closest associates in the Florida recount were Warren Christopher and Bill Daley. "Chris" Christopher was the paragon of the Los Angeles bar, an immaculately dressed, buttoned-down corporate lawyer. Cautious by nature where Baker was aggressive, Christopher played the careful, methodical Union general George McClellan to Baker's wily, opportunistic Robert E. Lee.

When his "client," Gore, showed agitation or anger or, worse, aggression during the recount, Christopher would counsel patience. Christopher was seventy-five, Gore fifty-two, at the time. The Tennessean had all the time in the world. Did Gore really want to ruin his chances for another run for the presidency by his obduracy this time? Clinton's former commerce secretary, Daley, seemingly more concerned about his future than Gore's, typically offered weak or even poor counsel. Following the election, Daley would find himself in

Texas, as the president of SBC, as the former Southwestern Bell and future AT&T was then known.

If, as Toobin says, "Gore and his lieutenants were so worried about appearing too aggressive that they were always hedging, compromising, and, in effect, undercutting their own work," Jim Baker "suffered no such agonies." There was nothing Baker would not do to ensure his candidate's victory in Florida, and if that meant repudiating "decades of Republican thought about judicial activism and state sovereignty, Baker would—and did—do it in a flash."

The Gore team had made a terrible strategic miscalculation early on. Thinking to stave off public criticism, they asked for a limited recount, rather than the ballot-by-ballot, statewide recount that would almost surely have favored their cause. Turning the issue on its head, Jim Baker claimed that the Democrats were fearful of a statewide recount. Besides, said Baker, "The vote in Florida was counted. . . . The vote in Florida has been recounted."

Skilled lawyer that he was, James Addison Baker III surely knew that this was not the case. For, in eighteen counties—with a total of 1.58 million votes, or more than a quarter of all those cast in the 2000 election—there had been no recount at all.

Once arrived in the Florida capital of Tallahassee, Baker and Allbaugh had quickly set up shop. At the top of the heap stood Baker himself, aided by his longtime associate Robert Zoellick. A whip-smart Swarthmore- and Harvard-educated lawyer, Bob Zoellick had served as ambassador, counselor, and undersecretary of state to Baker in the Bush I administration.* As their consigliere, Baker and Zoellick had the hyperaggressive Ben Ginsberg, an election law specialist at Washington's best-known law-and-lobby shop, Patton Boggs. (Ginsberg would, during the 2004 election, represent the notorious Swift Boat Veterans for Truth group.) Joe Allbaugh was there to handle the politics, while another longtime Baker aide, former State Department

---

*He would later serve Condoleezza Rice in the number two job, deputy secretary, and in a Bush II cabinet-level job, as U.S. trade representative.

spokeswoman Margaret Tutwiler, would deal with the press. The Bush team—in reality, the Baker team—was as organized, polished, and political as the Gore team wasn't. From Austin, the candidate would occasionally weigh in. The real, hands-on decision-making was done by others, in this case James A. Baker III.

The local contingent from Steel Hector and Greenberg Traurig numbered in the dozens, but there were also high-flying specialist lawyers on hand. The well-known Republican federal appellate law specialist Ted Olson had flown in from Washington. Olson and his colleague George Terwilliger were expected to handle appeals at the federal circuit court level and beyond.

Barry Richard and the Greenberg Traurig crew were expected to handle most of the state court litigation. Steel Hector lawyers serviced Secretary of State Harris. Governor Jeb Bush was represented by his lawyer, Frank Jimenez. And quietly, in the background, offering high-level legal advice were two rising stars of the Republican legal community, former Supreme Court clerks John G. Roberts Jr. and Miguel Estrada. Hogan & Hartson law firm partner Roberts, the future chief justice of the United States, was there to advise Governor Jeb Bush—about just what, neither man will now say.

A dozen or more lawyers came from a familiar source, Houston's Baker Botts. The planes that ferried them to and from Florida came from energy giants Enron, Halliburton, and Occidental, according to *The Austin Chronicle.* These were led by two veteran litigators, G. Irvin Terrell and B. Daryl Bristow. Terrell and Bristow, notoriously tough antagonists in a courtroom, were the best Baker Botts had to offer.

The older of the pair, Bristow, was an Oklahoman by birth, but with a Harvard Law degree (1964, cum laude). In his more than thirty years in the courtroom, Bristow had represented virtually all the biggest energy providers in town save for Enron (which was a Vinson Elkins client). Dynegy was his client; Reliant too; and CenterPoint as well.

Irv Terrell was a Texan, schooled at the University of Texas and its law school. UT had the reputation of being the best law school in the state, probably the best in the Southwest, and save for Virginia in the South as well. Terrell had made his name representing Penzoil

Company in its tortuous interference claim against Texaco. That was one time Baker Botts had gladly brought a tort action.* Penzoil— George H. W. Bush was great pals with the company's CEO, Hugh Liedtke, a Rice University trustee—walked off with a record $10.53 billion judgment and a $3 billion cash settlement. Texaco went into bankruptcy.

Terrell and Bristow didn't arrive in Florida alone either. Their bulging briefcases were toted by some of Baker Botts's best and brightest.† Jeffrey Toobin—himself a magna cum laude graduate of the Harvard Law School—described the team assembled by Jim Baker as "an armada of legal firepower."

The armada set off against a Democratic fleet whose most prominent sails—Microsoft lawyer David Boies and famed Harvard Law constitutional scholar and Supreme Court advocate Laurence Tribe— reflected the sun, all puffy and bright, but which were notably creaky in the billows. Christopher and Daley couldn't even agree on who their chief advocate should be, whether Boies or Tribe. Worse still, the Democratic war council kept wavering between peace offers and threats of attack.

Jim Baker made his position abundantly clear. When the Florida Supreme Court ruled unanimously in favor of Gore and for a hand count in the three big Democratic strongholds of Broward, Miami-

---

*And in doing so, the conservative firm had turned to flamboyant Houston plaintiff's lawyer Joe Jamail to argue its case in federal court. With some of the proceeds of his share of the record settlement, Joe Jamail went on to endow his old law school. His name now graces one of the finest buildings on the University of Texas at Austin campus: The Joseph D. Jamail Center for Legal Research.

†Among these was a young associate named Samuel Cooper. Sam Cooper had a pedigree that would make even Terrell and Bristow take notice. Cooper was the son of a longtime Rice political science professor—a distinguished specialist in congressional politics—named Joseph Cooper. The elder Cooper was a Harvard man (all his degrees were from that university) who had enjoyed a rapid rise at Rice, through the ranks to department chairman and dean. Later, at Johns Hopkins, he had been provost. Son Sam had gone the same Harvard undergraduate path (summa cum laude, Phi Beta Kappa), but diverged long enough to receive a law degree at Stanford, where he had been managing editor of the law review. He'd then gone on to clerk for Judge J. Harvie Wilkinson III of the U.S. Fourth Circuit Court of Appeals.

Dade, and Palm Beach, James Addison Baker III hit back. The Florida Supreme Court, Baker declared, had "changed the rules and . . . invented a new system for counting the election results." What the court had done was "unfair and unacceptable." Then he dropped his bombshell: "One should not be surprised," Baker warned, "if the Florida legislature seeks to affirm the original rules." In other words, as Toobin has it, Florida's Republican-controlled house and senate "could simply vote to give the election to Bush." No one could have imagined the more liberal Gore or Christopher or Daley making such a threat. But Baker had done so with alacrity.

Nor had Baker hesitated to send in the mobs. One of the forgotten moments of the Florida recount occurred soon afterward. That's when, in the midst of recounting the Miami-Dade vote, a voice rang out, "He stole a ballot! He's stealing a ballot! Thief!" The so-called thief turned out to be the chair of the county Democratic Party. He was not stealing ballots, but rather trying to test a single sample ballot. No matter. A mini-riot ensued, his pursuers led by a howling pack of Brooks Brothers–clad Republican activists. Among them was the future upstate New York Republican congressman John Sweeney, who was overheard shouting "Shut it down!" Among the other taunts were "No justice, no peace!" and "The whole world is watching!"

The Gore legal team, advised by Tribe, believed that the U.S. Supreme Court would stay out of the case. All those conservative states'-rights Republicans on the Court—led by the archconservative chief justice William Rehnquist and the brilliant right-wing associate justice Antonin Scalia—would surely not have the federal courts interfere in what was clearly the state's bailiwick.

Baker felt otherwise. His strategy, all along, as we have seen, called for the Supreme Court to be the final arbiter. Baker was a politician, he wasn't a jurist, and he certainly wasn't a philosopher. But he could count, and he was shrewd.

The U.S. Supreme Court was as deeply divided as the nation. On one hand, you could count to four. These were the four middle-of-the-road, moderately liberal jurists: John Paul Stevens (the senior member), David Souter (the shrewd William Brennan of this Court), Ruth Bader Ginsburg, and Stephen Breyer. On the other hand, there was the trio of reactionaries led by "The Chief," William Rehnquist himself, followed in close order by Scalia and Clarence Thomas. That left the conservative-but-not-reactionary Sandra Day O'Connor and Anthony Kennedy seemingly in the middle.

Some in the Bush camp feared that the Gore strategists were right. Perhaps the Court would not take up the case. Perhaps states' rights would win out. Baker believed otherwise. And in the legion of conservative former Supreme Court clerks working for the Bush team during the recount, Baker had confirmation of his beliefs. There were more than a dozen such men. Four had clerked for Scalia, three for Rehnquist. Tellingly, however, three more had clerked for the supposedly moderate O'Connor. In their Court days, many in the group had referred to themselves, perhaps "half-jokingly" (as Toobin has it), perhaps not, as "the Cabal." Virtually all were now members of the Federalist Society, the umbrella group favored by conservative and neoconservative legal intellectuals. Among these, here in Florida now, were Roberts (who had clerked for Rehnquist), Estrada (Kennedy), and Timothy Flanigan (Burger). Two (Estrada and Roberts) would soon find themselves on the U.S. Court of Appeals for the District of Columbia, the so-called D.C. Circuit, widely considered the most important court in America other than the U.S. Supreme Court itself. Flanigan, a future Tyco general counsel, would be nominated by George W. Bush as deputy attorney general of the United States. Roberts, of course, would find himself named to replace Justice O'Connor, and then, Chief Justice Rehnquist.

The former clerks now assured their masters that the current set of justices would take the case. The Supremes, especially the conservative Supremes, would *want* to take the case. No matter the legal niceties, no matter that states' rights would be trampled on and the members of the Florida Supreme Court made to look like fools. The Supremes in Washington would itch at the bits for a case like this, for such an opportunity seldom ever came their way.

And in this, the former clerks—and Jim Baker—were right. When word came that the Supreme Court had agreed to take the case, President Bill Clinton was stunned—though more stunned by his vice president's complacency than by the Court's action. Clinton fulminated. "The fix," he declared to friends, "is in. This thing stinks." Clinton would have had Gore go before the television cameras and denounce the Court. "These are not apolitical people," Clinton had said of the Supremes, so why not denounce them?

Had he been fighting this fight, Clinton bitterly told friends, he would have the people out in the streets. It would have been a case of the people versus the plutocrats and the reactionaries on the Court. And then the O'Connors and the Kennedys would see how they liked that kind of language, how they liked seeing thousands, maybe millions, of Americans in the streets of the nation's cities demanding a recount, a full, unfettered Florida recount.

But Gore wasn't Clinton, and the impassioned calls were not made to the public.

Clinton knew whereof he spoke too. Toobin, in his book *Too Close to Call: The Thirty-Six-Day Battle to Decide the 2000 Election,* has recounted how, on Monday, December 4, the very day that the Supreme Court delivered its first opinion on the election, Sandra Day O'Connor and her husband attended a private party. When the subject of the election arose, O'Connor went "livid." She didn't hesitate to speak her mind either, telling fellow guests, "You just don't know what those Gore people have been doing. They went into a nursing home and registered people that they shouldn't have. It's outrageous." It wasn't the sainted O'Connor's only off-the-cuff comment about the evils of the Gore campaign. On election night when it first appeared that Gore had won, O'Connor had vented her anger at another private party: "This is terrible." Her husband, John, explained to fellow guests why his wife was now so upset: "She's very disappointed because she was hoping to retire."

Retire and let President George W. Bush name her replacement.

It was a fool's errand to suppose that O'Connor—or the Republican Kennedy—would be the swing vote on the Supreme Court in the case of *Bush v. Gore.*

At some point, O'Connor did want to retire; while Justice Kennedy no doubt imagined himself Rehnquist's successor. O'Connor got her wish, Kennedy didn't.

The vote was 5–4.

The celebrations broke out in Tallahassee and Miami and Palm Beach, in Austin and in Houston. The Cabal—the former Supreme Court clerks—had been been right after all. They knew their judges.

And so too did James Addison Baker III.

CHAPTER SEVEN

★

The Price of Friendship

The presidential contest wasn't the only electoral squeaker of 2000. Congressional elections, both in the House and Senate, showed once again just how divided America was. The Republicans did, in fact, lose seats in the House, but the loss turned out to be a mere two seats. The same team—Hastert, Armey, and DeLay—would continue their rule uninterrupted, though, as before, real power lay more and more with the whip. DeLay's former deputy Hastert apparently didn't mind—so long as he occupied the biggest office—while Armey seemed resigned to a diminished role. The Big Boss, whatever the title, was clearly now the bullwhip-cracking DeLay.

Were he only plugged in to power in the House, Jack Abramoff would have continued as he had for the past six years, working the right-wing Republican side of the fence to stop Democratic legislation emanating from the White House.

But, of course, that was no longer the case. Not only was the House Republican, but so too was the Senate—where the tie-breaking vote of newly elected Vice President Dick Cheney ensured that the evenly divided (50–50) upper chamber was organized under Republican management as well.

Still, it was George W. Bush's disputed presidential victory that fundamentally changed Jack Abramoff's role in the world of Washington power politics. With the ascendancy of Bush and the Texas Republican crowd—along with the "tax reformers," "tort reformers," and Christian evangelicals attached to them—Abramoff was now in a position to influence the making of policy and the staffing of executive department offices.

Whereas in the old days—the bad old days of the Clinton administration—Abramoff was all too aware of the workings of the Department of the Interior (and how he despised those petty Democratic bureaucrats), now he was in a position to help staff some of the highest offices within the department. Abramoff would, with good reason, later boast to Indian tribal clients of his service on the Bush administration's Interior Department transition team.*

Created in 1849, the Department of the Interior had been transformed under President Theodore Roosevelt (1901–9) from a stronghold of patronage and political corruption into a defender of the public lands, guardian of the nation's Indian tribes, and voice of early-day environmentalism. But then TR *was* the last liberal Republican president.

The newly incumbent president was anything but. For one thing, this president didn't believe much in government. All the better then to put conservation in the hands of anticonservationists; and the bureaucracy in the hands of former lobbyists dedicated to destroying it.

With Colorado lawyer and antienvironmentalist Gale Norton named secretary of the interior, the search was on to staff the highest levels of the department with like-thinking right-wingers. One of

---

*Abramoff also found time to schmooze. His "in" at the Department of the Interior was non-profit-foundation executive Italia Federici, a close friend to both Interior Secretary Gale Norton and her number two, Deputy Secretary J. Steven Griles. In a March 1, 2001, e-mail, Federici wrote Abramoff, "Steve [Griles] really enjoyed meeting you and was grateful for the strategic advice on BIA [Bureau of Indian Affairs] and Insular Affairs. You definitely made another friend." But there was more: an invitation from Federici to Abramoff to attend "a very small cocktail party for Gail [*sic*]." Madame secretary was being feted by Federici and Jim Nicholson on March 6 at 6:30 p.m. Federici closed her e-mail: "Bye, for now." This and subsequent e-mails, letters, and other exhibits, together with statements and testimony before the Senate Indian Affairs Committee regarding the Abramoff scandals, are to be found online at the Web site of the committee (http://indian.senate/gov), under "Oversight Hearings on In RE Tribal Lobbying Matters, et al."

those helping guide the search: Jack Abramoff. Among those vetted by Abramoff in the quest to ensure quality at the top of the department was Norton's right-hand man, Deputy Interior Secretary J. Steven Griles, a former coal lobbyist.

Carlos Hisa, one of the leaders of the Texas Tigua tribe, recalled a conversation he had with Abramoff at this time. Hisa remembered Abramoff boasting of how "the president assigned him to staff some of the open slots for the Department of the Interior and such. And Jack Abramoff recommended some of the individuals that were placed in those positions."

Hisa's account is supported by that of tribal political consultant Marc Schwartz. Abramoff, Schwartz says, didn't hesitate to claim the connection: "He had spoken quite highly of his association with President Bush's transition team back in 2000, where he had . . . been involved with the selection of various individuals at the Bureau of Indian Affairs." The bureau was, of course, part of the U.S. Department of the Interior.

For the previous eight years, the Interior Department had been under siege. The besiegers had ranged from energy companies eager to drill in the arctic wilderness (while equally eager to escape paying royalties to the federal government for their offshore drilling) to lumber giants salivating over mighty stands of Western timber to mining companies with their eyes on the nation's immense coal deposits. Now the siege was over. The citadel had been stormed, and the former besiegers—Jack Abramoff among them—were the masters of America's natural treasures.

The importance of being Jack Abramoff was soon made manifest when he left Preston Gates Ellis & Rouvelas Meeds for a similar but higher-paying job as director of governmental affairs in the Washington office of Miami-based Greenberg Traurig. Now he could at last begin to call in IOUs from College Republican buddies, among them influential White House adviser Grover Norquist and Counselor to the President Karl Rove.

The move to Greenberg had long been in the works. Abramoff's style "had clashed with others at Preston Gates," write Susan Schmidt and James Grimaldi of the *Washington Post.* Many at the firm felt that the high-profile lobbyist "was moving too fast and being careless." Emanuel Rouvelas, the firm's founding partner in Washington, had told Abramoff, "If you're not careful, you will end up dead, disgraced, or in jail."

Greenberg's lobbying fees soared with the arrival of Jack Abramoff, more than quintupling, from $1.7 million in the first half of 2000 to $8.7 million in the first half of 2001. At Preston Gates, during this same period, lobbying-derived fees were cut in half.

All Washington took notice. In a lengthy profile of the $500-an-hour lobbyist, the *New York Times*'s David Rosenbaum wrote, "Mr. Abramoff tries hard to persuade his fellow Washington lobbyists to give more generously to the Republican Party, its candidates and conservative organizations. He expects to raise as much as $5 million this year, he said, and plans to donate as much as $250,000 personally."

Rosenbaum added that Abramoff's "interest in raising money for Republicans and conservative causes is the foundation of Mr. Abramoff's relationship with Mr. DeLay, who is determined to meld the lobbyists on K Street here into the Republican Party's political, legislative and fund-raising operations."

Abramoff went on to describe the bond between himself and Majority Whip DeLay: "We are the same politically and philosophically. Tom's goal is specific—to keep Republicans in power and advance the conservative movement. I have Tom's goal precisely."

Different though the two men seemed at first glance, they were the Janus heads of the same right-wing Republican coinage. For coinage, it was. Abramoff's $500-an-hour fee was matched, Rosenbaum noted, by few if any other lobbyists in Washington. No wonder given the praise showered on Abramoff by William Worfel, vice chairman of the Coushatta Indians, the rich Elton, Louisiana–based tribe: "I call Jack Abramoff, and I get results. You get everything you pay for."

And Worfel did pay, too, to the tune, eventually, of more than $32 million.

For his $32 million, alas, Worfel didn't get quite the full treatment accorded Mississippi Choctaw chief Philip Martin, whom Majority

Whip DeLay cited in the *Congressional Record* on January 3, 2001, for "all he has done to further the cause of freedom." To this encomium, DeLay attached an editorial that hailed the tribe's inspired "hiring [of] quality lobbyists."

Lobbyists such as Jack Abramoff.

As 2001 opened, Jack Abramoff appeared to be perched firmly atop the two worlds he now inhabited, that of D.C. power brokers and high-rolling gambling czars. Sometimes—oftentimes, when you got right down to it—the two worlds came together.

Take Super Bowl XXXV, for example. On Inauguration Day 2001, Mike Scanlon and SunCruz president Adam Kidan had celebrated the Republican ascendancy at a reception in the Capitol Hill offices of Tom DeLay. A week later, SunCruz vice president Abramoff took time off to fly key staffers at DeLay Inc.—that is to say, the Office of the House Majority Whip—down to Tampa aboard the company jet. Among the revelers were future DeLay chief of staff Tim Berry and former deputy chief of staff Tony Rudy, as well as two aides to Montana senator Conrad Burns (including Chief of Staff Will Brooke, who would later go to work for Abramoff at Greenberg). It was quite an affair too: not only impossible-to-get seats at Raymond James Stadium—where the Baltimore Ravens demolished the New York Giants, 34–7—but also a night of gambling aboard a SunCruz vessel.

But when it was all over and the privileged congressional staffers had settled back into their quotidian Capitol Hill jobs—having returned to D.C. via private jet—Jack Abramoff was left with another kind of reality. Down in Miami, it was all beginning to fall apart. While Adam Kidan and his partner were paying themselves $500,000 a year in salary as CEO and vice president, respectively—and flying around the world aboard private planes—Gus Boulis now smelled a rat and wanted the SunCruz sale rescinded.

Egged on by Boulis, the bankers had also begun asking impertinent questions of Abramoff and Kidan. The pressure was building. There had been a well-publicized fistfight between Boulis and Kidan at a

December 5, 2000, meeting. Kidan later claimed that Boulis had told him, "I'm not going to sue you, I'm going to kill you." Kidan accused Boulis of having stabbed him in the neck with a pen.

The new owners of SunCruz now responded by having the former owner barred from vessels he once owned. According to Matthew Continetti, writing in the *Weekly Standard,* Kidan, apparently fearing for his life, hired bodyguards and leased an armor-plated Mercedes (for $180,000).

Less than two months later, Gus Boulis—who would also perhaps have done well to lease an armor-plated car—was dead, the victim of a gangland-style slaying. On February 6, 2001, returning from a business meeting, Boulis was shot to death on a Fort Lauderdale street when a car pulled up in front of his car and another, a black Mustang, pulled up alongside. A shooter in the black Mustang then fired three hollow-point bullets into Gus Boulis's chest. The police investigation into the murder of onetime floating-casino magnate Gus Boulis would take more than four and half years to produce results. By the time the indictments were finally handed down in September 2005, the good-ship Abramoff was well on its way to sinking.

With Boulis dead, Kidan and Abramoff could run the cruise line any way they wanted. The partners now asked Foothill Capital for another loan to clear up their debts, stepped up plans to expand their casino operations to the Northern Marianas, and hired Greenberg (and Jack Abramoff) as their lobbyist in Washington.

The good times, however, soon began to wind down. The reason: money, or the lack thereof. Jack Abramoff, pressed by the bankers in the SunCruz deal, was in need of manna from heaven. He found it in Texas. Pending before the Texas state legislature that same spring of 2001 was a gambling expansion bill—a bill to legalize casino gambling, including Indian casino gambling, within the state—just the sort of thing to send Abramoff's biggest and richest client, the Louisiana-based Coushatta tribe, into a check-writing frenzy.

Needless to say, the Louisiana Coushattas didn't want other tribes horning into their wealth. Across the state line, over in Texas, the confusingly named Alabama Coushatta tribe presented a potentially grave danger. Living on a forty-six-hundred-acre reservation located near the small lumbering town of Livingston, in the heart of the East Texas piney woods, the 550-member Alabama Coushatta tribe was threatening to open a rival casino. And because Livingston was but seventy-three miles from Houston (an hour and seventeen minutes by car if you obeyed the law—less than an hour if you put pedal to metal), an East Texas casino was sure to draw customers away from the Louisiana casino.

The Alabama Coushattas tribe did, in fact, open a rival casino. Their prosperity would be short-lived, as would that of the Ysleta del Sur Pueblo tribe—better known as the El Paso Tiguas—owners for a time of the Speaking Rock Casino, located in the far western corner of the state, some 747 miles from Houston.*

The 1,250-member Tigua tribe had only received federal recognition as a tribe in 1987—at a cost of pledging to obey Texas gaming laws. But once Texas voters approved a state lottery in 1991, the Tiguas jumped—somewhat precipitously, it turns out—into the casino business, believing that they were no longer bound to seek a "covenant" with the state. In 1993, the impoverished tribe opened the doors of its liltingly named Speaking Rock Casino. With fifteen hundred slot machines, the casino attracted one hundred thousand visitors annually and began generating $60 million a year in revenues. Soon, the tribe's unemployment and dropout rates went from more than 50 percent to nearly zero.

At the time, Democrat Ann Richards was still governor of Texas and Democrat Dan Morales the state attorney general. Both were opposed to Indian gambling. Neither, however, was interested in leading a crusade against it. George W. Bush felt differently. Bush professed himself deeply opposed to Indian gambling—especially once the Tiguas had given $100,000 to his Democratic opponent for governor, Land Commissioner Garry Mauro, in 1998. "There ought not to

---

*This amounted to a ten-hour-forty-nine-minute car ride—long, even by Texas standards— much of it through brutally hot, barren West Texas via Interstate 10. The drive was longer still if you were coming from Elton, the home of the Louisiana Coushattas: thirteen hours fifty-three minutes (931 miles). Doubtless few if any gaming customers ever did drive the distance from Louisiana.

be casino gambling in the state of Texas, any shape or form of it," Bush said at the time. Following his electoral victory in November of 1998, Bush asked the legislature for a special appropriation for new Republican attorney general—and longtime Karl Rove client—John Cornyn to take up the legal cudgel against Indian gambling. Cornyn promptly filed suit in federal court to shut down the Speaking Rock Casino.

By then Jack Abramoff was known, far and wide, to be the man Indian tribes went to see when they had a problem, especially if the problem involved shutting down a rival casino owned by some other tribe. In this, Abramoff had plenty of help, not only from former DeLay chief of staff Buckham but also old friends Grover Norquist and Ralph Reed.

In March 2001, Ralph Reed e-mailed Abramoff, newly ensconced at Greenberg Traurig, that if the client (the Louisiana Coushattas) would approve his $397,200 "Texas Anti-Gambling Project," he would press the start button for a "grassroots" campaign to end all "grassroots" campaigns. What Reed proposed to do was whip the Texas evangelical ministers into a froth—and then have them, mullahlike, drive *their* followers into a tizzy over the evils of gambling. Indian gambling. *Texas* Indian gambling.

By the time the campaign ended, Reed's Century Strategies had been paid some $4.2 million—by Indian gambling interests, via various Abramoff conduits. Not that Reed didn't know where the money came from.*

While the public focus of the campaign was the El Paso Tigua tribe and its Speaking Rock Casino, the real focus—and real fear of the Louisiana Coushattas—was their East Texas brethren, the Alabama Coushattas.

In a suit filed against Abramoff, Reed, Scanlon, and fellow lobby-

---

*Back in 1999, Abramoff had e-mailed Reed regarding his work on behalf of the Mississippi Choctaw in their campaign to stop the Poarch Creek Indians from opening a casino in nearby Alabama: "Get me invoices as soon as possible so I can getChoctaw [sic] to get us checks ASAP."

Choctaw political and legal adviser Nell Rogers—she was the tribe's liaison with Abramoff—had been made to understand that Reed "did not want to be paid directly by a tribe with gaming interests. It was our understanding that the structure was recommended by Jack Abramoff to accommodate Mr. Reed's political concerns."

ists Neil Volz and Jon Van Horne by the Alabama Coushatta tribe in July 2006, one of Reed's former employees detailed how the grassroots effort to shut down the Texas casinos worked its magic. Among other things, some one hundred thousand antigambling postcards were sent to lawmakers' constituents.

For another, as many as eight thousand phone calls were patched through to members of the key state house committee considering the legislation. How this worked is instructive: "Bogus organizations were set up to make phone calls. The organizations were just telephones in a drawer. When a phone would ring, the employee would open the drawer, figure out which phone was ringing, and answer in the name of that organization."

Suzi Paynter, a lobbyist for Southern Baptists in Texas, later recounted to a reporter from the *Atlanta Journal-Constitution* — Reed's hometown newspaper — how, "in the spring of 2001, while strolling the grounds of the state Capitol [in Austin], her cell phone rang. A local state senator screamed in her ear, 'Stop it. Stop the phone calls.'" It seems that the state senator's office had been swamped with antigambling phone calls. Paynter, the reporter wrote, was puzzled. Lieutenant Governor Bill Ratliff had made it clear that he wasn't going to put the bill on the senate calendar. It was, therefore, doomed to failure. What's more, Paynter couldn't imagine any of the antigambling groups with which she worked having the money for automated phone banks. She was frankly puzzled. "I didn't know who it was," Paynter told the Atlanta reporter. Four years later, she thought differently: "Now I think I do." In retrospect, two words sprang to mind: Ralph Reed.

Paynter was right about the size of the operation — and its cost. In an e-mail to Abramoff, Reed submitted a "working budget" totaling $549,190. This for a mere two months' work (February/March 2001). Among the proposed charges: $60,000 for "activist postcard mailing (80,000 quantity)," $36,290 for "church membership mailing (95,500)," $24,000 for 80,000 computerized calls, $70,200 for 200 hours of "patch-through" calls, $25,500 in contributions to "coalitions," $60,000 for "legislative strategy/coordination," $142,000 for a two-week antigambling radio blitz, and $90,000 as Reed's own "management fee."

Scanlon was worried about the costs. In an e-mail to Abramoff, he wondered whether Reed had spent "all the money he was given to fight this—or does he have some left?" Abramoff replied, "That's a silly question! He 'spent' it all the moment it arrived in his account. He would NEVER admit he has money left over. Would we?"*

The question, under Texas law, is whether Reed was acting as an unregistered lobbyist in 2001–2. He maintains that he wasn't and was merely acting in a "fact-finding, informational nature," in the words of a spokesman. If Reed was prosecuted and found guilty, the maximum penalty would be twelve months' imprisonment and a $4,000 fine. So far, he has not been charged.

Appropriately enough for a DeLay Inc.–related nonprofit organization, the Reed-inspired Committee Against Gambling Expansion was headed by a lobbyist, in this case Andrew Biar.† They were successful in derailing the gambling expansion act. Though the bill passed the state House of Representatives, it died in the senate in May 2001 when, as predicted, Lieutenant Governor Ratliff refused to bring it to a vote.

After the bill failed—to the delight of Abramoff's biggest client, the Louisiana Coushattas—the Washington lobbyist offered the Alabama Coushattas of East Texas a new deal. For a price—a mere ten percent of their gaming revenues in perpetuity—Abramoff would get federal legislation passed that would trump the Texas state laws and make the Livingston casino legal.

---

*Reed was also doing plenty of flesh-pressing in the state. On April 2, he e-mailed Abramoff, "I am moving forward with the following: 1) Visiting with the staff of Rep. Talmadge Heflin to see where Rep. Heflin is on the H.B. 514 (the Tigua bill); Meeting with Christian Coalition [Texas] Family Policy Council, Eagle Forum to make sure H.B. 514 has the total focus of conservatives."

Former lieutenant governor Ratliff says he talked to Reed only once—and over the telephone at that. "My recollection is he called me about redistricting," Ratliff told the *Atlanta Journal-Constitution*, "but I can't say that for sure. I don't remember it being about gambling."

Jack Abramoff would seem to have remembered things differently. In a 2003 e-mail, Abramoff warned that the Indian casino bill had been resuscitated yet again in the Texas House and that "the current speaker, Tom Craddock [*sic*], is a strong supporter." Worse still, there would be no Bill Ratliff to fall back on in 2003: "Last year we stopped this bill after it passed the House using the Lt. Gov., Bill Ratcliffe [*sic*], to prevent it from being scheduled in the State Senate."

†The president of Houston-based Strategic Public Affairs Inc., Biar was active in the R-Club (whose Web site describes its members as "Responsible Conservatives for Limited Government"; "a gathering of gentlemen," in the words of the *Houston Chronicle*); a Life Member of the Houston Livestock Show; and a board member of the Houston Chapter of Citizens Against Lawsuit Abuse.

He failed, however, to mention his role in shutting it down in the first place.

But that was just talk. And in the end, the Alabama Coushatta tribe didn't buy into the talk.

Meanwhile, though, money—real money—was still flowing into the coffers of Jack Abramoff. Choctaw money was flowing, Coushatta money too. At Greenberg Traurig—where at least some legal work was being done on behalf of the tribes—governmental affairs director Abramoff's billing practices were anything but straightforward. In a business in which most attorneys bill by the hour and keep careful track of their time, Abramoff didn't bother. Instead, he made it up as he went along.

Not everyone on Team Abramoff was comfortable with the arrangement. Shawn Vasell, a manager in the governmental affairs unit—he would later work for Senator Conrad Burns as his Montana political director, before returning to Greenberg in 2003—e-mailed Abramoff on June 21, 2001, to warn, "Choctaw still has not gone out. The bill is a disaster (again). . . . People's entries compared to time imputed and work performed is a joke. . . . Not fun!!! And a big problem for me!!!"

The boss clearly wasn't on the same page as his worried associate: "What's the total on the bill now? How much time do you need from me?" Going to the heart of the matter, Abramoff e-mailed Vasell, "Tell me how much you need me to cover to get the bill up to around $150k."

The by now exasperated Vasell responded, "This is a very bad system that I am very uncomfortable with."

One day later, on June 22, 2001, SunCruz filed for bankruptcy. The lenders were demanding repayment. That same day, Jack Abramoff resigned as vice president of SunCruz Casinos. His partner in the Sun-Cruz deal, Kidan, would resign as president just days later. Abramoff, hurting for cash, and Mike Scanlon now came up with a name for another kind of project, one that was even more dubious than the takeover of the SunCruz Casinos line. They called it Gimme Five.

Over the previous six years (1995–2000), as we have seen, Abramoff had extracted millions of dollars in lobbying fees from the likes of the Commonwealth of the Northern Mariana Islands and its garment magnates. The goals had often been questionable, the fees astronomical, and surely Jack Abramoff had stretched the limits of credulity and legality, but that was nothing compared to what was to come.*

His and Michael Scanlon's clients: some of America's richest and poorest Indian tribes. Scanlon had set up his own political consulting firm, Scanlon Gould Public Affairs (which also did business as Capitol Campaign Strategies or CCS). Like his old boss Abramoff, Scanlon had yet to truly cash in.

In early 2001, Scanlon began to rectify that situation, with the help of Jack Abramoff. By now, Abramoff had become increasingly irritated with Reed and, especially, Norquist. Why, after all, should they have to give Norquist a $25,000 cut on every "pass through" handled by Americans for Tax Reform (ATF)? Reed was no better. Scanlon complained of Reed and his efforts to shut down one of the Texas casinos, "I'd like to know what the hell he spent it on—he didn't even know the dam [*sic*] thing was there—and didn't do shit to shut it down." To which Abramoff replied, "I agree." The little wizard from Georgia was, in Abramoff's words, merely "a bad version of us; no more money for him."

That's where Scanlon, CCS, and an obscure Scanlon-run nonprofit, the American International Center (AIC), came in. Beginning in the late winter of 2001, Norquist found himself cut out of the picture. In the place of ATF were substituted AIC and CCS.

The American International Center was strictly a shell. On paper, AIC was said to be an "international think tank" run "under the high-

---

*Among the more questionable clients Abramoff represented during his Preston Gates years was the government of Pakistan, beginning in May 1995. Disclosure statements show that Preston Gates was retained to lobby to overturn sanctions barring the delivery of American-made weapons to that country in light of its nuclear weapons program. The initial six-month contract called for a $165,000 retainer plus expenses. The firm continued to represent the Pakistani government until April 1997. Before being cut loose by the Pakistanis, Abramoff led a congressional delegation to visit there—without telling the lawmakers that he was the country's registered lobbyist. The cost of the trip came to more than $350,000, charged to Abramoff's personal credit card.

powered direction of David A. Grosh and Brian J. Mann." The two men were, in fact, old lifeguarding buddies of Michael Scanlon's. Grosh, who had known Scanlon since he was fourteen, remembered that there had only been one board meeting—it lasted fifteen minutes. As to his duties at AIC, Grosh testified, "I had asked him [Scanlon] what I had to do, and he said nothing. So that sounded pretty good to me."

Still, in the late winter and early spring of 2001, the checks started flying. Between March 16 and April 27, for example, the Louisiana Coushatta tribe cut four checks (for $400,000; $258,000; $298,000; and $397,000) and made them out to the American International Center. At about the same time (late April) the same tribe made out its first check (for $200,000) to CCS. A few months later, the Mississippi Choctaws cut their first check (also for $200,000) to CCS. By year's end, the Choctaws alone had delivered a whopping $1,485,656 to AIC.

Now, in the summer of 2001, Mike Scanlon had his brainstorm— "a plan," he e-mailed Abramoff, "that will make serious money." And result in criminal convictions for both men.

Scanlon and Abramoff had been having discussions about going into some sort of partnership since "the beginning of the year," but Abramoff's needs were now, thanks to the failure of SunCruz, far greater. Time was wasting. Or, as Scanlon put it, "I think we can really move it now."

He continued, "Here are the broad strokes; I have been making contacts with some larger Public Affairs companies in town for a few months. . . . The problem is that there is not much in CCS right now. However, if we build up Capitol Campaign Strategies enough I can get it acquired by a large firm by the end of next year at 3x the firm revenue. Bottom line: If you help me get CCS a client base of $3 million a year, I will get the clients served, and the firm acquired at $9 million. We can then split the up [sic] the profits."

And split up the money they did. Bank and tax records indicate that Capitol Campaign Strategies paid Jack Abramoff personally and Kaygold, a company owned and controlled by him, over $21 million over three years.

How the scheme worked—and how little the Indian tribes received for their millions—can be inferred from this May 31, 2001, e-mail from Scanlon to Abramoff regarding their "grassroots" campaign on behalf of the Mississippi Band of Choctaw Indians: "Here is the overall plan. We need about $200,000 to run the operation, leaving $1.3 million to split or $650,000 apiece. To make you whole, the idea was to get the $150,000 to CAF directly then have AIC cut Kaygold a check for the remaining 150,000." In the world of Abramoff and Scanlon, "grassroots" was just another word for Gimme Five.*

From the beginning, though, at the heart of the scheme was Capitol Campaign Strategies. There wasn't "much in CCS" then—or ever. In the end, it was just a hollow shell for a con game. But a con game that went so well for so long that Jack Abramoff and Michael Scanlon soon forgot about selling the company.

Why sell for $9 million, when you could make, oh, say, $42 million, split down the middle over the next three years?

More opportunities beckoned. Ralph Reed had e-mailed to say that he'd been having discussions with Pastor Ed Young.

Pastor Young was a man well worth knowing. Especially if your name was Ralph Reed. For Homer Edwin Young held in his hands the hearts, minds—and votes—of some forty thousand Houstonians. In the words of its Web site, "Second Baptist Church is one church in multiple locations. Under the leadership of its senior pastor, Dr. Ed Young"—son Ben served as associate pastor and another son, Ed Jr., was pastor of the Fellowship Church in Grapevine, Texas—"the church has experienced phenomenal and unprecedented growth."

In the nearly three decades of Young's pastorate, Second Baptist had

---

*The Senate Indian Affairs Committee would later find that Abramoff alone had used at least ten conduits to funnel his share of the take: From Kaygold to the Capital Athletic Foundation (CAF) and the boys' school Eshkol that it ran to Archives (owner of a kosher deli), Grassroots Interactive, Livsar Enterprises (owner of his upscale restaurant Signatures), and Sports Suites (which rented luxury skyboxes at sports venues such as MCI Center and FedEx Field). Abramoff even found time—and the money—to support a sniper workshop in Israel, as well as the $75,000 he needed to pay off a loan from his days as a Hollywood producer.

Entities owned or controlled by Scanlon ranged from Scanlon Gould and the AIC to Atlantic Research and Analysis (used to pay Abramoff) to the utterly fictitious Christian Research Network and the equally fictitious Concerned Citizens Against Gaming Expansion. Ten in all.

swollen in size, from two thousand to forty thousand members, an almost twentyfold increase. The immaculately coiffed minister was no mere local celebrity either—he was, after all, not only the host of an internationally syndicated television show, but the author of such best sellers as *Total Heart Health, The 10 Commandments of Parenting,* and *The 10 Commandments of Marriage.* In June 1992 and again in June 1993, Young was elected president of the Southern Baptist Convention, with its sixteen million members, forty-two thousand churches, five thousand "home" missionaries and five thousand "foreign" missionaries. The SBC offered strongly held conservative political views, evangelical Christian "outreach," Baptist2Baptist Web site links, and GuideStone Financial Resources, providing its churches and members with (in the words of the SBC's official Web site) "retirement plan services, life and health coverage, risk management programs and institutional investment programs."*

Reed reported to Abramoff and Scanlon that Pastor Young was "incredibly engaged and excited" and had already made plans to host "a breakfast with the top pastors in Houston to get them all mobilized" in the cause of defeating the pro-Indian gaming bill pending before the legislature.

Not only was Louisiana Coushatta money flowing during the fall of 2001, so too was Choctaw money. "The first wave of money is in," Scanlon informed Abramoff on September 1. "Its [*sic*] pretty good 1.5 mil."

"So let me see," Abramoff replied. "That's 700k for each of us and 100k for the effort? Seriously, what do you think we can score?"

Seriously, Scanlon told him, the Choctaws were probably good for

---

*With five separate "campuses"—Woodway, West, North, Pearland, and Willowbrook—the SBC's flagship church offered a mixture of "Worship," "Bible Study," and "Prayer & Care," not to mention "Sports & Fitness." Via the Web site, you could "Watch Online," "Give Online," and "Update My Info." You could also "Request Prayer" and, if necessary, get "Divorce Care" too. Forty thousand members, five campuses, one all-inclusive Web site— and the ministry of Pastor Ed Young—the Second Baptist Church of Houston, Texas, had it all. Years later, in May 2006, Pastor Young would be the final defense witness in the federal fraud and conspiracy trial of disgraced Enron Corp. executives Ken Lay and Jeff Skilling. Young testified that former CEO Lay was a trustworthy man: "I believe he loves God, I believe he works hard, and I believe he's a man who keeps his word."

another $1.5 million. Scanlon worked out the Gimme Five aspects of the deal thusly: "I can slide you 350 with no sweat. Plus you have 313 sitting here—so if you want, $663,000 is yours on Tuesday. When the next clip comes in another 350, which will put you over 1. But that's not all, there will be more when the dust settles. . . . Not bad."

After 9/11, America, as President Bush liked to say, was a different place. Enron had begun its collapse, the World Trade Center was no more. And within days of the tragedy, Abramoff was e-mailing Ralph Reed asking for his help in getting a federal contract for SunCruz. The Federal Emergency Management Agency (FEMA) would need a place to billet relief workers in New York. Why not put them up on cruise ships anchored in the harbor? Reed responded by promising to "put in a tag call to Karl [Rove] to find out the best contact at FEMA."

Four months later Abramoff was back on the Internet with Reed in a further attempt to enlist Rove's aid. Abramoff e-mailed Reed that he needed some "serious swat from Karl" to get the Justice Department to release $16.3 million in federal funding for a jail on the Mississippi Choctaw reservation. In the words of *Time*, "Abramoff had caught Reed at a ripe moment." Reed's reply, e-mailed from his Black-Berry, read, "Am at a lunch with Rove at the [Republican National Committee] meeting and just talked to the AG [then Republican Texas attorney general John Cornyn]."

The message in the bottle: Abramoff didn't have to attend meetings—or even venture forth to the White House—not when he had surrogates such as Ralph Reed to do his bidding.*

☆   ☆   ☆

---

*As the report (*The Abramoff Investigation*) of the House Government Reform Committee, released on September 29, 2006, subsequently made clear, there were plenty of other surrogates as well. E-mails recovered by the committee showed that Team Abramoff member Tony Rudy had pressed then White House political director Ken Mehlman—the longtime associate of Karl Rove who was until recently the chair of the Republican National Committee (RNC)—to put the squeeze on Justice to release the funding for the Choctaw jail. Having learned, from Rudy, that the Choctaws were big givers to the right party, Mehlman "said he would take care" of the problem.

Texas attorney general Cornyn was the hero of the day among the antigambling pastor set, having filed suit against the Tiguas in 1999, claiming that the Tiguas had in 1987 made a legally binding agreement not to establish a gambling facility on its reservation as a condition of its becoming a federally recognized tribe.

On September 27, 2001, U.S. district judge Garnett Thomas Eisele ruled in favor of the state—and against the Tiguas. A month and a half later, on November 12, the Tiguas took their case to the public, with full-page ads in the Austin, Dallas, Houston, San Antonio, Fort Worth, and El Paso newspapers—along with a full-page ad in the *Washington Post.* Scanlon reported to Abramoff the next day, "The *Post* spot is framed as a letter to President Bush and asks him to convince Cornyn to back off. 'We'd like to invite [Cornyn] to take a moment to see the community he's about to destroy,' the Tiguas said in their ad."

"Look out!" Scanlon warned. Shortly thereafter, Reed e-mailed from Texas, advising that Team Abramoff better get the pastor-led phone banks up and running. Reed recommended that they "start doing patch-throughs to [new Republican governor Rick] Perry and Cornyn" at once.

Cornyn was expected in El Paso that very day—and expecting a hostile reception from the Tiguas and their Democratic supporters. Reed advised, "We are sending 50 pastors to give him moral support."

A few weeks later, on November 30, Reed again e-mailed Abramoff to announce that Ed Young along with fifty fellow pastors would be meeting with Cornyn, this time to urge him to shut down the Alabama Coushatta's newly opened casino in Livingston.

Reed added, "We have also choreographed Cornyn's response. The AG will state that the law is clear, talk about how much he wants to avoid repetition of El Paso [where the Tigua casino was] and pledge to take swift action to enforce the law. He will also personally hand Ed Young a letter that commits him to take action in Livingston."

Cornyn would later tell the Associated Press that "he did not remember receiving a letter from Young or Reed, or providing a letter to Young." Cornyn did, however, "acknowledge . . . meeting with the minister," Pastor Young.

If anyone really wondered why Attorney General Cornyn had

such a bee in his bonnet for the Texas Indian tribes, all one had to do was check out the front page of the December 4, 2001, *El Paso Times.* That's when the Tiguas' hometown newspaper reported that the tribe had contributed more than $500,000 to political candidates during the past two election cycles (1998 and 2000).

Ears perked up in Houston, Atlanta, and Washington, where Reed, Scanlon, and Abramoff each read the story and pondered its meaning.

In 1998 and in 2000, virtually all the Tigua political money had gone to Democrats ($410,000 versus $91,000 to Republicans). The *El Paso Times* story noted that, large as the Tigua political gifting had been, the tribe still lagged "far behind the political contributions" of doctors, trial lawyers, and real estate owners—not to mention the biggest player of all, Texans for Lawsuit Reform (TLR), whose political contributions, almost all of them to Republicans, had topped out at $1.1 million in *each* of the past two election cycles.

Influential Austin lobbyist Bill Miller* had some advice for the Tiguas. The tribal elders, Miller told the *El Paso Times,* "might have been better off investing in the legal side of their fight" rather than in political donations.

Republican lobbyist Miller was sending a message: forget the damn Democrats. And, oh, by the way, you might think of signing up a Republican lobbyist or two. Before it's too late.

Cornyn, of course, got nothing from the Tiguas, but a small slice of the tribal political pie—more than $20,000—had gone to then lieutenant governor candidate Perry. On discovering this from reading the story in the *El Paso Times,* an outraged Jack Abramoff e-mailed Reed, "Perry has to return that contribution!"

A few days later, Abramoff was truly in high dudgeon when Reed informed him that the new governor—apparently remembering the $20,000 contribution—had told the *Dallas Morning News* that he

---

*Miller was known as one of the most powerful lobbyists in Austin. His HillCo Partners client list was headed by the Farmers Insurance company, the second-largest such company in Texas. During the 2002 election cycle, Farmers Employee & Agent PAC of Texas would be the number two corporate donor ($150,000) to Tom DeLay's TRMPAC. At the time, Farmers was much in the news for having purportedly overcharged customers and for allegedly employing deceptive trade practices.

wanted to help the Tiguas find new jobs should the courts rule against them and order the Speaking Rock Casino to be shut down.

Abramoff's terse reply to Reed: "What is he thinking?"

While Abramoff was still trying to fend off the bankers in the failed SunCruz deal, Mike Scanlon was starting to enjoy the high life. In September 2001, as befitting his new station on the K Street landscape, Scanlon purchased not one but two Washington houses for a total of $1.2 million. It was then too that Scanlon, by now divorced, and Emily Miller became engaged. The former DeLay communications director proposed to the current DeLay communications director over dinner at a swank Los Angeles restaurant called The Ivy. Two months later, in November, Scanlon paid $1.6 million for a beach house in Rehoboth Beach, where he had once been a lifeguard, and had it completely refurbished.

So much activity, so many love nests. For this, you have to do *some* work. It was time to call on Mike and Emily's old boss, Tom.

In a December 11, 2001, letter to Attorney General John Ashcroft, DeLay demanded that the Alabama Coushatta casino in Livingston, Texas, be closed: "We feel that the Department of Justice needs to step in and investigate the inappropriate and illegal actions by the tribe, its financial backers, if any, and the casino equipment vendors." DeLay's letter was cosigned by fellow Republican congressmen Pete Sessions, John Culberson, and Kevin Brady, all of Texas. Other recipients of the letter included Interior Secretary Gale Norton; the U.S. attorney for the Eastern District of Texas; and Texas governor Rick Perry.

The cost of mailing a letter: two weeks prior, on November 28, DeLay's TRMPAC received a $1,000 contribution from the Choctaws. Three months later, Sessions's PAC received $6,500 from Abramoff's tribal clients.

Busy though he was in Texas, Jack Abramoff had not forgotten his old friends in the Marianas. Nor they, he.

When Willie Tan associate Benigno "Ben" Fitial—he of the "Happy Birthday" Tom DeLay singing salute—announced plans to run for governor of the Marianas in 2001, old pal Jack Abramoff gave him a helping hand.

In October of that year, Abramoff asked his friends in the White House to withhold an endorsement for Fitial's Republican primary opponent.

The reply—from the office of senior adviser and chief political strategist Karl Rove—came swiftly, in the form of an e-mail from Rove's executive assistant Susan Ralston, who, until recently, had been Jack Abramoff's executive assistant.

"You win :) Karl said no endorsement."

When, in December 2001, Republican activist Angela Williams was under consideration for appointment as head of the Interior Department's Office of Insular Affairs—with oversight for the Marianas and Guam, among other U.S. possessions—Abramoff set out to block her appointment. Exactly what Williams had done to deserve the Abramoff treatment is unclear. Presumably, though, she was unacceptable to the Marianas textile magnates.

Normally, the appointment of someone like Williams to so obscure a post would have caused little commotion within the White House. After all, Williams's husband, former Marine Corps colonel Orson Swindle, had strong Republican bona fides. Shot down while flying his jet fighter over North Vietnam, Swindle had been held for six years (1966–73) as a POW in the infamous "Hanoi Hilton," where he befriended fellow POW John McCain. Swindle went on to serve in the Reagan administration as assistant secretary of commerce and later worked with big-name fellow former Reaganites Jack Kemp, William Bennett, and Jeane Kirkpatrick in the Empower America movement. A failed Republican candidate for the House from Hawaii in 1994 and 1996, Swindle eventually settled into a sinecure as a Republican commissioner on the Federal Trade Commission (1997–2005).

If this Republican power couple had a weak spot, however, it was Orson Swindle's close connection to John McCain. In a White House where *McCain* often passed for a four-letter word, Abramoff decided to exploit the connection to the fullest. In one of their interminable e-mail exchanges, Abramoff and Ralph Reed pondered how to do this under the hysterically flawed header "Were you able to whack McCain's wife yet?" *Time* would later describe this misstatement as "practically Freudian in what it reveals about their animosity towards McCain." Freudian or no, Reed wrote to say that he had "weighed in heavily" with the White House personnel office to block Williams's appointment. "Any ideas on how we can make sure she does not get it?" Abramoff asked. "Can you ping Karl on this?" Reed assured Abramoff, "I am seeing him tomorrow at the WH and plan to discuss it with him as well."

Needless to say, Williams didn't get the job.

In truth, though the Marianas were thousands of miles from Washington—and from Houston—the distance was deceiving. The story of Williams was but part and parcel of Jack Abramoff's greater plan to take over the U.S. Department of Interior.

CHAPTER EIGHT

✦

High Energy

Not all of the nation's new masters were marauders. At least a few were men and women of integrity and substance. One such was Paul O'Neill.

O'Neill, the former Alcoa CEO, had joined the Bush administration as secretary of the treasury, having been persuaded to do so by Vice President–elect Dick Cheney. O'Neill had served with a young Cheney in the administration of President Gerald R. Ford, and they had remained friends. Like Ford, O'Neill was a centrist; and like an even closer friend from those days, Federal Reserve Board chairman Alan Greenspan, he was a pragmatist. O'Neill was a believer in process: good policy resulted from rigorous thinking and even more rigorous questioning.

Pragmatic, moderate, questioning, O'Neill stood out in the early Bush cabinet. For one thing, O'Neill was almost painfully honest. None of this played well with the boss. As Ron Suskind recounts in *The Price of Loyalty,* President Bush found O'Neill's honest-to-a-point reputation at best an irritant, at worst a cause for firing. The president even took to taunting his treasury secretary. At a meeting of his inner circle, for example, Bush was heard calling out, "Hey, there, Big O. You know something? You're getting quite a reputation as a truth-teller. You've got yourself a real cult following, don't ya?" The president, O'Neill noticed, wasn't smiling, "and everyone knew not to laugh. It wasn't a joke."

Eventually, O'Neill was shown the door—his dismissal coming in a curt telephone call from old friend Dick Cheney—but not before some of the innermost workings of the administration had been revealed to him. Much of what O'Neill saw, from behind the curtain, came as a shock to him.

For one thing, O'Neill discovered that the administration was obsessed with Iraq. Within the highest circles, as early as February of that first year, writes Suskind, "the talk was mostly about logistics. Not the *why,* but the *how* and *how quickly*" America would go to war with Iraq. All that was lacking, O'Neill feared, was a casus belli.

The coming war—if war was to come—O'Neill perceived as being directly linked to oil. The new treasury secretary learned that documents were already being prepared by the Defense Intelligence Agency (DIA) mapping Iraq's oil fields, some of them marked "super-giant oilfield," others with the notation "earmarked for production sharing." More disconcertingly still, the maps indicated "exploration areas and [listed] companies that might be interested in leveraging the precious assets." One particular document was headed "Foreign Suitors for Iraqi Oilfield Contracts."

The man presiding over the planning for war in Iraq, Secretary of Defense Donald Rumsfeld, was another old friend from the Ford White House.* Where O'Neill had been a senior budget official, Rumsfeld, a former congressman from Michigan (like Ford), had been the White House chief of staff.

O'Neill thought he knew Cheney and Rumsfeld well, but he was no longer so sure about that. O'Neill wondered if a decade as the highly paid CEO of Dallas-based Halliburton, an energy services

---

*The story of Donald Rumsfeld has been told recently in Andrew Cockburn's *Rumsfeld: His Rise, Fall, and Catastrophic Legacy* (New York: Scribner, 2007). James Mann also points out in his *Rise of the Vulcans: The History of Bush's War Cabinet* (New York: Viking, 2004), that under President Ronald Reagan, a top-secret program existed to give the nation leadership in time of nuclear "decapitation." The program called for a rotating group of highly skilled team leaders—the regulars included Cheney and Rumsfeld—to act as chief of staff to a rotating series of cabinet officers who would take on the mantle of president in time of nuclear war should the president, vice president, and their constitutionally mandated successors be killed in the attack. The point being that such responsibilities fall upon an essentially unqualified low-level cabinet secretary, and the chief of staff would serve as "the real President." One wonders: did Cheney and Rumsfeld learn something from this?

company, had not fundamentally changed Cheney. The ambitious, middle-class striver from Wyoming was now a Texas multimillionare. Cheney's circle too had expanded since the Ford White House days, now encompassing Texas billionaires, international energy company CEOs, and a host of neoconservative thinkers.

Always reserved, Cheney seemed now almost sphinxlike. At the same time, Cheney's fine hand could be discerned, if not seen, behind almost every major White House decision.

Like his close friend Dick Cheney, Don Rumsfeld had made millions since leaving the Ford White House. As CEO of pharmaceutical manufacturer G. D. Searle & Company (1977–85) and, later, as CEO of General Instrument Corporation (1990–93), Rumsfeld had joined the ranks of America's multimillionaires. A single outside directorship alone, at the Swedish engineering giant ABB, paid Rumsfeld $190,000 a year (1990–2001).

By the time Rumsfeld returned to government service, he was long since used to running the show—whatever the show—his way. The former Princeton wrestler had become an autocrat. Old friends were struck by how bullheaded and aggressive, all-knowing and arrogant, Rumsfeld now was.

In stark contrast, the inexperienced president struck the new treasury secretary as lacking in inquisitiveness. Worse, the president was all too willing to sign on to ideological positions that hadn't been thought through. But that, O'Neill thought, was the very nature of ideology: "Thinking it through is the last thing an ideologue wants to do."

Under the influence of Cheney, Bush had quickly flip-flopped on the issue of global warming. Christine Todd Whitman, the former Republican governor of New Jersey and Bush's cabinet-level choice to lead the Environmental Protection Agency (EPA), was appalled. That was, however, but an augury of what was to come.

Within weeks of the inauguration, Cheney had begun a reassessment of the country's national energy policy. The former energy company executive, "America's CEO," George W. Bush, seemed remarkably disengaged from the process.

Cabinet meetings, O'Neill had quickly learned, were scripted affairs. Someone—almost certainly Cheney or his staff—would prepare discussion points, and these would be distributed in advance to the participants. Cabinet members, the treasury secretary included, were expected to stay on point—and be brief. The president's attention span was short.

So it was too with the president's energy task force. The members of the National Energy Policy Development Group, O'Neill included, were all high-ranking executive branch officials. Among them were the secretaries of energy (nuclear-energy industry apologist Spencer Abraham), interior (the strident antienvironmentalist Gale Norton), commerce (George W. Bush's closest friend in the cabinet, Texas multimillionaire oilman Don Evans), transportation (the one Democrat in the cabinet, Norman Mineta, a virtual cipher), agriculture, and state. Other members included EPA administrator Whitman and former gubernatorial chief of staff and 2000 presidential campaign manager Joe Allbaugh, the head of FEMA (the Federal Emergency Management Agency).

Since the members were all executive branch officers, the minutes of their meetings would not be subject to Freedom of Information Act (FOIA) requests. The meetings would thus be kept secret, and the outside attendees unknown by the public.

A dead giveaway as to the intentions of the Cheney energy task force lay in the selection of its staff director, Andrew D. Lundquist. A former top aide to conservative Alaska Republican senators Ted Stevens and Frank Murkowski—the leading congressional advocates for opening the Arctic National Wildlife Refuge (ANWR) to drilling—Lundquist was also a former staff director of the Senate Committee on Energy and Natural Resources. A lawyer, Lundquist would later reemerge through the mirror as one of the leading energy lobbyists on K Street.

The work of Vice President Cheney's energy task force continued unabated throughout the spring and summer of 2001. Former treasury secretary O'Neill's personal files show that the task force met almost exclusively with executives and lobbyists from energy companies, such as Chevron, the National Mining Association, and the National Petrochemical and Refiners Association. Interior Secretary Gale Norton, for example, met with Rocky Mountain–based petroleum companies looking to lease federal land. Cheney himself met with Enron chairman Kenneth Lay.

As the old Washington hand O'Neill saw it, "process drives outcomes." And in the case of the White House energy task force, "this combination of confidentiality and influence by powerful interested parties," in Ron Suskind's words, meant that important environmental concerns went unheard. These were of no interest to the energy companies—or to the administration.

Meeting with the members of the task force, Bush "threw out a few general phrases, a few nods, but there was virtually no engagement." He did not ask questions.

The truth, O'Neill thought to himself, was that "the president [was] like a blind man in a roomful of deaf people." While, behind him, solemn, stone-faced, and shrewd, Richard Cheney pulled the levers of power.

That was how the White House was really run in the Age of the CEO President.

Bush might have been a hands-off chief executive, but Dick Cheney certainly wasn't. High-level meetings with Cheney could prove intense. Former treasury secretary O'Neill vividly recalled one such meeting between himself, Federal Reserve chairman Greenspan, and Cheney. The discussion was wide-ranging. Cheney, as usual, "mostly listened, not offering much." Greenspan and O'Neill emphasized how any tax cuts the new administration might propose should be limited, "sober and very responsible." Cheney nodded, his demeanor, as usual, "earnest [and] opaque."

The centerpiece of the administration's economic policy was the Economic Growth and Tax Relief Reconciliation Act of 2001, known as EGTRRA and pronounced "egg-terra." It would be the first of three massive tax cuts whose benefits primarily extended to the nation's rentier class.

It's often forgotten now, but at the time—the late winter and early spring of 2001—administration spokespersons, led by the president, spent much of their public face time talking down the economy and insisting that only such a massive tax cut for the investor class could stimulate the markets.

The talking points worked. In late May, the Republican House voted 240 to 154 in favor of the "stimulus package" (all Republicans plus 28 Democrats and 1 independent voted in favor, while 153 Democrats and 1 Republican voted no). Significantly, thirty-nine members were recorded as nonvoting.

The bill lowered the top income tax bracket from 39.67 percent to 36 percent, lowered the capital gains tax from 10.8 percent, and would repeal the estate tax in 2010. The bill also had the unintended effect of pushing hundreds of thousands—if not millions—of middle-class American taxpayers into the waiting arms of the alternative minimum tax (AMT). In deflecting taxes away from America's richest citizens, EGTRRA cast the middle class into tax hell.

Only when discussion turned to the California energy crisis did Cheney became voluble. Cheney's years as CEO at Halliburton had, O'Neill thought, "granted him a sense of mastery" in the area of energy policy. What was happening in California wasn't just a matter of policy. Crisis was in the air. In the wake of perceived shortages and rolling blackouts, energy prices in the Far West had soared throughout 2000 and 2001. The blackouts had begun in June 2000, when ninety-seven thousand customers in the San Francisco Bay area were left without electricity in the midst of a heat wave. Over the next several months, it only got worse. On January 17, 2001, California's Democratic governor Gray Davis declared a state of emergency. Between March 19 and 20, blackouts affected some 1.5 million customers.

For his part, Cheney insisted that the problem wasn't supply—and certainly not a manufactured crisis of supply—but rather, as O'Neill recalled him saying, a "malfunctioned distribution system, not a fundamental inadequacy of capacity." The fault lay with the usual cast of left-wing environmentalists and the many needless regulations that had been imposed on the industry during the Clinton years.

The crisis lasted about as long as Enron lasted. The rolling blackouts ceased in September 2001, just as Enron cratered.

Freed now of the constraints imposed by a Democratic White House, conservative Republicans in the House and Senate were working on a parallel track with the Cheney energy task force. The Friends of Big Oil were led, as usual, by the hard-driving House majority whip, DeLay. Working closely with him were two senior Republican members of the House Energy and Commerce Committee, Chairman W. J. "Billy" Tauzin of Louisiana and Joe Barton of Texas.

First elected to represent a suburban Dallas district, the Texas Eighth, in 1984, Barton had arrived in Washington as a member of a freshman minority Republican class that also included the retired exterminator from Sugar Land. The two right-wing soul mates quickly formed a friendship.

DeLay and Barton had much in common. Both men favored a virulent, take-no-prisoners approach to politics, and both were sponsored by the oil and gas industry. Barton publicly boasted of his work as a former "natural gas decontrol consultant for Atlantic Richfield Oil and Gas Company." DeLay was known as "the congressman from Enron," while Barton was often called "the congressman from Exxon," the international energy giant based in Dallas.

And while DeLay early on secured a place on the powerful Appropriations Committee, Barton was assigned to the House Commerce Committee (today's Energy and Commerce Committee, the title reflecting its change of focus under Republican leadership).

Under Chairman Tauzin, a former Democrat turned Republican, the full Energy and Commerce Committee was a hotbed for oil and gas state conservatives, anxious to preserve and expand the prerogatives of the industry. No member of the committee was more anxious than subcommittee chairman Barton.

As the spring and summer of 2001 unfolded, Chairman Barton's big push on behalf of Big Oil was a comprehensive piece of legislation known in congressional parlance as H.R. 4 (The Energy Policy Act of 2001).

H.R. 4 was an omnibus energy bill whose stated goal was further deregulation of the industry, as spelled out by Enron lobbyists. But like so many of the bills introduced by the Bush administration and its congressional cohort, H.R. 4 was also an arrow aimed straight at the heart of the New Deal.

Almost seventy years after Franklin Roosevelt had made the New Deal the centerpiece of his first administration, Republicans on Capitol Hill were still fighting to repeal it, virtually bill by bill. Only now, with a Republican president and a Republican Congress, they were actually succeeding in doing so.

The Senate version of H.R. 4, for example, sought to repeal an important piece of New Deal legislation, the Public Utilities Holding Company Act of 1935 (PUHCA). The impending repeal of PUHCA would, however, result in disastrous, unintended consequences—for Tom DeLay and for a Kansas-based energy company called Westar.

Back in the days when it was known as Western Resources, Westar was just another old-fashioned public utility. As was the case with most traditional public utility companies, Western's principal business lay in generating and delivering energy—in this case electricity for over a half million electric customers and more than a million natural gas customers in Kansas, Nebraska, Oklahoma, and Missouri.

As Western Resources, the company had been a good, solid moneymaker, rich in cash, low on debt, but low too in its profit margins. But then a new generation of leaders emerged on the scene beginning in 1995. Led by a new CEO, a former Wall Street investment banker named David Wittig, the former Western Resources was given not only a new name (Westar Energy) but a new goal as well: it was going to be "the Enron of the Midwest."

In the end, it almost was.

Not content just to think big, David Wittig liked to live that way too. In a city where "mansions" cost $300,000, Topeka's "old Landon place"—built in 1923 by newspaper publisher and politician Alf Landon, the 1936 Republican nominee for president—went for $700,000. The winning bidder was newly ennobled CEO Wittig. Before he was done renovating it, the Landon mansion would include not only a gym but also a regulation-size basketball court. The cost of these home improvements: more than $6 million.

The high-living Wittig had some big ideas for the former Western Resources. Spurred on by the prospect of energy deregulation, Wittig intended to take Westar into nonregulated, nonenergy businesses. With that end in mind, Westar began buying an ever-larger stake in ADT, the largest home-security-monitoring company in America. By the fall of 1996, Westar had increased its stake in ADT to nearly 22 percent. Westar then announced an unsolicited tender offer for all the remaining shares of the home-monitoring company. ADT management rejected the offer as "inadequate."

While publicly fending off Westar, ADT management secretly negotiated a friendly merger with Tyco International. The failed merger with ADT, ironically, turned out to have a huge and unexpected upside for Westar. It sold its shares in the home-monitoring company to Tyco for a substantial premium. The payout after taxes to Westar amounted to $519 million.

Westar would never again have it so good.

When Westar failed to acquire ADT, Wittig turned his sights on Protection One, the third-largest home-security-monitoring company. By the end of 1997, Westar owned 87 percent of the company.

A year later, with the Kansas City Royals on the block, Westar made a failed attempt to purchase the local baseball team.

Strange to say, the Enron of the Midwest began to experience growth pains. By 1999, with Protection One in danger of going into bankruptcy and Westar saddled with the debt service from a host of other lesser deals, the company's stock began to sink.

In response to the mess he had created, CEO Wittig proposed in 2000 to separate the company into two parts: a regulated utility business and a nonregulated business. The creation of these two new companies, Wittig assured the board, would result in "increase[d] shareholder value." The board agreed to the plan.

Westar now went before the Kansas Corporation Commission

(KCC) for permission to raise rates by $151 million. The request stirred up a hornet's nest in Kansas. Local newspapers began running stories about Wittig's $8 million annual pay package; and a Kansas-based corporate gadfly began asking questions about Westar's two Citation jets (one costing $10 million and the other $18 million).

Left unreported at the time were other, vastly bigger numbers. Under terms drawn up by Wittig and his right-hand man, Westar "chief strategist" Douglas Lake, the new nonutility company (to be named Western Industries) would be left with $1.45 billion in assets—and virtually no debt. Westar, on the other hand, would be left with the regulated utility business—and $3 billion in debt, plus millions more in pension obligations.

By virtue of "change-in-control" provisions in their personal service contracts, Wittig was set to walk off with somewhere between $37 million and $65 million, while Lake would have made off with between $18 million and $35 million.

The train appeared to have left the station when Westar struck a merger deal with Public Service of New Mexico (PNM) in a $1.5 billion all-stock swap. As part of the September 2000 deal, Westar proposed to spin off its non "pure-play" businesses into the new Western Industries, whose CEO and COO would be David Wittig and Douglas Lake, respectively.

And so it all might have gone—exactly as to plan—leaving Messrs. Wittig and Lake a couple of very wealthy men indeed, but for two jokers in the deck, one of them named Tom DeLay, the other Joe Barton.

By the fall of 2001, Westar CEO Wittig and strategist Lake knew they had some problems at the Enron of the Midwest. For one, on July 20, the KCC had issued an order enjoining the company from proceeding with its new rights offering. For another, the U.S. House of Representatives on August 1 passed Joe Barton's H.R. 4, a bill that had been set in motion by lobbyists from the real Enron.

Normally, an Enron-sponsored energy bill could have been expected to work to Westar's advantage as well. This one would have—

if Westar had remained one big happy, old-fashioned utility company. But it hadn't.

Denounced by angry ratepayers at home, denigrated by the KCC, its business plans all gone astray, the company was also being forced into fighting a faraway battle on Capitol Hill.

The problem lay in the Senate version of H.R. 4, which, it will be recalled, proposed repealing the Public Utilities Holding Company Act (PUHCA). The repeal of PUHCA would, however, make Westar subject to ("grandfathered into") another classic piece of New Deal legislation, the Investment Company Act of 1940 (ICA).

The rationale behind all this was spelled out in a handwritten briefing paper entitled "PUHCA Repeal & The Investment Company Act: An Unintended Problem." The paper was written in advance of a meeting with DeLay staff policy adviser Jack Victory.

The briefing paper went right to the point: "IC Act 1940, if 40% or more of the value of your assets is passively owned stuff, you're an investment company."

In December of 1995, Westar had entered into a deal with ONEOK, Inc., a Tulsa-based natural gas distributor. In spinning off its natural gas business, Western had received a passive 45 percent equity in ONEOK.

Thanks to its large minority ownership stake in ONEOK and its majority stake in Protection One, among other properties, Westar's balance sheet was now ladened with passively held assets—more than 40 percent of the entire value of the company. With PUHCA repealed, Westar would become subject to ICA.

And, subject to ICA, Westar could not proceed with its spin-off without transferring some of the $3 billion in debt to the succeeding company—the one Wittig and Lake intended to run. To do that, they would have to escape the clutches of ICA.

Wittig, Lake, and Westar now turned to K Street. In March 2001, Governmental Strategies, a Virginia-based firm, registered as a lobbyist for Westar. Governmental Strategies, as just about everyone in Washington knew, was a major recipient of lobbying business thanks to Tom DeLay's K Street Project. In short, Governmental Strategies was a Republican firm with close connections to some of the top right-wing legislators on Capitol Hill—especially on the House side.

Westar wanted its lobbyists to have a major hand in the drafting of energy deregulation legislation. In particular, Westar—and its two top executives—desperately wanted a provision that H.R. 4 notably lacked: a section that would specifically grandfather Westar from PUHCA.

In search of some kind of quick fix, the Westar lobbyists began scheduling meetings on Capitol Hill. The first known meeting occurred on June 27, 2001, when Westar lobbyist Richard Bornemann sat down with Representative Joe Barton and House Energy and Commerce Committee staff members.

Lobbyist Bornemann made it known that Westar was going to be badly hurt if H.R. 4 passed without specific relief for the company. No mention, apparently, was made of just how badly CEO Wittig and strategist Lake would be hurt by H.R. 4. Barton, the lifelong friend of Big Oil and Big Energy, was sympathetic.

The goal was clear: to save the Enron of the Midwest from the clutches of the New Deal. The question was, how to slip the language into the law.

The real Enron was in worse trouble still.

Six times, *Fortune* magazine named Enron "the most innovative company in America." By the year 2000, Enron boasted twenty-one thousand employees, while claiming $111 billion in revenues.

The problem was that while the twenty-one thousand employees existed, the $111 billion in revenues didn't. Enron—and its billions in profits—was a house of cards.

The story of Enron has been told many times by a number of gifted authors, among them Kurt Eichenwald, whose *Conspiracy of Fools* may well be the best of all the full-length accounts of the extraordinary rise and disastrous fall of the energy giant.

Enron shares that had traded as high as $90 had been halved by the fall of 2001. A white knight, in the form of Houston-based archrival Dynegy, now appeared on the horizon. Enron chairman Ken Lay feared that the white knight might ride away. When Moody's, the big bond-rating agency, threatened to downgrade Enron's debt, Lay turned to his old friend Secretary of Commerce Don Evans. The two men ran in the same circles, oil and right-wing Republicanism being the common denominator. Lay also turned to Treasury Secretary O'Neill. Lay, O'Neill quickly realized, was making the case for a federal bailout of the troubled energy giant.

When O'Neill brought up the subject with the president, Bush paused and told him, "We should tell the media that this happened, immediately . . . get it on the record."

Truth, O'Neill replied, "is best—always best."

Moments later, Bush told a group of reporters that he had had only one recent conversation with Ken Lay, and, no, they hadn't talked about the company's business. Not a single word did the president say of Ken Lay's phone calls to Don Evans and Paul O'Neill.*

In the wake of Enron's December 2001 bankruptcy—the largest in American economic history—the truth began to emerge, not only the truth behind Enron's complicated trading schemes, but also the truth

---

*By 1982, writes Kevin Phillips in *American Dynasty*, "the upper tier of U.S. wealth . . . was top-heavy enough with oil money, much of it Texan, to constitute a virtual Petroleum Club of the United States." Phillips's book is particularly good as to the connections between the first Bush administration and the rise of Enron, noting that it was President George H. W. Bush who ordered his then secretary of energy to develop a new energy strategy that eventually spawned the Energy Act of 1992, which mandated the deregulation of electricity at the wholesale level and required utilities to carry privately marketed electricity on their wires. Helping open the door wider still for Enron was a 2–1 vote by the Commodities Futures Trading Commission to define energy derivative contracts in such a way as to exclude them from CFTC oversight. The vote was taken on January 14, 1993, just days before President Bill Clinton was to take office. The chair of the CFTC: Wendy Gramm, the wife of Texas Republican senator Phil Gramm. Wendy Gramm would go on to serve as an Enron director from 1993 to 2001, earning somewhere between $915,000 and $1.853 million for her efforts. Not for nothing were the Gramms widely known in Texas as "Mr. and Mrs. Enron." The power of Enron could be measured in other ways as well: between 1993 and 2001, Enron pumped $5.3 million into the campaigns of federal candidates, most of them Republican. In a two-year period (1999–2000), Enron lobbyists spent $3.4 million pushing their deregulation agenda in Congress; and during the 1997–98 and 1999–2000 election cycles, the company spent more than $1 million in Texas campaigns and PACs and $4.8 million lobbying the legislature. Among the recipients of the company's largesse: governor George W. Bush ($238,000); Lieutenant Governor Rick Perry ($187,000); and Attorney General John Cornyn ($158,000).

behind the California energy crisis of 2000. The crisis had, like Enron's revenues, been a fraud. Megawatts had been laundered, the market manipulated. "Congestion fees" were paid for illusory "death star" market manipulations.

But Enron wasn't alone in manipulating the markets. A federal grand jury in San Francisco would later bring an indictment against Reliant Services, a wholly owned subsidiary of another major Houston energy player, Reliant Energy, charging that it had plotted to hide a multimillion-dollar trading loss in June 2000 by shutting off four of its five California power plants, thereby causing a spike in prices to consumers. According to the indictment, Reliant subsequently brought the power plants back online to take advantage of the higher hourly rate. The cost to California taxpayers, federal prosecutors charged, was in the tens of millions of dollars.*

Reliant too would crater as a result of the Enron disaster. But it would barely manage to skirt bankruptcy and the attendant public relations disaster that would entail. In the run-up to the California energy crisis the company's board included some of the most powerful political players in Houston, among them two Baker Botts partners, firm chairman E. William Barnett and senior partner James A. Baker III.

Barnett and Baker were more than law firm partners. They were best friends. Barnett was the chairman of the Rice University trustees and a major Bush fund-raiser, having raised tens of thousands of dollars for the 2000 presidential campaign. Like old Captain Baker before him, Barnett had his hands in every pie in town, from the Houston Zoo to the bar association, the University of Texas Law School Foundation, and J. P. Morgan Chase Texas (where he was a director).

Reliant senior vice president, general counsel, and secretary to the board of Reliant Hugh Rice Kelly led the negotiations with lawyers representing the company's many creditors. Kelly, a former Baker Botts partner and TLR tort reformer, turned as a last recourse for legal

---

*The San Francisco grand jury handed up the indictment against Reliant on April 9, 2004.

advice not to his old firm but to a famous Wall Street law firm. The plan the New York lawyers offered was for Reliant to put a "poison pill" in place.

The Reliant board went with the plan—and the company survived. Its executive leadership, did not.*

By the summer of 2001, Chairman Joe Barton had begun circulating in draft form a second major energy bill, this one to deregulate energy transmission.

On September 21, 2001, Barton passed around a draft of his proposed new legislation to members of the Energy and Air Quality Sub-

---

*The relationship between Reliant, Barnett, Baker, and Baker Botts was explored—unsuccessfully—in a so-called shareholders derivative suit filed in 2003 in Harris County, Texas, district court, *Hudelson v. Letbetter* (Cause No. 2002–25241, 269th Judicial District of Texas). At issue was alleged round-trip trading of electricity made by Reliant during the California energy crisis. Defendants in the case included former Reliant CEO Steve Letbetter and former Reliant board member James A. Baker III. A special litigation committee (SLC) was appointed by Reliant's board on December 5, 2003, to investigate the claims asserted in the Hudelson lawsuit. The SLC report went on to exonerate the individual defendants. But according to plaintiffs' subsequent filing, only four former Reliant employees were personally interviewed by the SLC and only two bankers' boxes of documents were reviewed during the yearlong investigation. And while James A. Baker III was a named defendant in the suit, his old friend and former law partner, recently retired Baker Botts managing partner Bill Barnett, was on the special committee to the board investigating the charges. Counsel to the SLC was the Houston law firm of Zummo & Mitchell, whose two name partners were also former Baker Botts partners. Baker Botts was, moreover, counsel to the defendants, James A. Baker III, included. The effect, plaintiffs' lawyers argued in their March 3, 2004, motion to compel defendants and the SLC to produce documents, made for a neat little circle. The Texas court felt otherwise: the case was dismissed.

Though they were no longer officers of the company, Letbetter and Kelly did well for themselves. SEC filings (available at http://sec.edgar-online.com/2003/05/01/0000951019-03-002622/Section11.asp) show that former CEO Letbetter earned a base salary of $983,750 and a bonus of $1.739 million in 2001—chicken feed, by Enron standards perhaps; while Kelly earned a base salary of $431,250 and a bonus of $322,575 that same year. On leaving the company in April 2003, Letbetter received a severance of $6.9 million and a pro rata bonus of $747,946. His 551,890 shares of restricted stock would vest to him provided that he did not breach his noncompete agreement. In addition, Letbetter received financial-planning services up to a maximum of $25,000, outplacement services up to a maximum of $100,000, and medical insurance until age sixty-five. He also received a minimum twelve-month consultancy to the tune of $83,333—per month. In addition, he was set to receive fifteen annual installments of $49,152 per month under the company's deferred compensation plan, and would be provided with office space, parking, and "support" for a three-year period, including home-security monitoring. His unvested options would become immediately exercisable.

For his part, general counsel Kelly received $2.3 million in severance, together with a pro rata bonus of $96,164, along with "outplacement services, financial planning, extended medical and life insurance coverage." He too walked away with a large package of stock options.

committee. Contained within the draft, appearing as Section 125, was the grandfather clause that Westar executives wanted so badly.

On December 5, Barton formally introduced the proposed legislation as H.R. 3406 (The Electric Supply and Transmission Act). Like H.R. 4, H.R. 3406 was widely viewed as Enron-inspired—so much so that opponents took to calling 3406 the Enron Act. Ironically, the Houston-based energy giant was already in its death throes by then.

Conveniently, Westar lobbyist Bornemann had donated $1,000 to Barton on October 17; and when Barton introduced H.R. 3406, Western's grandfather clause (Section 125) was part of the language of the bill as originally offered.

Democratic staffers on the House Energy and Commerce Committee were, in fact, perplexed by Section 125. So much so that, on January 30, 2002, the ranking Democrat on the committee, Representative John Dingell (Mich.), and the ranking Democrat on Barton's subcommittee, Representative Edward Markey (Mass.), wrote to then SEC chair Harvey Pitt asking for an analysis of Section 125. They were concerned, Dingell and Markey wrote Pitt, that the language of 125 seemed to open the door, post-Enron, for a host of former utility companies to become unregulated mutual funds.

Pitt, a former Wall Street securities lawyer widely viewed as being sympathetic toward the very companies he was supposed to oversee, nevertheless sent the Dingell letter on to SEC staff for review. Two weeks later, Pitt forwarded a memo to Dingell stating SEC staff opposition to Section 125.

The strange history of Section 125 did not, however, end there.

On March 28, a partner at the Washington law firm of Wilmer Cutler, a woman named Marianne Smythe—herself a former top SEC administrator—joined the fray, with a letter to Dingell and Markey setting forth new language for Section 125. The revised Section 125, Smythe claimed, "would offer a very narrow range of companies (we believe, in fact, just one company)" to be grandfathered. Nowhere in her letter, however, was the word *Westar* mentioned.

Less than a week later, investigators say, Westar lobbyist Bornemann began obtaining fund-raiser schedules for Energy Committee chairman Tauzin and subcommittee chairman Barton. The fund-raisers for both men were arranged by the same Virginia-based Republican-oriented company, Epiphany Productions, yet another beneficiary of the DeLay K Street Project.

With the Senate preparing to vote on its own version of H.R. 4, Westar and its lobbyists were, more than ever, determined to get H.R. 3406, with its Section 125, made into law.

That same month, lead lobbyist Bornemann e-mailed a Westar vice president named Douglas Lawrence a proposal strongly suggesting that the company should pursue a "Platinum Package" of campaign contributions, beginning with $25,000 in "soft money" to DeLay's TRMPAC and another $31,000 in "hard money" going to various candidates associated with Chairman Tauzin and subcommittee chairman Barton.

Bornemann followed up with another e-mail to Lawrence: "I absolutely detest asking you for money. We all prefer to think that our powerful personalities and strategic brilliance transcends such grubbiness." That said, warned Bornemann, Westar was going to have to keep to the "Platinum Budget" if it expected results on the Hill.

A good start would be the $25,000 marked for Tom DeLay and his TRMPAC. With H.R. 4 having long since passed the House and moving toward a vote in the Senate—the bill passed the upper chamber on April 26*—daughter Dani DeLay Ferro and former DeLay legislative director Drew Maloney, a lobbyist for the Federalist Group, decided that the time was right to throw a fund-raiser for TRMPAC. The event, held at the Homestead resort in Hot Springs, Virginia, took place on the heels of the Senate vote.

For $25,000 per company, representatives of the energy corporations most impacted by H.R. 4 could wine and dine and even play a round or two of golf with Whip DeLay. Among the attendees were representatives of Reliant Energy, the Williams Companies of Tulsa, the El Paso Corp. of Houston—and Westar Energy.

On May 19, 2002, Doug Lawrence, Westar's vice president for public affairs (the chief in-house lobbyist), wrote a memo to senior

---

*The House had passed its version on August 2, 2001.

company management outlining the need "to get a seat at the table" of the House-Senate Conference Committee that would would have to resolve the differences between the competing bills.

The Lawrence memo called for senior management to give $56,500 in "soft" and "hard" money to candidates supported by leading House and Senate Conference Committee members: Senator Richard Shelby (R-Ala.), chair of the Senate Banking Committee and a member of the Senate Energy Committee; Representative Barton; Representative Tauzin—and House majority whip DeLay.

The memo went on to spell out the exact amount of money required of each Westar executive. Of the total, $25,000 had already been delivered to TRMPAC, the rest (virtually all of it would be paid out) went to various protégés of the four powerful Republican legislators.

If it sounds confusing, it was. On May 20, Douglas Lake e-mailed Lawrence to ask, "Who is Shimkus, who is Young? Delay [*sic*] is from TX what is our connection?"

As Lawrence explained to Lake in a subsequent e-mail, "We are working on getting our grandfather provision on PUHCA repeal into the Senate version of the energy bill. It requires working with the Conference Committee to achieve. We have a plan for participation to get a seat at the table."

Lawrence explained that the contributions were intended not for the congressmen themselves—all four held safe seats—but for the congressional campaigns of close associates.

After describing Senator Shelby as "our anchor on the Senate side," Lawrence wrapped up the discussion: "Ultimately the plan is directed at getting a strong position at the table on both the Senate and House side."

When you got right down to it, the simplest part of the whole equation was also the most fundamental: passing an energy bill—any energy bill, whether H.R. 4 or H.R. 3406—that contained the language found in Section 125 of 3406.

Throughout that spring and summer of 2002, Westar lobbyist Bornemann was busy, attending numerous barbecues and other fundraisers on behalf of the energy companies' principal water carriers, Congressmen Tauzin and Barton—and their protégés.

The socializing—and the hefty contributions to Tauzin, Barton, DeLay, and company—eventually bore fruit. Later that summer, the House and Senate—temporarily in Democratic hands—had their conferees meet to iron out their differences over H.R. 4. The contingent from the lower chamber was notable for the presence of many of its most powerful "old bulls," among them Whip DeLay himself, Chairman Tauzin, and fellow chairmen James Sensenbrenner, Michael Oxley, and Bill Thomas. Also among the conferees were the redoubtable pork-barrel-roller supreme, Don Young of oil-producing Alaska, and no less than four congressmen from Texas (DeLay and Barton, plus lesser lights Lamar Smith and Larry Combest). On the House side, the Democrats—led by Dingell and Markey—were overwhelmed, 28–20.

It didn't take a genius to see that this was an important bill—one that Whip DeLay intended to have passed just the way he wanted it passed.

No doubt Westar CEO Wittig thought he had a lot on his mind that summer. He didn't know the half of it. A close friend, local bank president Clinton Odell "Dell" Weidner II, already knew that he—and Wittig—were in hot water.

Weidner had lent Wittig the millions he had needed to fix up the former Landon mansion, and the two men had drawn close over time. Thus, in early April 2001, Weidner had come to his pal Wittig with an investment opportunity. Weidner proposed that Wittig invest $1.5 million in a Scottsdale, Arizona, real estate project. Wittig, however, declined to put his money into the venture.

Weidner suggested that Wittig lend him—the banker—the $1.5 million, so *he* could invest in Eagle Ride. According to Wittig, Weidner told him that he preferred not to apply for a loan himself "because he wanted to show Frank Sabatini, the owner and chairman of the board of Capital City, that he could do the deal himself."

The Westar CEO countered that if Weidner would increase Wittig's credit line at the bank from $3.5 million to $5 million, he would be only too happy to lend his banker friend the necessary capital.

On April 26, 2001, Weidner contacted Cap Cities Bank customers

Michael Earl and Tim Burns, who were already negotiating to acquire the Eagle Ride real estate. Four days later, Weidner had $1.5 million wired into Wittig's personal account at the bank. Weidner then transferred the money to a Phoenix bank—and with that became a 50 percent owner of the renamed Scottsdale Sierra Eagle Ridge LLC. The next day, May 1, Weidner gave Wittig a promissory note for $1.5 million.

The story could have ended there, with Dell Weidner a minor real estate mogul. But it didn't. Weidner's secretary, upset by what she perceived as the unethical way in which the deal had gone down, revealed the boss's little secret to another officer at the bank. The bank officer, in turn, notified federal authorities.

On July 17, while Wittig was on vacation, FBI agents arrived at company headquarters in Topeka with a grand jury subpoena for the Westar CEO. The subpoena, dated July 16, made specific reference to a questionable $1.5 million loan that Wittig had made to a banker friend in April 2001.

Unbeknownst to outside directors of Westar, Wittig had been interviewed by the FBI in August and appeared before a federal grand jury on September 12. As far as can be ascertained, he told no one at the company—besides his second-in-command, Douglas Lake—about it.

On September 17 and 18, agents from the FBI served grand jury subpoenas on Westar. The subpoenas ordered Westar to produce documents relating to Wittig, the company's aircraft, and annual shareholders' meetings. Again, company directors were not apprised.

In Washington too the wheels just kept on moving. Six days after Wittig's federal grand jury appearance—and one day after the first federal grand jury subpoena had been served on Westar—Joe Barton moved to reinsert the Westar grandfather clause (now designated as Section 136) into the conference version of H.R. 4.

The next day, September 19, Representative Markey offered an amendment to strike 136. The House conferees voted the amendment down, 8–6. Barton cast his vote as well as votes he held in proxy— including DeLay's—against the amendment.

That same night, Wittig, for the first time, told an outside company director about the FBI probe. Four days later, on September 23, the

Westar board met in special session. The primary reason for the meeting was neither to advise the board of the grand jury subpoenas nor to form a special committee. Instead, it was to approve Wittig's proposal for new employment contracts for himself and Douglas Lake.

Only at the end of the meeting, with the proposal having passed, did Wittig tell the board that the FBI had interviewed him. Four days later, the Westar board authorized the formation of a special committee—the members of which had all been recommended by Wittig himself.*

With the woeful tale of David Wittig and Westar now out in the open, Republicans on the House-Senate Conference Committee withdrew Section 125 (or 136, as it had been redesignated) from Joe Barton's "Enron Bill."

Enron itself was long since dead. But now, in October 2002, the would-be masters of the Enron of the Midwest had also come acropper.

Just how far acropper they—and their friend Tom DeLay—had come we will soon see.

---

*In February 2003, Wittig and Clinton Odell "Dell" Weidner were found guilty by a federal jury of falsifying bank documents. Weidner was sentenced to six years and six months in prison. Wittig was sentenced to four years and three months in prison and fined $1 million. In the fall of 2004, Wittig again went on trial in federal district court in Kansas City, Kansas, this time in company with his former number two at Westar, Douglas Lake. The trial ended in a hung jury in December.

Tried again before U.S. district judge Julie Robinson, during the late summer of 2005, both men were found guilty this time. Wittig was found guilty on thirty-nine counts and sentenced to eighteen years in prison and fined $5 million in addition to $14.5 million in restitution. On January 5, 2007, the Tenth Circuit Court of Appeals overturned the convictions. The appeals court said that evidence at the trial did not justify the verdicts, and the U.S. Attorney's Office in Topeka announced that it would not try to reinstate the conviction on money laundering and wire fraud. The defendants would, however, be retried on lesser courts. The appeals court also reduced Wittig's earlier sentence. Judge Robinson then cut it to two years. See, for example, Andrew Longstreth's excellent account of the trials, "Disorder in the Court" (*The American Lawyer*, July 2005).

CHAPTER NINE

✭

What's the Matter with Texas?
Part I

"Government Preparing to Tell Texas About Texans" was the headline of an Associated Press dispatch dated February 26, 2001. "Texans," the AP noted, "are about to find out who they are, where they live and why it all matters." The U.S. Census Bureau would be releasing the first set of detailed figures sometime in the next month. The numbers already released showed that, with 20,851,820 residents, Texas had become the nation's second-largest state, surpassing New York, and behind only California in population.

Once the detailed statistics arrived, the Texas State Data Center at Texas A&M University in College Station would then process the numbers for use by the state legislature in its redistricting efforts. The raw data would be broken down by race, ethnicity, and gender, broken down too among the state's 254 counties and thousands of cities, but also down to the most basic political division, the precinct level.

State Representative Delwin Jones, a Republican from Lubbock and the chairman of the House Redistricting Committee, told the AP that he expected to have the Census Bureau figures in hand before March 15. The legislature, meeting in its regular biennial session, would then have until May 28 to redraw the lines for the state house, senate, and board of education districts. More crucially, the legislature would also have until then to redraw the lines for the state's thirty-two congressional districts. Or, as an Associated Press reporter explained it, somewhat inaccurately, as history would show, "Redistricting is the redrawing of political boundaries once a decade after new census figures are released."

The thirty-two seats were a gain of two, with most of the additional population coming in the suburban reaches of the Dallas–Fort Worth, Houston, and San Antonio–Austin metropolitan regions.

One thing was already clear, said Jones, "Rural Texas is going to lose."*

When reporter Hector Tobar of the *Los Angeles Times* looked at the changed landscape that was Texas circa 2000, he found that "the Lone Star State has become a place ever more divided by great stretches of highway and fortune, booming in both glitzy high-tech suburbs and ramshackle border colonias, while its old cattle towns lose people and influence."

The big news was that the state had added over 2 million Latino residents (2,018,310, to be exact) in a decade—a 47 percent increase, meaning that "Tejanos" now made up roughly a third of the state's population.

The New Texas was suburban—and Latino. On the one hand, there were the suburbs, whose growth had largely been fueled by the success of computer companies such as Dell, Compaq, and Texas Instruments. These were, in essence, sprawling, white, middle-class enclaves. And they were Republican.

A perfect example was provided by Tom DeLay's own Sugar Land, a former sugarcane plantation that had exploded in size in less than a decade, the surrounding Fort Bend County having grown 57 percent between 1990 and 2000. Where once had been cane fields and pastures,

---

*University of Texas law professor Steve Bickerstaff's *Lines in the Sand: Congressional Redistricting in Texas and the Downfall of Tom DeLay* (Austin: University of Texas Press, 2007), appeared in print after the manuscript of this book was completed.

sugar silos, and barns, today there were quaintly named developments, First Colony here, New Territory there. The Fort Bend County Chamber of Commerce's Louis Garvin told Tobar that he reckoned, "If we can keep pouring enough concrete to build the freeways, we'll keep the people coming here."

But another Texas was poor and Latino. And it was growing faster still. Demographers were predicting that by 2005, the state's population would no longer be majority white. The growing number of Spanish-speaking Texans was evident just about everywhere in the state, but particularly on the border with Mexico. Laredo, for example, grew 45 percent. Such growth did not come without problems attached. State-provided services—never among the nation's best— were now stretched to the limits. You name it, there was a problem. The welfare system, notoriously underfunded, was a disgrace; adult literacy services hardly existed in places; by treating the poor and indigent virtually pro bono, hospitals were bleeding money; the prisons were overcrowded; and, the biggest worry of all, the public school systems were under court orders to reform the existing system of local and state funding, much of it currently dependent on property taxes, which in many cases were capped.

Looked at this way, Texas as it entered the new century was one big pressure cooker. It didn't take a genius to know that the valve on the cooker was eventually going to blow.

Republicans were almost certain to pick up the additional two seats in the House. The 2000 census figures showed that eight of the ten fastest-growing districts were Republican—ranging from 20.43 percent growth in DeLay's own suburban Houston district to a whopping 29.76 percent growth in Majority Leader Dick Armey's suburban Dallas district. Only one Democratic district—that held by liberal Austin congressman Lloyd Doggett—broke the 20 percent growth mark (21.41 percent). With the Texas congressional delegation currently composed of seventeen Democrats and thirteen Republicans in the House, the odds were strong that in 2002, the numbers would be 17–15, maybe even split down the middle, as congressional expert

Charlie Cook predicted in his May 22 "Off to the Races" column. Cook, however, offered this caveat: if Republicans "get some breaks, either through the state legislative/gubernatorial redistricting process or in the courts . . . the chances of Republicans scoring larger gains are certainly there." Cook also warned, "At this point, it looks likely that the map will end up in the courts."

But first, legislators would focus on themselves, by redrawing state house and senate districts. In the senate, the Republicans held a 16–15 edge; whereas in the house, the Democrats, led by Speaker Pete Laney, held a 78–72 advantage. There were, moreover, a number of Republicans on the conservative West Texas cotton farmer Laney's team, among them House Redistricting Committee chairman Delwin Jones. By late April, the seventy-seven-year-old Jones was already well on his way to becoming a pariah within his own party. Speaker Laney, said a Texas Republican Party spokesperson, "is once again attempting to deny the political voice of Texas voters in order to protect the political careers of incumbent politicians."

Come mid-May, and the battle over redistricting the state legislature had reached a level of ferociousness seldom seen even in Texas politics. By late April, when the house and senate redistricting committees unveiled their maps, tension was high—and political posturing was in the air.

Republican Party officials proclaimed themselves pleased with the senate plan—drawn by Republicans—but were quick to call the house map a "thinly veiled attempt to protect the career of Speaker Pete Laney." New governor Rick Perry played coy, refusing to say whether he would veto the redistricting plans.

Should that happen, the map-drawing would fall to a five-member committee, the Texas Legislative Redistricting Board, which had a 4–1 Republican edge (Lieutenant Governor Bill Ratliff, Attorney General John Cornyn, Comptroller Carole Keeton Rylander, and Land Commissioner David Dewhurst, plus Democratic speaker Laney). Ultimately, as Charlie Cook predicted, the federal courts would have the last say.

That became a far likelier possibility when the state house and senate failed to redraw their own district lines. In the senate, where redistricting, in effect,* required a two-thirds vote to pass, a dozen Republican legislators had decided—no doubt with a little help from Tom DeLay—that the lines drawn, especially in the house, weren't Republican enough for them. *Austin American-Statesman* political reporter Laylan Copelin wrote that the state's leaders were resigned to "sift[ing] through the ashes of redistricting." The question now was whether Governor Perry would call a special session and ask the legislators, having failed to draw their own lines, to try to draw congressional lines—the ones that meant something not just to the people of Texas, but the American people as a whole, since the future occupants of those congressional seats would be voting on national legislation.

Meanwhile, it would all be up to the 4–1 Republican Legislative Redistricting Board to draw the state legislative lines, for both house and senate. As the *American-Statesman*'s Copelin put it, under Texas law, the legislators "don't get a second chance to do their own districts in a special session."

Reporter Copelin also drew a revealing portrait of Attorney General Cornyn, one that emphasized the critical role that he played in this little drama: "As the state's top lawyer, Cornyn has the dual role of voting on a map and then defending it in court." He quoted Cornyn, "This is not just a political process. . . . It's a legal process. No matter how much you want to draw lines to help your political party, it must clear the Justice Department and the courts."

What the silver-haired fox Cornyn saw no need to add, however, was that the Justice Department, under former Republican senator and current attorney general John Ashcroft, was now under the sway of a highly politicized White House, with a former Texas Supreme Court justice as White House counsel (Alberto Gonzales); a former Texas Lottery Commission chair (Harriet Miers) as deputy White House staff secretary; and Cornyn's own longtime political guru in the pivotal role of counselor to the president (Karl Rove). What were the odds that the professionals in DOJ would be able to stop a Republican gerrymander—at any level, legislative or congressional?

---

*By tradition, it took a two-thirds vote to bring legislation to the floor of the Texas State Senate.

Or that the federal courts would declare such a gerrymander unconstitutional? For what Cornyn also failed to mention was that the U.S. Fifth Circuit Court of Appeals had, under Presidents Reagan, Bush, and Bush, gone from being among the most liberal federal courts (especially with regard to civil rights issues) to a bastion of conservatism, only a step or two removed from the notoriously right-wing Fourth Circuit in Richmond, Virginia.*

No, like the AP's earlier, reassuring nod that congressional redistricting only happens once every ten years, Cornyn's reluctance to spell out the full truth meant that most Texans—including most well-read Texans—would continue to assume that the Department of Justice and the federal courts would right whatever injustices the Legislative Redistricting Board and the Republicans meted out. Political innocents, they were about to be proved very wrong indeed.

House Redistricting Committee chairman Jones, the seventy-seven-year-old veteran legislator, was still trying to play the game the way it had long been played in Texas, with the goal being to sustain the state's long-standing, built-up seniority in the state house. And that, of course,

---

*The Fifth Circuit, which sits in New Orleans, was created in 1891, with federal appellate jurisdiction over the states of Louisiana, Mississippi, Texas, Alabama, Georgia, and Florida. In 1981, the court was split, with Alabama, Florida, and Georgia moved to the new Eleventh Circuit. Today, the court consists of nineteen judges, four of whom are on senior status. Of the remaining fifteen, four were appointed by President Ronald Reagan; one by President Jimmy Carter; four by President George H. W. Bush; three by President Bill Clinton; and three by President George W. Bush. The count, in other words, stands at eleven Republican appointees versus four Democratic appointees. Of these, the most notable appointments have all been Republican: former chief judge Patrick Higginbotham of Dallas; Judge Edith Brown Clement of New Orleans; and Judge Priscilla Owen of Houston. Higginbotham, named to the federal district court in Dallas by President Ford in 1975 (at age thirty-seven), was elevated to the Fifth Circuit by President Reagan in 1982. One of the court's most conservative members, Higginbotham was considered by both Presidents Bush as a possible nominee to the U.S. Supreme Court. In late August 2006, Higginbotham took senior status, but prior to that time, he presided over the three-judge federal panel hearing the various Texas redistricting cases in recent years. Judges Brown Clement and Owen were both widely reported to have been considered by President George H. W. Bush as possible nominees for the U.S. Supreme Court. Owen, born 1954, was for seventeen years a lawyer at Houston's Andrews & Kurth firm—James A. Baker's old firm—and served on the Texas Supreme Court from 1995 to 2005, when she joined the Fifth Circuit. The more radical of the two well-known female jurists on the court, Owen served on the board of advisers of the Houston and Austin chapters of the conservative Federalist Society.

meant retaining the sitting members, whether Democratic or Republican. Though a Republican, Jones pushed through his committee, 9–6, a plan supported by Democratic speaker Laney. The plan, which reporter Copelin predicted "would go nowhere," went nowhere.

By the end of June, Governor Perry was telling reporters that he was getting "negative vibes" as to the ability of legislators to draw new congressional lines. As a result, the Associated Press reported, there was an increased likelihood that the governor would not call a special session of the legislature—and that congressional redistricting would be left up to the courts. The governor added, "We will not waste taxpayers' money on a special session if we can't feel a very clear positive ending."

Once again, the AP dispatch emphasized the comforting old saw "redistricting is done every ten years." No mention, of course, that, in the hands of sharpers, it might be done multiple times every ten years.

As yet there was no mention of multiple redistricting, but with a massive dust cloud having settled upon Austin—the result of Saharan dust having been carried to North America by westward trade winds—the political forecast was now "crazy and hazy," in the words of a local reporter. While most politicians readied for the ritual July Fourth handshaking and baby-kissing events, other politicians had been plotting in near secret. Two days before the Fourth, Senate Redistricting Committee chairman Jeff Wentworth, a right-wing San Antonio Republican, announced that his committee had come up with a congressional map that would flip the state's delegation from 17–13 Democratic to overwhelmingly Republican.

That, of course, didn't sit well with Democrats in the Democratic-controlled state house. Governor Rick Perry soon made it official. He would not call a special session of the legislature to deal with congressional redistricting. The state's most influential congressman, Martin Frost, pronounced himself pleased, telling reporters, "I am very confident that the courts will craft a fair plan that protects minority voting rights and honors Texas tradition." Frost, the ranking Democrat on the powerful House Rules Committee and the fourth-highest-ranking member of the party's leadership, as chair of the House Democratic Caucus, had been among those marked for extinction under the Wentworth plan, along with Congressmen Lloyd Doggett, Ken Bentsen, and Nick Lampson.

The real mischief—as the Democratic congressmen would later learn—would come much sooner, with the workings of the Texas Legislative Redistricting Board, the five-member Republican-controlled body that would now tackle state legislative redistricting.

Speaker Pete Laney, the lone Democrat on the board, offered the map that had been voted out by the house. The Laney plan was expected to have turned the house Republican, 80–70, but with enough rural, pro-Laney Republicans to keep the speaker in office. Attorney General Cornyn, as chair of the board (the LRB, as it was known), presented his own plan, one that would add still more Republican seats—most of them from urban and suburban areas—to yield a super-Republican majority of 90–60 and lead to Speaker Laney's certain downfall. The Cornyn plan was a bloodbath in the making, pairing no less than forty-two incumbents—thirty-two of them Democrats—against one another. With the state senate already in Republican hands (16–15) and with the new plans under consideration sure to add three to five Republicans, the work of the LRB would also prepare the way for a Republican-controlled second effort at congressional redistricting. Yet in the hurrah over legislative redistricting—and the assurance that the federal courts would be left to handle the congressional side of things—that possibility received scant attention.

The LRB voted 3–2 in favor of the Cornyn plan. Republican lieutenant governor Bill Ratliff—the former Democratic state senator from East Texas—sided with Speaker Laney, but the other three Republicans on the board held firm. His plan, the sanctimonious Attorney General Cornyn said, would create "competitive races" and "reinvigorate our politics so that the public becomes reengaged." Among those now facing a competitive race was Speaker Laney, who found himself thrown into a district that was two-to-one Republican.

☆ ☆ ☆

Meanwhile, the fine hand of Baker Botts's election lawyers was being felt. As reporter Laylan Copelin had it, "Gov. Rick Perry conspired with Republican lawyers to gain an advantage in a race to find a friendly judge to draw the state's 32 congressional districts."

On July 3, Perry had notified legislative leaders that he was not going to call a special session to deal with congressional redistricting. Yet, even as Lieutenant Governor Ratliff and Speaker Laney were receiving their hand-delivered notes, lawyers from Baker Botts were filing suit in a Harris Count (Houston) state court. In the court papers, the Baker Botts lawyers wrote, "Governor Perry has announced that he will not call a special session of the Texas Legislature."

The timing and locale, said a Democratic lawyer, were no accident. The Baker Botts lawyers clearly had inside information from the governor's office, and they were clearly "forum-shopping" for a friendly court in a friendly venue. Republican lawyer Andy Taylor—a sometime official in Cornyn's office, Taylor would later argue in favor of the state's congressional redistricting efforts in federal court as a private attorney on retainer—claimed that the hand-delivered letters were merely formal notifications of what had been announced on June 29 by Perry (when he told the press he had "bad vibes").*

A Baker Botts spokesman referred calls to new partner Sam Cooper—one of the Florida recount lawyers. Speaking for Attorney General Cornyn, Andy Taylor denied that Republicans were looking for a Republican judge to hear the case.

Speaking for himself, Cornyn said: "My decisions as attorney general aren't motivated by how they may be perceived in campaigns," adding that the LRB's plans "were drawn to represent the future of Texas." Later, in a November appearance before a three-judge federal court, Taylor would be forced to admit that at least one senate seat, in the coastal city of Beaumont, had been redrawn solely in order to "flip it" from Democratic to Republican.

---

*Taylor later joined Locke Liddell & Sapp—the politically connected Dallas law firm whose former chair had been White House counsel Harriet Miers. There he was hired by Cornyn to represent the state in its congressional redistricting appeal work, for which the firm was paid $804,478. He later joined the Texas Association of Business (TAB) as its general counsel, while representing DeLay's TRMPAC in its civil lawsuits.

But John Cornyn surely did have the future of Texas in mind when he helped draw the lines. For, in doing so, he and his two Republican colleagues ensured that the political future of Texas would meet the 3-R Test. Thanks to Cornyn & Co., the political map of Texas at the turn of the twenty-first century could be expected to be Republican, reactionary, and radical. Reliably so at that—and in ways that the moneymen behind TLR, TAB (Texas Association of Business), and TRMPAC would wholeheartedly agree with.

But then again, there was nothing to be gained by going out in public and saying *that.*

What was clear now was that congressional lines for 2002 would be in the hands of the courts. The question was, which courts? With hearings scheduled to begin on September 10, "Texas politicians and political aficionados submitted congressional redistricting plans to an unknown court and an unknown judge," in the words of *San Antonio Express-News* reporter Bob Richter. Predictably, a Democratic plan aimed to keep the state's delegation Democratic, 17–15. A plan submitted by Attorney General Cornyn "on behalf of the state of Texas"—and a separate plan submitted by the state's Republican Party—aimed at a 21–11 Republican margin.

On September 12, the state's by now all-Republican supreme court ruled 8–1 that the redistricting lawsuits should be tried in a Travis County (Austin) state district court, a venue favored by Democrats. Of course, what the state supreme court judges knew well was that a decision at the district court level was sure to be appealed—sure too to find its way into their own hands.

Following a two-week trial, Judge Paul Davis, a Democrat, unveiled *his* congressional redistricting plan. In public at least, Republican leaders cried foul, citing the supposed similarity between Judge Davis's plan and that of Lieutenant Governor Bill Ratliff's, a Democrat turned Republican. State Republican Party leaders claimed that the judge's plan would likely create sixteen Republican districts, thirteen Democratic districts, and three toss-up districts—well short of their stated goals. The state's senior Democratic congressman, Martin

Frost, at first seemed to take a wait-and-see approach, telling local reporters that the decision would leave the state with a Democratic house delegation. Still, Frost believed, the plan divided too many Hispanic and black communities and was, thus, likely in violation of the federal Votings Rights Act.

Privately, Frost was stunned by the ruling. The decision, in reality, seemed to threaten the careers of no less than five sitting Democratic house members: Ken Bentsen (the nephew of former Democratic U.S. senator and treasury secretary Lloyd Bentsen), Chet Edwards, Charles Stenholm, Max Sandlin, and Jim Turner. As an anonymous Democrat involved in the redistricting effort told the *Washington Post*'s Tom Edsall, "What really hurt us in Texas is that a Democratic judge made the ruling." Worse still, Judge Davis's decision was also likely to have a national impact. As the *Post* headline put it, "Texas Setback Rattles Democrats; If Redistricting Plan Is Upheld, Prospects in House Look Bleak." Thanks to Judge Davis's ruling, Republicans, currently holding on to a nine-seat margin, would likely retain control over the new post-9/11 House.

A week later, Judge Davis shocked political observers, Democrats and Republicans alike, by reversing himself. In his new decision, Davis seemed to marry aspects of Speaker Laney's congressional mapping plan with his own. Republicans, this time, were genuinely outraged. "We are dumbfounded by the bizarre actions taken undertaken by Judge Davis," said state GOP chair Susan Weddington. Under the new plan, all but one of the endangered Democrats—Ken Bentsen, a white Houstonian, who was put in an overwhelmingly black and Latino district—would seem to have emerged somewhat safer. Their leader, Martin Frost, fared best of all, as his district went from leaning Republican to solidly Democratic. Suddenly too Democratic prospects for regaining control of the House—Majority Whip Tom DeLay's House—improved dramatically.

One week later, the Texas Supreme Court showed its true colors, rejecting by a 6–3 vote the revised congressional redistricting plan. Judge Davis, the court ruled, had improperly switched plans at the last minute. Parties, the court said, should have been given time to examine and cross-examine witnesses. Democratic lawyers pointed out that the evidence in the case had, in fact, been presented over two weeks.

Even as the Texas Supreme Court was voiding Judge Davis's plan, the "third act" in the state's congressional redistricting battle had already begun in a federal district courtroom in Tyler. The date was October 15.

It was, at first glance, an obscure venue for a case with such profound implications for the state and the nation. Yet, strange to say, Tyler had history on its side, for many of the most important and wide-ranging federal court decisions affecting Texans over the past four decades had been handed down from the federal bench there.

Tyler's city fathers had long styled it "The Rose Capital of America." There was an annual Rose Parade, a Rose Festival, and even a Rose Queen. But what Tyler was mostly known for was oil—and, in the political realm, a tight-fisted, old-fashioned, unyieldingly right-wing sort of conservatism.

Indeed, Tyler might well have been the most conservative city in a conservative state. With its population of about eighty-five thousand, Tyler had long been the banking center of oil-rich, people-poor East Texas. Once populist country—where many a Democrat would truly have voted "for a yeller dog" rather than a Republican—East Texas, a land of piney woods, poor whites, and poorer blacks, had in recent decades turned more and more conservative and Republican thanks mostly to their disdain for Lyndon Johnson's Great Society and the impact of federal-court-ordered school integration.

Ironically, at one point, the most hated federal judge in the South might well have been William Wayne Justice of Tyler. It was U.S. district judge Justice who, in the late 1960s and early 1970s, ordered massive school integration across district after district throughout mostly rural, Baptist East Texas—the Texas heart of the Old Confederacy—and had had crosses burned on his lawn, by way of thanks.

It was Justice—a brave, crusading judge, to be sure—who also ordered the Texas prison system reformed. Justice too who ordered bilingual education mandated for the state's public schools.

But by 2001, Judge Justice—sometimes referred to as "the real governor of Texas"—was in semiretirement. His eventual successor on the federal district bench in Tyler, former U.S. attorney John Hannah Jr., wasn't quite the firebrand that Judge Justice had been, but he was certainly liberal by the standards of the place—and well known for his ethical approach to politics and the law.

President Carter had appointed Hannah as U.S. attorney for the Eastern District of Texas. In that position, Hannah had prosecuted some two dozen local officials on corruption charges. A failed run for state attorney general in 1982 was followed by a term as secretary of state under Governor Ann Richards. Her new secretary of state's primary task, the governor vowed, would be to reform state ethics laws.

President Bill Clinton, in turn, had appointed Hannah to the federal district bench in Tyler. Now, in tandem with fellow Clinton appointee T. John Ward,* a district judge sitting in the nearby East Texas town of Marshall, and the eminent conservative Chief Judge Patrick Higginbotham of the Fifth Circuit Court of Appeals, Hannah was to be one of the three federal jurists handling the Texas congressional redistricting case.

With the Texas Supreme Court having thrown out Judge Davis's map, the three-judge federal panel meeting in Tyler now had a blank slate to work with. They were free to draw Texas's congressional map as they saw fit—within the guidelines of the law, as they interpreted it.

Final arguments in the case came on November 2, but not before Judge Higginbotham had ordered the state to draw up a new map overnight. The sudden request came after the state's lawyer in the redistricting case, Andy Taylor (on behalf of Attorney General Cornyn), questioned the state's star witness, John Alford of Rice University, as to how the judges should draw up a thirty-two-seat Texas congressional map.

Alford was an associate professor of political science at Rice. His

---

*In his courtroom in the small town of Marshall, Judge Ward presided over one of the nation's most celebrated federal "rocket dockets," personally presiding over an enormous number of the nation's biggest and most high profile intellectual-property and patent cases.

specialty was congressional voting patterns. Alford's advice to the court: start by drawing the nine existing "minority-opportunity" districts, then determine whether and where to draw new minority districts. Should the court take his advice, the impact would strongly favor (mostly Democratic) minority candidates—but also a larger host of white, conservative Republican candidates. In concentrating large numbers of black and Hispanic voters in majority black and Hispanic districts, the side effect would be to dilute those same voters from districts held by white Democratic congressmen. It was an insidious process, particularly if you were a white Democratic House member in a marginal district. For the end result was almost sure to be fewer Democrats going to Congress.

Not surprisingly, lawyer Taylor told the court that he would have a map ready the next day.

However carefully the three-judge Fifth Circuit Court panel pondered Taylor's Republican-drawn map, in the end they drew their own. What they came up with did not leave the state's Republican Party bosses cheering. The court's November 15 ruling essentially awarded the Republicans the two new House seats, yet left the status quo ante. The howls—some of them of the most cynical sort imaginable—could be heard from Tyler to Houston to Austin to Washington. Tom DeLay told reporters, "The essence of the map drawn by the federal court is incumbent protection at the expense of our growing minority population."

But in a separate ruling dated November 28, the same three-judge federal panel ordered that the Republican-drawn state senate map would stand. Following objections from the U.S. Department of Justice's Civil Rights Division, the court chose to draw its own map for the state house; but the court's map also strongly favored Republicans, almost as much as the plan drawn by the LRB. Pete Laney's days as speaker were coming to an end.

More ominous still, Republicans now began talking aloud about how they would redraw the congressional map once they got hold of both houses of the state legislature.

This they would do not in ten years, as newspaper accounts had long suggested—but as soon as a newly elected Republican legislature could be called into regular session.

Forget about 2012; the Democrats' day of reckoning was fast approaching, like a freight train bearing down on Little Nell.

The Tom DeLay Express was roaring round the bend.

CHAPTER TEN

★

What's the Matter with Texas?
Part II

C ame the November 2002 general election, and Republicans did as expected, picking up an additional two Texas seats in the new House of Representatives. The breakdown among the Texas congressional delegation was now 17–15 in favor of the Democrats.

The real breakthrough for Republicans came in the state legislature. The state senate, previously16–15 Republican, now had a decisive 19–12 GOP margin. The state house, formerly 78–72 Democratic, was now 88–62 Republican. For the first time in 130 years—since Reconstruction—Republicans controlled both houses of the Texas state legislature.

Exactly how this happened has been chronicled before, most notably in an August 29, 2003, piece "The Rise of the Machine" by Jake Bernstein and Dave Mann in the *Texas Observer*. As Bernstein and Mann showed, the stage had long been set, "thanks to Rove, Bush and Democratic bungling." By 2000, Republicans controlled the governor's mansion and the courts, but had yet to gain control over the legislature.*

The big push was launched that fall when the Houston-based Tex-

---

*This and much of what follows is closely informed by Bernstein and Mann's excellent deconstruction in "The Rise of the Machine," *Texas Observer*, 8/29/03.

ans for Lawsuit Reform (TLR) combined with the Texas Association of Business (TAB), a virtual appendage of the Republican state party, to plow close to $1.5 million into legislative races—all but $30,000 of which came from the tort-reforming millionaires of TLR. They largely succeeded, but fell short of their stated goal by six votes in the state house.

Stalemated during the 2001 legislative session by Democrats—and even some of their own, more independent Republicans—in the state house, the combined forces of DeLay, Rove, TLR, and TAB were determined to turn it around in 2002.

But as Bernstein and Mann say, they "needed money quickly and in a quantity most easily found through corporate sources." The heart of the matter was that under Texas's 1905 election law, a corporation could not spend its own money for nonadministrative election activities.

Hence the creation not merely of "the Money Machine," but also of an effective money-laundering process designed to circumvent that 1905 law.

While TAB, under its rotund leader, former Dallas Republican legislator Bill Hammond—a member of the state House of Representatives class of 1983, along with close pals Tom DeLay, current Republican state house leader Tom Craddick, TRMPAC treasurer Bill Ceverha, lobbyist Bill Messer, and Governor Rick Perry's chief of staff, former and future lobbyist Mike Toomey—could try to skirt the fine lines of the 1905 law, outright corporate gift-giving was clearly illegal.

What TAB could—and did—do was to finance "issue ads" that avoided "magic words" such as *vote for* and *elect, defeat,* and *cast your ballot for.*

But, Travis County district attorney Ronnie Earle would later allege, TAB and its running mate TRMPAC went beyond that—way beyond that.

In the general election, TAB targeted twenty-two house races and two senate races, spending a staggering $1.9 million in corporate money.

TRMPAC—Texans for a Republican Majority—had been founded by Tom DeLay in September 2001 in response to the legislature's having failed to redistrict the state's congressional districts. From the get-go, TRMPAC was designed to be the not-so-country cousin of DeLay's ARMPAC. In reality the two were virtual twins. Seed money for TRMPAC came from predictable sources: $50,000 from ARM-PAC and $25,000 each from right-wing Dallas Republican Louis Beecherl and Houston multimillionaire Bob Perry, the principal moneyman behind the future Swift Boat attack ads and a key financial supporter of TLR. Perry, in the words of Bernstein and Mann, was "an ardent opponent of the civil justice system, and not surprisingly, a perpetual focus of lawsuits." He was, in other words, a man who hated plaintiffs' lawyers with his whole soul.* As such, Bob Perry was the very embodiment of the "tort reformer," stripped of fancy-sounding "reformist" veneer. He was also the largest single donor to the Republican Party in the 2002 election cycle, having written close to $4 million in checks to various Republican campaigns and PACs.

A chart by the nonprofit Texans for Public Justice shows that in the 2002 Texas state legislative election, a combination of right-wing PACs and individuals—TAB PAC ($118,844), TRMPAC ($639,642), ARMPAC ($47,000), the RNSEC (Republican National State Elections Committee) PAC ($234,000), TLR PAC ($1,208,032), and Bob Perry ($642,500)—raised a total of $7,968,218. And if you included the $1.9 million TAB raised from corporations for "issue ads," the number reached $9,865,218. And that was money targeted at only twenty-three legislative seats.

There you had it. The Money Machine had spent an average of over $425,000 on each of twenty-three key legislative seats. Not congressional seats, mind you, but legislative seats. Nothing like it had ever been done in Texas before. Not content merely with beating Democrats, the Machine spent money heavily on defeating "the

---

*Who, one might ask, is Bob Perry? A man rich enough to have spent $16 million on political efforts in 2006, for one thing, almost all of it having first passed through shadowy so-called 527 issue groups. The ultimate recipients: the likes of Texans for Lawsuit Reform ($601,000), the Republican Party of Texas ($780,000), and the Harris County Republican Party ($125,000). A seventy-four-year-old homebuilder in Houston, Perry is believed to be worth somewhere between $385 and $652 million. His Perry Homes has had revenues as high as $593 million. In 2005, the company built 2,688 homes—all of them within state, most of them ranging in price from $150,000 to $500,000. See S. C. Gwynne's sympathetic profile, "Bob Perry Needs a Hug," *Texas Monthly* (April 2007).

wrong kind of Republicans," in particular those rural Republicans allied with Democratic house speaker Laney. The message: they (and especially TLR) would eat their own if their own strayed off the reservation.

The money behind TAB was widely believed to have come largely from the state's insurance industry, where the big four insurers had recently increased homeowner's and car insurance by as much as 110 percent and now faced calls from an angry public for reform. Predictably, the insurance companies threatened to pull out of Texas—even though it was the second-largest state in the union. Insurance companies claimed—somewhat improbably—that the rate hikes were the result of increased mold and water claims. Independent analysts disagreed. The real reason for the massive increases, many believed, was that the industry was hurting from the collapse of NASDAQ tech stocks and the post-9/11 hit taken on all the world's stock exchanges. The insurance industry, Bernstein and Mann wrote, "had lost big in the stock market and wanted to recoup losses by passing them on to consumers."

Another prominent gift-giver to the cause was communications giant AT&T, in danger of having its near monopoly on the Texas high-speed Internet market stolen away by San Antonio–based SBC. (In 2003, AT&T's pet legislation died a sudden death at the hands of Republican legislators.)

Had the leaders of TAB and TRMPAC stopped with "issue ads," they would perhaps not have found themselves in the courtrooms.

But in September 2002, TRMPAC sent a check for $190,000 (most of it from corporate contributions) to the RNSEC in Washington, and the RNSEC sent the same $190,000 in seven separate payments to seven separate Texas state legislative candidates.

On October 18, with the pressure now mounting rapidly toward Election Day, TRMPAC executive director John Colyandro ordered the PAC's accountant to send fourteen checks totaling $152,000 to Republican state House of Representatives leader Tom Craddick. The subject line of the e-mail read, "Hard $ checks." The money was sent "Fed Ex'ed for Monday delivery" to Craddick at his district office at 500 West Texas, Suite 880, Midland, Texas, ATTN: Susan Wynn." Wynn headed the district office. With the money came specific instructions as to how to disburse it. Fourteen Republican candidates for the legislature were each to receive a check.

The die was now cast.

A month earlier, on September 9, a TRMPAC employee named Susan Lilly had boarded an early-morning Austin-to-Houston flight for a day of intense preelection fund-raising.

In a whirlwind five-and-a-half-hour tour, Lilly and freshman Republican state representative Beverly Woolley met with a series of Houston energy and finance executives.

Among the executives they met with was Bruce Gibson of Reliant Energy. A former state legislator, Gibson had joined the executive-tower crowd—his office was on the forty-seventh floor of Reliant's downtown office building—as chief lobbyist for the energy giant. (Later, following the 2002 election, he would walk back through the mirror and emerge as chief of staff to new Texas Republican lieutenant governor David Dewhurst.)

The last meeting of the day was with Houston billionaire Charles Hurwitz, the CEO of a holding company called Maxxam, with, among many other things, interests in the Texas horse-racing industry. Hurwitz's biggest claim to fame, however, lay in the billion-dollar collapse of a San Antonio savings and loan controlled by Maxxam. Throughout the 1990s, the Clinton administration and the Federal Deposit Insurance Corporation (FDIC) had sued Maxxam seeking to recover $821 million. The Clinton administration had offered to forgive a portion of the amount in return for a stand of virgin redwoods owned by Maxxam, California's Headwaters Forest. Maxxam—and Hurwitz—had declined.

It was undoubtedly a successful trip for the tireless twosome. Maxxam's PAC gave TRMPAC $5,000; and Reliant contributed $25,000.

As the *Texas Observer*'s Bernstein and Mann pointed out in their subsequent piece "Rate of Exchange," it was also a successful trip for the banking, energy, and pipeline industries being courted that day by TRMPAC.

The banking industry—Lilly and Woolley's first visit of the day had been with bankers—wanted a bill passed that would, for the first time in Texas history, allow them to offer home equity loans on lines of credit.

Reliant was splitting its production and electricity-line divisions (renamed CenterPoint) from its electricity-provider division (renamed Reliant Resources) and wanted a bill passed that would allow gas companies and pipelines to charge customers more on their gas bills at the discretion of city governments. The bill was being sold as a means for the corporations to recoup the money they spent on improvements, but it was, in fact, open-ended.

Charles Hurwitz of Maxxam wanted more than the Texas legislature—even a Republican state legislature—could grant him. He wanted to get the Feds off his back in the case of the failed San Antonio S&L.

In the end, all the parties got what they wanted. The newly Republican Texas state legislature passed both the pipeline law and the banking act in 2003. Charles Hurwitz, arguably, did better still. Majority Whip DeLay castigated federal banking regulators for their unfair treatment of the Houston billionaire, TRMPAC contributor Hurwitz. Eventually, following a House Republican committee investigation of FDIC and Office of Thrift Supervision "misconduct," the government settled for $206,000 in return for dropping the case.

No redwoods, no $821 million, no admission of guilt.

The saga came to an end in August 2005 when U.S. district judge Lynn Hughes of Houston issued a 133-page opinion that assailed the FDIC staff "for its betrayal of public trust [and] its vindictive political assault on a private citizen." Judge Hughes, a conservative jurist appointed to the court in 1985 by President Ronald Reagan, went on to describe the Clinton administration bureaucrats as "corrupt individuals within a corrupt agency." The judge then slapped the FDIC with an unprecedented $72 million sanction. "They were not content with stealing from Hurwitz," the judge wrote in his opinion. "Through this case they sought to 'cause him pain.' They sought to humiliate him."

A sympathetic article in *Texas Monthly* in April 2006 by S. C.

Gwynne dismissed the government's case as a "Tree Ring Circus," and declared that the prosecution of the poor old billionaire Hurwitz was a case of "your tax dollars at work." Wrote Gwynne, "Charles Hurwitz did not cause the failure of United Savings. He did nothing wrong at all, in fact." The media's version of the Hurwitz affair, he added, was "deeply flawed."

After thirty-four years in the Texas House of Representatives—much of it in the obscurity of being a minority within a minority (a super-right-winger among mere right-wingers), Tom Craddick was poised to be speaker. When Craddick held a press conference to announce that he had the necessary pledges to make him the boss of the house, the boss of a still more important House was there to savor his old friend's—and his own, greater still—triumph.

Tom DeLay, employing the money machine that was TRMPAC, had helped make Tom Craddick speaker; but Craddick, with his control over the newly Republican state house, was about to make Tom DeLay the permanent boss of the U.S. House of Representatives. Or so it seemed.

In time, questions would arise about DeLay's involvement with TRMPAC and its alleged use of corporate money—legal questions. In time too questions would arise about Speaker Craddick and his acceptance of that $152,000 from TRMPAC in the form of fourteen checks destined for fourteen Republican candidates for the state House of Representatives. The reason: those archaic—but still effective—Texas election laws stemming from the Populist Era.

How very appropriate it was too. The Populist Era legislators— men like Sam Rayburn and his friend Sam Johnson (Lyndon's legislator father)—had written those laws in response to the excesses of the Gilded Age. The robber barons, the Wall Street tycoons, and railway magnates and their surrogates—the fancy Houston lawyers like Captain Baker and his partner Bob Lovett—had run Austin from afar. Rayburn and Johnson and men like them had, for a time at least, taken the state capitol back.

Rayburn and Johnson, the successors to the turn-of-the-century populists, had been members of the house together. Eventually, Sam Johnson fell back into obscurity and near poverty, a broken man. But Rayburn went on to make his mark in Washington, the greatest House Speaker since James G. Blaine, since Henry Clay even.

Great man that he was, Rayburn never ceased being an East Texas populist. And while never a conventional liberal, he pounded the gavel that made possible Franklin Roosevelt's New Deal, Harry Truman's Fair Deal, and the beginnings of John F. Kennedy's New Frontier. And his protégé, Sam Johnson's big-eared, rawboned son Lyndon, added the Great Society to the list of Democratic achievements.

But now, a different kind of Texan was master of the House. And everything about Tom DeLay ran counter to Rayburn and Johnson. Whatever their shortcomings, the two Texas Democrats could never— would never—shake the old populist impulse that had so long ago run like an electric charge through Sam Ely Johnson.

DeLay was all about destroying the Democratic domestic agenda of a half century and more. Down with the Great Society! Down with the New Frontier! Down with the Fair Deal and the New Deal! Hell, Tom DeLay wanted to destroy Teddy Roosevelt's Square Deal. Trust-busters! Meat inspectors! Drug regulators! Conservationists! Environmentalists! Damn them all.

The world of Tom DeLay, with its unfettered lobbying, money machines, and money laundering, was also a world bereft of a social conscience. And a world bereft of a safety net, not merely for undocumented workers, but for American citizens. It was pure laissez-faire capitalism of a sort that would have been immediately recognizable to the old robber barons and their political minions.

Social Darwinism was knocking at the door, and Tom DeLay was primed and ready to open it wide.

First, however, Speaker Craddick, newly elected Lieutenant Governor Dewhurst, and Governor Perry would need to prepare the way.

This they did, though the way proved rockier than anticipated. When the legislature returned to Austin in the spring of 2003, Tom DeLay had sprung into action with a congressional redistricting map designed to turn the 17–15 Democratic margin in the House of Representatives into a red-state 20–12 in favor of the GOP.

Now it was time for Democrats to howl. Suffice it to say that the Democrats were outnumbered and outvoted from day one in Austin that spring and summer. Suffice it to say too that, famously, Democratic legislators fled the state, first for Oklahoma, later for New Mexico, to avoid a vote. In the first instance, house members retreated to a motel in Ardmore, Oklahoma, for four days. Successfully, so it seemed, for the regular session of the legislature came to an end without producing a congressional redistricting bill.

Not so successfully the second time. Newly transformed, newly powerful House Calendar Committee chairwoman Beverly Woolley—she of TRMPAC fund-raising fame—announced that whatever Democrats thought, she wasn't ready to move on yet. Nor were Tom Craddick, Tom DeLay, or Governor Rick Perry, who promptly called "the lege," as it's known in Texas, back into special session, beginning on July 1.

This time, it was the senate where the holdouts gathered. When the house passed the DeLay measure, 84–61, Democratic senators vowed to block its passage under a decades-old rule that required a two-thirds vote to bring a bill to the floor. Ordinarily, the Republicans would have had the numbers, but former lieutenant governor Bill Ratliff, angered that northeast Texas's congressional district (long occupied by Sam Johnson's populist friend Wright Patman) would be gutted under the plan in order to deny it to incumbent Democrat Jim Turner, now promised to vote against bringing the bill to the floor. But Ratliff hadn't counted on the power of the White House. The *Austin American-Statesman* was soon reporting that Ratliff "has gotten an arm-twisting from Karl Rove."

Eventually, desperate senate Democrats decided to follow the scenario written by their house colleagues, fleeing as a group, under cover of night, to Albuquerque, New Mexico, on July 28. There they stayed through the end of the first and second special sessions.

On September 15, Governor Perry called yet another special session, and this time it did the trick. On October 12, the senate Democrats returned home after one of their own, Houston senator John

Whitmire, announced that he would vote in favor of Tom DeLay's redistricting plan.

Suffice it to say, Governor Perry signed the redistricting bill as soon as it reached his desk. The story didn't quite end there, however. Under federal law, the Civil Rights Division of the Department of Justice had first to approve the changes in the congressional map. On December 19, 2003, the Department of Justice did just that.

The *Washington Post*'s Dan Eggen would later report that political appointees in the Department of Justice had, in fact, barred professionals in the Civil Rights Division from commenting in public on the Texas redistricting. As it happened, the professional staff had not only not approved the DeLay plan, they had rejected it. Only no one outside "main Justice" knew the truth. Eggen went on to report that the DOJ's Civil Rights Division had lost about a third of its three dozen staff lawyers over the past nine months alone. Wrote Eggen, "Many current and former lawyers in the section charge that senior [Bush administration appointees in the department] have exercised undue political influence" in redistricting decisions, citing in particular the Texas redistricting effort. Eggen quoted former voting rights section chief Joe Rich: "The voting section is always subject to political pressure and tension. But I never thought it would come to this."

Back in Texas, the three-judge panel of the U.S. Fifth Circuit Court of Appeals returned to the issue of congressional redistricting. On Thursday, June 9, 2005, the newly reconstituted panel—U.S. district judge John Hannah Jr. having died in the interim—upheld congressional redistricting in Texas.

The chief judge of the panel remained the archconservative Fifth Circuit Court judge Patrick Higginbotham of Dallas, a Reagan appointee to the bench, widely believed to have been considered by both the Bush I and II administrations as a possible Supreme Court candidate.

The panel voted unanimously to uphold the redistricting plans, and voted 2–1 to dismiss arguments by university professors that the legislature should have used updated census figures rather than numbers that were now three years old. Republican governor Rick Perry rejoiced.

In Washington, a DeLay spokesman said that the ruling "is just another confirmation that redistricting brought about fair representation." Voting with Higginbotham was U.S. district judge Lee Hyman Rosenthal of Houston, a former Baker Botts litigation partner, and U.S. district judge T. John Ward of Marshall.

"We suffer no illusion of commission or ability to cleanse the air of partisan politics and self-interest, or to otherwise make angels of men," wrote Higginbotham. A cynical observer might have wondered if the words had been chosen in jest.

Tom DeLay might have trouble with judges in general—but he would have no complaints that day with Judges Higginbotham and Rosenthal.

Later still, the U.S. Supreme Court would also hear the Texas redistricting case—and would also let stand the gerrymander, excepting only that a border-country district would have to have its lines redrawn.

After the November 2004 election, the Texas congressional delegation consisted of two Republican senators and 21 Republican House members. Of the two senators, the senior, Kay Bailey Hutchison, was the former Rove client who had been indicted on felony offenses by District Attorney Earle. A Texas state district judge had dismissed the case against her. The new junior senator was another former Rove client, John Cornyn, the former state supreme court justice, attorney general, and chairman of the Texas Legislative Redistricting Board (LRB), the man who more than any other drew the lines that made the Texas legislature Republican in 2003.

Of the twenty-one House Republicans, few were men of stature— for men they all were—though two towered above the others, majority-leader-in-wait DeLay and Energy Committee chairman-to-be Barton. The rest were widely regarded as "furniture," in the parlance of the Texas legislature.

Of congressional Texas Democrats, there were now but eleven.

CHAPTER ELEVEN

✴

The Heart of the Matter

January 2002 had been an eventful month in the lives of many in the world of DeLay Inc. In Washington, Emily Miller resigned her position as DeLay's communications director to prepare for her August 10 wedding to Mike Scanlon.

Down in Texas, Ralph Reed continued to feed information to Abramoff. On January 7, 2002, he e-mailed Abramoff: "we [sic] have talked to the AG's office. here's [sic] the skinny." The Fifth Circuit was scheduled to rule on the Tigua case that Wednesday (two days later). A similar case, concerning the East Texas–based Alabama Coushatta tribe, was also shortly to be heard before a federal district judge. Attorney General Cornyn's office was "very confident of victory."

To further tighten the screws, Abramoff advised Reed to "get one of our guys in the legislature to introduce a bill which disqualifies from state contracts any vendor who provides goods or services to a casino in the state." That way, Abramoff advised, Governor Perry and Attorney General Cornyn "can sit back and not be scared."

Not to worry, replied Reed. "We have tigers." In other words, there were state representatives and senators more than willing to introduce just such punitive legislation designed to make "life tough on the tribe."

After all, as Abramoff wrote to Scanlon in an e-mail dated January 16, "We need that moolah. We have to hit $50M this year (our cut)."

Just as Cornyn and Reed had anticipated, on January 17, 2002, a three-judge panel of the Fifth Circuit ruled against the Tiguas. Speaking Rock would have to be shut down. Cornyn, who was already running for the U.S. Senate, professed himself pleased as punch. He was especially appreciative, Cornyn told the press, that the Fifth Circuit panel had expedited its ruling.

Republican state comptroller Carole Keeton Rylander—she was the mother of Bush spokesperson Scott McClellan—told the press that closing Speaking Rock would cost twenty-two hundred jobs and result in the loss of $55 million in annual personal income.

No matter. The only remaining question was when Speaking Rock would be shuttered. On February 5, 2002, Reed e-mailed Abramoff to say that a source in the attorney general's office had told him that the court order closing the Speaking Rock Casino would be issued six days later, on February 11. Abramoff's response: "Whining idiot. Close the f'ing thing already ! !"

A twenty-four-hour-a-day operation that had attracted one hundred thousand visitors a year and generated nearly $60 million in annual income for the tribe—lifting the Tiguas out of abject poverty—Speaking Rock was now on the road to being nothing more than a bitter memory.

The Tiguas were indeed in a desperate fix. Desperate enough to call for Jack Abramoff's services.

Abramoff e-mailed Scanlon on February 6 with the news: "I'm on the phone with Tigua! Fire up the jet baby, we're going to El Paso." Scanlon's reply: "I want all their MONEY!" To which Abramoff breathed a hearty "Yawzah!"

In an e-mail to Ralph Reed—the same Ralph Reed who always professed ignorance of the real sources for the money paid him for his antigambling crusades—Abramoff wrote, "I wish those moronic Tiguas were smarter in their political contributions. I'd love to get my hands on that moolah!! Oh well, stupid folks get wiped out." Abramoff also asked Reed to forward him a newspaper article about "our client" the Coushattas. The date was February 11, 2002.

The next day, Abramoff met with Tigua leaders in El Paso. He offered to work for them pro bono—until they got their casino reopened, when he would begin charging the tribe his standard $150,000–$175,000 monthly retainer. But he also insisted that the Tiguas hire Michael Scanlon to help organize a "grassroots" campaign for them.

In an e-mail to Tigua adviser Marc Schwartz, Abramoff explained, "While we are Republicans, and normally want all Republicans to prevail in electoral challenges, this ill advised decision on the part of the Republican leadership in Texas must not stand, and we intend to right this using, in part, Republican leaders from Washington." In short, what Abramoff proposed, was a "legislative fix" from the D.C. side of the Texas Republican Party aimed at putting the kibosh on the state side of the Texas Republican Party. Or as Scanlon would later describe it, "Simply put, you need 218 friends in the U.S. House and 51 senators on your side very quickly, and we will do that through both love and fear."

By February 18, Abramoff was back in El Paso laying out Scanlon's grassroots campaign, Operation Open Doors. The next day, Scanlon e-mailed Abramoff with news of a story that had run in that morning's *El Paso Times*: "This is on the front page of todays [*sic*] paper while they will be voting on our plan!" The story told of how Speaking Rock had been closed down, and how, as a result, "450 people received their final termination notice and 60-day severance packages Monday. A line wound out the door at Speaking Rock Casino."

Abramoff's reply to this dismal news: "Is life great or what ! ! ! !"

When a few days later an e-mail, presumably sent from Tigua consultant Schwartz's office, included Abramoff among the mass recipients, the Washington lobbyist was furious: "Marc, if this came out of your office, please tell them NEVER to include my name on a list like this. Our presence in this deal must be secret. . . . Some of the people on this list are real dangerous knowing that I am involved."

Abramoff was still steaming when he e-mailed Scanlon to complain about Schwartz: "That fucking idiot put my name on an email list! What a fucking moron. He may have blown our cover!! Dammit. We are moving forward anyway and taking their fucking money."

Not to worry—too much. On March 5, 2002, the papers were signed: "Scanlon Gould Public Affairs (Scanlon Gould) and the Tigua Indians of Ysleta del Sur Pueblo El Paso (the Tribe) hereby enter . . . into an agreement" for "Operation Open Doors." As a result of Abramoff's second meeting, the tribe had managed to get Scanlon's fee reduced—to $4.2 million, with a nonrefundable $2.1 million due within the month, the full fee coming due three months from the signing date.

The plan, as outlined by Abramoff, called for amending the applicable federal act, Public Law 100–89, by striking section 107, which allowed the state of Texas to prohibit Tigua gambling. The language amending the law would quietly be slipped into an unrelated bill. One idea, seriously discussed, would have been to slip it into a terrorism insurance bill, which had passed the House and was moving in the Senate and heading for conference committee, where the deed would be done. Another possibility was the Energy Act of 2002, but that, Abramoff wrote, seemed "more problematic. Might not become law."

In the end, Abramoff and Scanlon settled on the 2002 Election Reform Act as their conduit—and that great and good friend of the American Indian Congressman Bob Ney of Ohio as their instrument in committee. Once the bill reached the House floor, Majority Whip DeLay would take over. On the Senate side, Connecticut's Christopher Dodd would act as the bill's shepherd. No one seems to have bothered to ask why Dodd, a liberal Democrat, would do Jack Abramoff's bidding. The answer, no doubt, is that desperation was in the air that day at Speaking Rock—while dreams of millions of dollars swam before the eyes of Abramoff and Scanlon.

And in their desperation and despair, the Tiguas did as they were told, making the $300,000 in political donations demanded of them by Abramoff. Checks went out, beginning in March, to ARMPAC, Missouri congressman Roy Blunt's Rely on Your Beliefs PAC (ROY PAC), and Chairman Bob Ney's American Liberty PAC.

Another prominent recipient was Friends of the Big Sky, a PAC controlled by powerful Montana Republican senator Conrad Burns, the chairman of the Interior Subcommittee of the Senate Appropriations Committee and vice chairman of the Public Lands and Forests Subcommittee of Energy and Natural Resources.*

Other recipients of Abramoff-inspired Tigua largesse included the Missouri Millennium Fund—a PAC dedicated to fair and honest redistricting, the Republican way—Kansas senator Sam Brownback's Restore America PAC, and California congressman John Doolittle's Superior California Federal Leadership Fund.

On March 20, Abramoff e-mailed Scanlon, "Just met with Ney!!! We're fucking gold!!!!! He's going to do Tigua."

Six days later, Abramoff e-mailed Schwartz in Texas, directing him to send $32,000 in checks to two of Congressman Ney's political action committees and to his campaign committee. Meanwhile, Ney's chief of staff, Neil Volz, made the circle complete by officially joining

---

*In total, Burns would receive $150,000 from Abramoff and his Indian clients. Burns, a right-to-lifer, NRA fan, and big-business advocate, returned the favors, most notably by helping another Abramoff Indian-tribe client, the wealthy Saginaw-Chippewa—the "Sag-Chips"—get an earmark for a $3 million federal grant to upgrade their tribal schools—over Interior Department opposition. A Burns spokesperson told the *Washington Post* that the senator was just trying to "help these tribes get a leg up and help the children get a good education." The senator himself told a Montana newspaper, the *Missoulian,* that the current school buildings on the Sag-Chip reservation "were in such bad shape that you wouldn't keep livestock in them." His terse explanation for his vote: "I did it for the kids."

Later, when Burns's relationship with Abramoff had become the subject of Washington cocktail chatter—and a matter of discussion among federal prosecutors—Burns became increasingly snappish. Jack Abramoff—"I wouldn't know that man if he walked through that door," Burns insisted to reporters—had nothing to do with his vote in favor of the $3 million for Sag-Chip school repair. Asked about "special interests," Burns told a group of reporters and editors, "You are a special interest." Lobbying, he added, was part of the American system of government. "That's been the way this government was built since its inception."

Still, it did seem a bit strange that the senator from Montana should have shown so much interest in the plight of a Michigan-based tribe, except for various coincidences of the Jack Abramoff variety. It didn't hurt, for one thing, that both lobbyist Abramoff and Senator Burns shared the services of political operative Shawn Vasell. While at Greenberg, Vasell had acted as client manager on the Mississippi Choctaw account and had registered as a lobbyist for the Choctaw and Coushatta tribes in 2001. A year later, Vasell turned up as political director for Senator Burns; and passing through the revolving door yet again, Vasell found himself back on staff at Greenberg in 2003.

Nor was Vasell the only Burns staffer in the pay of both the Senate and Greenberg Traurig. Within weeks of the passage of the 2004 Interior Department appropriations bill—in which quietly resided a $3 million earmark for Sag-Chip school repair—Burns's chief of staff, Will Brooke, resigned and went to work at Greenberg. Said Jack Abramoff, "He's a big hire for us."

Team Abramoff in the governmental affairs department of Greenberg Traurig.*

That same month, in March 2002, Scanlon paid $4.7 million in cash for yet another home for himself and his fiancée, Emily Miller—an ocean-side mansion and guesthouse in Rehoboth Beach, Delaware, that had once belonged to members of the DuPont clan.

Scanlon's behavior grew stranger during the spring and summer of 2002. According to one account in the *Wall Street Journal,* Scanlon actually returned to his summer lifeguard job at Rehoboth Beach, while "occasionally visiting Washington and staying at his Ritz-Carlton apartment." The rent on Scanlon's Ritz-Carlton apartment: $17,000 a month.

Mike Scanlon wasn't the only one living the high life that year. Over a seventeen-month period in 2002–3, Jack Abramoff's Signatures restaurant gave away some $180,000 in free food and drink to power-ful guests—eighteen of whom were designated *FOO Comp,* for "friend of owner," or *A Comp,* for "associate of owner." According to the *New York Times,* Abramoff's own tab during the same period came to roughly $65,000.

At the head of the list of those being comped: Thomas D. DeLay. In anticipation of a visit from the congressman and his wife, Christine, Abramoff e-mailed orders to his managers: "Table of 6, put it where I sit and remove the other table. Their meal is to be comped." At a restaurant where a steak cost $74, that was indeed a sweet deal.

From his personal Table 40, Abramoff could look around the room

---

*A few years later, at an open hearing of the Senate Indian Affairs Committee, Chairman McCain named the recipients of Tigua funds, one by one. Vice Chairman Dorgan then asked, "As Senator McCain read some of the names of those things, it's like the Association of God-Fearing Citizens. Who's that? Did some of these names ring a bell, or did you ask, who are these people that we're being asked to contribute to?"

No, replied Tigua tribal leader Carlos Hisa, "I never asked." Hisa also testified that nei-ther he nor political adviser Schwartz were aware of Ralph Reed's surreptitious role in the game.

SENATOR DORGAN: Does it surprise you to know that while he was working with you, [Jack Abramoff] was paying Mr. Reed to help shut down your casino?

MR. SCHWARTZ: That's probably one of the most disturbing details. Yes, it was a complete surprise.

of a D.C. power restaurant frequented by such worthies as White House counselor Karl Rove and Speaker Denny Hastert, a restaurant that was conveniently located on Pennsylvania Avenue between the White House and the Capitol, a restaurant too whose walls were lined with historic documents. In light of what was to come, perhaps the most fitting of these was the copy of former president Richard Nixon's pardon.

And if Washington's truly powerful could sometimes be found at Signatures, its lesser lights—powerful figures in the world of Jack Abramoff—were veritable denizens. Denizens, that is, on the comp. Among them, Congressman Dana Rohrabacher, who had served as one of Abramoff's references in the SunCruz deal; Congressman John Doolittle, whose name also appeared on the FOO list; and "another regular visitor," Chairman Bob Ney of the House Administration Committee, who, employees told the *Times,* "frequently ate and drank without paying."

So passed the spring and summer of 2002—for the privileged few who enjoyed being on the owner's list—at Signatures. For the meat-eating Tom DeLay, freed now of his earlier, Come to Jesus prohibition vows, it was truly the summer of Napa Valley cabernets and $74 steaks.

Collecting was another matter—and one in which Tom DeLay's appetite was every bit as voracious as Jack Abramoff's. That summer, DeLay set about raising money for his various political war chests by asking Abramoff to raise money via his own private charity, the Capital Athletic Foundation (CAF).

"Did you get the message from the guys that Tom wants us to raise some bucks from Capital Athletic Foundation?" Abramoff asked in a June 6, 2002, e-mail. "I have six clients for $25K," he advised former DeLay deputy chief of staff Tony Rudy, who was by now part of Team Abramoff at Greenberg. "I recommend we hit everyone who cares about Tom's requests. I have another few to hit still." The goal was to raise $200,000 for DeLay.

Rudy's job was to pass on a request for $25,000 from the wealthy

Saginaw-Chippewa tribe of Michigan. The request, Abramoff wrote, would "look better coming from you as a former DeLay COS [chief of staff]." Then he added, "We're gonna make a bundle here." Whether he meant "make a bundle" for DeLay or for himself and Scanlon, Abramoff didn't say.

Rudy, a few weeks later, e-mailed Greenberg colleague Todd Boulanger about the status of one of those $25,000 contributions to CAF; he noted, "Jack wants this. It is something our friends are raising money for."

Boulanger replied, "I'm sensing shadiness."*

Jack Abramoff didn't let up the pressure on the Tiguas. Of course, he also still had plenty of time for golf, with Scanlon and his other good friends Congressman Bob Ney, Ney's former chief of staff Neil Volz, Ralph Reed, and White House procurement officer David Safavian, the former Internet-gambling lobbyist. The venue: a summer 2002 trip to London (via Gulfstream II private jet) and from there to the fabled St. Andrews golf course in Scotland. As usual, in the world of Jack Abramoff, pleasure and business came together seamlessly. Ostensi-

---

*Rudy wrote back to congratulate Boulanger on his astuteness: "Your senses are good. If you have to say Leadership is asking, please do. I already have."

But then Leadership didn't stop asking. E-mails disclosed by the Senate Indian Affairs Committee in late 2005 showed that DeLay had, in the words of a *New York Times* story, "made an unusual personal call to Mr. Abramoff's office on July 17, 2002, to press for [a] contribution to [a $25,000-a-plate] Republican fund-raiser."

Abramoff's assistant Holly Bowers e-mailed the boss—he was down in El Paso on Tigua business that day—to say that she'd received a phone call from the majority whip "about the President's dinner contribution you owe. . . . It was the Congressman himself [who had called]. Needless to say, I was a bit nervous." DeLay, she added, said he would "call you again this afternoon or possibly see you at Signatures tonight."

The President's Dinner was a reference to the major Republican fund-raiser held a month earlier, on June 19. In the words of the *New York Times*'s Philip Shenon, "News reports at the time said that Mr. DeLay and other members of the House Congressional leadership were each expected to raise at least $500,000 for the dinner." According to the *Times* account, the dinner, which was held at the Washington Convention Center and featured a speech by President Bush, raised nearly $30 million.

If Jack Abramoff was in arrears on his payments, he didn't intend to stay that way. In a reply e-mail, he told Bowers, "I played with your email a bit (quite a bit) to scare the Tiguas into getting me that check. I hope you don't mind. I wanted you to see this in the unlikely case that they call and mention it to you."

The Tiguas did not contribute to the cause that day. But the Mississippi Choctaws did. To the full extent of the $25,000.

bly, the bill would be paid for by Abramoff's Capital Athletic Foundation; but the $120,000-plus tab for the visit would actually be left to Abramoff's two Texas tribal clients, the Tiguas and the Alabama Coushattas. In an e-mail, Abramoff asked the Tiguas "if you guys could do 50K" and warned that the trip would be expensive because two years earlier "we did this for another member—you know who."

In the end, the West Texas–based Tiguas turned down the opportunity to support Congressman Ney's golfing habit, but not before convincing their East Texas brethren, the Alabama Coushattas, to pick up the tab. Carlos Hisa, the lieutenant governor of the Tiguas, later explained, "We told [the Alabama Coushattas] it was for a golfing trip and certain individuals from Congress were going to go, that were going to help us with our cause." Jack Abramoff, Hisa said, "had told us even from the very beginning the entire thing was top secret." The plan as Hisa understood it was for Ney to slip language into pending legislation that would eliminate the federal ban against commercial gaming for the Alabama Coushattas. Added Hisa, "Only a few could know because the language was going to be sneaked in." As a result, the Alabama Coushattas wrote a check for $50,000, made payable to the Capital Athletic Foundation, never knowing that CAF *was* Jack Abramoff. The very day that the foundation cashed the tribe's check (July 24, 2002), the Alabama Coushatta tribe was forced to shut down its casino in Livingston, Texas.

Ney would later claim—falsely—that the purpose of the trip was for him to give a speech "to Scottish parliamentarians" and attend the Edinburgh Military Tattoo, described by the *Los Angeles Times* as "an annual parade of kilted soldiers marching to bagpipes and drums at Edinburgh Castle." But there was no record of Ney's having given any such speech. What's more, the Scottish Parliament, having gone on recess, wasn't even in session at the time.

In August, recently returned from a few rounds played on the world's most celebrated links, Ney met with Tigua tribal representatives and praised Abramoff's work. He also indicated that he would support placing the key language in the election bill.

There was just one problem: Democratic senator Chris Dodd wasn't on board for the deal. Not that Abramoff and Scanlon hadn't tried. On July 25, Abramoff e-mailed Scanlon, "I just spoke with Ney who met today with Dodd on the bill and raised our provision. Dodd looked at him like a 'deer in headlights' and said he has never made such a commitment. . . . Ney feels we left him out to dry. Please call me!!!"

Without Dodd, the jig was up. No one, of course, told the Tiguas that.

According to news accounts, Scanlon attempted to approach Dodd via Democratic National Committee vice chair Lottie Shackleford, a former Little Rock, Arkansas, mayor and member of Dodd's finance committee. According to investigators for the Senate Indian Affairs Committee, Shackleford and two associates—one a former executive director of the DNC—were paid $50,000 by Scanlon's CCS to pressure the senator.

When it didn't work, Abramoff went ballistic. Imagine that: Jack Abramoff had been gypped! "Hold tight," Abramoff e-mailed Scanlon, "but get our money back from that mother fucker who was supposed to take care of dodd [*sic*]."

In an e-mail to Scanlon on October 4, Abramoff reported, "Too many crises right now. We HAVE to win this Tigua thing." Three days later, he reiterated his chagrin: "We still have to deal with the fuck up on the Tigua thought [*sic*]."

Years later, interviewed by Michael Crowley, Abramoff was still chagrined about the licking he took on the Tigua congressional effort. "That," Abramoff told Crowley, "was the only time I can think of that we failed to achieve our goal. That was one loss against ten thousand wins." Collecting himself, Abramoff "stared at me intently," wrote Crowley. " 'We never lost,' he said, stabbing the table to punctuate each word. 'We. Did. Not. Lose. One. Fight. Ever.' "

It even reached the point where Scanlon feared that their friendship was cracking, e-mailing Abramoff, "Hey—I know you are pissed about the Tigua thing but we gotta do the best we can to recover."

Abramoff replied, "We'z cool. I was not really pissed at you." Seemingly undeterred, he e-mailed Tigua consultant Schwartz in late December to say that he and Scanlon had come up with a new idea: "We are coordinating efforts to attach our legislative fix to the upcoming omnibus appropriations bill. Specifically, we are working to attach it to the Indian Health Care section of the labor, Health and Human Services portion of the legislation."

A week later, all was back to normal. "Hey, how about 11 am rb and then 1 PM lunch?" asked Abramoff, who was proposing a racquetball game. To which Scanlon replied, "You fucking lame ass—you better start pulling some real opponents or I am going to beat your ass to a pulp next time we get out there!"

The e-mail exchange continued in the same vein:

ABRAMOFF: Hey bitch, I am ready fo yo ass, but yu a big time faggot and afraid of a real man!

SCANLON: We will see about that fucko.

ABRAMOFF: I love this bitch talk you punk ass bitch. As soon as I get yo ass on the court, you be crying like a baby! :)

The wheels on the Abramoff Money Machine almost fell off in November 2002—but not because of his and Scanlon's recent dealings with the Alabama Coushattas and Tiguas. Indeed, the near disaster had nothing to do with any of Jack Abramoff's Indian tribal clients, whether in Texas or elsewhere.

The venue was instead the U.S. territory of Guam.

There, acting U.S. attorney Frederick A. Black was conducting a grand jury investigation into Jack Abramoff's congressional lobbying efforts on behalf of the local superior court.

In short, a bill pending before Congress would have made that island's superior court inferior to its supreme court. Abramoff had, in turn, been hired, apparently under the table, by the superior court to lobby against the bill.* All this seemed a little strange to Acting U.S. Attorney Black, a career federal prosecutor. Once he got wind of it, Black promptly opened a grand jury investigation into the scheme.

Black was himself already in hot water with Abramoff's other Pacific islands clients, having earlier put in motion a post-9/11 review study

---

*Stranger still, as the *Los Angeles Times* would later report (5/06/05), Abramoff's payment for his services—$324,000—was delivered in a series of thirty-six separate $9,000 checks. The "pass through" in this case was a Laguna Beach, California, lawyer named Howard Hills. In the succinct wording of the *Times*, "Hills said he was a middleman."

that cited "substantial security risks in Guam and the Northern Marianas" as a result of loose immigration regulations. Why this should have infuriated Marianas boss Willie Tan and his friends is easy to see: those same loose regulations, in effect, made possible the cheap immigrant labor so beloved of garment-manufacturing magnates such as Tan.*

Abramoff was quickly on top of the threat, warning his Marianas clients, "It will require some major action from the Hill and a press attack to get this back in the bottle." Greenberg Traurig records show that Abramoff and his aides expected to meet with Justice Department officials.

In the end, that's exactly what happened. The federal grand jury having subpoenaed Guam superior court records concerning Abramoff on November 18, Fred Black found himself removed from office precisely one day later.

A position that had gone unfilled for more than a decade—Black had held office as acting U.S. attorney that whole time—was now deemed worthy of a full-time political officeholder. Immediately.

Black's successor, Leonardo Rapadas, came highly recommended by the Guam Republican Party—and by Karl Rove.†

Jack Abramoff, one might suspect, breathed a sigh of relief.

Meanwhile, the wedding date for Mike Scanlon and Emily Miller— August 10—had come and gone. Unknown to Miller, Scanlon had fallen for a twenty-four-year-old waitress at a Rehoboth Beach restaurant. They were already secretly dating.

---

*Abramoff also paid to have conservative think-tank Cato Institute senior scholar Doug Bandow write a column for the Copley News Service in 2001, in which Bandow declared that fighting terrorism was no excuse for "economic meddling" in the Marianas and Guam. The federal government, Bandow wrote, "should respect the commonwealth's independent policies, which have allowed the islands to rise above the poverty evident elsewhere throughout Micronesia." It was not the first time that the right-wing free-market advocate Bandow had written on behalf of Abramoff clients. When *BusinessWeek Online* confronted Bandow in late December 2003 with revelations that he had served as a paid advocate for Jack Abramoff and his clients, Bandow resigned his position at Cato.

†According to the *Los Angeles Times,* which broke the story, "Fred Radewagen, a lobbyist who had been under contract to the [territorial] administration, said he carried that recommendation to top Bush aide Karl Rove in early 2003."

In November, the former lifeguard and the waitress were married. Three weeks later, according to an account in the *Wall Street Journal,* "Ms. Miller was a bridesmaid at the Houston wedding of another former DeLay aide." Amidst much joy, and some tears, Ms. Miller confessed "that she had helped Mr. Scanlon spread negative stories about Mr. Rudy." She also apologized to her old boss DeLay, who hugged her and said, "We are all part of the DeLay family."

Shortly afterward, Miller, having returned to Washington, called on Scanlon's ex-wife, Carrie Liipfert. The two scorned women soon became close friends. So much so that when Liipfert filed a motion in a suburban Washington court for increased child support payments, she did so with the benefit of critical information afforded her by Miller. Court papers show that Liipfert argued that her ex-husband's "financial circumstances . . . have improved dramatically" and that "it is believed he earns millions of dollars per year now."

Mike Scanlon's salary in his last year as Tom DeLay's communications director had been $155,000, while his debts amounted to $39,000, including $19,400 in credit card debt. Now, suddenly, he was a multimillionaire.

Jack Abramoff, who should have been just as rich as Scanlon— together they reaped some $82 million from the Indian tribes, according to Senate investigators—was instead in a financial pinch. Why this was so has never been made entirely clear. Former SunCruz partner Ben Waldman had settled with the bankers at Foothill Capital for $450,000, while Abramoff had also settled for an undisclosed amount. Kidan was said to be still in litigation over the failed deal. Surely, the SunCruz debacle must have contributed to Abramoff's plight, but that doesn't seem a sufficient answer. Perhaps too the cost of running a group of Washington, D.C.–based restaurants—there were three now—had become a serious financial drain. Or perhaps the answer lay in Abramoff's exuberant way of life.

During the first nine months of 2002, Jack Abramoff collected $12.2 million in fees from Indian tribes. He spent $232,000 on his personal travel, including $69,000 for a Passover family vacation. According to details released by the Senate Indian Affairs Committee, he also then spent $134,000 for a new BMW; $69,000 for his driver's salary;

$103,000 in credit card charges; and $36,000 in fees to accountants and other personal advisers. He also wrote checks to the tune of $28,000 for various political campaigns.

Whatever the exact reasons, Jack Abramoff was hurting. On February 19, 2003, the biggest lobbyist in town was forced to e-mail his partner, the recently remarried Michael Scanlon, who was vacationing in St. Barts, "Mike!!! I need the money TODAY! I AM BOUNCING CHECKS!!!" After Scanlon promised to send him money, Abramoff wrote, "Sorry I got nuts, but it's a little crazy for me right now. I am not kidding that I was literally on the verge of collapse."

The question again arises, why? Records show that the two partners split at least $42 million over three years—this, out of the $66 million that was paid by tribes to Scanlon's Capitol Campaign Strategies (CCS) and that company's "alter ego" Scanlon Gould Public Affairs.

The same bank and tax records show that Capitol Campaign Strategies paid Abramoff personally and Kaygold, a company which he owned and controlled, over $21 million.

Precious little, it would seem, was ever spent on grassroots organizing. No wonder then that the two partners rhapsodized about their relationship. The vast majority of the money paid Scanlon's various companies went straight into their personal bank accounts.

"You are a great partner," Abramoff e-mailed Scanlon. "What I love about our partnership is that when one of us is down, the other is there. We are going to make dollars for years together."

To which Scanlon replied, "Amen. You've got it boss. We have many years ahead."

And so it no doubt seemed in February 2003. The country was on the precipice of war with Iraq. President Bush's approval ratings were still high. The Congress was Republican again—and the Democrats were but a dispirited minority, almost entirely shorn of power and moral authority.

This was as good as it was going to get.

CHAPTER TWELVE

★

Master of the House

Boss now of Texas as well as Capitol Hill, Tom DeLay basked in the glow of his reflected power. Never more so than in the spring and summer of 2003.

In Austin, the House gerrymander had shown who really ran the state of Texas. Showed too how DeLay could harness his own needs and wants with those of the White House, the Republican National Committee, local Republican hopefuls, right-wing Christian fundamentalists, TAB and TLR and the Bob Perrys and their ilk—all with their own agendas.

How Delay—and the White House—worked their way with important economic legislation can be seen in the passage of two bills. On May 23, the new Congress passed the Job and Growth Tax Relief Reconciliation Act of 2003, known as JGTRRA (and pronounced "Jagterra"). This third round of tax cuts for the rich in the guise of "job stimulation" for the poor and middle classes was estimated by the nonpartisan Congressional Budget Office to increase the now yawning deficit by "as little" as $60 billion in 2003 and as much as $340 billion in 2008. By lowering taxes on dividends and capital gains and accelerating the 2001 tax cuts, the import of the bill was to make federal tax revenues as a percentage of GDP to their lowest level since 1959.

The vote was, as usual, razor-thin: 231–200 in the House, with all but one Republican voting yes. In the Senate, Vice President Cheney cast the deciding vote, 51–50.

Nothing, though, so well illustrated the power of DeLay the congressional boss than the vote over the Medicare Prescription Drug, Improvement and Modernization Act of 2003. The vote would also demonstrate what could happen when Texan Bush and Texan DeLay combined their considerable might. Passage of the "MMA" legislation would show off every skill possessed by Tom DeLay. Like "tort reform," or like the Senate's vote on the Iraq War, the Medicare Drug, Improvement and Modernization Act was a Trojan horse—designed to marginalize the opposition. Some, like the AARP—so desperate for any kind of prescription relief that it would accept the proverbial half a loaf rather than no loaf—would be forced into bed with DeLay and Big Pharma. Others, almost all of them Democrats, would then find themselves painted as having "gone against AARP" or of "trying to deny drug benefits to our seniors." And like a vote against the war, a vote against the AARP was seen to be a career-killer. Only in this case the battleground was not the Senate but the House.

The root of the problem lay in the spiraling cost of prescription drugs, something no one expected at the time of the passage of the act creating Medicare in 1965. Medicare had, of course, been the capstone of Lyndon Johnson's domestic agenda, the Great Society. First envisioned by Harry Truman in the late 1940s, federal-sponsored medical coverage for seniors had floundered for years, opposed as it was by the American Medical Association (the AMA) and Republican legislators in Congress.

Only with the overwhelmingly Democratic Congress elected alongside him in 1964 was even legislative genius Johnson able to pull that rabbit out of the hat. But now he had, and over time Medicare had become, like Social Security, an entitlement that not even the most right-wing Republicans dared bad-mouth for long.

That did not mean, however, that conservative Republicans wished to extend the benefits of Medicare—though AARP, with its enormous demographic base of seniors, certainly did. The genius of the Medicare Prescription Drug Act was that it gave AARP—and the seniors—just enough to push them on board, while giving billions to Big Pharma.

On the one hand, MMA provided a subsidy for large employers to discourage them from eliminating private prescription coverage to retired workers. That was a key AARP goal—and one that pleased traditionally Democratic labor unions even more. But the encouragement took the form of huge subsidies to the corporations affected by the bill. IBM, for example, was estimated to benefit to the tune of $400 million over six years, beginning in 2006.

On the other hand, MMA prohibited the federal government from negotiating discounts with drug companies. Big Pharma would be getting paid full freight.

And MMA prohibited the federal government from establishing a formulary, a list of accepted medications, while allowing private providers, such as HMOs, to do just that, thus restricting drug choices. The act also provided that care could be restricted to networks of providers; prescription coverage could be deferred; and care, other than emergency care, could be restricted by region. The act also funded a six-city trial of partly privatized Medicare (by 2010), gave an extra $25 billion to rural hospitals, and mandated means testing for Medicare B patients beginning in 2007, meaning that the next generation of Medicare recipients would have to pay virtually full price for Medicare B benefits beginning at retirement, thus in effect eliminating Medicare B over time. That was the genie in the bottle—and the worst aspect of the bill if you were a boomer rather than a current senior.

From the point of view of current seniors, the worst part of the act was that it provided for a "doughnut hole" in the middle of coverage, meaning that enrollees were 100 percent responsible for costs between $2,250 and $5,100 (a gap of $2,850).

Clearly, this bill was no AARP dream.

But it was the reality Tom DeLay and the administration presented AARP with. It was also, as was almost everything else pending before Congress in the Age of DeLay, written in large measure by industry lobbyists.

And who better to write such legislation than one of DeLay's closest colleagues on the Hill along with a former DeLay chief of staff? For such were the chief strategist and the chief tactician of MMA.

After representing south Louisiana's Third Congressional District, the famed Cajun country, for twenty-five years (1980–2005), the former-Democrat-turned-Republican Tauzin would retire only to take up the reins at Big Pharma's trade association. The very day he left Congress, January 3, 2005, Tauzin took over as president of the Pharmaceutical Research and Manufacturers of America (PhRMA). It was widely reported at the time that his asking fee had been $2 million—and that the former congressman had gotten it. Big Pharma knew the value of talent.

But in the summer of 2003, Billy Tauzin was still chairman of the House Energy and Commerce Committee, and thus the man chosen to shepherd MMA through the House.

The day-to-day legislative tactics were left to Susan Hirschmann, the former DeLay chief of staff. Hirschmann's conservative, even right-wing credentials were impeccable. She had been a big shot both in her native Alabama and later in D.C. with the College Republicans. One of her closest female friends in Washington was said to be right-wing think-tank executive Amy Ridenour, Jack Abramoff's former friend and money-mover. And her husband, David, was a vice president of the U.S. Chamber of Commerce.

So sought-after had Hirschmann been when she made it known that she was ready to leave DeLay's office and cash in on her contacts that an auction was held for her services. Williams & Jensen won that battle. The fees from her client list there soon mounted into the millions. Of these, Big Pharma and its various individual members were the ne plus ultra.

What a cast of characters had lined up behind MMA: the Bush White House and Karl Rove, Big Pharma, the AARP, Boss DeLay, his Energy and Commerce chairman Tauzin, DeLay and Tauzin's right-hand man on the committee, Joe Barton of Dallas, and, making the trains run on time, Susan Hirschmann.

Considering the brains and brawn lined up behind the thing, it's astonishing that the vote was even close. But it was—very, very close.

And when the time came, in the early hours of June 27, 2003, the vote stood 214 in favor—and 218 against. But the DeLay train was not done, not by a long shot. In the next few minutes, one Republican House member was made to change his vote to "present," while two others switched their votes from no to aye.

After the Senate voted 76–21 to pass its own version of the bill, a joint House-Senate conference committee was called to "unify" the two measures. The critical, final House vote on the Medicare Prescription Drug Act came on November 22, 2003, at 3 a.m. After forty-five minutes, the bill seemed lost, with the vote at 219–215 against. Once again, contrary to House precedent, the vote was held open. This time it was for all the marbles. DeLay, Blunt, and even Speaker Hastert could be seen on the floor of the House, buttonholing and cajoling, promising this member rewards and threatening to wreak vengeance on that member.

Even Republicans were appalled. One senior Republican remembered it as "the ugliest night I have seen in twenty-two years in politics." Representative Walter Jones of North Carolina recalled that night, "It was horrible. I saw a woman—a member of the House—a lady—crying."

At 5:50 a.m., all the threats and all the promises, the sweet nothings of pure power politics, had done their charm. When Republican John Culberson of Texas reversed his vote, the deed was done. The Medicare Prescription Drug, Improvement and Modernization Act of 2003 had passed.

It was soon revealed that the true cost of the MMA had been hidden. Medicare's nonpartisan chief actuary admitted that he had been ordered not to reveal the cost. While Bush administration spokespeople—and their legislative lackeys—pronounced the cost a mere $395 billion, the real number was in excess of $500 billion.

The lead negotiator from the Department of Health and Human Services joined the ranks of K Street lobbyists ten days after the passage of the act. At least fifteen congressional staffers involved went the same way.

With his twin triumphs in Austin and Washington, DeLay now appeared at his zenith. The passage of the various Texas redistricting plans guaranteed a decade or more of Republican ascendancy in the Lone Star State and augured a Republican-controlled—*DeLay-controlled*—House of Representatives for at least that long. In Washington, the passage of the Medicare Prescription Drug Act by a single vote was all the testimony that any White House—much less one run by Karl Rove—needed to appreciate the value of DeLay's arm-twisting prowess.

The Pest Man, the Bug Catcher, the Exterminator: it didn't matter what the highfalutin Bush I crowd or the pointy-headed intellectual Rove called him behind his back. The message was the same: whether it was in Austin or in Washington, Tom DeLay delivered.

As 2003 folded into 2004, and the months slipped away, the November 2004 election would yield everything that DeLay could have asked for: a second term for George W. Bush, a Republican Senate, a stunning reversal of fortune within the Texas congressional delegation (the ever so slight 17–15 Democratic edge that had turned solidly Republican, 21–11), and, best of all, renewed control over the House of Representatives for Majority Leader DeLay.

The master of the House whatever his title, Tom DeLay was clearly the dominant member of the Republican congressional leadership. Denny Hastert, the inarticulate teddy bear decorously perched in the Speaker's big chair, held symbolic power but little else. Large of girth, with pawlike hands, furrowed brow, yet ready grin, Hastert had been DeLay's deputy in the whip's office, and in reality he was still DeLay's deputy. Gingrich vanquished, Armey sloughed away, Hastert alone was left, a placeholder.

DeLay was now one of the most powerful men in American government. And within his particular realm (Republican Party ideology, domestic and economic policy, and, especially, energy policy), his only serious rivals were his fellow Texans Karl Rove and Dick Cheney.

Time, though—*his* time—was already growing short.

The value of Tom DeLay could be measured in all sorts of ways. Consider that ARMPAC contributed more than $900,000 to more than a hundred House Republican candidates in the 2004 election cycle alone. Since 1994, Republican congressional and presidential candidates had received more than $4.2 million from the same DeLay-controlled political action committee.

Or consider this: lobbying fees at the top fifty K Street shops increased 11 percent in 2004 alone. That year, a total of more than $840 million was spent on lobbying in Washington.*

Of this, a significant share went to former DeLay staffers. Bloomberg News would later report that the eleven lobbyists who had at one time or other worked for DeLay brought in at least $45 million in lobbying fees during 2002–3. Topping the leaderboard was Medicare Prescription Drug Act strategist Susan Hirschmann of Williams & Jensen. Among her clients: the drugmaker Wyeth, which, Bloomberg News reported, had set aside $21 billion to pay for claims that its diet drugs caused heart and lung complications. Not surprisingly, lobbyist Hirschmann was a pillar of the "tort reform" movement, while earning $1.4 million in lobbying fees from Wyeth during the same period.

The *Washington Post*'s Jeffrey H. Birnbaum sketched "The Road to Riches Is Called K Street." Since 2000, Birnbaum found, the number of lobbyists in the city had doubled to 34,750, with amounts charged up 100 percent.

Robert L. Livingston, former congressman from Louisiana and once would-be Speaker of the House and now the president of a thriving six-year-old lobby shop, was quoted as saying, "There's unlimited business out there for us." In explaining this profusion of lobby excess, Livingston noted that the tax cuts President Bush had signed into law also vastly curtailed federal regulation of big business. Meanwhile, federal outlays had grown all out of proportion. "The result," reported Birnbaum, "has been a gold rush on K Street, the lobbyists' boulevard."

Another congressman enjoying newfound attention in the spring of 2005 was Dallas's own Joe Barton. Barton, fifty-five, had finally ascended the heights, succeeding Billy Tauzin in the 109th Congress as chairman of the House Energy and Commerce Committee.

---

*The cost of winning a congressional campaign was up too. In 1976, it had cost an average of $86,000 to win a House seat. By 2006, the number had risen to $1.3 million. For a Senate seat, try $8.8 million (*Washington Post*, 4/9/07).

As newly crowned chairman, Barton promptly hired a passel of energy-company lobbyists and insiders to serve as his top staffers. Among them were C. H. "Bud" Albright, the chief lobbyist for Reliant Energy Inc.,* as chief of staff; Margaret Caravelli, a lobbyist for MTBE (methyl tert-butyl ether), a gasoline additive that is the subject of groundwater-pollution litigation nationwide; and Kurt Bilas, a former senior counsel at Reliant Energy, as committee counsel.

The energy bill pushed by Barton and passed by the House in April 2005 was a boon to the industry—and to the tort reformers. The bill contained a waiver against lawsuits to manufacturers of MTBE. Congressman Henry Waxman, the then ranking minority member of the House Committee on Government Reform, later estimated that the waiver could be worth billions to the affected companies. The major beneficiaries would be Exxon, which, according to the Center for Responsive Politics, contributed $942,717 to candidates in 2004, Valero Energy ($841,375), Lyondell Chemical ($342,775), and Halliburton ($243,946).

The *Washington Post* found that since 1997, oil, gas, electric, nuclear, coal, and chemical companies had contributed $1.84 million to Barton—more than to any other House member. During the 2000 and 2004 election cycles, these same companies gave $9.2 million to Republican presidential candidate Bush. The top source for both Bush and Barton proved to be the same: the Southern Company, the leading electric supplier to Georgia, Alabama, Florida, and Mississippi. Southern donated $103,390 to the Barton and $172,922 to the Bush campaigns. Barton, in turn, funneled a staggering $6 million–plus to House colleagues and the NRCC.

Not surprisingly, the network of former Barton staffers plying their trade on K Street was almost as formidable as DeLay's own and included lobbyists for Reliant Energy, Philip Morris, MCI, the American Chemical Council, AT&T, Duke Energy, and the Ford Motor Co.

Like DeLay, Barton was not known to be close to President Bush,

---

*Reliant, the *Post* pointed out, had contributed $160,000 to DeLay and $50,000 to Whip Roy Blunt's Roy B Fund.

though the president, Barton told the *Post,* affectionately called him Big Dog. In Barton's words, "They don't invite me to Kennebunkport or to the ranch in Crawford, unless it's a political event."

A framed motto in Barton's office said it all: FEAR GOD, TELL THE TRUTH, MAKE A PROFIT.

CHAPTER THIRTEEN

✦

Schiavo Spring

On September 21, 2004, three of Tom DeLay's closest associates—Jim Ellis, the former R.J. Reynolds operative; fund-raiser Warren RoBold; and TRMPAC executive director John Colyandro—were indicted by a Texas grand jury.

The three men were charged with felony counts for having accepted political contributions from corporations. Colyandro and Ellis were also indicted for money laundering. At the heart of the case was the century-old statute that forbade corporations from contributing directly to political campaigns. By indicting Ellis, RoBold, and Colyandro, Travis County district attorney Ronnie Earle was aiming at the heart of DeLay Inc.

A little more than a week later, on September 30, Majority Leader DeLay found himself admonished by the Committee on Standards of Official Conduct (the so-called House Ethics Committee). Ironically, the admonishment stemmed from the surreal events surrounding one of DeLay's greatest triumphs: the infamous one-vote victory in favor of the Bush administration's Medicare Prescription Drug Act. Republican representative Nick Smith now claimed that DeLay had offered him a quid pro quo for his vote on the bill that night.

As outlined by Smith, the deal was simple, straightforward—and unethical. If the Michigan representative voted in favor of the Prescription Drug Act, DeLay promised to support Smith's son, a candidate (unsuccessful, as it turned out) to succeed his father in Congress, in the upcoming Republican primary.

The contest boiled down to an issue of trust: would the committee take the word of the retiring congressman from Michigan or that of the powerful House majority leader? The Ethics Committee took Smith's word, but refused to "censure" DeLay, letting him off instead with an "admonishment."

Just one week later, on October 6, the same House Ethics Committee again "admonished" the leader, this time for having involved the Federal Aviation Administration in the 2003 battle over Texas congressional redistricting. The FAA had been used, at the behest of DeLay, to track down the Democratic state legislators who'd fled the state aboard a private plane to avoid having to vote on the Republican-drafted redistricting bill. The "admonishment" was DeLay's third by the committee. The leader's fury was subsequently turned on Chairman Joel Hefley (R-Colo.), who would find himself the ex-chairman of the Ethics Committee in the next Congress—and on his way to being a lame-duck congressman.

With rumors of more criminal indictments swirling about Austin, House Republicans voted on November 17 to amend their own intraparty leadership rules. No longer would a felony indictment automatically result in a member of the leadership being required to resign his position. Now, only a *conviction* for a felony crime would suffice. No one was under any illusion as to why the rules' change had been made.

Under pressure from watchdog groups and the press—and at least a handful of their own more independent members—Republicans soon reversed course. Not even DeLay could get away with such a naked maneuver for long. Something new was now in the wind, and it did not bode well for the leader.

Nor did the civil trial that opened in state court in Austin on February 28, 2005. The trial would focus on allegations that the treasurer of TRMPAC, Bill Ceverha, a former television newsman and former state legislator from Dallas, had illegally raised and spent corporate campaign funds during the 2002 election cycle.*

The suit had been filed in 2003 by a group of defeated Democratic legislative candidates. The five charged that TRMPAC used $600,000 in corporate contributions for political purposes and had failed to report as much to the Texas Ethics Commission. Plaintiffs claimed that the money was then funneled into twenty state house elections. The result of that election, as we have seen, was to have profound implications and not merely for the five defeated Democrats. The state House of Representatives turned Republican for the first time since Reconstruction, and Tom DeLay's close friend Tom Craddick of Midland thus became speaker. This was the body that, in 2003, pushed through DeLay's congressional redistricting agenda.

A lawyer for the defeated candidates, Chris Feldman, demonstrated in court just how the TRMPAC-to-ARMPAC scheme worked. TRMPAC first moved $190,000 (most of it in corporate money) from its own account to that of the Washington-based Republican National State Elections Committee, an arm of the Republican National Committee (RNC). The RNSEC, in turn, donated the very same money, dollar for dollar, to seven Republican candidates for the Texas state House of Representatives. When you got down to it, there was nothing fancy about the play. It was a lot less fancy, in fact, than some of the money-moving tactics employed by Jack Abramoff using Indian tribal gambling money or by Ed Buckham with the Russian oil money at the U.S. Family Network (USFN). And a lot cheaper to execute, there being no greedy third-party hands stretched out for their Reed-like, Norquist-like—or Mrs. Ed Buckham–like—cuts.

Ceverha and company, however, continued to offer the same line of defense. The same "I'm shocked, shocked" line. Shocked that anyone could possibly think that TRMPAC and ARMPAC had anything to do with each other. Shocked too that anyone might imagine that TRMPAC's $190,000 donation to the RNSEC had anything to do

---

*Much of the evidence given in the trial, in effect, ran parallel with the allegations that Travis County district attorney Ronnie Earle had earlier marshaled in his indictment of Ellis, RoBold, and Colyandro—and later used to indict DeLay himself.

with the $190,000 the RNSEC had, in turn, given to the seven Republican candidates for the state house.

In a video deposition played at the trial, John Colyandro claimed that TRMPAC "was modeled only in passing" after ARMPAC. But Colyandro was also forced to admit that he and Jim Ellis had named DeLay and Ceverha as advisory directors of TRMPAC.

At the trial, Feldman made much of a September 2002 e-mail exchange between TRMPAC fund-raiser Warren RoBold and Drew Maloney, the Washington lobbyist who had previously been DeLay's legislative director.* Maloney, whose clientele included Reliant Energy (a major contributor to TRMPAC), offered RoBold a list of possible corporate donors, adding, "I finally have the two checks from Reliant. Will deliver to T.D. next week." TRMPAC's records show that it received $25,000 from Reliant that month.

The *New York Times* headline of March 13, 2005, told the story: "As DeLay's Woes Mount, So Does Money." Clearly, someone was worried. In the article, the *Times* reported that the Tom DeLay Legal Expense Trust had taken in more than $250,000 since the September 2004 indictments of Ellis, Colyandro, and RoBold in Austin. Among the corporate donors were some familiar names: Reliant Energy ($20,000) and Bacardi USA; AMR (the Dallas-based parent company of American Airlines); Bell South; the Coors Brewing Company; Dallas-based ExxonMobil; and two of DeLay's oldest and best corporate friends, tobacco giants Philip Morris and R.J. Reynolds.

There were also a host of congressional donors to the DeLay legal defense fund: newly elected majority whip Roy Blunt of Missouri ($20,000), who, without DeLay's support, would never have been able to ascend to the post; Texas Republican Henry Bonilla ($15,000), the congressman from "the border country"; former Louisiana congress-

---

*Maloney famously held a baby shower for Tom DeLay's daughter Dani DeLay Ferro at the Washington offices of his client Reliant Energy. Maloney and DeLay Ferro put together the 2002 TRMPAC golf-outing-cum-fund-raiser that would result in a House Ethics Committee "admonishment" for DeLay. Among the attendees were representatives of Reliant and other industry giants.

man Billy Tauzin ($15,000); Judiciary Committee member Lamar Smith of Texas ($10,000); and Tom Cole of Oklahoma ($5,000). The contributions from the latter two members raised eyebrows. Earlier in the year, in a movement widely assumed to be "the prevent defense," Smith—who had hosted a 2002 fund-raiser for TRMPAC—and the even more right-wing Cole had been named to the House Ethics Committee. Now they were also seen to be contributors to the Boss's defense fund.

Embattled though he might be, the majority leader was certainly feeling the love that spring. Asked by pesky reporters if he planned to step down as leader anytime soon, DeLay only chuckled. No wonder. A few hours later, he found himself standing before an audience of a thousand donors at a Washington luncheon for the National Republican Congressional Committee (NRCC). There, keynote speaker DeLay took a shot at new Democratic National Committee (DNC) chair Howard Dean. "Republicans from Texas aren't known for our *eloquicity*," DeLay told the roaring crowd. His keynote speech ended, DeLay walked off the stage to the tune of "Still the One."*

DeLay had always operated best when he was in the backroom: his strength was in the quid pro quo, the wink-and-a-nod, in reducing grown men to jelly behind closed doors. None of this played well in public. The spotlight was no friend to Tom DeLay.

But by early spring 2005, the spotlight was on DeLay, like it or not. At first, it was an unwanted spotlight—the ethics charges, the Earle investigation down in Austin, the budding Abramoff scandal. Now, though, there came the opportunity for Tom DeLay to stand in the spotlight on his own terms—if he chose. If the past was predictive, then DeLay would remain in shadow.

He, instead, chose the light.

---

*At the same event, another close DeLay protégé, upstate New York congressman Thomas M. Reynolds, the chair of the House Republican Campaign Committee—who would, in that same role, find himself at the center of the Mark Foley House page scandal in the fall of 2006—hailed DeLay as a man who had "refused to back down from those who oppose the principles and values of the Republican Party."

His very public performance in the days and weeks to come would be the moment of Tom DeLay's triumph—and the moment of Tom DeLay's undoing. In retrospect, it was a desperate move on the part of a desperate man. An act of bravado, reckless and foolhardy—and destined to failure. But, it must surely not have seemed that way to DeLay in March 2005.

For DeLay believed that he had a cause, *the* cause that would save him from his critics, harden his base, make the right-wing Christian bastion that surrounded DeLay Inc. impenetrable, and perhaps even save him from indictment.

The cause had a name too: Terri Schiavo.

By late March, the case of the tube-fed, brain-damaged Mrs. Schiavo had all but knocked the war in Iraq off the front pages. Schiavo's husband had petitioned a Florida court to remove her feeding tube, an action opposed by her parents, pro-life advocacy groups, and Governor Jeb Bush. But no one else in the Republican Party leadership—not Senate majority leader (and presidential hopeful) Bill Frist, nor even the born-again president George W. Bush—was as loud or as public as Tom DeLay in demanding that the federal government intervene in the Schiavo case. DeLay was front and center. Day after day.

The Senate hastily approved at a rare Sunday session legislation to allow the federal courts to intervene in the case. "Every hour is incredibly important to Terri Schiavo," a teary-eyed Tom DeLay told the cameras. Whipped forward by the majority leader—and prayed over and encouraged by the high command of the Christian right, the Family Research Council's Tony Perkins and Focus on the Family's Dr. James C. Dobson—the House passed the Schiavo legislation in the wee hours of Monday morning. One hundred fifty-six Republicans and forty-seven Democrats voted for the legislation. Fifty-three Democrats and five Republicans voted against it. President Bush almost immediately signed the bill into law. Every hour was indeed "incredibly important" to someone—if not necessarily for the brain-dead Schiavo, who had been in a persistent vegetative state for approximately fifteen years.

Less than a week later, on March 27, Walter F. Roche Jr. and Sam Howe Verhovek wrote in the *Los Angeles Times* of "DeLay's Own Tragic Crossroads." The majority leader had, it turned out, been among family members who'd had to decide in 1988 whether to let the comatose Charles DeLay—Tom's father—live or die. A sixty-five-year-old drilling contractor, Charles DeLay had been injured in a freak accident at his home. A backyard tram had run away with him, wife Maxine, brother Jerry, and Jerry's wife, JoAnne. Charles had been thrown headfirst into a tree. The others emerged badly injured. Doctors advised that Charles DeLay, left to live, would "basically be a vegetable." The family—Tom included—chose to let him die. When, on December 12, 1988, Charles DeLay expired, family members—Tom included—were in attendance.

The Schiavo case proved disastrous for the Christian right—and thus for Tom DeLay. The courts, state and federal, ruled at every turn against Terri Schiavo's parents and in favor of her husband, Michael. Poll after poll showed that the vast majority of Americans did *not* want government to intervene in these life-or-death family matters.

As an indirect result, months before Katrina, the Schiavo case had begun to make Americans rethink the fundamental relationship between themselves and the Republican leadership. And what they saw of Tom DeLay, they did not like. The polls all said as much. The behind-the-scenes Republican powers took note.

By month's end, Leader DeLay was being assailed in the most unexpected places. On March 28, the devoutly right-wing editorial board of the *Wall Street Journal* castigated its former hero in a stunning leader entitled "Smells Like Beltway." Leave it to the *Journal* editorial writers, though: surely, only they could have discerned that it was Washington that had corrupted DeLay and not the other way around.

DeLay, meanwhile, fumed, as his real supporters—the Christian right—formed around him. Two days later, DeLay challenged his liberal critics—conveniently failing to mention that his most dangerous critics were now to be found on the right—to "bring it on."

DeLay had, of course, been correct about one thing: his support, always firm on the Christian right, was now, post-Schiavo, rocklike. The unfortunate lesson from this would be that the Christian right, adrift from its moneyed Republican corporate allies, would not suffice.

And still they tried. The *Washington Post* reported on March 31 that a consortium of right-wing nonprofits had pledged to use their grass-roots data banks in defense of Leader DeLay. The leading lights of the effort included David A. Keene of the American Conservative Union, Heritage Foundation boss Ed Feulner, and the Family Research Council's Tony Perkins.

On April 10, Mike Allen of the *Washington Post* told the behind-the-scenes story of that meeting in "DeLay's Backers Launch Offense." The resistance movement, Allen wrote, had been launched two weeks earlier when DeLay flew back to Washington from Houston over Easter recess to speak to a group of thirty conservative leaders in the conference room of the Family Research Council. The wily DeLay knew what he was about: "Officials working with DeLay said he is trying to lock in support by sowing the message that an attack on him is an attack on the conservative movement."

GOP sources told Allen, "Top Republican aides now have a daily conference call in which they trade intelligence about upcoming DeLay stories so they can form a united front in responding."

It would be a united front in what DeLay fervently hoped would be a fight to the finish—with his team, that is, left standing.

Even in defeat, it was still the Schiavo spring; and the silver-haired first-term senator from Texas, John Cornyn, helped give it that surreal edge. As recalled in a stinging *New York Times* editorial, "The Judges Made Them Do It," Cornyn had risen on the floor of the Senate "in a moment that was horrifying even by the rock-bottom standards of the campaign that Republican zealots are conducting against the nation's judiciary." The former Texas attorney general (and longtime Rove client) smoothly explained away the recent cases of violence directed against the nation's judiciary. These acts of criminal violence should,

Cornyn argued, be seen as a response to those judges who "are making political decisions yet are unaccountable to the public." The frustration, Cornyn continued, "builds up and builds up to the point where some people engage" in violence. The judges, the former Texas Supreme Court judge declared, "make raw political or ideological decisions." Cornyn—the Bush administration (and Big Oil's) most dependable senator—the *Times* concluded, had "thumbed his nose at the separation of powers, suggesting that the Supreme Court be 'an enforcer of political decisions made by elected representatives of the people.' "

Even Bill Frist retreated before that kind of rhetoric, saying, "I believe we have a fair and independent judiciary today."

DeLay's hometown newspaper, the *Houston Chronicle,* was also getting tough with him. In early April the *Chronicle* revealed that the Texas Office of State-Federal Relations—an agency overseen by Republican speaker Tom Craddick—had put former DeLay legislative director Drew Maloney on the payroll not two months after Craddick became speaker in 2003.

Craddick, of course, was the man DeLay and TRMPAC had made speaker of the Texas House. Maloney, meanwhile, had worked not only for DeLay but also with daughter Dani DeLay Ferro in putting together a $25,000-a-pop golf outing for the corporate friends of Tom DeLay. That event took place in April 2002, just in advance of a House-Senate conference on H.R. 4, the Joe Barton–sponsored energy act. Attendees included Maloney's number one client, Reliant Energy, along with a host of other industry giants, including Westar.

Now, it turned out, Craddick had gifted Maloney and his Federalist Group lobby shop with a $180,000-a-year contract to represent the State of Texas in its efforts to lobby the U.S. Congress. The sheer circularity of such a proposition was breathtaking—Tom DeLay's hand-picked speaker pays Tom DeLay's former legislative director to lobby Tom DeLay, whose TRMPAC (using money in part supplied by Maloney's biggest client, Reliant, then moving it through DeLay's ARMPAC and over to the RNC, and only then back to Republican state legislative candidates in Texas) furnished the dough that made Craddick speaker. A veritable triple play of politics and breathtaking indeed—unless you were familiar with the world of DeLay Inc. In which case, it was just par for the course.

The Christian right had not turned its back on DeLay, nor had the National Rifle Association. The NRA was expecting sixty thousand attendees at its April 2005 annual convention in Houston. Many of them would be present in the George R. Brown Convention Center to hear the keynote speaker, Majority Leader Tom DeLay, deliver the homily "Right to Carry."*

The *Houston Chronicle* headline told the story: "Arms key to free society, DeLay tells convention." The *Chronicle* also reported that since 1989, the NRA's PAC had donated $45,800 to DeLay's reelection campaigns.

By early April, with the attack on the judiciary still in full swing, Majority Leader DeLay spoke before the Judeo-Christian Council for Constitutional Restoration. The title of the meeting: "Confronting the Judicial War on Faith." Among the other notable attendees was Representative Lamar Smith of San Antonio, who, it was reported, cochaired with DeLay the so-called Judicial Accountability Working Group.† At the two-day conference run by evangelist Rick Scarborough, former pastor of the First Baptist Church of Pearland, attendees were encouraged to pick up a free copy of "In Defense of . . . Mixing Church and State."

While the Christian right kept the faith, other supporters on the right were losing patience with DeLay. For the first quarter of 2005, the Tom DeLay Legal Expense Trust was reported to be far off the pace from the $430,000 it took in during the second half of 2004. Repeat

---

*George R. Brown was, with his older brother Herman, the cofounder of what is today Kellogg, Brown and Root, a division of Halliburton. The Brown brothers were, as Robert Caro's magisterial biography of Lyndon Johnson shows in detail, Johnson's chief financial backers.

†Other members of the group included fellow Texas right-wingers Representatives John Culberson of Houston and John Carter of Round Rock.

donors included American Airlines, Bacardi USA, and R.J. Reynolds. Other givers to the cause included Nissan USA and Verizon. An additional thirty or so donors—mostly GOP congressmen—had also sent in about $50,000 over the past three months.

Meanwhile, TRMPAC's woes mounted with almost every additional story about it in the news. The Associated Press, in an April 11, 2005, report, quoted TRMPAC fund-raiser Warren RoBold asking Drew Maloney, "What companies that you know of would be interested in tort reform in Texas with asbestos problems that might support TRMPAC?" To which the Reliant lobbyist Maloney replied, "I would say Dow Chemical (they have a big asbestos problem), other cos. with asbestos problems including ... Owens Illinois ... Halliburton I believe."

This, however, was small change compared to the bombshell buried in Michael Isikoff's April 18 *Newsweek* story, "With Friends Like These . . ." In an exclusive interview, Isikoff had found Jack Abramoff "somber, bitter and feeling betrayed," "glumly sitting at his corner table at Signatures, the tony downtown restaurant he owns [and] that remains his last redoubt." When Isikoff noted that Tom DeLay and his aides had repeatedly said that they were unaware of Abramoff's shenanigans, the former "Casino Jack" replied bitterly, "Those SOBs." Then, pulling himself together, Abramoff told Isikoff, "DeLay knew everything. He knew all the details."

After that, the fear grew strong.

On April 12, 2005, DeLay walked over from one side of the Capitol to the other in order to meet with Republican senators over lunch. At the ninety-minute affair, DeLay implored his fellow Republicans to stick with him. Afterward, DeLay told reporters that his message had been simple: "Be patient; we'll be fine." For the Master of the House— used to criticizing the weak-kneed senatorial crowd—it must truly have been a humbling experience.

Jack Abramoff, facing far worse, still had a few friends left. College classmate Representative Dana Rohrabacher of California told the *Houston Chronicle,* "Jack has made some mistakes ... but he is not the dishonest, malevolent, arrogant wheeler-dealer that people are portraying. He is a fine man." Of Abramoff, Rohrabacher would later say to the *Washington Post,* "He's a very honest man."

Meanwhile the hue and cry from the Schiavo case lingered. Would-be president Frist announced that he had agreed to join in a telecast portraying Democrats as "against people of faith" for blocking Bush's court nominees. The telecast was organized by the Family Research Council and was scheduled to originate from a "megachurch" in Kentucky on the evening of April 24, now dubbed Justice Sunday. Among the other scheduled participants were Chuck Colson, the former Nixon White House top aide and Watergate felon and founder of the Prison Fellowship Ministries; and Dr. Al Mohler, the president of the Southern Baptist Theological Seminary. Said Tony Perkins, leader of the Family Research Council, "As the liberal, anti-Christian dogma of the left has been repudiated in almost every recent election, the courts have become the last great bastion for liberalism."

Minus Frist, the organizers of Justice Sunday were the backbone of DeLay's defenders. On that much, DeLay had bet right.

But among the Frists of the world—fellow Republican politicians with their own careers to consider—it was another matter.

That same day Elisabeth Bumiller of the *New York Times* reported, "Bush Is Seen as Unlikely to Seek DeLay's Ouster."* The reason was simple, argued a GOP strategist said to be "close to the White House": "They need DeLay, and they particularly need him on Social Security."

Meanwhile, the money continued to flow in, even if not as fast as in the past. DeLay's reelection campaign raised $438,235 in the first three months of 2005, more than half of it ($221,000) from corporate

---

*Bumiller's story contained a fascinating insight into the relationship between president and leader. At age thirty-three, DeLay, she reported, first met Bush, then thirty-four, shortly after Bush's defeat in a 1978 congressional race. She quoted DeLay as having said of Bush, "He was, what's the word I want? *Passionate* is too feminine, but he was gung ho for his daddy. He was kind of oil-field trash—that's an endearing term, by the way—and when I first met him, he was trying to find himself." Bush did his part too, giving DeLay a ride back to Washington from Texas on Air Force One later in the month. After the flight, DeLay reported himself "very humbled" by Bush's support.

PACS or trade associations. Among the individual donors were Tony and Lisa Rudy, who each gave $2,000; and Swift Boat Veterans for Truth sugar daddy, "tort reform" activist, and TLR bedrock Bob Perry, the multimillionaire Houston homebuilder ($8,000).

It was a good thing that the givers continued to give, for the cost of DeLay's defense was going up every day. E-mails are the cheapest form of advertising. Mailers and phone calls cost real money. The embattled DeLay now began sending out e-mails to supporters back home asking them to accept his version of recent events, "the real story." DeLay titled his e-mail message "What the Press Isn't Telling You." He also stressed that his three admonitions did not constitute a "sanction." And he signed the message "Take care and God bless, Tom."

Seriously bad news came the next day, when the House overturned its new, DeLay-inspired ethics rules. Said Speaker Dennis Hastert, "I am willing to step back." Under the newly reversed changes, complaints could have been dismissed within forty-five days if the ethics committee could not decide how to proceed. By reverting to the old rules, the committee might well be forced to open an investigation into DeLay's overseas travel and his relationships with lobbyists.

A story in the *New York Times,* detailing the two-way street that was DeLay Inc., didn't help either. Jack Abramoff's college buddy Representative Dana Rohrabacher of California had taken in $5,000 from ARMPAC, only to give back $5,000 to the DeLay Legal Expense Trust. Representative E. Clay Shaw Jr. of Florida had received $30,000 from ARMPAC—and had returned $15,000 to the DeLay legal fund over three electoral cycles. The Texas congressional delegation was full of contributors to the fund. These included Representatives Michael Burgess, $15,000 from ARMPAC (and gave back $5,000 to the defense fund); Kenny E. Marchant, $10,000 (and returned $5,000); John Carter, $20,000 (and returned $5,000); Henry Bonilla, $10,000 (and returned $10,000). Ethics Committee member Tom Cole of Oklahoma also participated; having received $15,000 from ARMPAC, he returned $5,000 to the legal defense fund. Of the five Republicans on the House Ethics Committee, every single one had given—and many had been gifted in return. The faithful Lamar

Smith got $5,000; new Ethics chairman "Doc" Hastings, $10,000; Judy Biggert of Illinois, $10,000; and Melissa Hart of Pennsylvania, $15,000.

Less than a week later, the Associated Press reported that Cole and Smith, their gift-giving and gift-receiving now in public view, had stepped down from the Ethics Committee.

By early May, mighty Tom DeLay had become an object of derision.

Writing in the *Washington Post,* columnist Dana Milbank noted, "DeLay Tries, Without Much Success, to Duck the Media Pack." Milbank's story began, "Tom DeLay sneaks around the Capitol like a fugitive these days, using back doors and basement passages to avoid television cameras. . . . And it still doesn't work." When a reporter shouted, "[Ronnie] Earle says you're America's problem. . . . What do you say to that?" DeLay said nothing, while scrambling away through a crowd of tourists.

A day later, DeLay could be found addressing the fifty-fourth annual National Day of Prayer gathering on Capitol Hill—and calling for "greater humility." "Just think of what we could accomplish," he told his listeners, "if we checked our pride at the door. . . . If we spent less time ducking responsibility and more time welcoming it. If we spent less time on our soapboxes and more time on our knees."

DeLay received a standing ovation for his talk. Speaking to the press afterward, DeLay explained, "Humility is something I work on every day."

The opening prayer at the event was led by James C. Dobson, the chairman of Focus on the Family. The $2,000-a-plate evening event to honor DeLay was held at the downtown Washington Hilton and sponsored by the American Conservative Union. Cochairs included Dobson and Tony Perkins. Guests wore HOORAY FOR DELAY stickers on their lapels, while a band played "If I Had a Hammer." Though former representative Bob Livingston spoke, fewer than two dozen congressmen showed up for the event.

Among the few Republican congressional stalwarts who did show were Majority Whip Roy Blunt, desirous of succeeding the Boss if the time ever came, New York conservative Tom Reynolds, the head of the Republican House Campaign Committee, and Ohio's John Boehner, who had openly feuded with DeLay—and been punished for his efforts.

Among the other notables who showed up was Abramoff buddy and Rove protégé Ken Mehlman, the then head of the Republican National Committee. Mehlman sat at the big head table with DeLay. He was there, Mehlman said, "to salute a leader." Mehlman's mentor Rove was not present.

"The message tonight," said Tony Perkins, "is, if they pick a fight with Tom DeLay, they pick a fight with all of us." "A nice hootenanny," L. Brent Bozell, president of the Media Research Center, called it. There were videotaped testimonials from Speaker Dennis Hastert—not in attendance—Mississippi governor Haley Barbour; former North Carolina senator Jesse Helms; Majority Whip Blunt; and James Dobson. Pastor Dobson warned that liberals know that the way "you win the battle is to shoot the brave soldiers first. And Tom DeLay is a brave soldier."

Writing in the *Texas Observer*, Lou Dubose reported, "Entire tables were filled with 20-somethings from the 501(c)3 and 501(c)4 nonprofit foundations that do the thinking and issues advocacy for the conservative movement."

Bob Perry flew in from Houston. The multimillionaire homebuilder and "tort reform" sponsor—and chief bankroller of the Swift Boat Veterans for Truth—told reporters that he'd talked to his lawyers, and they "tell me Tom DeLay doesn't have any legal problems. So he's going to be all right. You can fix a public relations problem."

Back in Texas, state district judge Joe H. Hart found that TRMPAC treasurer Bill Ceverha had indeed violated state election laws by failing to report $684,507—including $532,233 in corporate donations used for campaign activities—in 2002. The judge awarded $196,600 in damages to the five defeated Democrats who were plaintiffs in the case.

The news in Washington wasn't good either, where it turned out that newly installed House Ethics chair "Doc" Hastings (R-Wash.) had received campaign contributions from the Seattle-based Preston Gates law firm and its former star lobbyist Jack Abramoff and had put remarks in the *Congressional Record* in 1996 reflecting his opposition to the Clinton-backed reform package for the Marianas, warning that imposition of minimum wage "could crush its fragile economy." Curiously, Hastings's chief of staff told reporters that his boss didn't even know what Abramoff looked like: "Until we saw his picture in the paper, we wouldn't have known Jack Abramoff from Jack and the Beanstalk."

While Hastings might not have known Jack Abramoff from Jack and the Beanstalk, many members of Congress did—including some on his committee. In time—and the time would be soon—they would all know who Jack Abramoff was.

CHAPTER FOURTEEN

✫

Bush Justice

The administration of George W. Bush began life on the margins—a point that is seldom sufficiently remarked upon. A few facts are well known, beginning with the election of a presidential candidate who lost the popular vote—and who profited mightily by the fiasco that was the Florida recount. Other facts tend to remain obscured behind the haze of the past.

To recite the most obvious of these: George W. Bush lost the popular election by 539,947 votes in 2000 (50,456,169 or 47.8 percent to Al Gore's 50,996,116 or 48.4 percent). Less well remembered is that when Green Party candidate Ralph Nader's 2,831,066 votes—most of which would almost surely have gone to Gore in a straightforward two-way race—are added to the equation, the combined opposition lead stretches to almost 3.5 million, adding up not merely to a plurality, but to the 51.1 percent majority of Americans who voted against Bush.

The Bush presidency thus began as a minority presidency, with a minority president and a minority vice president. Not only in the presidential vote, but, in effect, everywhere there were signs of a deep, abiding divide, an almost cataclysmic fissure within American politics, beginning in the Congress, where both houses were now split, almost down the middle.

Typically, historically, such a presidency with such a divided Con-

gress would emerge weak from the contest, weak from the very get-
go. It would, like the first administration of Texas governor George W.
Bush, be, by necessity, devoted to compromise.

This proved not to be the case.

Given the numbers—and to make it work, as the architect of the
Republican ascendancy, Karl Rove, and, still more so, Vice President
Cheney would have it work—the system would have to be rigged.
And it was. "Bush Justice," as we shall see, was but one part of that
effort.

First consider the other elements in the rigging. Within the
White House, as we have seen, Vice President Cheney was fast accu-
mulating powers that none of his predecessors had ever held—much
less imagined. Frustrated by having to work under the more liberal,
Machiavellian Franklin Roosevelt, John Nance Garner, known as
Cactus Jack, had memorably complained that "the vice presidency
isn't worth a pitcher of warm piss." In his time, Al Gore had been
reckoned "a powerful vice president" by some—taking the lead, for
example, on environmental issues, such as global warming, under
President Clinton. Still, Gore was but a useful helpmate compared
to his successor, the aggressive old hand and practiced schemer
Cheney.

More than six years into the Bush presidency, Washington reporter
Joshua Micah Marshall would find a nugget buried in the government
directory known as *The Plum Book*; it was a definition of the vice
presidency as construed by the office of Vice President Dick Cheney:
"The Vice Presidency is a unique office that is neither a part of the
executive branch nor a part of the legislative branch, but is attached by
the Constitution to the latter. The Vice Presidency performs functions
in both the legislative branch (see article I, section 3 of the Constitution) and in the executive branch (see article II, and amendments XII
and XXV, of the Constitution, and section 106 of title 3 of the United
States Code)."

The assertions put forth by Cheney's legal team—and the construction here spoke loudly of lawyers (and especially Cheney's longtime counsel, David Addington)—were breathtaking in their sheer
audacity: the vice president, the argument seemed to go, was an inde-

pendent actor, virtually coequal to the president, especially were he a weak president.*

But then nobody knew anything about *that* in 2001. Nor, at the time, did Americans know that Cheney, secure in the White House bunker, had on 9/11 taken on presidential powers—the power to order the U.S. Air Force to shoot down commercial airliners and thus, in effect, to command the military of the United States.

Only later too would we learn that Cheney had, with the apparent blessing of his president, given himself the power to declassify the highest state secrets—at will. These were all hints that this was surely not going to be an ordinary presidency. And, of course, Cheney had early in the first term put into motion the work of the secret energy-policy committee. This was important work that would be almost entirely hidden from public view, by virtue of an Addingtonian legalism (the fact that the formal membership of the committee was drawn exclusively from the executive branch).

So too with much that would transpire on Capitol Hill in the first years of George W. Bush's presidency. The Senate emerged from the November 2000 election evenly divided, 50–50, but with the vote of a minority vice president giving a clique of die-hard conservatives—again, led by the administration's indispensable man, Cheney—the power to organize the upper chamber along Republican lines. Staff directors, counsel, investigators: the vast majority of these would now come from Republican ranks. The chairmen would all be Republicans—and many would be taken from the ranks of the most unyielding right-wingers in the Senate, among them Ted Stevens of Alaska (Appropriations), Pete Domenici of New Mexico (Energy and Nat-

---

*In truth, there was a measure of historical precedent to the argument. The Constitution, as envisioned by the framers, had not reckoned on party-based presidential tickets. Thomas Jefferson, for example, had run as the Democratic Republican candidate for president against John Adams, the Federalist candidate, in 1796. Adams had won the presidency, 71–68, but Jefferson had also been thrust into the vice presidency. Four years later, Jefferson, once again running as the Democratic Republican candidate against Adams, finished with 73 electoral votes—the same number enjoyed by his running mate, Aaron Burr. (Adams had come in third with 65, and his vice-presidential running mate, Charles Pinckney, fourth with 64.) The 1800 contest was eventually settled by the House, but only after Burr's bitter rival Alexander Hamilton had thrown the Federalist vote to Jefferson. The problem was rectified almost immediately with passage of the XII Amendment ("Present mode of electing president and vice president by electors") in June 1804, in time for that year's presidential election.

ural Resources), and, beginning in 2003, James Inhofe of Oklahoma (Environment and Public Works).

Appropriations chairman Stevens was the leading advocate for opening the Arctic National Wildlife Refuge (ANWR), a project near and dear to Dick Cheney's heart. There was nothing "kinder or gentler" about the then seventy-eight-year-old Ted Stevens, who was often said to be "the meanest man in the Senate." No "compassionate conservative," he.

Environment and Public Works chairman Inhofe of Oklahoma, meanwhile, was the leading congressional opponent of global warming theory. Stevens, Inhofe, and Domenici were senators so far to the right that liberal groups often rated their voting records in the teens.

The tip-off came in May and December 2001. First, moderate Vermont senator Jim Jeffords—Inhofe's predecessor as chairman of the Environment Committee—crossed the aisle and temporarily allowed the Democrats to reorganize the Senate. Just five months into the new administration, Jeffords already felt himself frozen out by the right-wingers in his party, especially those in the White House.

The onus for this disaster should have fallen on Karl Rove, but, instead, it fell on Senate Republican leader Trent Lott of Mississippi. Lott was deeply conservative, but he had a mind of his own. He was therefore considered unreliable by Rove and the White House. But then Lott "misspoke" at the one hundredth birthday party of the veteran segregationist senator Strom Thurmond of South Carolina—and laid himself open for removal: "I want to say this about my state. When Strom Thurmond ran for president, we voted for him. We're proud of it. And if the rest of the country had followed our lead, we wouldn't have had all these problems over the years, either."

Lott was quickly made to walk the plank, his successor as minority leader being the Rovian favorite Bill Frist of Tennessee, a mere second-term senator and a virtual neophyte among Republican ranks. The message was obvious: no matter one's years of seniority or experience, independence would not be tolerated on Capitol Hill.

Still, for a brief time, or roughly from May to September 2001, the Senate was capable of discomforting the minority president and his administration. Judicial appointments were held up, tax breaks to the rich moderated at least somewhat, and minor investigations launched. The operative word was *discomfort,* but *impediment,* not.

But after 9/11, it was all downhill. The Senate, as much as the House, would now be committed to the "Global War on Terror," whatever its terms, no matter how outrageous that might prove to civil rights and the Constitution, and in the hands of an increasingly fanatical cadre of right-wingers. "The Rights of Man" were a thing of the past. The country—and the Congress—were in the grip of hysteria.

The so-called Iraq War Resolution, passed by this same, ostensibly Democratic Senate on October 11, 2002, was, as we now know, the last straw. Few indeed wanted to speak truth—old Senator Robert Byrd of West Virginia, Ted Kennedy of Massachusetts, and a mere handful of others—but the essence of the thing was that Dick Cheney, Karl Rove, and the White House had the senatorial Democrats by the short hairs, and they knew it. Vote against the resolution and, especially if you were up for reelection in November 2002, you were likely a goner. The overwhelming 77–23 vote in favor of the open-ended resolution showed that Rove had it right: the words *Profiles in Courage* had little meaning left, at least in the halls of Congress.

In the House, a mere nine seats separated the Republican majority from the Democratic minority. Yet here too a coterie of far right-wingers ran the show, ostensibly led, as we have seen, by Speaker Denny Hastert, but, in reality, by the bullwhip-cracking Tom DeLay.

By now DeLay had thoroughly rigged the system such that committee chairmen were chosen not by seniority but by their appeal to a Republican leadership panel overseen by DeLay. The result, in almost every case, was personal fealty on the part of the chairmen to the whip.

Small fry with little experience suddenly found themselves powerful chairmen—Abramoff-saga protagonists Richie Pombo and Bob Ney, among them. Dependable veterans wishing to remain chairmen— "Old Impeacher" Henry Hyde and "Tampon Millionaire" Jim Sensenbrenner—toed the line too. Hyde had run out his six-year term as chairman of Judiciary, but on the promise of continued good behavior, he was switched to International Relations. Sensenbrenner of Wisconsin—he really was a "tampon millionaire," his family's great wealth having stemmed in part from the manufacture of such a product—was the House's equivalent of Ted Stevens.

Widely loathed and despised—a *New York Times* profiler could find almost no one willing to go on record, despite numerous complaints of arrogance and high-handed behavior—Sensenbrenner succeeded Hyde at Judiciary where he served as a wall against congressional investigations into alleged political tampering at the Department of Justice. When the opinions of civil rights lawyers in Main Justice were ignored in important redistricting cases—including Tom DeLay's redistricting project in Texas—the committee failed to find sufficient interest or cause to investigate. Why look after a bunch of liberal Democratic crybabies? Why indeed?

So it went everywhere in the House That Tom Built, nowhere more so than in the powerful Rules Committee. Once upon a time, Rules had set not only the calendar but the tone for debate in the House. Historically, the committee had been a highly independent body.

At its worst, under a succession of obstructionist Dixiecrat chairmen, the Rules Committee had sat for decades on important civil rights legislation. At its best, under the distinguished historian of the House, Richard Bolling, the committee had acted as the strong right arm for Speaker Tip O'Neill and the Democratic leadership. Bolling, who had three times tried and failed to win the House leadership himself, was nobody's minion—and nobody's fool either.

But under DeLay, Rules, presided over by the handsome, articulate—and predictably conservative—David Dreier of California, dutifully sped forth the White House's pet projects, while deep-sixing virtually all the major Democratic-sponsored legislation.

Dreier, though perceptibly brighter than most, was not unique among House chairmen. Indeed, no less than five major committees would be presided over during the DeLay years by right-wing Republicans from California: not only Rules, but also Armed Services (Duncan Hunter), Appropriations (Jerry Lewis), Ways and Means (Bill Thomas), and Resources (the aforementioned Richie Pombo). And, like Energy and Commerce chairman Billy Tauzin of Louisiana and his right-hand man, subcommittee chairman Joe Barton of Texas, they were all men from energy-producing states. They were the Men from Big Oil and Big Money. They knew where their bread was buttered too.

And since, as we have seen, Tom DeLay's interests lay in oil and gas, appropriations and taxes, rather than foreign affairs—save for the odd foray to the Marianas or a golfing trip to Scotland or a chance to break bread in Moscow with oil oligarchs—these more esoteric national and international issues were largely left to the Senate.

Which did not mean that the administration was going to leave the House to find its own way on matters of war and peace. Vice President Cheney, who in his guise as presiding officer of the Senate already possessed an imposing set of offices on the other side of the Capitol, arrogated for himself the grand suite of offices traditionally occupied by the chairman of the House Ways and Means Committee. It was a perfectly outrageous power grab—one that no doubt gratified the former House Republican whip Cheney's enormous (if well-hidden) ego.

In another Congress in another time, such an overreaching vice president would have been asked to vacate the Ways and Means chairman's suite, *tout de suite.* But in 2001, Cheney was not only president of the Senate, but also national energy-policy czar, de facto House foreign-policy overlord, and, in the opinion of some people, the real president of the United States. And with Cheney and DeLay around to call the shots, the Congress of the United States was little more than a lapdog to power.

With such clear—and frightening—top-down management on daily display, it was no wonder that the troops, from the most senior to the most junior, fell in line. The nine-vote House majority would seldom fail DeLay—or the president, or Dick Cheney.

On votes to reduce taxes—vote after vote after vote—to give breaks to Big Oil while ignoring the environment, to appropriate money (for the war in Afghanistan and, later, by the bucketfuls for the military buildup prefatory to the coming war in Iraq), the ranks held. A razor-thin nine-vote majority came to seem like a vast hundred-vote majority. Under Cheney and DeLay, it was all "Landslide George" in the halls of Congress.

And, meanwhile, no one seemed to want to peer beneath the curtain. *Oversight,* like courage, was just another forgotten word.

☆　☆　☆

But then so too was *justice.*

To understand how the system came to be rigged and justice perverted in the age of Bush—and by whom—it is necessary to let history unroll itself.

The time is 1995, the place, Texas.

Consider again for a moment the political landscape George W. Bush inherited as governor of Texas in 1995. The governorship had required a careful balancing act. On the one hand, there was Bush himself, inexperienced and callow, carried into office by a narrow margin over a popular, one-term Democratic governor. Most Texans hardly knew what they were getting, save for an athletic and seemingly affable young man with a famous name, an Ivy League education, and a cultivated twang.

As opposed to all that were the still highly functioning remnants of the old Texas Democratic establishment. The lieutenant governor, speaker of the house, attorney general, both houses of the state legislature, most of the judiciary, and virtually all the lesser county and municipal offices were still safely in Democratic hands as 1994 gave way to 1995.

Unsurprisingly, then, compromise became the norm. The modus vivendi of that first term was that, as old Speaker Sam Rayburn had memorably put it, "If you want to get along go along." In general terms, this is what they did too.

But beginning with Bush's second term as governor in 1999, the lieutenant governorship and the attorney generalship flipped. In part, this had been a matter of pure luck. In part, it was the result of Democratic miscalculation. Much too could be chalked up to the machinations of Karl Rove, still operating as a Republican political consultant in Austin.

Ailing, his many years of serious health problems having reached a dangerous crescendo, Lieutenant Governor Bob Bullock—still shrewd and capable and as profane as ever—had given way to the Republican Rick Perry, an unexceptional if nevertheless predictable right-wing former state legislator. Bullock had been unbeatable in his time, but near death now, he withdrew from the political arena. The way was open for Land Commissioner Perry, swept along in the wake of "moderate" governor George Bush's 1998 electoral triumph.

As we have seen, the longtime Rove client, former Texas Supreme Court justice John Cornyn—the faux-populist crusader against the "billionaire tobacco lawyers"—was also swept into office in the Bush landslide of 1998, as state attorney general. Where Perry, save for the inevitable cowboy boots, had the well-trained look of a minor California Republican congressman—tie tied tight, shirt buttoned down, hair sprayed against all winds—Cornyn came equipped with the twenty-first-century Republican senatorial look: well-coiffed white hair and honeyed voice—all of it perfectly judged to cloak a far-right agenda. Cornyn's day in the senatorial sun was already nearing even as he took up his office as state attorney general.

Behind the scenes—never far from the surface—the work of "the Iron Triangle" went apace. Here were Governor George W. Bush's three closest advisers, each with defined areas of interest. Karen Hughes, the tall, tough-talking former Texas television news reporter—she had been raised a "military brat," her father having been the former governor of the old Panama Canal Zone—fended off the press, a human flyswatter to some, but also capable of handing out choice morsels to the favored few. Joe Allbaugh, the chief of staff, minded the day-to-day operations of government. Rove took care of political strategy. Not a member of the Iron Triangle, but perhaps closer still to the governor, was Clay Johnson, Bush's old roommate at Phillips Andover and Yale, whose job it was to oversee boards and commissions. (Johnson would also play a key behind-the-scenes role in Bush's White House.)

In the governorship of George W. Bush, there was no éminence grise, no true power behind the curtain. Herein lies the key as to why the apparently "moderate" governor metamorphosed so suddenly into the adamantly reactionary president. For, in short, there was no Richard B. Cheney among the inner lot that fed the ego and helped chart the way for George Walker Bush to govern Texas. There was no one even close to a Cheney among that number.

But there was a fourth member of that inner Texas team. Not a "decider" like Cheney, not a promulgator of policy, nor an ideologue either, nor a consummate political insider of the highest order, skilled in forcing the bureaucracy to bend to his will. But rather an enabler gifted in making sure the wheels turned—and turned on time.

Every administration needed one: a functionary. A smooth, hard-working functionary, utterly beholden to the boss, utterly devoted to the man himself. In the Texas governorship of George W. Bush, there was just such a fellow. His name was Alberto Gonzales, and he was a quiet man. A very quiet man.

So great was Bush's electoral victory in Texas in November 1998 that an unheard of 27 percent of black voters and an even more astonishing 49 percent of Hispanic voters cast their ballots for the Republican governor. For a time—a short time, as it turned out—Texas seemed to be experiencing not only a Republican Revolution, but also a Hispanic Revolution. Or more precisely a Hispanic Republican Revolution.

The principal beneficiary of that revolution would be a then rather obscure former Vinson & Elkins partner named Alberto Gonzales, Bush's appointee successively as counsel to the governor and secretary of state. Where William Jefferson Clinton had famously come from Hope, Arkansas, Alberto Gonzales came from Humble, Texas. Indeed, the Man from Humble could boast of origins that made Clinton's look privileged.

Al Gonzales had been one of eight children, the progeny of Pablo and Maria Gonzales. His alcoholic father worked maintenance in the rice-mill silos, a dangerous job to be sure, but especially so for a man with a serious drinking problem. His mother kept a two-bedroom house on the far edge of Houston, while, as Gonzales's biographer Bill Minutaglio has it, "planes from the airport that would later be named the George Bush Intercontinental Airport still thundered overhead."

Seeking a way out of poverty, Gonzales had at age eighteen enlisted in the U.S. Air Force. The date was August 24, 1973, at a time when George W. Bush was rounding out his service in the Texas Air National Guard. A few years later, Gonzales found himself at the U.S. Air Force Academy in Colorado Springs, a cadet officer in training. It was no secret that the air force was anxious to expand its minority presence, especially among the officer corps. The young Al Gonzales was among the beneficiaries of this liberal-minded minority-admissions program.

With thoughts of becoming a fighter pilot, Gonzales had matriculated at the academy, taken course work, become president of his freshman-class council—and shortly thereafter dropped out. Having completed only 91.5 hours of course work, Gonzales submitted his request to leave the academy. Gonzales's "Record of Disenrollment" from the academy indicates, "His military performance as a cadet was average while his academic performance was above average." His "separation agreement" with the air force tells us that Gonzales's goal now was "to pursue a career in law . . . [and] attend Rice University in Texas, to study Political Science and hopefully be admitted to their law school next year." Rice, in fact, had no law school. Indeed, it had never had a law school.

But it did have a cavernous football stadium, capable of holding thousands and built largely with funds provided by Lyndon Johnson's principal "sugar daddy," the multimillionaire Houston contractor and longtime Rice University board chairman, the late George R. Brown. Al Gonzales knew Rice Stadium well, for as an impoverished Latino boy of twelve, he had sold soft drinks to fans sitting in the stands. Now he was returning as an undergraduate. Now he would be the one drinking Coke and watching the Rice Owls play football.

Quiet and reserved—but athletic too—Gonzales did well at Rice, graduating in 1979 with a bachelor's degree cum laude in political science. While at Rice, Gonzales seems to have made no particular impression on fellow undergraduates. But he did make an impression—a significant impression, as it turned out—on political science professor Gilbert Cuthbertson.

Known as Doc C, Cuthbertson was a Rice institution, a kindly, decent, soft-spoken, middle-aged professor whose popular courses were notoriously studded with jocks. In Doc C's classes the "gentleman's C" of yore had long since evolved into "the people's B." At a college where few indeed graduated with honors and where an A-minus was a mark of honor, Gil Cuthbertson was known to be not only a kindly soul, but a generous grader.

When the time came for Gonzales to apply for admission to law school and letters of recommendation were required, Cuthbertson, a Harvard Ph.D., waxed enthusiastic about his young protégé.

Far older than Rice, far grander too, the university on the Charles River in faraway Massachusetts nevertheless obliged; and three years later, Alberto Gonzales emerged, at age twenty-six, a graduate of the famous Harvard Law School. Father Pablo did not live to see his son's triumph. The older man, only fifty-two, instead died in January 1982 from injuries suffered in a fall at a grain silo.

Pablo Gonzales's son, the newly minted Harvard-trained lawyer began work as an associate at Houston's Vinson & Elkins in 1982. As it would so often be in his later life, Gonzales's timing was perfect. V&E had hired its first black attorney in 1974, its first Latino attorney in 1977. Five years later, the firm had yet to have a Latino partner.

What better story could a young man impart than the one Al Gonzales brought to the table? And it was all true too. Talk about your rags-to-riches story: a childhood spent in poverty, four years in the military—no shirker, he—a sojourn at the Air Force Academy, an undergraduate honors degree from Rice, and the patina of Harvard Law School—Al Gonzales looked, on paper at least, to be perfect.

Known almost universally as V&E, Vinson & Elkins was a newcomer compared to its rival Baker Botts. Founded in 1917 by James Elkins and William Vinson, the lawyers of V&E had made their bones litigating oil and gas cases. But much like Captain Baker and Mister Bob Lovett before him, the shrewd and calculating Elkins had developed tentacles that reached far and wide. Allying itself with the old Jesse Jones interests—now in the guise of a purported nonprofit (Houston Endowment Inc.), which also, conveniently, controlled the city's main newspaper, the *Houston Chronicle*—Elkins's First City National became Houston's dominant financial institution.

In the process, V&E developed a distinct corporate culture. It was, as Bill Minutaglio says, a culture of discretion: "In the madcap, dangerous world of Texas oil and big business—where the level of backstabbing, treachery, illegalities, subterfuge, and deceit was unmatched except maybe in a book that combined the Bible and the collected works of Shakespeare—V&E had earned a justly famous reputation for keeping its clients protected. If you were a V&E client, high or low, and as long as your money was good, you found yourself working with a brass-knuckled firm that bent over backward to protect your privacy, to keep you out of court and jail, to keep the revenue spigot completely unclogged."

The client list of V&E had grown golden over time: not only First City National, but Brown & Root, its successor firm Halliburton, and an increasingly profitable energy company called Enron. Eventually, Enron became V&E's biggest and most important client, its billings accounting for nearly $32 million in 2001. By then, Minutaglio writes, "At times some of the V&E lawyers were working so closely, so intimately, with Enron, they simply set up temporary offices there." Wags took to calling the firm Vinson & Enron, though others, perhaps more perceptive still, had it as Enron & Vinson.

When the deluge came, in the fall of 2001 and subsequently, V&E would pay for that sort of closeness, in both reputation and dollars. But, as the 1980s gave way to the nineties and the nineties gave way to the new century, the fate of V&E was increasingly tied to that of Enron. As Enron grew, so did V&E. And, as V&E grew, so did its partners' paychecks. If you were a young, first-year associate such as Al Gonzales, there was much to aspire to at V&E, not least an annual salary that could stretch to seven figures if you were among the most favored partners.

Like Enron, the other names on the firm's client list were often newer than those on Baker Botts's list, and more political too. For a long time, V&E had been seen as a more political law firm than Baker Botts. V&E had come to employ such notables as former conservative Texas Democratic governor turned Republican John B. Connally (as a name partner) and former Senate majority leader Howard Baker in its Washington office. At V&E, they knew how to play both sides of the political fence—and make it pay.

And if the firm knew how to attract famous older talent such as Connally, it also knew how to develop young talent. In part, the way to do both was the same: V&E paid well. But Vinson & Elkins was also a little more hospitable to talented strivers than its rival Baker Botts. V&E had legal talent aplenty, but its lawyers were also less predictably white-shoe than those of Baker Botts.

Still, in a town in which there was a definite legal hierarchy, V&E stood at the top of the heap, coequal or nearly coequal to the older firm. And into this closed and privileged enclave of discreet but tough-edged Texas lawyers, Alberto Gonzales arrived in June 1982 as a first-year associate. There too he would spend the next thirteen years of his life.

By the time Gonzales joined V&E, at least some firm partners thought that the words *equal opportunity under the law* might have pragmatic meaning. The time was right to promote the careers of talented black and Latino lawyers. V&E chairman Harry Reasoner—himself an honors graduate of Rice—reckoned that Al Gonzales was just such a man. With his innate tendency to "play things close to the vest," Gonzales seemed to be made for V&E. And he was. Eight and a half years later, along with two other minority lawyers, Gonzales was made partner.

"Empires of Paper" was how the lawyer-writer Griffin Smith had memorably termed Houston's legal citadels, of which V&E and Baker Botts stood supreme. Now, the quiet Latino from Humble, the poor boy who had scaled the heights of Rice and Harvard Law, had arrived at the very summit of one of those "Empires of Paper."

At V&E, Gonzales had practiced transactional law. He was, in other words, a corporate lawyer—a man who made the dealmaking work, whether it was in real estate or in M & A work (mergers and acquisitions).

He had also, by now, gone through one wife and found a second, a tall, attractive, blond, green-eyed divorcée named Rebecca Turner. The couple—she was a banker and already the mother of a son—married in late August 1991. That same year, Gonzales was elected to the board of the state bar of Texas. There, he met a soul mate of a different sort—a lawyer as quiet and serious and loyal as Alberto Gonzales himself. Her name was Harriet Miers, and she would become president of the state bar the very next year. Miers was also, already by now, a close associate of a Dallas businessman, Texas Ranger CEO George W. Bush.

The two made an unlikely pair: the privileged Dallas lawyer Miers, with her Southern Methodist University education, and the Hispanic from Humble, Al Gonzales. But, in fact, they were a great deal alike. No one ever confused either one for an Ivy League law professor. They were both, instead, "legal process wonks." As Minutaglio says, "Neither of them was famous for being on the short list of the great intellectuals in Texas, or the great constitutional scholars, or the most dazzling practitioners of extemporaneous law . . . they weren't rabbits, they were turtles."

It would thus, Minutaglio adds, "only be a matter of time before they were bound by their enormous fascination, loyalty, and admiration for George W. Bush."

For Miers, the fascination with Bush—the intellectual subordination, even—had already begun. For Gonzales, the moment would come soon enough. Elected governor in November 1994, sworn into office in the winter of 1995, Bush was looking to find in-house legal counsel. Prodded by Miers, he had no farther to look than the offices of Vinson & Elkins in Houston, and the thirty-nine-year-old Al Gonzales. Fredo, Bush called him, but not, apparently, after Michael Corleone's dim-witted, weak, and doomed brother in *The Godfather*, but because it sounded (to Bush at least) like a shortened version of *Alberto*. Other times, Bush called him "Alfredo."

Taking the job of counsel to the governor meant an enormous cut in the nearly half-million-dollar-a-year salary Gonzales had become used to by now. As counsel, Gonzales quickly developed a reputation as a hard worker, arriving at the office regularly at six-thirty in the morning. Like his friend Miers, Gonzales was also known to be exceptionally loyal to the boss. A good thing since the Bushes demanded total loyalty. George W. and his elder brother Jeb were both said to ask the same of their underlings: are you willing to throw yourself on a grenade to protect the Bush family? Al Gonzales was.

Gonzales proved as much too when he traveled to the state prison in Huntsville to witness executions—or listened as they were described to him over the telephone in the silence of his office in Austin. (The executions took place after midnight, in the early-morning hours, the deadly details as recorded being at once dull and chilling: *6:26: prisoner strapped to gurney. . . . 6:28: needle inserted. . . . 6:35: lethal dose administered. . . . 6:45: prisoner is pronounced dead.*) During Bush's terms in

office as governor, 152 people were put to death in Huntsville—Old
Sparky, the electric chair of old, having given way to death by lethal
injection.

Gonzales had also to vet and write the clemency memos for the
governor, the most infamous of which derived from a case in which
the defendant's lawyer had slept through major portions of the trial.*

Alberto Gonzales truly cemented his relationship with George W.
Bush in 1996. That's when a summons for jury duty in Travis County
arrived in the mail, addressed to 1010 Colorado Street—the gubernatorial mansion in Austin. While the governor told the *Dallas Morning News* that he would be "glad" to serve, the truth was quite the
opposite.

Under Texas law, the governor, like any other prospective juror,
would be asked, "Have you ever been accused, or a complainant, or
a witness in a criminal case?" The governor had, in fact, been charged
with disorderly conduct in 1968 and drunk driving in 1976.

The particulars were thus: as a Yale undergraduate, the twenty-
year-old Bush had gotten caught in a Christmastime prank in New
Haven in 1966. He "might have had a few beers," Bush later recalled.
In any case, the jolly DKE frat brother had grabbed a storefront
wreath and run with it. He was caught almost immediately by New
Haven police officers. The charges were later dismissed.

A year later, Bush again got himself into trouble with the police,
this time at a Yale-Princeton game in Princeton. The date was November 18, 1967. Bush and a bunch of his DKE buddies had traveled to
Princeton for the event. When it was over—with Yale winning the Ivy
League football title, 29–7, behind the stellar play of fellow DKE members Brian Dowling and future NFL Dallas Cowboys running back
Calvin Hill—pandemonium erupted on the field. Bush found himself
detained, questioned—and told to leave Princeton Township before
sundown. Later still, in 1976, Bush, while at the family summer com-
pound in Kennebunkport, Maine, was charged with drunk driving.

---

*Questioned by Senator Russ Feingold of Wisconsin at his 2005 confirmation hearings as
attorney general of the United States, Gonzales would claim to be unable to recall the particulars of the case.

What made the governor's problem all the greater was that he had been called for jury duty in a case of drunk driving. Worse still, the defense attorney in the case—which involved a stripper from the Austin club Sugar's—planned to ask potential juror Bush questions under oath about his own DWI record.

As Harriet Miers would with Bush's Air National Guard records, so Al Gonzales did with his arrest record: he brushed it away neatly, a mere grain in the sands of time. Gonzales convinced the judge in the case that his client, the governor, would have a "conflict" serving on the jury. The "law-and-order, CEO governor" was dismissed. And George W. Bush walked away with his public reputation intact.

After that, the sky was the limit for Al Gonzales: appointment as Texas secretary of state was followed by appointment to the state supreme court; followed by, upon Bush's 2000 recount victory, appointment as White House counsel. Alberto Gonzales had come a long way indeed.

On inauguration eve 2001, Vinson & Elkins gave a dinner party for Alberto Gonzales. The firm had much to celebrate: its former partner was now about to become the first Hispanic White House counsel. The next day, V&E threw one of the most elaborate of the several "Texas inauguration parties," hosting no less than fourteen hundred revelers at its "parade-viewing party," held at the elegant Willard Hotel. On offer were celebratory drinks the better to wash down "Vinson & Elkins inaugural barbecue sauce."

As White House counsel—old friend Harriet Miers was just down the hall, serving as staff secretary to the president—Gonzales brought with him but one fellow Texan, attorney Stuart Bowen, who had been among the lawyers dispatched to Florida for the recount.*

Bowen aside, the staffing of the counsel's office had been done elsewhere, by other hands. Virtually all were members of the neo-conservative Federalist Society. Among these were at least some of the

---

*He would later emerge as a thorn in the administration's side in his role as inspector general of the Iraq reconstruction effort.

former Supreme Court clerks who had been so instrumental in the
Florida recount. Others among the cast bore other stamps of
approval: Brett Kavanaugh, for one, the former senior deputy to Kenneth Starr and coauthor of the *Starr Report*. As deputy counsel, there
was Florida-recount lawyer and Burger clerk Timothy Flanigan. Two
among the number were not formally members of the team, yet were
frequent guests at the counsel's staff meetings: David Addington, the
longtime counsel and deputy chief of staff to Dick Cheney; and
William Haynes II, general counsel to the Department of Defense and
right-hand man to Secretary of Defense Donald Rumsfeld.

A wise man might over time have perceived that the brains behind
the White House counsel's office resided elsewhere, in Cheney's and
Rumsfeld's inner circle.

The team player, the facilitator, the transactional lawyer Gonzales
would make the papers move. But he would not fashion the policy
behind the papers. That was for others to do. Among his accomplish-
ments in his first year of service: the drafting of Executive Order
13233, which was issued by President Bush on November 1, 2001,
which tried to constrict the Freedom of Information Act by limiting
access to the records of former presidents.

In the wake of 9/11 and, especially, in the buildup to, execution,
and wake of the Iraq War, the policy was fixed by Cheney and Rumsfeld, the legal buttressing left to the lawyers. At the top of the legal
heap stood Addington and Haynes, and no doubt too the former Wall
Street lawyer and Cheney chief of staff I. Lewis "Scooter" Libby.
Finding legal justification for the policies wrought by Cheney and
Rumsfeld was Gonzales's job, first as White House counsel and later
as attorney general. The litany of policies approved and given the
stamp of supposed legality by Gonzales—most of them dubious—is
long and well known, whether the decision to have the CIA "render"
alleged Al Qaeda and Taliban members to secret prisons in eastern
Europe, after first abducting them off the streets of western European
cities in Germany and Italy in some cases; or the decision to allow
secret wiretapping without court orders; or the vast overstepping of
presidential authority (not the least of which were the Presidential
Signing Statements, in which President Bush announced that he would

not follow the letter of laws he had just signed); or simply to ignore the Constitution and congressional mandates, such as the Foreign Intelligence Surveillance Act of 1978 (FISA), requiring that legal justification be presented before a secret FISA court for such wiretapping to take place; or the questionable, possibly unconstitutional, holding of unproven Al Qaeda and Taliban suspects at a specially constructed military prison at Guantánamo Bay, Cuba.

And because no one—or hardly anyone—thought that Al Gonzales was a constitutional scholar, the tortured legal basis for torture fell instead on a certified egghead, the Federalist Society academician John Yoo, in the Justice Department's Office of Legal Counsel. Gonzales, it was said, liked Yoo, respected his intelligence, and particularly admired his fifteen-page memo "The President's Constitutional Authority to Conduct Military Operations Against Terrorists and Nations Supporting Them."*

The question, of course, was how far the government could go in prosecuting the war. Could the Constitution really be so parsed as to allow torture and the virtual elimination of habeas corpus?

In the hands of John Yoo—backed up not only by the vice president and his coterie, but also by the White House counsel and future attorney general of the United States—it could.

Because of the Bush administration's continuous attempts to widen presidential powers and narrow constitutional protections, the specific

---

*John Yoo, the author of many of the so-called torture papers governing the treatment of war on terror prisoners, remembers White House counsel Gonzales as a jolly fellow, always good for a laugh, a man both earnest and loyal. Gonzales, says Yoo, "came to Washington with no agenda but that of providing his client, George W. Bush, with the best legal advice possible." Meetings, however—meetings like the ones where the torture papers were drawn up and approved—were run by Gonzales's deputy, Tim Flanigan, the former Burger Supreme Court clerk, Florida-recount lawyer, and Federalist Society member. At the meetings, writes Yoo, Flanigan typically "play[ed] the role of the inquisitor." Many of the most critical meetings, Yoo adds, were held in the "Empire-style Old Executive Office Building" in December 2001, at a time when the White House "held its procession of Christmas parties and receptions." Yoo was one of four deputies to assistant attorney general Jay Bybee, a former University of Nevada law professor who headed the Office of Legal Counsel (OLC). Yoo, a professor of law at the University of California at Berkeley today, had been a Supreme Court clerk for Justice Clarence Thomas. Bybee is today a federal appeals court judge.

milestones of Gonzales's six-year tenure as both White House counsel and attorney general have largely been blurred.

But it might be worth revisiting one of them. In November 2004, following his narrow presidential victory over Senator John Kerry, Bush nominated Gonzales to replace John Ashcroft as his attorney general for his second term. He was confirmed by the Senate by a vote of 60–36 and sworn in on February 14, 2005, the highest-ranking Hispanic in U.S. government history.

No one ever said that being attorney general was a ticket to the pantheon of American history. Most attorneys general, like most presidents, have been mediocre men. Many an attorney general has, in fact, been a hack, while others were mere fixers. Some even managed to cover the Department of Justice with a coating of ethical soot, among them the Harding administration's Harry M. Daugherty (leader of the Teapot Dome era "Ohio Gang") and Nixon's Watergate-era John Mitchell.

Called upon to testify before a federal grand jury in 1926, former attorney general Daugherty declined the honor, saying: "I refuse to testify and answer questions put to me, because: the answer I might give or make and the testimony I might give might tend to incriminate me."

The great and good have been far outnumbered by the mediocre and even bad. A few, though, managed to transform themselves. During the trust-busting presidency of Theodore Roosevelt, the attorney general of the United States had been a small, prim, dapper man named Philander Knox, and his story is worth retelling in light of Alberto Gonzales, onetime Texas lawyer and longtime friend of George Bush's.

As a Pittsburgh lawyer, Knox had played a prominent role in the organization of the United States Steel Corporation. The consolidation of U.S. Steel had made Andrew Carnegie a millionaire many times over and had given Wall Street financier J. P. Morgan control over America's (and much of the world's) steel industry.

But under President Teddy Roosevelt, Knox carried out the crusade to bust the trusts. The archdefender of the status quo, the corporate counsel par excellence, turned on a dime, beginning with John D. Rockefeller's Standard Oil Trust. When an investor friend rang up

Knox one day to ask why the attorney general hadn't tipped him off to the filing of one of the early trust-busting cases, Knox famously replied, "There is no stock ticker in the Department of Justice."

The lesson in the tale of Philander Knox can explain much about the public service provided by Alberto Gonzales. The question, as 2005 opened, was whether Alberto Gonzales would somehow transform himself.

Would Gonzales be able to go from serving George W. Bush to serving the nation? Would Al Gonzales, the Quiet Man from Humble, be the man who stands up to power and speaks truth? The answer was no. Gonzales was no rabbit. He was a turtle. He was not a leader. He was a lawyer. A lawyer's first obligation—legal ethics insist—is to his client. As White House counsel, there was no question as to Gonzales's obligations. They were to his client, the president of the United States.

But as attorney general, he had other, more pressing obligations, to the people of the United States and to the Constitution.

Or, so it says.

CHAPTER FIFTEEN

✫

Trouble in Texas

Down in Georgia, another prominent member of Team Abramoff, Ralph Reed, was preparing to make his first run for elected office, vying in the Republican primary for that party's nomination for lieutenant governor. Reed, an Associated Press reporter wrote, had "for two decades . . . made his mark as a squeaky-clean political operator," but was now facing charges that he "had raked in money from the same gambling interests he once called 'a cancer on the American body politic.'" Just where and with whom Reed was supposed to have made a mark as "a squeaky-clean political operator" was open to question, but there was no doubt that the former Christian Coalition leader's role in the Abramoff Indian tribal gambling scandals was now front and center in the news.

And there was more to come. Just as the Senate Indian Affairs Committee hearings into the Abramoff scandals were set to open, reports surfaced in June 2005 that Abramoff's former law firm, Preston Gates, had paid for some of Tom DeLay's overseas travel, including $70,000 for the infamous May 2000 trip to London and the St. Andrews golf course in Scotland.

When the Senate hearings opened the next day, the paper trail was made manifest in the form of e-mails and invoices: "Wire all funds.

Professional Services. $3,405,000.00" read one such invoice sent to the Louisiana-based Coushattas in 2002.*

Coushatta tribal leaders told Senators McCain and Dorgan of the Indian Affairs Committee how they had paid some $32 million to Jack Abramoff, Michael Scanlon, and their associated enterprises. The question now was "why money they intended to benefit DeLay causes was often disguised or routed elsewhere."

Why indeed?

Among the charges to the tribe was $185,000 for a Washington-arena skybox—the same skybox used by Tom DeLay to treat high-rolling donors to a performance of the Three Tenors in May 2000. Another was the $70,000 used to reimburse Preston Gates for DeLay's London and Scotland visit.

One tribal leader noted, "We still haven't gotten to the bottom of it. We have no idea of the extent of it." They would eventually—to the tune of more than $82 million.

Meanwhile, as the noose around Abramoff tightened, so too did the noose tighten around the neck of DeLay. For what the Senate hearings were making abundantly clear was that Tom DeLay and Jack Abramoff were joined at the hip.

The news out of Texas wasn't any better. On July 7, Westar Energy admitted in court papers that the company—one of the eight corporate and three individual defendants in the criminal action filed in Austin by Travis County district attorney Ronnie Earle in September 2004—had, in fact, made a $25,000 donation to the cause to secure pre-

---

*In another, Abramoff directed the tribe on how to proceed with its political gift-giving: "Enclosed please find a check for $10,000 to the Texans for a Republican Majority. This check needs to be reissued to America 21," a Nashville-based, Christian-right grassroots group, whose voter turnout efforts contributed to Republican successes in the 2002 midterm House elections. In much the same fashion, Abramoff ordered the tribe to cancel a $25,000 check to ARMPAC and send it instead to Sixty Plus, the Big Pharma–backed front group that was intended as a Republican alternative to the more liberal AARP. The tribe, of course, had no business sending $25,000 to Sixty Plus, but Sixty Plus had significant political juice behind it in 2002: in this case, the Bush administration and Majority Whip DeLay, who were trying to get a Medicare prescription drug benefit—its very terms written by Big Pharma lobbyists such as former DeLay chief of staff Susan Hirschmann—through Congress.

cious face time with DeLay at his June 2002 golfing spree at the Homestead resort in Hot Springs, Virginia.

One week later, Texas district judge Robert Perkins refused to overturn the indictment of one of the three individual defendants in the same case. John Colyandro, identified in the *Washington Post* as "a veteran of White House political adviser Karl Rove's direct-mail firm," had sought to have the charges against him dropped on grounds that the decades-old Texas law under which he was being prosecuted was "poorly drafted." Less than a month later, the judge also denied arguments by Colyandro and codefendant Jim Ellis that the charges were based on an unconstitutionally vague law.

In reality, Colyandro and Ellis—and their codefendant, Warren RoBold—were small fry. Just weeks later, in late August 2005, the big fish were hauled in. DeLay and his longtime close friend and associate new Texas House speaker Tom Craddick met separately with Travis County prosecutors. DeLay and his legal team sat with prosecutors for ninety minutes on August 31. Afterward, DeLay's press spokesman announced that the leader had voluntarily met with the prosecutors—a notion quickly countered by "a source familiar with the meeting," who told reporters that DeLay appeared only after being threatened with a subpoena. DeLay's Austin attorney told the press that his client had had "a very pleasant conversation" with prosecutors.

The same day (September 8) that the *Austin American-Statesman* reported on the leader's "very pleasant conversation," it also reported that four indictments had been issued against TRMPAC and its right-wing running mate TAB, the Texas Association of Business. The charges mirrored the earlier ones lodged against Colyandro, Ellis, RoBold, and the eight corporate givers in September 2004: a total of 128 counts against TAB and two against TRMPAC for having illegally used corporate money to fund Republican state political campaigns in 2002. By its own proud reckoning, TAB spent $1.7 million in that election cycle. All 130 counts were third-degree felonies. TAB faced up to $7 million in damages and fines, and its president, Bill Hammond—a former Dallas Republican state house member—called on its twenty-five-hundred employer members and two hundred chambers of commerce to pony up for war with Ronnie Earle: "Please do not abandon us in our hour of need. Please help our struggle with your wallet and voice." As TAB put it in an e-mail to members, "This is the heart and sole [sic] of this case: will TAB and other organizations be able to communicate with the public or will the only source of information be left to the news media?" To hear TAB tell the tale, all it was being accused of was "sharing." TAB, in its own words, had "created an impartial voting record outlining how many members of the Legislature voted to maintain an out-of-control justice system and voted time and time again to raise taxes on hardworking Texans. We then took this information and shared it with the folks back home." There was no mention in the e-mail of the $1.7 million—most of it donated by big insurance companies—or that the money had been spent entirely on the candidates of one party in twenty-four legislative races in 2002.

The corker, though, was saved for the end: "Someone once said a representative republic cannot remain a republic for long when its representatives become increasingly immune from public scrutiny and criticism. If Mr. Earle succeeds, many critics will be silenced." Mr. Earle's defenders would, of course, probably have said exactly the same thing—of Mr. DeLay.

At sixty-three years of age, Ronnie Earle had served as Travis County district attorney for almost half his lifetime—having spent nearly thirty years in office. While Austin was far from the largest city in Texas, it was the state capital; and, as such, the public integrity unit of the DA's office had been empowered with a wide-ranging oversight function. An elected Democrat, Earle had not hesitated to indict alleged offenders whether Democratic or Republican. The list was long and mostly consisted of Democrats—twelve of fifteen, to be exact. The notable exception had been U.S. senator Kay Bailey Hutchison, whom Earle had indicted on charges of official misconduct and record tampering in 1994. After a state judge ordered an acquittal for Hutchison, Earle had been forced to drop the case. Republicans, however, were still citing Earle's failure a decade later as proof of his Democratic leanings—and alleged incompetence. "A bogus indictment," "a political witch hunt," a legal "shenanigan" were some of the more polite descriptions thrown about. Curiously, for such a "partisan fanatic," Earle had chosen to stay in the same job for all those years—in September 2005 he was in his eighth four-year term of office, having first been elected in 1976—without aspiring to higher preferment.

In truth, Ronnie Earle was like a pleasant but firm old country doctor whose job it was to treat the sores on the body politic. His task, as Earle liked to remind voters, was simple: "Our job is to prosecute abuses of power and to bring those abuses of power to the public."

When, on September 28, District Attorney Earle charged Congressman DeLay with one count of criminal conspiracy, the leader called a press conference to decry "this all-too-predictable result of a vengeful investigation led by a partisan fanatic."

The most blatantly partisan majority leader in the history of the U.S. House of Representatives went on to denounce Earle in the most personal of terms: "This morning, in an act of blatant political partisanship, a rogue district attorney in Travis County, Texas, named Ronnie Earlier charged me with one count of criminal conspiracy." It was, DeLay contended, "one of the weakest, most baseless indictments in American history."

The exact language that DeLay used that morning at his press conference is revealing as evidence of either sheer bluster or utter delusion. Most likely, it was a bit of both. The man who had for more than ten years used the powers of his office in the most startlingly political fashion—vengeful, mean, and retributive—seemed now to see himself reflected in Ronnie Earle: "Mr. Earle is abusing the power of his office to exact personal revenge for the role I played in the Texas Republican legislative campaign in 2002 and my advocacy for a new, fair, and constitutional congressional map for our state in 2003."

New and, according to the federal courts, constitutional it may have been, but few indeed would ever have called that map "fair."

To hear Congressman DeLay tell it, his connection with TRMPAC was tenuous, but nevertheless suited to the underhanded goals of "Mr. Earle, an unabashed partisan zealot . . . targeting a political action committee on whose advisory board I once served."

It was, of course, all semantics, on a par with the countless times DeLay had insisted with cable news interviewers that he had never been "censored by the House," figuring (usually rightly) that the follow-up question would never come: "But, you *were* admonished three times, were you not?"

The latest Austin indictment arose out of District Attorney Earle's earlier investigation, the one that had led to criminal charges being filed against DeLay operatives Ellis, Colyandro, and RoBold. The charge was essentially the same, only now focusing on the boss rather than his minions. DeLay, Earle charged, had acted as the ringleader of a money-laundering scheme that sought to circumvent the state's law prohibiting corporations from contributing directly to state political campaigns. In short, Earle alleged that DeLay had conspired to have corporate money raised by TRMPAC be funneled through the Republican National Committee and back to Texas state Republican candidates: a neat $190,000 handed off, passed, and received.

Word of this latest Austin indictment put others in the spotlight as well. Among them was Terry Nelson, the political director for President George W. Bush's 2004 reelection campaign. According to the indictment, Nelson, acting on behalf of the Republican National Committee (RNC), had accepted TRMPAC's check for $190,000—$155,000 of it coming from corporate donations—only to funnel that same $190,000, dollar for dollar, back to individual Republican state legislative candidates in Texas.

What all this amounted to, said Fred Wertheimer, the head of Democracy 21 and a longtime advocate of strict campaign finance laws, was a classic example of the DeLay system at work, in which "you had corporations who really weren't interested in Texas politics giving large sums to TRMPAC because they were interested in the power of House majority leader DeLay."

DeLay, Democratic lawyer Stan Brand noted, had written a new chapter in campaign financing history, "which was exporting the federal power of his office back to his state."*

The real drama now shifted to Washington, where Leader DeLay was, at long last, forced—if only temporarily—to relinquish his hard-earned title.

Within hours of the indictment being made public in Austin, House Republicans met and chose Whip Roy Blunt of Missouri as their acting leader.

Conservative senior Republican Zach Wamp of Tennessee expressed the feelings of many that day: DeLay, Wamp admitted, might be right, but it didn't matter. The party had a PR disaster on its hands. And there was nowhere for Tom DeLay to go but back into shadow.

Ever since *l'affaire* Schiavo, DeLay had seemed to increasingly relish the spotlight. His successor, Blunt, was the opposite. Blunt, said Democratic representative Barney Frank, was just a "very, very low-profile guy for this kind of job."

Low profile, but well experienced. At age fifty-five, Blunt was a longtime protégé of John Ashcroft, the former Missouri governor, U.S. senator, and attorney general in the Bush II administration.† Blunt's father had been a state representative. His son Matt was the current governor, having previously served as secretary of state. Blunt himself had once been Missouri secretary of state—and, for four years, president of his alma mater, Southwest Baptist University. His wife, Abigail Perlman, was a lobbyist for Altria Group Inc., the parent com-

---

*Brand was a former general counsel to the U.S. House of Representatives when it was under Democratic control. He is widely recognized as a leading expert on campaign finance laws. *New York Times*, 9/29/05.

†Ashcroft himself had joined K Street a mere ten months after resigning the attorney generalship. Corporate America, he told the *New York Times*, "need[s] someone who can take threatening circumstances and neutralize them. I'll be a lightning rod for people facing serious challenges." Ashcroft's staff boasted a former chief of staff to the attorney general, David T. Ayres; a former press secretary to Vice President Dick Cheney, Glover Weiss; and Republican fund-raiser C. T. Gaynor II, who helped raise more than $300 million in the 2004 election. *New York Times*, 3/17/06.

pany of Philip Morris.* His other son, Andrew, was a Missouri-based
Philip Morris lobbyist. And his daughter, Amy, made it a threesome:
she too was a lobbyist.

Elected to the House in 1996, Blunt had been leapfrogged by
DeLay over other, more senior members and made chief deputy whip
in only his second term in office. Blunt was said to be a better listener
than DeLay, but no less dogged in his doctrinaire approach and hard-
ball style. "Roy would listen to me, and then he would beat me the next
day anyway," recalled moderate Delaware Republican congressman
Mike Castle, adding, "These guys are all right out of the school of Tom
DeLay." Both men employed fund-raiser Jim Ellis—simultaneously at
times—and neither was squeamish about taking money from Jack
Abramoff.

As the Associated Press's John Solomon and Sharon Theimer
demonstrated, the thread running through DeLay Inc. also found its
way into Blunt's PAC, the Rely on Your Beliefs Fund (known as the
ROY B Fund). In short, Solomon and Theimer concluded, "Tom
DeLay deliberately raised more money than he needed to throw parties at the 2000 [Philadelphia Republican] presidential convention,
then diverted some of the excess to longtime ally Roy Blunt through a
series of donations that benefited both men's causes." But then, according to an aide to Blunt, "The fact that DeLay's charity, Christine
DeLay's consulting firm, and Blunt's son were beneficiaries was a
coincidence."

All you had to do was follow the money. Take, for example, the
$150,000 transferred from the DeLay side to the Blunt side of the
equation in the spring of 2000.

Well in advance of that summer's GOP national convention,
ARMPAC's convention fund had sent $50,000 to the ROY B Fund on
March 31. Eight days later, on April 7, the ROY B Fund reciprocated
by donating $10,000 to DeLay's private charity for children (the
DeLay Foundation). That same day, the ROY B Fund made the first
of several payments during a three-week period (April 7–May 1) total-

---

*During the 2003–4 election cycle, Blunt's "527" committee brought in a total of $109,452 in
contributions from the Altria Group. *Washington Post*, 1/29/06.

ing $40,000 to Ed Buckham's Alexander Strategy Group, where worked one Christine DeLay.

There was more.

On May 24, 2000, just as DeLay was about to leave for Scotland with Abramoff, the ARMPAC convention fund transferred $100,000 to the ROY B Fund. Three weeks later, on June 15, the ROY B Fund turned around and donated the same amount—surprise, surprise—to the Missouri Republican Party, which then spent more than $160,000 to help son Matt in his successful campaign to become secretary of state.

Nor did the exchanges end with the November 2000 election. Shortly before the election, ARMPAC gifted the Missouri Republican Party with $50,000. A month later, the Missouri Republican Party sent the same $50,000 back to ARMPAC's nonfederal account, the one that could be tapped for contributions to Republican candidates for state office.

In the words of the longtime Blunt aide, these were all just a bunch of "unrelated activities."

In a September 29, 2005, editorial, "Tom DeLay Behind the Curtain," the *New York Times* called on DeLay to resign his leadership position. "The imperious Texan," declared the *Times*, "is an increasing embarrassment to his party, turning its majority into an undisguised fountain of patronage and an ideological cudgel while skirting the bounds of campaign law." But then that was just the liberal *Times* expressing itself. The White House didn't much care what the *Times* had to say, and Tom DeLay cared even less.

Unfortunately for the leader, the bad news that summer wasn't lost on fellow Republicans. First there had been the Schiavo debacle—now thought to have been badly bungled by one and all, but especially by the Rove favorite Senate majority leader Bill Frist. Then, Rove, along with Vice President Cheney's close confidant and chief of staff, I. Lewis "Scooter" Libby, had both been hauled before a federal grand jury. At issue were the alleged roles they played in the outing by right-wing columnist Robert Novak of CIA covert operative Valerie Plame, former U.S. ambassador and White House critic Joe Wilson's wife. Meanwhile, the stench of the Abramoff scandal was growing daily.

Then there had been Katrina. As far as the public was concerned, a single photograph had apparently said it all: the image persisted of the airborne president, seemingly disengaged, peering out the window of Air Force One, while far below him, fanning out over the vast Mississippi Delta, the immensity of the damage wrought by Katrina lay exposed like a gaping wound.

It was, for many, the defining moment in the second Bush presidency. And it gave new meaning to all the other mischances: the Iraq War, the Schiavo episode, the fight over the courts, the Plame case, the Abramoff scandals—and now Tom DeLay's Texas tribulations.

What was a good Republican operative to do—or say—in the face of all this?

"Even though DeLay had nothing to do with Frist, and Frist has nothing to do with Abramoff, how does it look? Not good" was how Bill Kristol put it. When the *Weekly Standard* editor, Fox News contributor, Murdoch media supremo, and Harvard-educated neocon intellectual Kristol was worried, it followed that the malaise within Republican ranks was both general and deep.

The latest *New York Times*/CBS Poll now showed Congress with an approval rating of 34 percent. The picture, said a Republican strategist, was "grim."

"But in the glass-and-steel buildings" of K Street, wrote the *Los Angeles Times*'s Tom Hamburger and Peter Wallsten, the former majority leader's influence was still strong. DeLay had, it turned out, assigned a member of the leadership to keep K Street in line: Roy Blunt, truly the man of a thousand lobbyists.*

Within the DeLay camp, despite the setback in Austin, there was

---

*Where a couple of years ago all those successful Republican lobbyists had been hot, hot, hot, now they were trying hard to escape attention. The most successful—and best connected—of the lot included former Michigan governor John Engler—whom George W. Bush had once considered for vice president—who now headed the National Association of Manufacturers; former commerce secretary Don Evans, now in charge of the Financial Services Forum; and Marc Racicot, the former Montana governor and chairman of the Republican National Committee during the Florida recount, who now headed the American Insurance Association.

no letup in braggadocio. Gary Bauer took time off from his busy work as president of the right-wing American Values group to call the former leader and "assure him of the robust support that awaited him at a planned speech to evangelical supporters of Israel that night." DeLay showed up for the event and pronounced himself unafraid: "I fear no evil." He was roundly cheered.

Down in Texas, while DeLay cronies went about denouncing Ronnie Earle, the veteran Texas Democrat A. R. "Babe" Schwartz, for twenty-five years state senator from the coastal region around Galveston, told a different story. The former leader, Schwartz said, had been "gut-shot politically." One of the wise old men of Texas politics, Schwartz said an early eulogy for DeLay: "You can take a glancing blow sometimes, you can be accused of many things and still get elected to public office. But an indictment for a felony, no matter how much yelling you do about how false and flimsy and how fake it is, the public says the guy got indicted, and where there's smoke there's probably fire."

With the November 2006 general election just thirteen months away, DeLay already had a formidable opponent, former U.S. representative Nick Lampson.

In part this was DeLay's own fault. Lampson, a four-term moderate Democrat, had been one of the victims of the Texas Republican congressional gerrymander. DeLay had then compounded his problem by shifting Democratic voters into his supposedly safe "Texas 22" congressional district. The strategy had almost immediately been called into question when a poorly financed and relatively unknown Democrat named Richard Morrison had held DeLay down to 55 percent of the vote in 2004, 10–15 percentage points less than in previous years.*

A forceful reminder of just how rich Tom DeLay's legacy was came by way of an October 3 story in the *Washington Post*. "DeLay's Influence Transcends His Title" ran the headline. In a way, the story was the usual

---

*DeLay spent $3.1 million in the race versus Morrison's paltry $685,000.

one of the leader and his flock, mostly former staffers become lobby-ists. Many of the familiar names were there: K Street Project cofounder, Pennsylvania Republican senator, and Schiavo family spokesman Rick Santorum; Ed Buckham of the Alexander Strategy Group and a host of former DeLay staffers including Susan Hirschmann, Tony Rudy, and Karl Gallant; former U.S. representative turned lobbyist Bill Paxon of New York (a plotting-mate in the failed effort to oust Speaker Gingrich those many years ago); Acting Majority Leader Blunt, Republican Congressional Campaign chairman Tom Reynolds of New York, and Deputy Whip Eric Cantor of Virginia (all of them "social conservatives who support such pro-business policies as deregulation and tax cuts"); and, of course, Grover Norquist.

Some members of the old gang merited special praise. Speaker Hastert's deputy chief of staff Mike Stokke—he would later be found at the center of the purported cover-up of the Mark Foley affair in September 2006—singled out former DeLay chief of staff Hirschmann, recently minted as a lobbyist for Big Pharma, among other clients. "Having DeLay in her background is a strength," said Stokke. "Having worked for Tom brings credibility."

As the authors pointed out, Tom DeLay's Texas problems had as yet to change anything on K Street: "Rather than going under-ground, the project has gone unabashedly public," with a Web site that provided news about lobbying jobs. The site was, as the authors also pointed out, maintained by Grover Norquist.*

☆　☆　☆

---

*The K Street Project Web site is still in business. A quick visit to the site takes a first-time visitor to "The True K Street Project Revealed." There we learn that "the goal of the K Street Project was and is quite simple. We advise companies and trade associations to hire men and women who understand free-market economics, who support their principled positions for free trade, against tort law abuse, and for lower and more transparent taxes."

Of course, the Web site also offers "K Street Project Job Postings," a weekly compilation of lobbying-shop jobs, from entry level to executive suite; "Word on the Street: The Latest K Street Buzz," mostly about hirings; "Street Cleaning: Moving 'em Up or Out," about promotions, retirements, and resignations on K Street; "Corner Gang," about new hires and new accounts; and links, including one to UnionFacts.com ("The Center for Union Facts has gathered a wealth of information about the size, scope, political activities, and criminal activity of the labor move-ment in the United States of America"). For more, go to http://www.kstreetproject.com.

Six days after Tom DeLay was indicted on conspiracy charges, a third Texas grand jury indicted him on the far more serious crime of money laundering, a first-degree felony that could carry a long prison sentence. (The earlier conspiracy charge was a fourth-degree felony, punishable by a two-year sentence in state prison.)

DeLay's lawyers claimed that District Attorney Earle had only returned to the grand jury after defense attorneys had filed a motion to dismiss the first count as based on a law that did not exist in 2002.

Earle countered, saying that the two new charges—money laundering and conspiracy to commit money laundering—had been filed in response to new information that had come to the attention of his office over the weekend.

And, indeed, based on an account in the next day's *Washington Post* (October 7), the basis for the new charges was not hard to fathom. "DeLay Meeting, RNC Actions Coincided: Financial Transactions Began on Day Texan Met with Fundraiser" read the headline. The story recounted how DeLay had met at his Capitol office for at least thirty minutes on October 2, 2002, with top fund-raiser Jim Ellis, who had earlier given the Republican National Committee a check for $190,000. Later that same day, the RNC began processing checks written out to seven Republican candidates for the Texas legislature. The total value of the checks: $190,000.

The *Post* article went on to quote from Travis County court papers. The key sequence of events in the alleged money-laundering scheme, District Attorney Earle charged, began on September 11, 2002, when DeLay fund-raiser Ellis "did request and propose" that an arm of the RNC make payments to the Texas candidates following receipt of the $190,000 from TRMPAC. The next day, according to the indictment, a check in that amount was delivered to the Republican National State Elections Committee, an arm of the RNC. The indictment also charged that the check came with a list of Texas state candidates to whose campaigns exact amounts of money should be funneled.

According to other documents, already disclosed in the earlier civil trial of former TRMPAC treasurer Bill Ceverha in Austin, a staff member in then RNC chairman Mark Racicot's office requested on October 2 that checks be cut and sent to the Texas Republican candidates.* The next day, Racicot arrived in Texas to join a series of events sponsored by TRMPAC, including a dinner with Republican governor Rick Perry. The checks to the seven Texas Republican candidates were cut and mailed one day later, on October 4.

Back in Washington, the former majority leader was showing that he had not lost his touch—and that he had learned much from the 2003 fight over the Medicare Prescription Drug Act. At issue this time was an oil refinery bill carried by Joe Barton of Dallas. In the wake of Hurricane Katrina, prices at the pump had spiraled. Polls—as if anyone needed to consult a poll—showed that Americans were angry, mighty angry about paying $3 and more a gallon for gas.

Energy-company-friendly House Republicans were quick to seize on a good thing, tying a purported crackdown on price gouging at the pump with a measure to expedite construction of new refineries. This "bold plan for the nation's energy future," in the words of Speaker J. Dennis Hastert was basically a sweetheart deal for the industry.

It could have been worse: the White House had added language that would have made it easier for utilities to expand—without adding new antipollution devices. That was too much even for some House Republicans.

Sherwood Boehlert, the moderate New York Republican who chaired the House Science Committee, argued against the measure: "We're enriching people, but we are not doing anything to give the little guy a break."

As the "no" votes began to tally up, the leadership team—Speaker Hastert, Acting Leader Blunt, and, yes, former leader DeLay—could be seen twisting arms on the floor. There was Hastert, seen "repeatedly cornering" a senior Florida congressman, Bill Young, heretofore an opponent of the bill; here, Blunt going after a moderate Republican from the Philadelphia suburbs; and over there, in that corner, DeLay

---

*Mark Racicot would later trade in his RNC chairmanship for a job at the more lucrative K Street fraternity.

cajoling a Maryland congressman. In the words of the *New York Times*, DeLay might have been "officially out of power, but not out of practice as a persuader."

This time the Republican leadership didn't have to extend the vote for three hours. It only took forty-five minutes—it had been scheduled for five—to get what they wanted. In the end, a baker's dozen of Republicans, including Chairman Boehlert, voted "no," along with every single Democrat.

But the measure passed. The final tally was 212–210.

Henry Waxman, the veteran California liberal, got it best: "Doesn't this make the House a banana republic?"

A banana republic it might have been, but one whose real leader was at least temporarily shorn of office.

The title of a *New York Times* article perfectly encapsulated the situation as it then stood: "DeLay Is a King Without a Crown in the House." The piece cited not merely DeLay's leading role in the refinery bill, but a host of other illustrative tales. House Appropriations Committee chairman Jerry Lewis needs some advice on a particularly tough bill? Call for Tom DeLay. The top dogs on the Budget Committee hold a secret meeting. DeLay is asked to sit in. The Republican leadership is caught short on votes for an energy bill. The former leader is out on the floor acting suspiciously as if he's still the leader.

DeLay, a senior Republican told the *Times*, was "still driving the agenda." Then he added, "I guess he has to because he is the only guy who can get this done."

It was one of those little stories, buried inside the newspaper, but it had to ring bells everywhere in the world of DeLay Inc. An AP dispatch datelined Austin reported that Travis County district attorney Earle had subpoenaed telephone records for former leader DeLay's home in Sugar Land—and phone records for two numbers used by daughter and fund-raiser Danielle DeLay Ferro.

DeLay's lawyers were soon back in court, this time seeking a new trial judge. DeLay's attorneys argued that state district judge Bob

Perkins of Austin, having made contributions to the Democratic Party and to liberal organizations that had demonstrated "a personal bias" against DeLay, should be removed from the case.* Judge Perkins punted, ruling that the decision as to who should try the case would have to be made by the region's chief administrative judge, a Republican.

The same October 20 session also marked defendant DeLay's first appearance in open court. That in itself was occasion for press coverage, but what really raised eyebrows was how the former leader returned from Washington to Houston, via a corporate jet owned by R.J. Reynolds, a longtime contributor to DeLay causes (including his legal defense fund). Other R.J. Reynolds/DeLay connections would soon be revealed. When the House Ethics Committee announced that it had hired a new chief counsel, William V. O'Reilly, a former partner in the Washington office of the Jones Day law firm, the *Washington Post* reported that O'Reilly had previously represented the tobacco giant in antitrust litigation.

It was all musical chairs, though, from there on. First, Administrative Judge B. B. Schraub, the Republican appointee, removed Judge Perkins, the elected Democrat. But then, following an official complaint about Schraub's links with Republicans, Schraub removed himself. Next came the turn of Texas Supreme Court chief justice Wallace B. Jefferson, another Republican. Jefferson, an African-American appointed chief justice by Republican governor Rick Perry in 2004, had had as his campaign treasurer in 2002 none other than indicted TRMPAC treasurer Bill Ceverha—and had been endorsed by the same group. The hue and cry again went up from Democrats about Jefferson and his GOP ties.

Ultimately, the torch, if such it can be called, was passed to Judge Pat Priest, whose most recent political donations had been three checks of $150 each to Democratic state house candidates in 2004. "The last man standing" in the words of the *New York Times*'s Ralph Blumenthal, Priest was a sixty-five-year-old, semiretired judge from

---

*Judge Perkins had contributed $5,485 to Democratic campaigns since 2000, including $400 to the Democratic National Committee and $400 on MoveOn.org. *Washington Post*, 10/22/05.

San Antonio. He got the short straw, Judge Priest told Blumenthal, not because he had contributed large sums to political candidates, but because, unlike many of his fellow Texas judges, he had given so little. "That's it," said Priest. "I'm a tightwad."

If DeLay couldn't choose his judge, he surely couldn't choose his accuser. But he tried his best to put Ronnie Earle on the defensive. Throughout October, television ads sponsored by the right-wing Free Enterprise Fund flooded the airwaves in Austin. While the voice-over pronounced "Bad, Ronnie, bad," the screen showed a drooling attack dog.

In Washington, DeLay was behaving just as aggressively. When fellow House Republicans threatened to confront the former leader at a three-hour closed-door session, DeLay quickly put the dissidents in their place. The revolt went nowhere. While one anonymous Republican legislator told reporters that DeLay "knows [that] every day that goes by is a day he grows weaker," a senior House Republican, Ray LaHood of Illinois, put a different spin on things. DeLay's campaign to hold on to power had been "very effective," said LaHood. "People are still afraid of him."

Just as Tom DeLay was still afraid of Ronnie Earle. While DeLay's lawyers claimed that Earle had offered their client a deal—a guilty plea in return for lowering the charge to a misdemeanor—now it turned out that it was DeLay's lawyers who had first approached the district attorney with such a deal.

It was at an August meeting with Earle's staff that DeLay first acknowledged to prosecutors that he knew of—and supported—the transfers in 2002 of $190,000 in mostly corporate funds from TRM-PAC to the Republican National Committee. That, in itself, was not the problem. The problem was that DeLay also acknowledged knowing about—and supporting—the transfer of the same $190,000 from the RNC back to Republican legislative candidates in Texas.

Approached by DeLay's Washington lawyer, former Republican

congressman Ed Bethune, District Attorney Earle seemed prepared to accept the deal—if DeLay and fund-raiser Jim Ellis would also agree to serve three-to-four-month jail terms.

What everyone knew, in Austin and in Washington, was that a jail sentence would mark the end of the former leader's comeback trail. On that rock, the deal foundered. Said another of his lawyers, "DeLay was at peace with not doing that. He is ready to fight about it."

The impasse in Austin didn't keep DeLay supporters from raising more money on his behalf. When a group of sixty-seven lobbyists sponsored a fund-raiser in Washington for the former majority leader, the hosts included Federalist Group lobbyist and former legislative director Drew Maloney and Big Pharma lobbyist and former chief of staff Susan Hirschmann. As a Bloomberg dispatch put it, "DeLay has worked hard throughout his tenure to champion legislation favored by business lobbyists. Last night, those lobbyists were working hard for him."

The event was rich with energy lobbyists, including representatives of Reliant, ExxonMobil, Chevron Corp., the Washington-based trade associations the American Petroleum Institute and the Edison Electric Institute (whose members included nuclear-energy giant Entergy Corp. and San Francisco–based PG&E Corp.). Not exactly surprising since the recently passed energy bill had included $14.6 billion in industry subsidies.

When individual Republican congressmen began returning to Washington in January 2006, the handwriting was on the wall. The combination of mounting publicity from the Abramoff scandal along with the money-laundering indictments in Austin had made the former majority leader radioactive.*

"Tom DeLay's bid to return as Majority Leader in the House of

---

*On December 5, the judge in Austin dropped the conspiracy charges against DeLay, but let stand the more serious money-laundering charge.

Representatives," a dispatch from Reuters reported, "was in mounting jeopardy."

Now too, individual House Republicans were actually going on record saying they would not only not welcome a return, they were even prepared to vote down the former leader. Ray LaHood of Illinois, a senior Republican first elected in the Gingrich sweep of 1994, didn't mince words, telling Reuters, "I would not support him for majority leader."

Him, of course, was DeLay.

Others felt the same way. Indiana congressman Mike Pence, the chairman of the right-wing Republican Study Group—which DeLay had once headed—was unprepared to offer the former leader his support. Worse, Pence told Reuters, that he was "troubled" about the Abramoff allegations involving the congressmen and his staff.

The handful of moderate Republicans—most of them from the Northeast—were more troubled still. Connecticut congressman Christopher Shays, a frequent DeLay critic who had plenty of first-hand knowledge of just how harsh the bullwhip's sting could be when wielded by the master, was blunt: "Jack Abramoff's guilty plea and his close association with Tom DeLay underscore the need for a new majority leader."

With the leadership vote scheduled for January 31, when the Congress formally reassembled, the news was all bad now for the former leader.

The worst news of all came in published reports suggesting that Republicans within the leadership were quietly turning against DeLay. Acting Majority Leader Blunt was said to want to remove the word *acting* from his title, while Chairman John Boehner of the Education and the Workforce Committee was also reckoned to be close to throwing his hat into the ring. Boehner was an especially interesting case, having previously tangled with the Boss; but then also having, rather ostentatiously, come to DeLay's defense in the months leading up to his indictment.

With Blunt and Boehner lurking in the wings, DeLay's fate grew more and more precarious. A *Washington Post* headline of January 7 underscored the point: "Tide Turning Against DeLay." Shays, along with Representatives Charlie Bass (N.H.) and Jeff Flake (Ariz.), was reported to have prepared a petition supported by perhaps three dozen members calling for a special leadership election.

Besides Blunt and Boehner, others were now looking longingly at the big job. A host of GOP bigwigs—among them Appropriations Committee chairman Jerry Lewis of California; right-wing congressman Pence of Indiana; moderate conservative John Shadegg of Arizona; and the heretofore loyal DeLayite Tom Reynolds of New York, the chairman of the House Republican campaign committee—were all said to be interested in DeLay's old job.

Eventually, even the Boss knew the game was up. An Associated Press dispatch of January 7 told the story: "Text of Letter from DeLay to Hastert." The letter ran a very short three paragraphs and included this: "The job of majority leader and the mandate of the Republican majority are too important to be hamstrung, even for a few months, by personal distractions."

Personal distractions. Who but Tom DeLay could have phrased it so?

In his letter to Speaker Hastert—a suddenly much empowered Speaker Hastert—DeLay announced that he would be "reclaiming" his seat (and seniority) as an "Appropriator"—his long tenure presumably entitling him to become one of the "cardinals" of that most powerful of committees. He also promised that he would be seeking reelection to a twelfth term representing the Twenty-second Congressional District of Texas.

In closing, the former leader signed himself, "Sincerely, Tom DeLay."

The leadership battle royal that followed pitted Blunt, Boehner (whose close ties to K Street were also well known),* Pence, and Shadegg.

Washington Post reporter Tom Edsall reported that Boehner's Freedom Project PAC received $572,719 in 2003–4 alone, of which $292,570 came from employees or lobbyists of private student-lending companies and for-profit educational institutions. Boehner, who was instrumental in helping DeLay and Santorum set up the K Street Project, was by now

In the end, Boehner prevailed, while Blunt at last got to take the *acting* part out of his title. He was back to being majority whip.

The former leader soon discovered the pitfalls of being a former leader. Within weeks of resigning the leadership, DeLay learned that funding for his pet project, a $500 million project for research and development of "ultra deepwater" drilling for oil and gas, had been cut from the Department of Energy's 2007 budget. The fine print told a sadder story still: buried inside the 1,220-page report was word that the administration was seeking to forgo the project entirely.

Critics had long argued that the language of the bill virtually ensured that funding for the project would go to a nonprofit organization, the Research Partnership to Secure Energy for America. Headquarters for the partnership: Sugar Land, Texas.

Language for the project had not been included in the original energy bill, but had been slipped in overnight by four of the leading negotiators. Democratic congressman Ed Markey, a senior member of the Energy Committee, complained bitterly, "It was snuck in at the last minute as a virtual giveaway to the most profitable companies in the history of the world."

Well, now with the leadership gone, so was the $500 million.

Facing three challengers in a March 2006 Republican primary, the former leader was reduced not only to running for his political life, but scrounging for every penny he could find to finance his reelection campaign.

"I'm like a cemetery! I'll take anything!" DeLay hollered out as he hosted a GOP live auction in Houston. The "Sugar Land Republican and certified auctioneer," as the *Houston Chronicle* had it, raised all of $16,600 that night. Truly chicken feed by old-time DeLay standards.

It must have been quite an event though, for Houston bootmaker

---

chairman of the House Education and the Workforce Committee, whose oversight extended to for-profit educational institutions and issues such as student loans. *Washington Post,* 1/29/06.

Rocky Carroll was inspired to contribute five more pairs of handmade boots.

Well, every dime—and every pair of boots—counted. DeLay's Democratic opponent in November, former representative Nick Lampson, had already raised $1.8 million since announcing his candidacy in May 2005. DeLay, meanwhile, had raised more than $3.2 million and spent more than $2 million of it, much of it on direct mail and telemarketing between January 1, 2005, and February 15, 2006.

It was all part of the cost of "retail electioneering" in the age of DeLay.

To no one's particular surprise, DeLay handily survived the Republican primary. What he did not survive was the latest spate of news out of Washington, beginning with the guilty plea of his former deputy chief of staff Tony C. Rudy on March 31. The plea bargain with federal prosecutors directly implicated former DeLay chief of staff and Alexander Strategy Group lobbyist Ed Buckham, who remained the former leader's closest personal and political confidant.

It was now curtains for the former leader. On the evening of April 3, DeLay told allies in the House—among then Congressional Campaign chairman Tom Reynolds of upstate New York—that he planned on giving up his seat. The race against Nick Lampson in Texas, DeLay was quoted as saying, appeared "increasingly unwinnable."

The problem for Republicans lay in the fine print: under Texas election laws, a candidate must die, be convicted of a felony, or move out of the district to be removed from the November ballot. As yet, the Republicans seemed to have none of these working in their favor. About to turn fifty-nine that Sunday, DeLay's health appeared fairly robust. So far, he had not been convicted of anything. And for all anyone knew, the former leader was still a Texan.

Though DeLay told supporters that he was "at peace" with his decision to resign, friends found him a dispirited figure. The Reverend Rick Scarborough, the founder of Vision America and former pastor of a Houston church that DeLay sometimes attended, reported running into the former leader at the Sugar Creek Baptist Church the Saturday before he made his resignation announcement. DeLay, Scarborough said, had pulled him aside, saying that "he had finally made a decision that was going to be difficult for him to announce, but that God wanted him to get out of that race."

The deed was done: on June 9, 2006, Tom DeLay officially became not only a former leader, but a former congressman as well.

CHAPTER SIXTEEN

✶

Casino Jack Sinks

On September 21, 2003, reporter Julia Robb of the *Town Talk* newspaper in Alexandria, Louisiana, broke the story that the Coushatta tribe had paid Michael Scanlon's firm $13.7 million. Robb was arguably the unsung hero in the whole sordid tale of Abramoff and Scanlon, and her report, "Millions Misspent," opened a stream of inquiry. By early 2004, the Miami-based leadership at Greenberg Traurig had become worried—deeply worried—about its star D.C. lobbyist and his ways. News of the *Town Talk* story had begun reverberating among Indian tribal leadership, among the Washington press corps, among rivals on K Street, in the halls of Congress, and finally even in Miami.

Greenberg lawyers representing Abramoff in the SunCruz bankruptcy now demanded to meet with Scanlon.* Quizzed at the Miami headquarters of the law firm in January 2004, Scanlon confessed that he had paid Abramoff $19 million out of the fees paid him by Indian tribal clients. The bells were now ringing everywhere.

The dam burst wide on February 22, 2004, when a front-page story in the *Washington Post* detailed how Abramoff and Scanlon had charged Indian tribes more than $45 million for three years' worth of

---

*According the *New York Times*, Scanlon "at times used an office at Greenberg Traurig, although he was never a firm employee."

lobbying and "grassroots" work. At last glance, the number was $82 million—and still climbing.

A week later, on March 2, 2004, Greenberg Traurig fired its star lobbyist. And shortly afterward, the Senate Indian Affairs Committee opened an investigation, led by its then chairman, Native American Colorado senator Ben Nighthorse Campbell; and by Campbell's successors, John McCain and Byron Dorgan.

"The committee," Dorgan would later explain, "did not need a Deep Throat to tell us to follow the money." The reams of e-mails sent and received by Jack Abramoff and Michael Scanlon, Dorgan added, would be all that was needed to convict the two men—together with their minions and, likely too, their sponsors.*

Yet even as the unwanted spotlight shown ever brighter upon him, Abramoff remained, as one writer put it, "a lobbyist in full." As investigation after investigation swirled about him, Abramoff continued to involve himself in politics. For all his problems, Abramoff still managed to raise $100,000 for Bush/Cheney 2004—enough to earn him the cherished designation Bush Pioneer.

Evidently, it wasn't enough.

On August 11, 2005, Abramoff and his former SunCruz partner Adam Kidan were indicted by a federal grand jury in Fort Lauderdale. The pair were charged with five counts of wire fraud and one count of conspiracy. Each of the six counts carried a possible prison term of five years and a $250,000 fine.

It took four and a half years, but in late September 2005—just as Jack Abramoff's career as a lobbyist was cratering—Florida authorities arrested three men in connection with the murder of Gus Boulis, the former SunCruz owner.

---

*An AP account pointed out, "The Senate Indian Affairs Committee blocked out references to [Senator John] Cornyn in the e-mails it released last week." The former Texas Supreme Court justice and state attorney general had, after all, become Chairman John McCain's Republican colleague in Capitol Hill's upper chamber. Fortunately, as the AP's Suzanne Gamboa also noted, "In previous Reed e-mails released by the committee, Cornyn's name was not removed."

Anthony Moscatiello, sixty-seven, arrested in Queens, New York, was charged with murder, conspiracy, and solicitation to commit murder. The same charges were filed against Anthony Ferrari, forty-eight, who was arrested in Miami Beach. A third man, James "Pudgy" Fiorillo, twenty-eight, was arrested in Palm Coast and charged with murder and conspiracy.

Moscatiello, whom authorities identified as a bookkeeper for the Gambino crime family, had been indicted along with John Gotti's brother Gene in 1983. But while Gene Gotti went to prison, the charges against Moscatiello—who had also turned up in FBI wiretaps of the Gottis—were dropped.

News accounts at the time of the 2005 arrests noted that homicide detectives were investigating a payment of $145,000 from SunCruz to Moscatiello and his daughter for consulting work and "site inspections" in 2001. According to court documents, "There is no evidence that food or drink was provided or that any consulting documents were prepared." Ferrari too had been in the employ of SunCruz in 2001, having been paid $95,000 for "surveillance services."

Abramoff was clearly now in grave trouble. But in one of those moments that are so delicious to political junkies, a sideshow to *l'affaire* Abramoff soon developed, one that brought together such disparate but fascinating players as the Tyco company, Tom DeLay, Karl Rove, Harriet Miers, and Alberto Gonzales, and revealed yet another nest of connections that indicated how things were really run in the administration of George W. Bush. On September 21, 2005, the *Los Angeles Times* headlined, "Tyco Lobbyist Urges Senators to Support Tyco Lawyer Nomination."

In that story, Tyco International lobbyist Edward Ayoob acknowledged that he had been lobbying senators to approve the nomination of the company's top lawyer, Timothy E. Flanigan, to be deputy U.S. attorney general.

As we have seen, Flanigan, a former U.S. Supreme Court clerk, had been one of the Republican lawyers during the Florida recount of 2000. Prior to becoming general counsel of Tyco in late 2002, Flanigan had served as deputy to then White House counsel Alberto Gonzales. In that job, Flanigan had given legal teeth to the administration's policies regarding treatment of "enemy combatants."

Tyco lobbyist Ayoob had previously worked alongside Abramoff in the "governmental affairs" unit at Greenberg Traurig; Flanigan had employed Abramoff to lobby on behalf of Tyco. The Abramoff connection had come about in response to a 2003 bill before Congress that would have levied higher taxes on Tyco—the conglomerate made infamous by its convicted former CEO L. Dennis Kozlowski—after the company moved its corporate headquarters to Bermuda. The Democratic-sponsored legislation would have imposed higher taxes on companies, such as Tyco, that moved offshore to cut their tax bills.

Flanigan, in a written response to questions from Senate Judiciary Committee members, defended his hiring of Abramoff, noting that he had been advised, "Mr. Abramoff had good relationships with members of Congress, including Rep. Tom DeLay." Just how good those connections were was soon made apparent to Tyco. Abramoff, Flanigan said, "told us that he had contact with Mr. Karl Rove."

If Jack Abramoff had, in fact, ventured forth to the White House and the office of the counselor to the president on behalf of Tyco, he would have found a familiar face guarding the gate. Rove's personal assistant, Susan Ralston, had previously worked as Abramoff's personal assistant.

It was a small world, Washington was, in the glory days of Tom DeLay. Small enough so that, in 2005, Ralston herself became the subject of a thousand-word profile in the *New York Times*. Reporter Anne Kornblut wrote that "Susan B. Ralston, 38, has worked as an assistant and side-by-side adviser to Karl Rove since February 2001, helping manage his e-mail, meetings and phone calls from her perch near his office in the West Wing. That has made her an important witness in the C.I.A. leak investigation, as the special prosecutor has sought to determine whether Mr. Rove misled investigators."

A Filipino-American born in Chicago, married without children, living in the Virginia suburbs, Ralston was said to have testified twice before the grand jury in the Plame case and to have been interviewed as well by federal investigators with regard to the Abramoff scandals.

Though "published rumors suggest that Mr. Abramoff sought to place Ms. Ralston with Mr. Rove after the 2000 election to gain easy access to him," Kornblut wrote, "her colleagues said that was not the case."

Colleagues, in fact, portrayed her to the *Times* as "an up-close and innocent witness." Said a close friend, a Republican lobbyist, "Susan is sharp as a tack and straight as an arrow, and so that's hopefully going to pay off now. . . . Because if you were not straight as an arrow in the midst of this whirlwind, you'd be in a world of hurt."

Kornblut asked Grover Norquist for his take on this matter. His reply: "Karl was looking for the most competent person around and stole her."

Come the release of the House Government Reform Committee's report *The Abramoff Investigation* and a slightly different picture of Susan Ralston emerged. The report showed that Abramoff and his Greenberg Traurig colleagues had billed clients—mostly Indian tribal clients—for some 485 White House contacts, including eighty-two e-mail and other contacts with the office of Karl Rove, sixty-nine of which were directed to Ralston, who, the records also showed, was on nine occasions treated to tickets to sporting events courtesy of Jack Abramoff. Like her boss, Rove, Ralston used a Republican National Committee rnc.com account for her e-mail.

Among the high-ranking Bush administration figures with whom Abramoff and his team had contact were Cheney policy advisers Ron Christie and Stephen Ruhlen, Attorney General John Ashcroft, White House intergovernmental affairs chief Ruben Barrales, and U.S. Trade Representative Robert Zoellick. The list was long.

From her initial job as executive assistant to the senior adviser to the president, Ralston had by 2005 ascended to the position of special assistant to the president and assistant to the senior adviser. In the words of the *Times*: "When Mr. Rove moved to the first floor from his second floor [White House] office, Ms. Ralston moved there, too." Ralston wasn't just in proximity to power, she now had it herself:

"People familiar with Ms. Ralston's work said she functions as Mr. Rove's own chief of staff."

Consider: Jack Abramoff's former executive assistant was by now somebody special. Special assistant to the president of the United States and de facto chief of staff to the senior adviser to the president of the United States.

That's who Susan Ralston was.

Needless to say, Abramoff's efforts on behalf of Tyco had been successful—and costly. Flanigan told committee members that he later discovered that as much as $1.5 million of the $2 million Tyco had paid GrassRoots Interactive, at Abramoff's direction, had been diverted to "entities controlled by Mr. Abramoff and were not used in furtherance of lobbying efforts on behalf of Tyco."

Himself now under the microscope—the Judiciary Committee's ranking minority member, Senator Patrick Leahy (D-Vt.), described his selection as another example of the Bush administration's "cultural of cronyism"—Flanigan, on October 8, 2005, was forced to ask the White House to withdraw his name from consideration as deputy attorney general of the United States, the second-highest-ranking job in the Department of Justice.*

Citing Flanigan's role in drawing up the administration's "torture papers," the American Civil Liberties Union hailed his withdrawal: "Flanigan has no business supervising prosecutors responsible for investigating and prosecuting torture and abuse that his own policies helped facilitate."

Among the "torture papers" cited by the ACLU was the infamous 2002 Justice Department memo that defined torture as having occurred only if the pain inflicted led to major organ failure or death. While Gonzales and Flanigan were not its authors, they had been briefed on the opinion, which was later withdrawn in 2004 when it became public.

Flanigan, had he been confirmed, would have succeeded career prosecutor James B. Comey as deputy attorney general. That fact alone gives

---

*Flanigan would later reemerge as a member of the unofficial team prepping Attorney General Gonzales for his Senate testimony in the U.S. attorney's scandal in April 2007.

pause, for it was Comey, in the guise of acting attorney general of the United States (after his then boss, John Ashcroft, had recused himself), who named career prosecutor and Chicago U.S. attorney Patrick J. Fitzgerald to investigate the "Plamegate" leaks involving right-wing columnist Robert Novak; CIA undercover operative Valerie Plame; her husband, former ambassador Joseph Wilson; the *New York Times*'s Judith Miller; and a host of top administration officials.

In doing so, Comey had given Fitzgerald virtual carte blanche. Quoting from Comey's December 30, 2003, authorizing letter to Fitzgerald: "By the authority vested in the Attorney General . . . I hereby give to you all the authority of the Attorney General . . . and I direct you to exercise that authority as Special Counsel independent of the supervision or control of any officer of the Department."

Would Flanigan have made that choice—or signed those papers? And how would a Deputy Attorney General Flanigan have handled the Abramoff investigation? Or any of the several other scandals that would soon emanate from the Department of Justice?

On November 21, 2005, Michael Scanlon entered into a plea bargain agreement with prosecutors from the Department of Justice—the same Justice Department where Tim Flanigan had, a few weeks earlier, almost became deputy attorney general. In exchange for his cooperation, Scanlon pled guilty to bribery charges that could put him in jail for as much as five years—and agreed to repay the tribes some $20 million. He also implicated his partner Jack Abramoff (referred to in court documents as "Lobbyist A") and "Representative #1," whom reporters quickly identified as Representative Bob Ney of Ohio. As the charge made clear, Scanlon and Lobbyist A had "provided a stream of things of value" to Representative #1, who stood all but accused of violating, among other federal criminal statutes, the Hobbs Act and the Honest Services law.

The headline in the *New York Times* was ominous: "Corruption Inquiry Threatens to Ensnare Lawmakers." More ominous still were stories in the *Washington Post* suggesting that Scanlon's cooperation had led to "a major advance in the 18-month federal investigation into alleged bribery and corruption involving the lobbyist, members of Congress and executive branch agencies," and that the joint Justice/FBI team looking into Abramoff's activities could number as many as forty investigators and prosecutors.

For the first time, an outline of the investigation was beginning to emerge, and its scope was now seen to be wide indeed. The probe was not just going to be about Abramoff and Scanlon. Names—congressional names—were being affixed to the probe, names such as DeLay and Ney, Doolittle and Rohrabacher. "The scrutiny of Mr. Ney has caught the attention of anxious lawmakers who have lobbying relationships of their own," wrote Carl Hulse in the *New York Times*. Writing in the *Wall Street Journal,* reporter Brody Mullins named more names, including those of Senator Conrad Burns,* former Interior Department deputy secretary J. Steven Griles (about whom we will soon learn more), former White House procurement officer David Safavian, and Republican fund-raiser Julie Doolittle, the wife of Congressman John Doolittle of California. Mullins went on to suggest that as many as five former top DeLay aides might be under investigation—among them Tony Rudy, Ed Buckham, and Susan Hirschmann—as well as former Doolittle chief of staff Kevin Ring, a member of Team Abramoff at Greenberg.

Writing in the *New York Times,* Anne Kornblut warned that investigators were particularly interested in "how Mr. Rudy, who left Mr. DeLay's office in 2001 to join Greenberg Traurig, and Mr. Volz, who left Mr. Ney's office in 2002 for that firm, obtained their positions." At the heart of the investigation, Kornblut suggested, was whether Abramoff had "solicited help from both men and their supervisors on Capitol Hill while helping arrange for high-paying positions."

Their supervisors. Meaning, Tom DeLay and Bob Ney.

---

*The three-term senator Burns, with a highly competitive reelection campaign looming in 2006, would increasingly become the focus of media attention in his home state. In a combative interview with the local independent newspaper the *Missoulian,* in January 2005, Burns claimed that his political enemies were behind stories linking him to Jack Abramoff. Said Senator Burns, "Until I am or I am not [charged], what makes it a story? Just your opponents." Jack Abramoff, said Burns, "was one bad apple in a bushel," adding, "We use lobbyists. I can't run an airline. I can't run a power company. There's a lot of things that I don't know very much about."

Kornblut carried the thread even further: Rudy, she noted, was now a partner at the Alexander Strategy Group, the lobbying firm run by DeLay's former chief of staff and longtime personal minister, Ed Buckham; and Alexander Strategy was now "under scrutiny for its ties to Mr. Abramoff and for putting Mr. DeLay's wife, Christine, on its payroll for several years."

There you had it: the congressman, his wife, his minister—and their world. All of them under the microscopic scrutiny of a forty-member team of investigators and prosecutors. Thanks to Jack Abramoff, Michael Scanlon, and Adam Kidan. Even the most corruption-weary Washingtonians could see that the probe might well encompass virtually the whole of DeLay Inc.

The Boss and his posse were behind a DOJ eight ball.

Six weeks later, on January 3, 2006, with both of his former business partners having pleaded out before him—Kidan had entered a plea of guilty to two counts of fraud and conspiracy in Miami on December 15 ("I played with the big boys, and this is the result," Kidan told *Newsday*. "I wish I had never met Jack")—Abramoff entered into the first of *his* two plea bargain agreements, this with federal prosecutors in Washington. Standing before U.S. district judge Ellen Huvelle, Abramoff pleaded guilty to three counts of fraud, tax evasion, and conspiracy to bribe public officials, charges that could land him a decade in federal prison. He also agreed to pay back $26 million to the tribes. And he implicated Tony Rudy.*

A day later, Abramoff traveled to Miami and stood, head bowed, before U.S. district judge Paul C. Huck. The *New York Times* reported that Abramoff and his lawyers had been in negotiations with federal prosecutors for some eighteen months, beginning around July 2004.

---

*A January 10, 2006, story in the *New York Times* by reporter Neil Lewis, "Team of Career Prosecutors Negotiated Lobbyist's Deal," should perhaps have sounded warning bells. While Abramoff's Washington plea deal had been announced to much fanfare before the cameras by a political appointee, Assistant Attorney General Alice Fisher—she was a protégée of Homeland Security Secretary Michael Chertoff—the newly named head of DOJ's criminal division, the hard lifting had been done by a team of nonpolitical career prosecutors led by Noel Hillman, the chief of DOJ's Office of Public Integrity, assisted by a longtime career assistant U.S. attorney in Miami named Mary Butler. Now, Hillman was about to be named to the federal district court in New Jersey.

Investigators had another source as well. The *Wall Street Journal* reported that Emily Miller had for some time been aiding in the Justice Department probe of Abramoff—and her former lover Michael Scanlon.

On March 29, Abramoff was sentenced in Miami to five years and ten months in federal prison for charges arising out of the SunCruz fraud.

Two days later, on March 31, 2006, Tony Rudy pleaded guilty in a Washington federal courtroom to conspiracy. He could face as much as five years in prison. He was also fined $250,000. In his plea bargain, Rudy implicated Ed Buckham and Ohio congressman Bob Ney.

Later, David Safavian would be convicted on corruption charges. Arrested at his home in Alexandria, Virginia, on September 19, 2005, Safavian was charged on October 5 with five counts of lying to federal officials and obstruction of justice. The charges stemmed from the now infamous 2002 golfing trip to Scotland, but the federal complaint also detailed how Jack Abramoff had hoped to use his influence with Safavian to lease Washington's Old Post Office building for one of his Indian tribal clients and additional government property for the use of his Eshkol Academy.*

Neil Volz, Congressman Ney's former chief of staff and Team Abramoff member at Greenberg, would be the next to go, having, like Scanlon, Abramoff, and Rudy before him, pleaded guilty to corruption charges.

☆ ☆ ☆

---

*The chronology in the Safavian case reads like this: May 2002, Safavian becomes deputy chief of staff at the General Services Administration, having previously worked as a lobbyist with Jack Abramoff and later as a congressional staffer under Representative Chris Cannon (R-Utah); May 24, 2002, Abramoff contacts Safavian about finding a building for his Eshkol Academy; June 19, 2002, Abramoff "reaches out" to Safavian in an effort to redevelop the Old Post Office in Washington as a luxury hotel; July 11, 2002, Safavian promoted to chief of staff at the GSA, the number three job at the agency; August 3–9, 2002, Safavian participates, along with Representative Bob Ney and Ralph Reed, in the Scotland trip organized by Jack Abramoff; November 2004, Safavian promoted to chief of federal procurement policy in the Office of Management and Budget (OMB); February and March 2005, Senate Indian Affairs Committee questions Safavian about the Scotland trip—and he assures them he had GSA approval; September 16, 2005, Safavian resigns post at OMB; September 19, 2005, Safavian arrested.

By the spring of 2006, the Senate Indian Affairs Committee hearings began to wind down, with Senators McCain and Dorgan having painstakingly guided the investigation through one Abramoff lobbying effort after another, laying out his involvement with six Indian tribes in six states—Texas, Louisiana, Mississippi, New Mexico, Michigan, and California. Of particular interest to the committee was the tale of the Match-E-Be-Nash-She-Wish Band of Pottawatomi Indians— better known as the Gun Lake tribe—which in 2002 had wanted to build a casino on their 147 acres near Grand Rapids, Michigan.

Unfortunately for the Gun Lake tribe, the Michigan Saginaw-Chippewa tribe—the "Sag-Chips," in Abramoff parlance—already had a casino. And not just any casino, but one of the biggest Indian gambling joints in the country, the Soaring Eagle Resort and Casino. Represented by Abramoff and Scanlon, the Sag-Chips were determined to stop the rival Gun Lake tribe from poaching on their territory.

In short, it was the same old story, with a slightly different cast of characters. Rich tribe, poor tribe, big casino, no casino.

Sag-Chip political adviser Chris Petras e-mailed Abramoff to warn him that the Gun Lake proposal was wending its way through the various layers of Interior Department bureaucracy. It was up to Abramoff to stop it.

Abramoff had often boasted to his Indian tribal clients of his "in" with the Bush administration. Now he had a chance to prove it. The very day that Petras sent out his warning signal—December 4, 2002— Abramoff e-mailed a key, if seemingly improbable, contact, Italia Federici, the president of the Council of Republicans for Environmental Advocacy, also known as CREA. Grilled mercilessly by Senator John McCain at a Senate Indian Affairs Committee meeting, Federici outlined the story of CREA, which McCain persisted in calling "the CREA."*

The story of CREA was instructive, to say the least. The "environ-

---

*Federici having earlier eluded a committee summons, McCain made a point of having her sworn under oath. Reporter John Aloysius Farrell searched for CREA's Colorado offices, only to find one of them occupied by a university comptroller and the other by a flower shop.

mental advocacy" group had been founded in 1997 by conservative Republican activist and fund-raiser Federici. The group's honorary cochairs were Grover Norquist and right-wing Colorado lawyer and failed 1996 Republican U.S. Senate candidate Gale Norton. Its general counsel was another GOP heavyweight, Ben Ginsberg.*

With such as these as its advocates, the environment was in good hands. CREA, though, was anything but what the title proclaimed it to be. The raison d'être for CREA was disguised advocacy on behalf of big-business interests. Nakedly so, in fact, save for the title. In the words of a *Washington Post* account: CREA "received its financial backing from chemical and mining interests, leading some environmentalists to brand it a front for industrial polluters."

But then how many obscure antienvironmental advocacy groups could call Grover Norquist a founder or cite as his cofounder a member of the president's cabinet, the incumbent secretary of the interior, and the person to whom the Bureau of Indian Affairs (BIA) reported? Just one: CREA.

Needless to say, after that, Indian money began flowing in the direction of CREA. Hauled before the Senate Indian Affairs Committee by McCain and Dorgan, Federici remained unflappable even when presented with proof that hundreds of thousands of dollars in Indian tribal donations had flowed into CREA's coffers. Nor, Federici testified, had she been particularly inquisitive as to *why* the tribes were giving such large sums to CREA.

A monument to stubborn Plains-states rectitude, Senator Dorgan laid it all out for the CREA leader, Federici: "You are an environmental organization. You come into a lot of money from Indian tribes. My guess is that money had nothing to do with generosity, or had very little to do with energy or the environment, but had a lot to do with Mr. Abramoff saying to his contacts in these tribes, 'I want you to stick money into Ms. Federici's organization,' and they did."

---

*A longtime Republican activist and prominent cable news talking head, Ginsberg had been counsel to the Republican National Committee and would be counsel to Bush/Cheney 2000, playing a prominent role in the Florida recount. (Still later, Ginsberg would serve as legal adviser to the Swift Boat Veterans for Truth group in 2004.) His particular forte, however, lay in Republican redistricting efforts—so much so that his pet dog was named Gerrymander.

Senator McCain put it less gently: "It looks to me like you were working for Mr. Abramoff and you were getting money from Indian tribes to do it. That's what it looks like to me."

McCain also observed, "The way you describe it in this testimony is the Indian tribes are generous; Jack is generous; everybody is generous. That is unbelievable to me."

Unbelievable too was Federici's explanation for the open-wallet approach of Jack Abramoff's Indian tribal clients: there was nothing new about any of this, Federici solemnly informed the suddenly wide-eyed Senators McCain and Dorgan. America's Indian tribes had always been generous.

In his best "Aw-shucks, I'm a country boy, but I ain't a dope" manner, Senator Dorgan said, "Here is what it looks like. Now, I come from a really small town, but I think I can spot a pretty big lie from time to time. Somebody has been lying to us. Somebody sitting at this table has been lying to us. . . . The question is who."

But there was more from the senator from North Dakota, his straightforward, country-bred language a stark contrast with her looping sentences often punctuated with an insistent "Okay?"

DORGAN: "It almost sounds like a fairy tale, doesn't it? You get hundreds of thousands, up to five hundred thousand dollars, and the people that gave it to you really never reached out to you to talk to you about the issues that represented the main elements of your organizations. That is why I think this is unbelievable, Ms. Federici. We have a body of evidence here that suggests you got a substantial amount of money from Indian tribes, and then you were very busy working with Mr. Abramoff. . . ."

MS. FEDERICI: "But, Senator, I was not abusing nonprofit resources, okay? . . . I repeatedly offered to meet with our Native American donors [but] they did not want to be bothered with me."

Even from behind thick glasses, Byron Dorgan's eyes could be seen blinking. "Ms. Federici," he declared, "you must be the luckiest woman alive."

Little wonder then that Jack Abramoff had sought the aid of Italia Federici to help him in putting a stop not only to the Gun Lake casino, but also the casino that the Jena tribe proposed opening in Mississippi.

As 2002 wound down, both proposals had been moving forward; Jack Abramoff's proposed solution to these problems rested on the same two sources: Italia Federici and J. Steven Griles.

On December 2, Abramoff e-mailed Federici, warning her that the Jena "are on the march again." He added that he hoped that the CREA leader would do what she could to "make sure Steve squelches this again."

Federici's response: "I'll bring it up asap."

Not trusting Italia and Steve to carry all his water, Abramoff instructed Greenberg staffer Todd Boulanger to draft a letter to Gale Norton warning her that "we hold you accountable" for stopping "reservation shopping" on the part of the Jenas. The proposed signatories on the letter: the House leadership trio of Hastert, DeLay, and Blunt. Somewhat toned down, the letter would be sent in June 2003.

Chris Petras having alerted him that the Gun Lake proposal was also moving forward, Abramoff e-mailed Federici again, two days later, on December 4: "This is a disaster in the making. This is the casino we discussed with Steve and he said that it would not happen. It seems to be happening!"

"Steve" was J. Steven Griles, the former coal and oil industry lobbyist and now deputy secretary of the Department of the Interior. Or, as he preferred to style himself, "chief operating officer" of the Interior Department—the COO, in other words, to Secretary Gale Norton's CEO.

Griles was by then not only a powerful figure in Interior, but a friend of Abramoff's—and longtime close friend of Italia Federici's. Secret Service records show that Abramoff visited the White House on March 6, 2001. Two days later, Griles's nomination was forwarded to the Senate. As the Senate Indian Affairs Committee would later report, "According to an email dated March 1, 2001—just seven days before the President nominated Griles for the second highest position at Interior, Abramoff met with Griles. Apparently, Federici was present— later reporting to Abramoff that 'after I retrieved my coat I ended up sharing a cab with Steve. . . . He really enjoyed meeting you and was grateful for the strategic advice on BIA and Insular Affairs' "—the watchdog agency for U.S. territories and commonwealths, such as

Guam and longtime Abramoff client the Commonwealth of the Northern Mariana Islands. " 'You definitely made another friend.' " By summer's end, in e-mail to clients, Abramoff had begun referring to the Interior COO as "our guy Steve Griles."

Who was "our guy"? At Interior, Griles, in the words of an Associated Press story, quickly "earned a reputation as a go-to broker in [President George W.] Bush's program to lease out vast oil, gas and coal reserves below federally owned land in the West." The story noted that for almost half of his four-year tenure at Interior, Griles was under investigation by the department's own inspector general for possible ethics violations, including arranging meetings between department officials and his former clients and partners. The IG described Griles's behavior as "an institutional failure" and also noted that he "continued to receive $284,000 a year, in addition to his Interior salary, as part of a four-year severance package from his former lobbying and consulting firm," National Environmental Strategies Inc. (NES). The IG's office would eventually charge Griles with twenty-five possible ethical violations while in office. Secretary Gale Norton dismissed twenty-three of the charges and failed to act on the other two.

In a scathing 145-page report from 2004, the Interior Department inspector general, Earl E. Devaney, who had previously served for more than twenty years as a special agent in the Secret Service, described Griles as "a train wreck waiting to happen." What particularly incensed Devaney was the "bureaucratic bungling" of offshore oil and gas leases by Interior during the Griles years.*

Griles's government career had begun at the Virginia Department

---

*The leases, signed in 1998 and 1999 at the tail end of the Clinton years, allowed energy companies to escape the usual 12.5 percent royalty paid to the government for such leases. But the leases also had a threshold marker: should the price of oil exceed $34 a barrel, the government would be empowered to restore the royalty charges. Strange to say, while the price of oil soared above $34 during the Bush II years, Interior Department officials failed to charge royalties on the leases—on tens of millions of barrels of oil. Writing in the New York Times, Edmund L. Andrews noted, "Department officials kept quiet about their mistake for six years after they discovered it." The cost of their mistake—under COO Griles's watch—would, government officials predicted, "cost the Treasury as much as $10 billion over the next decade." To quote Inspector General Devaney in his report to the House Governmental Reform subcommittee on energy: "Simply put, short of a crime, anything goes at the highest levels of the Department of the Interior."

of Conservation and Economic Development (1970–81). It was there that the future Interior COO made his first important contacts in the surface-mining business—the business of strip-mining for coal. Griles continued to build up his interest and expertise in coal, serving as deputy director, Office of Surface Mining, in the Reagan-era Interior Department—run in those days by the notoriously antienvironmentalist secretary James G. Watt (1981–83). So in tune with the boss and his successors was he that Griles was promoted up the ladder at Interior, finishing his first stint there (under President George H. W. Bush) as assistant secretary.

After that, Griles emerged as senior vice president of the United Company, which was in coal mining, among other natural-resource endeavors. Fresh from his lobbying efforts on behalf of the same industry, Griles walked back through the door and, voilà, found himself Gale Norton's number two at Interior. There is abundant evidence that Jack Abramoff was on the "transition team" at Interior. The question is, did Abramoff put his own man in as deputy secretary?*

Whether or not he was Abramoff's man, Steve Griles was certainly Ms. Federici's man, at least according to the *Washington Post*, which reported that the two had long enjoyed "a personal relationship." And Ms. Federici was Jack Abramoff's go-to lady when it came to Interior. "The way to stop" the Gun Lake casino, Abramoff e-mailed Federici, "is for Interior to say they are not satisfied with the environmental impact report. Can you get [Griles] to stop this one asap?"

Federici's reply: "I will call him asap." Presumably she did too. Two days later, the CREA president sat down with the COO of the Interior Department and got some quality face time.

---

*One thing is for sure: more than two years later, Abramoff attempted to woo the deputy secretary of the interior into joining him as a lobbyist at Greenberg Traurig. In a September 9, 2003, e-mail to colleagues in the governmental affairs unit at Greenberg, Abramoff recounted how he had met with Griles that evening and reported that the deputy secretary was "ready to leave Interior and will most likely be coming to join us." Griles, Abramoff added, "had a nice sized [lobbying] practice before he joined Interior and expects to get that and more rather soon. I expect he will be with us in 90–120 days." Confronted with Abramoff's e-mail traffic, Griles admitted before the Senate Indian Affairs Committee that he had been made the offer—but had turned it down. He also insisted that there was nothing improper about his job discussions with Abramoff—despite the fact that federal law generally makes it a crime to open job negotiations while still working for the government.

"The meeting with Griles," Abramoff e-mailed Sag-Chip adviser Petras, "went well. We have a lot to do but we'll get there."

Mike Scanlon thought so too: "Hey," he e-mailed Abramoff, "I think a real quick way to blow this Gun Lake thing out of the water is to have BIA reject the land into trust, or lay some stipulation on their application that would buy us some time. Any word from Griles on this?"

Not only was Interior now suddenly—and inexplicably—hostile to the Gun Lake casino, but so too was the Department of Justice's Indian Law section. At issue, strange to say—strange because coming from an administration notably hostile to environmental issues—was the possible environmental impact of the casino.

Griles was becoming quite the Indian gaming expert.* For in 2003, he again went to bat against yet another proposed casino. This time it was the Jena Band of Choctaws and their plans for a casino that would rival that of the Louisiana Coushattas—the same gambling-rich Elton, Louisiana–based tribe that had bankrolled Ralph Reed's efforts to shut down the Tiguas at Speaking Rock.

In the Tigua case, Reed had received invaluable help from then Texas attorney general John Cornyn—amidst the hue and cry of Baptist ministers whipped up by Pastor Ed Young of Houston—but now Abramoff had better still: he had the aid of the deputy secretary of the interior. And Griles didn't disappoint, handing a binder full of legal arguments and objections to the Jena casino over to his fellow Interior officials.

At an open hearing of the Senate Indian Affairs Committee, former Interior Department counsel Michael Rossetti recalled how Griles had handed him the binder. Rossetti wanted no part of it—or Griles. At the hearing Rossetti testified, "I wanted Mr. Griles to know I had my eye on him." Griles's sudden interest in Indian affairs—and in the building of the Jena casino, in particular—"worried" Rossetti, so much so that he demanded that Gale Norton's number two tell him just "whose water was he carrying."

---

*Of obvious significance to Indian tribal lobbyist Abramoff was the long-running federal court case *Cobell v. Norton*, in which the tribes claimed that the Indian trust funds had been mishandled by the government over decades to the tune of as much as $176 billion.

Seated next to Rossetti at the Senate Indian Affairs Committee witness table, Griles, with his shock of white hair and chiseled Virginia-granite face, pearly teeth, big grin, and honeyed accent, cut quite a figure. Clearly unhinged, he shot back, "That is outrageous . . . and it is not true."

The Senate Indian Affairs Committee hearings came to an end, and one by one the DeLay/Abramoff shoes kept dropping. In early August 2006, Congressman Ney, "the Mayor of Capitol Hill," announced that he was no longer running for reelection. It was left to the *Washington Post* to provide the answer to the question Why Ney, why now?

To quote from the *Post*: "House Majority Leader John A. Boehner (R-Ohio)"—Tom DeLay's successor—"met with Ney last week to urge him to step aside, reminding him that with a son in college and a daughter nearing college age, he will need money, according to several congressional Republican aides. If he lost his House seat for the party, Boehner is said to have cautioned, Ney could not expect a lucrative career on K Street to pay those tuition bills, along with the hundreds of thousands of dollars in legal fees piling up."

Now it all made sense. Like just about everyone else in the world of DeLay Inc., Bob Ney's highest goal in life was to be a high-paid K Street lobbyist.

Alas, it was not to be. On September 15, 2006, the Justice Department announced that it had entered into a plea agreement with Congressman Ney. The six-term Republican from Ohio admitted in the words of a *New York Times* account that he had "effectively put his office up for sale." While he could have faced up to ten years in federal prison, along with a $500,000 fine, Ney was said to have gotten off light, thanks to a recommendation by prosecutors that he serve only twenty-seven months in jail. In a statement released by his attorneys, Ney suggested that his criminal acts were related to alcoholism.

Among the Abramoff-related charges was one that Ney, as chair of the House Administration Committee, had in 2002 helped direct a multimillion-dollar contract for wireless telephone service in the House to a technology company whose lobbyist was Jack Abramoff.*

Ney also admitted to taking a paid golfing trip to Scotland in 2002—the same trip that had brought down David Safavian—and a gambling jaunt to New Orleans in 2003; and to having taken free meals and drinks courtesy of the Greenberg lobbyist. In return for which, Ney admitted having "agreed to perform official acts."

Within the week, Ney had resigned his chairmanships of the Financial Services subcommittee on Housing and Community Opportunity and the "Franking Commission" (the Commission on Congressional Mailing Standards), which regulates the congressional privilege to use the public mail for free.

Resigning his seat in the House was another matter.

Despite being denounced by Speaker Dennis Hastert for his "unacceptable" and "illegal behavior," Ney refused to give up his $165,200-a-year job. After all, as Majority Leader John Boehner, a fellow Ohio Republican, had reminded him earlier, Bob Ney still had a family to feed.

Less than a week after Ney entered into his plea bargain with federal prosecutors, the Bush administration released records detailing the White House visits of figures connected to the Abramoff investigations between the years 2001 and 2006. The list was long, surprisingly so, given the White House's earlier reluctance to admit that the words *Jack Abramoff* had ever been uttered in its hallowed halls.

Among the visitors:

---

*Beginning in 1999, LGC Wireless—at the time, the largest provider of wireless-related antennas and repeaters—had begun working with the architect of the Capitol and various House officials to develop such a plan. But in 2001, just as Ney assumed chairmanship of the House Administration Committee, a second, competing firm began lobbying for the job. The otherwise obscure Foxcom Wireless, it turned out, had powerful friends. That same year, the Israeli-based telecommunications firm "donated" $50,000 to Jack Abramoff's personal charity, the Capital Athletic Foundation. A year later, on November 26, 2002—and over the objections of both LGC and nonpartisan Capitol Hill bureaucrats—Foxcom (subsequently renamed Mobile Access Networks) was awarded the wireless-equipment contract. As reported in the *Washington Post,* "Over the next two years, Foxcom paid Abramoff's team $280,000."

- Grover Norquist was found to have made ninety-seven visits to the White House, including a half dozen with the president himself.
- Ralph Reed, had had eighteen appointments at the White House, including two with the president.
- Recently confessed felon, former Ney chief of staff, and Team Abramoff member Neil Volz had also enjoyed White House hospitality eighteen times.
- Shawn Vasell, sometime political director to Senator Conrad Burns and Team Abramoff member, had also visited the White House eighteen times.
- Recently confessed felon, former DeLay deputy chief of staff, former Team Abramoff member, and onetime partner of Ed Buckham at Alexander Strategy Group, Tony C. Rudy had made his way through the pearly gates nineteen times.
- Former Doolittle chief of staff and Team Abramoff member Kevin Ring made thirteen visits.

To read the list was to wonder, why? Why now release the names and the numbers? The answer came barely one week later, when, on September 29, the House Government Reform Committee released its own report, *The Abramoff Investigation.* The White House was, clearly, preparing for some bad news.

The report was released, as bad news in Washington almost invariably is, on a Friday, so as to be buried in the Saturday editions of the newspapers. But, in this case, the report's findings were leaked the day before, Thursday evening, and so appeared prominently in the Friday-morning papers. The headline inside the *Washington Post* read, "Abramoff Put White House Contacts at 400."

Based on some fourteen thousand e-mails and other documents, the report actually found rather more Abramoff-related White House contacts than the *Post* headline indicated: 485 in all, including 82 with the office of the senior adviser to the president of the United States, Karl Rove. The report noted that Abramoff had billed clients for $23,981 in meals and drinks with White House officials.

Most of Team Abramoff's contacts with Rove's office were found to have gone through former Abramoff executive assistant Susan Ralston, not only Rove's chief of staff but also now special assistant to the president of the United States.

But it was on Rove himself—Rove and his fondness for good food, Rove and his love of sporting events, Rove and his immense power—that Team Abramoff had set its sights. The team, it would seem, scored repeatedly when it had to. For example:

With "March Madness" 2002 in bloom, and the NCAA's first- and second-round college basketball championship games scheduled to be played at Washington's MCI Center, Abramoff invited Rove to join him in the private box of NBA Wizards owner Abe Pollin. He then followed up with an e-mail to Ralston, telling her that her boss was "really jazzed" at the idea of sitting in the owner's box.

Evidently, Rove was too.

Ralston replied: "Karl is interested in Fri. and Sun. 3 tickets for his family?"

Abramoff: "Done."*

After the game, Abramoff e-mailed a colleague, referring to Rove and Ralston: "He's a great guy. Told me anytime we need something just let him know through Susan."

So great a guy that when, a few months later in July 2002, Abramoff learned that Rove and his party of eight to ten intended to dine at Signatures, he e-mailed a colleague, "I want him to be given a very nice bottle of wine and have Joseph whisper in his ear (only he should hear) that Abramoff wanted him to have this wine on the house." In a separate e-mail to the Signatures staff, Abramoff directed them to "please put Karl Rove in [sic] his usual table."

The prominent table, the special bottle of wine, the whisper in the ear that only the favored few should be allowed to hear.

The life of Abramoff had been sweet—while it lasted.

---

*As the 2007 U.S. Attorney's Office scandal revealed, Ralston's e-mail correspondence with Abramoff went via the Republican National Committee rnc.com accounts, used, one might surmise, to shield Rove and company from federal document preservation laws.

EPILOGUE

★

Day of Reckoning

As the November 2006 midterm elections loomed, many of the Republicans in both the Senate and the House who were running for reelection found themselves confronting millions of voters who no longer believed much, if anything, that their president had to say about why their country was at war in Iraq. The election threatened to become a referendum on Bush, no matter what other issues were at stake, and thus would every seat count, in both the Senate and the House.

In Texas, Tom DeLay was finished as a candidate. But he was still on the ballot, in accordance with Texas election law, and what Texas Republicans surely did not want was to have to wage a write-in battle in the election. In a gambit to enable Republican leaders in the Texas Twenty-second House District to take his name off the ballot and put in a successor candidate's name, DeLay suddenly announced that he was a *Virginian*. In a statement to reporters, a DeLay spokesperson explained how, "As a resident of Virginia, [DeLay] cannot legally be on the ballot in November."

Alas, a slew of judges, both federal and state, saw the matter differently. U.S. district judge Sam Sparks (a George H. W. Bush appointee to the federal bench, sitting in Austin) ruled that while DeLay was free to withdraw from the race, Texas Republicans could not remove his name from the ballot. Wrote Judge Sparks, "Political acumen, strategy and manufactured evidence, even combined with a sound policy in mind, cannot override the Constitution."

DeLay's legacy, meanwhile, lived on. Quite apart from the now swollen ranks of Republican K Street lobbyists and the odor wafting from that general direction, Tom DeLay had made the House his own and populated its highest ranks with his closest followers: Hastert, Blunt, and Barton, among them. But they were merely the most visible of these. In an article titled "All DeLay's Children," Ari Berman reported in the *Nation* how "the Hammer [had] left many nails behind among the lower tier of House GOP leadership members, committee chairmen, party spokesmen and fundraisers he propelled to power."

Among these were a quintet of ambitious DeLayites, all of them hoping no doubt "to grow up" (as Jack Abramoff had once put it) to "be like Tom" and grab the greasy ring of power: Eric Cantor (age forty-three), that rara avis, as Berman reported, "the only Jewish Republican in the House," who now held the title of chief deputy whip; Jack Kingston (age fifty-one), vice chairman of the Republican Conference Committee, who, when the Boss was first indicted, circulated a glossy brochure entitled "The Hammer Has a Big Heart," explaining the then majority leader's resilience in the face of adversity by saying, "He knows Jesus personally"; Patrick McHenry (age thirty), the youngest member of the 109th Congress, described as the party's "attack dog in training"; Richie Pombo (age forty-five), already a chairman, the House's most militant antienvironmentalist;* and Tom Reynolds (age fifty-five), the head of the National Republican Congressional Committee (NRCC), already marked as a "real comer" in the House of DeLay (the Boss, Reynolds once told reporters, "was a

---

*Richard Serrano and Stephen Braun, writing in the *Los Angeles Times* (January 8, 2006), described how Pombo and his fellow Northern California Republican John Doolittle had joined with DeLay in obstructing an investigation by federal banking regulators into the affairs of Houston billionaire Charles Hurwitz and the failed San Antonio savings and loan he once controlled. When a letter from DeLay failed to stop the investigation, Doolittle and Pombo used the power of the House Resources Committee to subpoena the FDIC's confidential records in the case. In 2001—drawing on the Bob Ney playbook—the two congressmen made public much of the most sensitive material by inserting it into the pages of the *Congressional Record*.

darn good mentor of mine"). This was, it appeared at the time, a crew with a future.

Yet it did not help that the Republican write-in candidate to replace DeLay in the Twenty-second District was named Shelley Sekula-Gibbs. Not only was Ms. Sekula-Gibbs a political unknown, her name was, well, difficult to remember, much less spell.

Nor did it help that the White House was hit with the perfect political storm on Friday, September 29, 2006: the release of the House Government Reform Committee's report on the Abramoff scandal, complete with hundreds of new e-mails (some of them directed to the White House itself and the office of Karl Rove); the leaking in the press of Bob Woodward's scathing third volume of "Bush at war," *State of Denial,* with its tales of White House infighting and administration incompetence; and first word on cable TV of a sex scandal involving Florida Republican congressman Mark Foley and a congressional page boy with whom he'd apparently enjoyed a torrid e-mail correspondence.

Ironically, the detailed report of the House Government Reform Committee on the Abramoff scandal was virtually lost beneath the mountain of other news that day. Still, it portended ill, especially if, as now seemed possible, the Democrats were to regain control of the House in November. Unusually, the report had been prepared by House Democrats under the leadership of the ranking Democratic committee member, Henry Waxman of California. The Republican chairman, Tom Davis, though he largely owed his position to his talents as a party fund-raiser, was known to be one of the more independent—and, certainly, shrewder—leaders within the House Republicans. Davis allowed the report to be released under the imprimatur of the committee as a whole, but with Waxman's name up front. It was a bold—and, no doubt, smart—move on Davis's part. But it also suggested what the House Government Reform Committee might look like under Chairman Waxman, who was known to be one of the most aggressive investigators on Capitol Hill. Lobbyists, administration officials, and big-business types alike could take no solace in the idea of a Chairman Waxman demanding that they raise their right arm and swear to tell the truth, the whole truth, and nothing but the truth.

No, it was the other news of the day that mattered most. The Woodward book, with its portrait of a disinterested president, a nonfunctional White House national security apparatus—presidential favorite Condoleezza Rice was described as having been the worst national security adviser in history—and a rogue Defense Department, was an instant best seller. *State of Denial* pulled back the administration curtain, to devastating effect. For the next two weeks, Bob Woodward seemed hardly ever to be off the television news.

And when Woodward wasn't on, it was the Mark Foley scandal, 24/7. The lurid accusations against the gay Florida Republican were bad enough, but the alleged cover-up by the likes of Speaker Hastert, his top aides, Majority Leader Boehner, Congressional Campaign Committee chairman Reynolds, Page Board chairman Shimkus, and Whip Blunt stood to finish off the House Republicans. The cable news networks trotted out an old saw, but they were right: the Republican leadership in the House had formed a firing squad—for themselves—and in a neat little circle.

Come the day of electoral reckoning, and, in the House at least, it was all over by 10 p.m. on the East Coast. The final count showed that the Democrats had not lost a single seat, while picking up their first majority since 1994. The House that convened in January 2007 would have 233 Democrats as against 202 Republicans, a thirty-one-seat margin for new Speaker Nancy Pelosi. Exit polls showed that while the war in Iraq remained the dominant worry for voters, the issue cited most often by voters was corruption. And in the public's well-deserved fury over corruption, many a head had been lopped off that day. The real shocker, though, came in the Senate, where the Democrats' seemingly impossible dream had taken shape, 51–49.

In whichever chamber of Congress they resided, the friends of Jack Abramoff—and Tom DeLay—had paid a heavy price. Gone was K Street cofounder Rick Santorum. Gone too was old Senator Burns of Montana. Over in the House, senior Armed Services subcommittee chairman Curt Weldon (under federal investigation for his ties to his lobbyist daughter and her Russian clients)* and Resources chairman Pombo both bit the dust. Former right-wing radio-talk-show host and Native American caucus chairman J. D. Hayworth did too. Many of the survivors, such as Doolittle of California, had run the closest races of their lives, in what had been thought to be ultrasafe "redder than red" Republican districts.

But it was down in Texas that the coup de grâce had been applied. Democrats of all stripes, from conservative Blue Dogs to the most liberal, e-mailed and telephoned one another in joy: Nick Lampson had crushed his write-in opponent, the surrogate for the fallen Tom DeLay. The Texas Twenty-second went blue.

In the aftermath of the rout, there was much finger-pointing. Speaker Hastert announced that he would step aside in the next Congress. Soon to be out of a job as Speaker, Hastert had neither the desire—nor the expectation that he would be asked—to stay on as minority leader. Despite his role in the Foley debacle, that would be John Boehner's consolation prize. Roy Blunt's would be that he survived to stay on as whip.

---

*In 2004, the *Los Angeles Times* reported that Weldon's daughter, Karen, had landed approximately $1 million in lobbying contracts with foreign clients whose work had been assisted by the influential congressman. Included among these was a 2002 contract for $500,000 from the giant Russian natural gas supplier Itera. Karen Weldon's partner in the lobbying firm proved to be Charles Sexton, the well-connected head of the Springfield Township Republican Party in suburban Delaware County, Pennsylvania.

Two years later, the *Los Angeles Times* broke the follow-up story of "A Small-Town Lobbyist and Her Big Connection" (January 28, 2006). The small-town lobbyist, Cecilia Grimes, proved to be a family friend of Representative Weldon, the vice chairman of both the House Armed Services Committee and the House Homeland Security Committee. A real estate agent in Media, Pennsylvania (population 5,469)—Media is the county seat of Delaware County, the heart of Weldon's district—Grimes and her partner, Cynthia Young, age twenty-eight, represented firms as far away as California. The retainer for such work: $20,000 per client. The lobbying firm was indeed well-connected: Young, it turned out, was married to the son of Florida Republican congressman C. W. "Bill" Young, the chairman of the House Appropriations Committee's defense subcommittee, with power of the purse not only over the Department of Defense, but also the House Homeland Security Department. Needless to say, many of the programs within the purview of the subcommittee were top secret, and their budgets remained hidden from the prying eyes of reporters and the public.

The other shoe dropped just in time for the 2006 midterm elections. In October, federal agents raided the homes of Karen Weldon and Charlie Sexton. In the subsequent election, the ten-term congressman Weldon was trounced by his Democratic rival, retired navy vice admiral Joe Sestak.

The story was widely reported, for example, in the *Philadelphia Inquirer*, October 17–18, 2006.

In Houston and in Austin, in the back rooms and the downtown clubs, political conversation had taken a new tone. Texas governor Rick Perry had been returned to office, but with a meager 39 percent of the vote. It didn't take a high-paid D.C. Republican strategist to know that if the self-styled "Texas Jew boy," the iconoclastic Kinky Friedman, had not siphoned off some 13 percent of the vote, former Democratic congressman Chris Bell (who polled 30 percent) might well have become the next governor.

Back at his home in Sugar Land, or perhaps it was the place in Arlington, Virginia, DeLay awaited trial on money laundering, while he no doubt also wondered about the fate of Ed Buckham and other old friends such as the stalwart Californians John Doolittle and Richie Pombo, Dana Rohrabacher, and Jerry Lewis. Perhaps too he shed a tear now and again for disgraced congressman Randy "Duke" Cunningham, who had begun serving eight years in federal prison for taking $2 million in bribes from defense contractors. The Cunningham indictment and conviction—much like Abramoff's—clearly presaged a wider investigation of lobbyists, corporate malefactors, and their congressional enablers.

Nor was Cunningham alone among Washington's formerly powerful. On Wednesday, November 15, 2006, Jack Abramoff arrived at the gates of a federal prison facility in Cumberland, Maryland, some 140 miles from the nation's capital. It was not how federal prosecutors would have had it. They had requested that Abramoff be allowed to remain free until finishing his allotted cooperation in their wide-ranging probe. The Federal Bureau of Prisons and a judge in Florida saw it differently. But at least Abramoff would have this much: a desk, paper, and pen with which to write his heart out.

In the dwindling days of the old Congress, the ghost of Tom DeLay briefly arose, as it were, from the political grave. Viewers of Don Imus's former MSNBC morning program will recall how Imus for a time made a personal crusade out of the Combating Autism Act of 2006. The bill, which had enjoyed overwhelming support in both houses of Congress, was bottled up in the House Energy and Commerce Committee. Day after day, the image and telephone numbers of Chairman Joe Barton were flashed around the world on *Imus in the Morning*. Why was this "fat little creep"—Chairman Barton—bottling up such a bill? Imus thundered. What did Joe Barton "have against autistic kids?"

The answer was nothing—and everything. Of course, Chairman Barton didn't have anything against autistic kids. But Barton's decision had everything to do with the will of Big Pharma, led, as we have seen, by an old buddy, former chairman Billy Tauzin, and lobbied hard for by former DeLay chief of staff Susan Hirschmann.

Big Pharma didn't have anything against autistic kids either, but it didn't want its constituent companies to be sued for making drugs that allegedly helped engender autism. In the end, the autistic kids and their parents prevailed. Wilting before the wrath of Imus, Barton freed the bill.

In the newly Democratic House, Speaker Pelosi wasn't the only woman who had risen to power. Louise Slaughter, a liberal from upstate New York, now exercised the gavel as chair of the powerful Rules Committee. When former Republican chairman Dreier rose on the floor of the House to decry the Democrats' new rules—backed by a 9–4 majority on the committee—Slaughter let him have it. There would be "Regular Order" in the Democratic House. No more five-hour votes. No more shenanigans on the floor. There would be no repetition, for example, of the infamous Medicare Prescription Drug vote, when, as Slaughter acidly recalled, former congressmen, lobbyists, and folks she didn't even recognize crowded the floor during the last-minute voting.

Change came about in both houses of Congress, but perhaps most notably in the House, where the grown-ups were now in charge of some of the most important committees, not only Rules, but also Armed Services, Appropriations and Budget. Gone from the helm of Armed Services was blustery, bug-eyed Duncan Hunter of California, he having emerged as one of the more improbable Republican presidential hopeful of 2008. In his place was quaint, scholarly Ike Skelton of Missouri, who, *Fiasco* author and *Washington Post* defense correspondent Tom Ricks reported, had written twice in advance of the Iraq War to President Bush, warning him of the grave dangers the country and its military might well face in the aftermath of that war. Skelton never heard back from the president. Now he was Chairman Skelton.

And on Appropriations, a committee so corrupt that it had become a byword for everything that was wrong in the old House, an owlish Wisconsin Democrat named David Obey had recaptured his old chair, lost twelve years back when the Republicans gained the majority. His first act as chair, Obey said, would be to restore an oversight subcommittee to Appropriations.

The dreaded word again: *oversight.* As predicted, the newly renamed House Government Oversight Committee almost immediately began a series of hearings under Chairman Henry Waxman. One of the most notable of these focused on "waste, fraud and abuse in Iraq reconstruction." While former Coalition Provisional Authority (CPA) czar Paul Bremer listened stone-faced, Inspector General Stuart Bowen described how American money had arrived in Iraq—237.3 tons in all, hundreds and hundreds of hundred-dollar bills bound in cellophane and heaped on pallets. Bowen reckoned that a staggering $12 billion of American money, meant for reconstruction efforts, could not be accounted for. Twelve billion dollars had just somehow gone missing.

In the upper chamber, the senators debated—or failed to debate—the rightness of the war and the president's "surge" proposal, which he announced in his January State of the Union address. There, the margin was razor-thin once more, especially after South Dakota senator Tim Johnson suffered a strokelike attack. After all, the forty-nine Democrats and their staunch ally, Vermont independent Bernie Sanders, were caucusing with the arch-adventurer, jowly Joe Lieberman of Connecticut. In order to remain the majority party, the Democrats would have to make do with perhaps the most outspoken defender of the war in the Senate. It would not allow for a comfortable relationship; and many were fearful that the day would come when Lieberman would walk across the aisle and become a Republican in name as well as spirit.

If much, in the Senate, remained unsettled, there was little doubt that the aftereffects of the Abramoff scandal would continue well into 2007 and beyond. In early January, former Interior Department deputy secretary Steve Griles learned that he was now officially the target of a federal criminal investigation. Days later, his name disappeared off the nameplate at Lundquist, Nethercutt & Griles. The K Street shop, led by former Cheney energy-policy director Lundquist, announced that it had "severed its ties" with the former coal-mining lobbyist.*

Meanwhile, former Ney chief of staff Will Heaton pleaded guilty to receiving illegal gifts and other "things of value" provided by Abramoff. Heaton was the second of Ney's former chiefs of staff to plead guilty on federal charges stemming from the Abramoff scandals. Those who had led the life of Abramoff when it was all prime ribs and cabernet, Scottish links and private jets, were now being treated to the downside. Some, indeed, were living the life in proximity to the man they all called Jack.

The resounding Democratic midterm election restored, at least temporarily, the sense for many that the basic machinery of American democracy worked. The voters had spoken, and many of their elected representatives had changed as a result. But it is a truism worth remembering that complete political change is rarely sudden, nor do those who remain in power willingly give it up or cease to exercise it.

---

*With the news that Griles was a target of a federal investigation came additional word that a senior Justice Department official had resigned her position. Sue Ellen Wooldridge, the assistant attorney general for environment and natural resources, had, it turned out, been rivals with Italia Federici for the heart of Steve Griles. Wooldridge, the former top lawyer at the Interior Department under Gale Norton and Griles, shared ownership of a vacation home with Griles and a ConocoPhillips lobbyist named Don Duncan. The Kiawah Island, South Carolina, home had sold for $980,000. The purchase had come mere months before Wooldridge approved a consent decree giving ConocoPhillips more time to pay a multimillion-dollar fine and meet pollution cleanup rules at some of its refineries.

Although the 2006 midterm elections may have cleaned out the last dregs of DeLay Inc., the other, symbiotic Texan strand of power still stood. The executive branch—and, above all, the White House operations led by Dick Cheney and Karl Rove—the defense and foreign policy apparatus, and the ideology-and-pure-politics shop with its close connections to the conservative media remained operative.

The 2006 midterms had, however, tarnished the Architect's gilt. Rove had been humbled back into the ranks of mere geniuses—and stripped of his policymaking role as White House deputy chief of staff. But as a schemer and operative par excellence, his presence was still required in the halls of the West Wing.* Cheney too, his staff now led by the arch-legalist David Addington, had had his wings clipped, if perhaps only at the edges. Cheney continued preaching his message of doom and gloom, his goal seemingly a never-ending global war on terror fought at any cost and at any price, Constitution, civil rights, habeas corpus—American lives and American treasure too—all be damned.

The new goals in the waning days of the administration of George W. Bush were much the same as the old ones: to reshape, no matter however bloody the undertaking, the Middle East; to prepare for war with Iran; to lower taxes even in a time of war, no matter the eventual cost to the country's children; to open still more of America's precious natural resources, lands and waters alike, to drilling and mining; to reduce the Democrats to shivering cowardice in the face of being denounced as "soft on terror," or for "not supporting the troops," or "failing to pay for the war." Yes, it was harder to make that kind of thing stick now that Iraq War veterans were in Congress. A Vietnam-era war hero and former Republican secretary of the navy, James Webb, sat in the Senate as a Democrat from Virginia, and a former vice admiral sat in the House, but, so accustomed were they to flinging these same old charges that the Republicans kept up the fire, whether the mess stuck or not. The important thing was to get as much of the

---

*At the trial of Scooter Libby in the Valerie Plame case in Washington, D.C., federal district court, Libby's defense attorneys even argued that the former Cheney chief of staff had been fed to the wolves to protect the really big dogs in the White House pound—Karl Rove, for instance.

agenda forced into reality as possible, as quickly as possible. For now the quest had a new note of urgency. The Bush Restoration was winding down.

And that meant that still more "Bush Justice" had to be enacted. It was now or never. No less than eight sitting U.S. attorneys ("The Gonzales Eight," the *New York Times* called them in an editorial)—most of them having previously received high performance evaluations—were now told that they were through. The orders had come from "on high," the Bush White House itself. In Arkansas, a highly distinguished lawyer respected by both Democrats and Republicans, H. E. Cummins III, was forced out. His acting replacement, J. Timothy Griffin, was a Rove protégé who had performed opposition research for the Republican National Committee, presumably the better to be in place on the old Clintonian turf and readied in advance of the dreaded Hillary candidacy in '08.

Another of the dismissed U.S. attorneys, Carol Lam, had been the force behind the prosecution and guilty plea of disgraced California congressman Randy "Duke" Cunningham. Plus, she had just indicted Kyle "Dusty" Foggo, the former number three official in the CIA. Her reward: a pink slip.

Lam was dismissed, so it would seem, because her investigation of Cunningham was resonant of so much that lay beneath the surface during the Bush years. Cunningham's particular claim on the affections of lobbyists and corrupt corporate executives was due to his position as a senior member of both the Homeland Security Committee and the House Defense Appropriations subcommittee, charged with oversight not merely of the Defense Department budget, but also those of the Central Intelligence Agency, Defense Intelligence Agency, and the National Security Agency. In total, some $300 billion in annual appropriations lay within the purview of Cunningham's subcommittee.

The question arose: what if the global war on terror had, at least in part, been the public face used to conceal millions—perhaps even billions—of dollars in corrupt appropriations being siphoned into top-secret contracts? What if a small coterie of Appropriations, Defence, Homeland Security, and Intelligence committee members were, in fact, on the take and engaged in a massive giveaway of federal funds.*

The question begged answering.

It was hard not to construe the firings as a message to other crusading federal prosecutors. Worse, it was discovered that someone—no one wanted to claim the credit—had, on the sly, slipped language into a 2005 bill renewing the Patriot Act, the passage of which Attorney General Gonzales had strongly supported. The nongermane provision allowed acting U.S. attorneys to serve long stretches of time in office without Senate confirmation. The message seemed to be that the Bush administration intended to keep its new, more political U.S. attorneys unscathed by the Senate confirmation process.†

The Supreme Court itself was now on the verge of being packed, former Florida-recount lawyer John Roberts, the pleasant-faced, but deeply conservative new chief, having been joined by the equally right-wing Samuel Alito Jr. In late February of 2007, Roberts and his running mate "Scalito," as wags dubbed the almost-as-reactionary-as-Scalia Mr. Justice Alito, were among the 5–4 majority in overturning a jury's $79 million punitive award in yet another of the tobacco cases. The "tort reformers" were beginning to reap their rewards.

---

*Cunningham's boss on the House Appropriations Committee, Jerry Lewis of California, had previously been the chairman of the Defense Appropriations subcommittee (1999–2005). In January 2005, Lewis became chairman of the full committee with control over $900 billion in federal spending. Even before Lewis took over as chairman of the full committee, there had been a tripling of the amount of monies appropriated in the form of "earmarks," funds specified for a specific purpose and often entered into the budget on the sly, having gone from 2,000 earmarks worth $10.6 billion in 1998 to 15,884 in 2004 worth $32.7 billion. By late 2005, reporters were asking some serious questions about Chairman Lewis and his relationship with defense-related contractors and lobbyists, among them his close friend, fellow former Appropriator and retired California Republican congressman Bill Lowery. See, for example, Copley News Service reporter Jerry Kammer's story detailing the Lewis-Lowery relationship (December 23, 2005). See also, the *New York Times,* June 3, 2006. Among the other prominent House Republicans on the Appropriations Committee: congressman John Doolittle, also of California.

†Almost immediately after the November election, the White House was forced to withdraw a number of its more outrageous federal appellate court nominees. The reason: none of these had a snowball's chance in hell of getting confirmed. Among them: William J. Haynes, the Cheney acolyte and Defense Department general counsel and staunch advocate of the "torture papers."

As for poor Harriet Miers, she resigned as counsel to the president in the early days of 2007 as the Bush administration remade its legal team in expectation of Democratic oversight committees boring into the foundations of the White House. It was, in a sense, a stunning fall for Miers. Had the president had his way, she would have graced the bench of the Supreme Court herself, rather than Alito. Her fall from grace had happened at warp speed: nominated to succeed Sandra Day O'Connor on October 3, 2005, she had pulled her name from consideration little more than three weeks later, on October 27. Now, suddenly, the woman who had been found worthy of a seat on the Supreme Court by George W. Bush was deemed not up to defending the legal bastion that had become the White House. It was time for Harriet to go home to Dallas.*

Miers did not, however, go gently into the night. When the U.S. attorneys scandal finally broke wide open in February 2007, the White House political shop pointed the finger at her. Miers, loyal to the end, was slated to play the fall guy in a seamy drama.

Alas, it did not work out so neatly. By mid-March, a slew of newly released White House e-mails showed that the idea for firing all ninety-three U.S. attorneys had originated not with the hapless Miers but with Karl Rove—a man no one ever thought to call hapless—as early as January 2005.†

Clearly, something bigger was at work here than just replacing a half-dozen or more U.S. attorneys—no matter what justifications the White House bandied about in excusing itself. Claims that this

---

*It bears remembering that many right-wing Federalist Society types had vehemently opposed her nomination. Intellectually, it was felt, Miers just couldn't hack it. But there was another reason: the White House counsel was in her sixties. She was, by Federalist standards, too old for the Court. The game plan had been obvious for years: pack the Court with young, aggressive, intellectual right-wingers, men whose opinions would not shift over time, and men who could be counted on to serve on the nation's highest bench for decades to come. Certainly, this had been the case with the likes of Chief Justice William Rehnquist, who had been appointed to the Court at age forty-seven in 1972 and went on to serve thirty-three years; Thomas (forty-three); Scalia (fifty-two); Roberts (fifty); and Alito (fifty).

†Longtime Rove observers recalled the close connection between the then-Texas political operative and FBI special agent Greg Rampton, who operated out of the U.S. Attorney's Office in San Antonio in the late 1980s and 1990s. It was Rampton whose 1990 investigation led to federal prison sentences for high-level officials in the Texas Department of Agriculture—and effectively ended the political career of their boss, liberal Democrat Jim Hightower.

U.S. attorney wasn't tough enough on illegal immigration or that U.S. attorney wasn't cracking down hard enough on violent crime were obviously just claims, and thin claims at that.

In a stunning *New York Times* op-ed (March 21, 2007), "Why I Was Fired,"one of the dismissed U.S. attorneys, David Iglesias of New Mexico, told the specifics of his own story and, in the process, blew the whistle on the scheme itself, by exposing its broader outlines. Iglesias, who had once been among the Justice Department's favorite U.S. attorneys, found himself in hot water when embattled New Mexico congresswoman Heather Wilson and the state's senior U.S. senator Pete Domenici, both Republicans, demanded that Iglesias bring indictments before the November 2006 midterm elections. What Wilson and Domenici claimed they wanted was for Iglesias to come down hard on alleged political corruption—Democratic political corruption.

By mid-April 2007, it was obvious that the Rove-inspired plan called for Democrats everywhere—and particularly those in key swing states—to be hounded for alleged political corruption and for alleged voter fraud. What this, in reality, amounted to was an effort to remove Democratic office holders and to curtail the votes of the elderly and the poor, along with those of African-Americans and Latinos. Anyone, in other words, who was likely to vote Democratic.

The scheme called for U.S. attorneys who were not sufficiently loyal to the administration to be removed. Disloyalty basically took one of two forms: either a lack of fervor in prosecuting alleged Democratic political corruption and voter fraud or, perhaps worse still, a no-nonsense approach to going after real political corruption, especially Republican political corruption. Iglesias's sins were the former; Lam's the latter. Both found themselves in the same boat, having been sacked not for the purported "performance-related issues" as stated, but for their noncompliance with the administration's political agendas.

But while Lam and Iglesias and six other U.S. attorneys went down, others remained untouched. Liberal *New York Times* columnist Paul Krugman, describing the "Department of Injustice," suggested that Congress and the media should take a hard look "at those who weren't fired." By late April, that was precisely what the Senate and House Judiciary Committees and the House Government Oversight Committee were beginning to do.

The picture was disturbing too: a U.S. attorney in New Jersey who had issued subpoenas not two months before the November 2006 midterm elections in a case that threatened to implicate Democratic U.S. senator Bob Menendez, up for reelection and in a tight race; another U.S. attorney, this time in Wisconsin, who, marked for dismissal, had apparently saved himself from the heap Lam and Iglesias found themselves in by suddenly going after an allegedly corrupt Democratic official; and an inexperienced thirty-three-year-old U.S. attorney in Minnesota named Rachel Paulose who seemed to have nothing in her favor save for her connection to resigned Gonzales senior counselor Monica Goodling. So inexperienced—and abrasive— was Paulose that within months of her ascendancy, the four highest-ranking career prosecutors in her office voluntarily took demotions rather than serve as her chief deputies.

Now too, high-ranking former career prosecutors at Main Justice, the department headquarters in Washington, began speaking out. Joseph Rich, the former chief of the voting-rights section, testified before the House Judiciary Committee about how the Bush administration had politicized the department. In his March 22 testimony, Rich noted the virtual mass exodus of career prosecutors in the voting-rights and civil-rights sections. He also made mention of something perhaps even more threatening: the decision by the Bush administration, carried out by Attorney General Gonzales, to put the hiring of future career prosecutors in the hands of political appointees such as Goodling and former Gonzales chief of staff D. Kyle Sampson. Gonzales, Rich said, had gone far beyond anything any U.S. attorney general had done in Rich's thirty-seven years at the department to politicize justice in America.

In two scant years, said Rich, Gonzales had taken politics and burned it into the fabric of the Department of Justice. In this, he had gone beyond John Ashcroft, beyond Ed Meese, beyond even John Mitchell.

This was the true meaning of Bush Justice—they thought. Then the next shoe fell.

★　★　★

By early May, the landscape was strewn with bodies. Not only the Gonzales Eight—now apparently grown to ten—but also Goodling, Sampson, and even the Justice Department's ostensible number two, Deputy Attorney General Paul McNulty. Others were on life support.

Revelation followed revelation. A senior aide to McNulty, Michael Elston, had called three of the dismissed U.S. attorneys to warn them to remain silent in advance of Attorney General Gonzales's testimony before the Senate Judiciary Committee. Paul Charlton, the former U.S. attorney for Arizona, was left with the impression that Elston "was offering me a quid pro quo agreement: my silence in exchange for the attorney general's."

John McKay, the well-regarded former U.S. attorney for Washington state, told House investigators that "I greatly resented what I felt Mr. Elston was trying to do: buy my silence." He added that "I believe Mr. Elston's tone was sinister and that he was prepared to threaten me further."

Come mid-May, and it was now apparent to all but the toadies on the Republican side of the House Judiciary Committee that something like a vast conspiracy had been at work in the halls of the Justice Department. The two young aides to Gonzales, Sampson and Goodling, it was revealed, had been given authority by the attorney general to hire and fire almost at will. All told, as many as a quarter or more of the ninety-three U.S. attorneys had at one point or other made the purge list.

But did anyone truly believe that two such inexperienced political appointees as Goodling and Sampson could have been behind the firings? Or would have acted without White House approval? And what was the real issue at stake? The Bush crowd made much of their discontent over the lack of immigration and gun prosecutions. "Voter fraud," however, was the issue that most dominated the discussion, even when most of their own Republican U.S. attorneys could find none.

The acting U.S. attorney in Kansas City, Brad Schlozman, had profited from the provisions of the renewed Patriot Act. Once in place, Schlozman had immediately gone after "voter fraud" suspects— just in time for the whisker-close November 2006 Senate election in

Missouri, which had been won by Democrat Claire McCaskill, thus tipping the balance of the United States Senate to the Democrats.

Schlozman's previous claim to fame lay elsewhere, for he had been the Bush political appointee in Justice who had rammed through the approval process for Tom DeLay's Texas congressional gerrymander. He was truly the definition of a "loyal Bushie."

Still, nothing prepared the press or public for the revelations of former deputy attorney general Jim Comey, appearing before the Senate Judiciary Committee in mid-May. Comey, in riveting testimony that left senators and staff slack-jawed, recounted how he had rushed, his car's siren blaring, to the hospital bedside of his boss, ailing attorney general John Ashcroft in March 2004, one step ahead of then–White House chief of staff Andy Card and then–White House counsel Alberto Gonzales.

The stakes had been high that night. Someone, presumably President Bush himself, had sent the dynamic duo to the hospital to try to get the gravely ill Ashcroft to sign off on the provisions of the secret, warrantless-wiretapping program, provisions that Ashcroft, Comey, and their two closest advisers had already decided were illegal. When Acting Attorney General Comey had refused to authorize renewal of the program, which was due to expire the next day, the White House had gone for a frantic end-run.

Comey beat Gonzales and Card to the hospital and explained as best he could the situation to the nearly comatose Ashcroft. When Gonzales and Card arrived on the scene—apparently ignoring Comey and his two aides—it was the White House counsel who pulled the authorization papers from his pocket and handed them to Ashcroft to sign.

The heavily sedated Ashcroft rose from his bed and, in "strong and unequivocal terms," refused to approve the renewal. What's more, said Ashcroft, pointing at Comey, "There's the attorney general." For his part, Comey was angry, having "just witnessed an effort to take advantage of a very sick man."

Senators, the press, and the public alike were left to make sense of this incredible tale and to wonder just what it was about the secret, warrantless-wiretapping program that had so appalled even a right-wing Republican regular such as Ashcroft.

But it wasn't just Al Gonzales, the quiet man from Humble, who now faced the cameras and the questions. There was Karl Rove—Harriet Miers too—and a cast of dozens caught in this parade. As an editorial in the *New York Times* intoned, even the Wizard of Oz had, at last, to emerge from behind the curtain.

Old faces, like those of Paul Bremer and Paul Wolfowitz, were also back in the news. None of those caught in the glare could have been happy with the unwanted publicity, the bright lights, and the noisy inquisition.

Tom DeLay too was back in the news. The *Houston Chronicle*'s Michael Hedges reported that federal investigators had begun to focus their attention on former DeLay chief of staff Ed Buckham and his employment arrangements with DeLay's wife, Christine.

So many scandals, so many spotlights. Nothing good was going to come of this, not from the perspective of those whom the bright lights now shone upon.

The Bush administration was sinking, and there was plenty of time left for it to sink farther. The rats were jumping ship. The war, which Wolfowitz had promised would pay for itself, had cost nearly a trillion dollars. Worse, it was now seen to be unwinnable. Of the $19 billion the CPA had shipped to Iraq, $8.8 billion was now found to be unaccounted for. Halliburton—Dick Cheney's old company—having gobbled up $7 billion in Iraq War contracts, was set to sever its last ties with its asbestos claims–laden KBR division, its own headquarters scheduled for removal to the Persian Gulf emirate of Dubai. Scooter Libby was a convicted felon.

Who was to say that, any day now, Patrick Fitzgerald might not reemerge from the Prettyman Courthouse in Washington with new indictments. Could a million or so White House e-mails have just disappeared without a trace? Not likely. And hadn't Fitzgerald specifically put the White House and its senior political adviser Rove on notice to preserve those e-mails? He had, and they hadn't. All those gwb43.com and rnc.com e-mails, where had they all gone? And who would find them and when?

And, all the while, Dick Cheney was still trying to connect Saddam to 9/11. The whole thing was surreal, about as surreal, in fact, as the last days of Richard Nixon, hunkered down in the White House.

Yes, the promised day would yet arrive. Cheney would decamp from the bunker and George W. Bush would return to his ranch in Crawford, Texas. The White House would at long last be delivered.

There would be sighs of relief all 'round. The great republic would roll on.

ACKNOWLEDGMENTS

This book represents a first pass at history. My obligations to the many fine reporters and authors who have so ably covered Texas and U.S. politics in the age of George W. Bush are too numerous to cite here. Some of these unsung heroes will find their names in the body of the text, others in the notes and footnotes. I thank them one and all.

Unlike those reporters, I did not cover the stories recounted here on a daily basis. But what I could do—and, I hope, did do—was to combine the sensibility of a trained historian with that of a reporter to connect a number of seemingly disparate threads.

In this, I hope that my old Yale teachers, Howard Roberts Lamar and the late C. Vann Woodward, would approve. Sometimes, in researching this book I felt a bit like Jack Burden, the historian-cum-reporter who is the narrator of Robert Penn Warren's novel, *All the King's Men*. Warren too was an old Yale friend—and an inspiration to me in writing this book, as was the late Willie Morris, raconteur extraordinaire, and author of *North Toward Home*.

Like Jack Burden with his "Little Black Book," I tried to keep careful track of events and characters. Early on, I began by amassing voluminous files, both printed and electronic, labeled "DeLay" and "Abramoff." At a certain point in time, I realized just how overlapping their stories were. What I had before me, I realized, was a vast web of intrigue.

This then is a map of my travels through the world of DeLay Inc. and the Abramoff scandals, connecting the rise of George W. Bush and the Karl Rove–crafted Republican ascendancy, the origins of "Bush

Justice," and the collapse of the tissue-thin house of cards that is this administration.

The link, of course, was the money. As Nan Graham of Scribner so quickly intuited, it was in fact all about "following the money."

The origins of this book date to a lunch at an Indian restaurant in New York City with Colin Harrison, of Scribner. A sixth-generation Texan, whose Anderson family progenitors first set foot in East Texas sometime in the early 1830s—at a time when Coahuila y Tejas was part of Mexico—I had long wanted to write a book about the politics and history of my native state. My great-great-great-grandfather Benjamin Anderson was, according to family lore, the only man ever to have fought in "both revolutions," the American and the Texan.

Colin was less interested in the distant past. And, eventually, he convinced me to write about present-day Texas.

Thus began our mutual journey. I am deeply grateful to Colin and his colleagues at Scribner for their belief in this project. The end point shifted over time and focus. Many another editor and publisher would have lost faith. Colin didn't.

My other everlasting debt of gratitude is to the Schumann Center for Media and Democracy. Without the support of Bill Moyers, Lynn Welhorsky, and their colleagues, this book would never have seen the light of day. Bless you, Bill; bless you, Lynn.

This book also could not have been written without the kindness of friends in the Lone Star State. Rick, Georgia, and Marty Bost entertained and educated me on many a visit. Kathryn and Craig Smyser did much the same, as did my friends the Kellys, Hugh, Molly, and Susie. Hugh will, no doubt, disagree, perhaps vehemently, with my conclusions.

That wise and good soul Mary Dix, her colleague Lynda Crist, Bob Patten, Ira Gruber, and Dennis Huston were among the many Rice University faculty and staff who made my visits to Houston happy ones.

Former lieutenant governor Bill Hobby and current Houston mayor Bill White did much to inform my understanding of Texas politics, as did Bob and Marty Stein. My old friend Phil Waller offered expert advice on congressional issues, present and historical.

In New York, my obligations are many, to Denise Martin, brilliant editor and counselor; Craig Unger, dear friend and wise reader; Aric Press and Anthony Paonita at the *American Laywer*; Howard Goldberg; and many another. In Boston, Michael and Dee Apstein were the best of listeners. In Washington, the late R. W. Apple, Jr., gave me encouragement and advice.

Lawyers are *good*, especially if you are a writer writing about sensitive issues. I thank my astute legal advisers, friends one and all: Dan Kornstein, Kevin Goering, Dan Weiner, George Sape, Frank Karem, and Mark T. Millkey. At Simon & Schuster I thank Elisa Rivlin for her expertise.

At Scribner, I thank Susan Moldow, Nan Graham, Karen Thompson, Steve Boldt, John Fulbrook, Laura Wise, Catharine Sprinkel, Elizabeth Hayes, and Molly Dorozenski.

My agent, Kris Dahl of ICM and her colleagues have done much to further this project.

Finally, there is my family: my wife, Hilary; son, Charlie; mother, Lois Croft Anderson Newton; and stepfather, Oakley Newton; and parents-in-law, Fran and Bob Hevenor; and sister-in-law, Martha. They alone know how much I owe them.

I thank each and all of these with my whole heart.

NOTES

Epigraphs

ix The committee did: Senate Indian Affairs Committee, "Oversight Hearings on In RE Tribal Lobbying Matters, et al.," http//indian.senate/gov. Henceforth cited as "Tribal Lobbying."

ix The government is: This is quoted in Edmund Morris, *Theodore Rex* (New York: Random House, 2001), hereinafter cited as *Theodore Rex*, 140.

Prologue: Third World Capital

xiii $5.28 billion in: AP, 2/1/07, as quoted in www.msnbc.msn.com/id/16922298.

xiv the Baker Institute's: http://bakerinstitute.org/Personnel.

xv Until Roosevelt fired: Bascom N. Timmons, *Jesse H. Jones: The Man and the Statesman* (1956); and William P. Hobby III, interview with the author.

xv James Addison Baker: Baker recently published an entertaining book of memoirs, coauthored by Steve Fiffer, *"Work Hard, Study . . . and Keep Out of Politics!"* (New York: G. P. Putnam's Sons, 2006), hereinafter cited as *"Keep Out of Politics!"*

Chapter One: The Changing of the Guard

1 This was the: On the political background, see, for example, Carl M. Cannon, Lou Dubose, and Jan Reid, *Boy Genius: Karl Rove, the Architect of George W. Bush's Remarkable Political Triumphs* (New York: Public Affairs, 2003), hereinafter cited as *Boy Genius*, 28–48.

1 Only in the: James Moore and Wayne Slater, *Bush's Brain: How Karl Rove Made George W. Bush Presidential* (New York: John Wiley & Sons, 2003), hereinafter cited as *Bush's Brain*, 193–94.

2 True, Texas had: On the Clements and White governorships, see, for example, *Bush's Brain*, 31–59; and *Boy Genius*, 18–23, 25–28, 29–37.

3 After his second: *Boy Genius*, 57–60; and *Bush's Brain*, 196.

3 Even so, Richards: On Richards and her administration, see *Boy Genius*, 59–75.

4 Ann Richards was: Author's interview.

5 Probably the most: Ibid., 162–63.

6 And on election: The 1994 gubernatorial election is discussed at length in *Bush's Brain*, 170–85; and *Boy Genius*, 68–75.

6 Current Houston mayor: Author's interview.

6 It hadn't helped: *Boy Genius*, 73–75; and *Bush's Brain*, 195–96.

7 The story of: My discussion of DeLay here and throughout the book owes much to Lou Dubose and Jan Reid, *The Hammer* (New York: Public Affairs, 2004), hereinafter cited as *Hammer*, and *The Hammer Comes Down: The Nasty, Brutish and Shortened Political Life of Tom DeLay* (New York: Public Affairs, 2006), hereinafter cited as *Hammer Comes Down*.

9 If Gingrich was: *Hammer Comes Down*, 91–92.

10 In this, Buckham: John Feehery, "Hammered: What I Saw at the Republican Revolution," *Washington Post*, 4/5/06, hereinafter cited as Feehery, "Hammered." See also *Washington Post*, 4/1/06. For more on the complicated relations between Buckham, Rudy, and Scanlon, see Brody Mullins, "End of the Affair: Behind Unraveling of DeLay's Team, a Jilted Fiancée," *Wall Street Journal*, 3/31/06, hereinafter cited as "End of the Affair."

10 Another of Rudy's: *Washington Post*, 4/1/06.

11 Born in Atlantic City: This and much of the following discussion is based on Michael Crowley, "A Lobbyist in Full," *New York Times Magazine*, 5/15/05, hereinafter cited as Crowley, "Lobbyist in Full"; and on Susan Schmidt and James V. Grimaldi, "The Fast Rise and Steep Fall of Jack Abramoff," hereinafter cited as "Rise and Fall," *Washington Post*, 12/29/05. For a useful chronology, see "The Abramoff Affair: Timeline," available online at the *Washington Post* Web site, http://www.washingtonpost.com. One of the best starting points for any study of the Abramoff scandal, "Investigating Abramoff," is also at the *Post* Web site and consists of a compendium of earlier *Post* stories: http://www.washingtonpost.com/wp-dyn/content/linkset/2005/06/22/LI2005062200936.html.

12 Abramoff's undoing at: "Rise and Fall."

12 Columnist Peter Carlson: Peter Carlson, "Abramoff as Auteur: He Was No Run of De Mille Movie Mogul," *Washington Post*, 11/27/05.

13 but in early: "Rise and Fall."

13 It was Buckham: Feehery, "Hammered."

Chapter Two: A Pig Roast on the Island

15 In the process: James Moore and Wayne Slater, *The Architect: Karl Rove and the Master Plan for Absolute Power* (New York: Crown Publishers, 2006), hereinafter cited as *Architect*, 181.

15 Gallant's first big: *Hammer Comes Down*, 125–28.

16 So-called for the: On the lobbying effort that paved the way for the building of the transcontinental railroad, see, for example, Stephen Ambrose, *Nothing Like It in the World: The Men Who Built the Transcontinental Railroad, 1863–1869* (New York: Simon & Schuster, 2000), 92–96, hereinafter cited as *Nothing Like It in the World*. On the Crédit Mobilier scandal, see again *Nothing Like It in the World*, 320–21, 373–75; also see Jean Edward Smith, *Grant* (New York: Simon & Schuster, 2001), 552–53, 560. The Crédit Mobilier scandal is dealt with in detail in David Haward Bain, *Empire Express: Building the First Transcontinental Railroad* (New York: Penguin Books, 2000), hereinafter cited as *Empire Express*, 675–711. The Teapot Dome scandal is dealt with in impressive detail in Francis Russell's controversial 1968 biography of Warren G. Harding, *The Shadow of Blooming Grove*. A better, or more riveting, study of a long-forgotten political age was never written.

17 Washburne knew whereof: *Nothing Like It in the World*, 95–96.

17 Less than a: Ibid., 273.

17 As the result: Ibid., 320–21.

18 The Crédit Mobilier: Ibid., 374; and *Empire Express*, 679.

19 Change came quickly: Elizabeth Drew, "Selling Washington," *New York Review of Books*, 6/23/05, 41–42.

21 Abramoff's first important: On the background to Abramoff's work in the Marianas, see, for example, Crowley, "Lobbyist in Full"; and "Rise and Fall." See also the chapter "Saipan," in *Hammer Comes Down*, 181–98.

22 The textile owners: "Saipan," in *Hammer Comes Down*, 181–98.

22 No longer a: David Rosenbaum, "At $500 an Hour, Lobbyist's Influence Rises with G.O.P.," *New York Times*, 4/03/02, hereinafter cited as Rosenbaum, "$500 an Hour."

22 Commonwealth governor Froilan: Office of the Public Auditor, Commonwealth of the Northern Mariana Islands, "M-01–05: Survey of CNMI-Contracted Lobbyist Activities, January 1994 through September 2001," 11/09/01.

22 It wasn't just: *New York Times*, 4/29/05, 5/04/05.

23 And what better: For a firsthand account, see Feehery, "Hammered"; see also "Saipan," in *Hammer Comes Down*.

23 When DeLay arrived: Feehery, "Hammered"; Rosenbaum, "$500 an Hour."

23 During the visit: Feehery, "Hammered"; "Rise and Fall." The pig roast is described in some detail in one of the seminal accounts of the Abramoff scandals, R. Jeffrey Smith's *Washington Post* piece "Former DeLay Aide Enriched by Nonprofit," 3/26/06, hereinafter cited as "DeLay Aide Enriched," which focuses on Edwin Buckham. For other accounts of the island pig roast see *Houston Chronicle,* 4/13/05; AP dispatch, 5/3/05; and *Los Angeles Times,* 5/06/06.

24 Congressman George Miller: Rosenbaum, "$500 an Hour."

24 Returning from Saipan: This and the following accounts are largely drawn from "DeLay Aide Enriched."

25 In servicing the: *Washington Post,* 2/27/07.

26 To the world: Rosenbaum, "$500 an Hour."

Chapter Three: The Fabulous Rise of Casino Jack and DeLay Inc.

27 The picture of: William N. Evans and Julie H. Topoleski, "The Social and Economic Impact of Native American Casinos," 8/7/02, www.bos.umd .edu/econ/evans/wpapers/evans_topoleski_casino.pdf.

28 In 1987, the: Ibid., 3, 5–15.

28 As a result: Ibid., 3.

28 That the casinos: Ibid., 3.

28 Connecticut politicians, for: *Pequot Times,* February 2007; www.igs .berkeley.edu/library/htIndianGaming.htm.

29 The Choctaws were: www.choctaw.com.

29 Still, by the: The invaluable sourcebook for material—investigative reports, e-mails, bank records, and the like—on the Abramoff scandals is *"Gimme Five": Investigation of Tribal Lobbying Matters: Final Report Before the Committee on Indian Affairs,* 109th Cong., 2d sess., June 22, 2006, available online at www.indian.senate.gov/public/_files/Report.pdf. Hereinafter referred to as *"Gimme Five."* Reference here is to page 16.

29 All that changed: Ibid., 18.

29 But the tribe's: Ibid., 18–19.

29 In the words: Ibid., 19; and *Washington Post,* 7/3/2000.

30 In 1996 and: *"Gimme Five,"* 20–21.

30 Two years into: "DeLay Aide Enriched."

30 In a fund-raising: Ibid.; and *Hammer Comes Down,* 128–32.

30 All was not: "DeLay Aide Enriched."

31 From those microscopic: Ibid.

31 Eventually, five years: Ibid.

31 The USFN did: Ibid.

31 Textile owners in: Ibid.

32　In little more: www.choctaw.com.

32　The Choctaws knew: R. Jeffrey Smith, "The DeLay-Abramoff Money Trail," *Washington Post*, 12/31/05, hereinafter cited as "Money Trail."

32　DeLay; his wife: Ibid.

32　One day after: Ibid.; *"Gimme Five,"* 33–38; and "DeLay Aide Enriched."

32　Coincidentally, a letter: "Money Trail."

33　The Coushatta tribe: www.coushatta.org.

33　The Louisiana Coushatta: Ibid.; *"Gimme Five,"* 40–58.

34　Reed, like his: Thomas B. Edsall, "In Ga., Abramoff Scandal Threatens a Political Ascendancy," *Washington Post*, 1/16/06, hereinafter cited as "In Ga."

34　Over the next: Ibid.

34　As Reed famously explained: Ibid.

35　In 1997, Reed: Ibid.

35　Freed of his: www.ralphreed.com.

35　As he put: *"Gimme Five,"* 23.

35　Among Reed's clients: Countless examples of how the process worked are to be found in the Senate report *"Gimme Five,"* but see, for example, pages xi, 20–21, 26–27.

35　With Reed preparing: Ibid., 27, 28.

35　It was a: *Hammer Comes Down*, 137–42.

35　DeLay, somewhat miraculously: Ibid.

35　Late that summer: "Money Trail"; *"Gimme Five,"* xi, 22, 36; and *Washington Post*, 6/7/06.

36　Records would later: "Money Trail."

36　Two months later: Ibid.

37　The common denomination: Ibid.

37　What exactly the: Ibid.

37　Other sources claim: Ibid.

37　According to an: Ibid.

37　Christopher Geeslin, a: Ibid.

37　The IMF funding: Ibid.

38　At first, DeLay: Ibid.

38　Coincidentally, the same: Ibid.; and "DeLay Aide Enriched."

38　The check for: "Money Trail."

38　The Russian oligarchs: *Boston Globe*, 2/23/06.

38　The money just: "DeLay Aide Enriched."

38　The largest contribution: "DeLay Aide Enriched"; and *Hammer Comes Down*, 130.

38　None of this: *Hammer Comes Down*, 128, 133.

39　The men running: Ibid., 132–33.

39 While the DCC: "DeLay Aide Enriched."

39 But not before: Ibid.

39 In the world: Ibid.

39 Another key figure: Reporter Brody Mullins's "End of the Affair," *Wall Street Journal*, 3/31/06, remains one of the milestone articles in the unfolding of the Abramoff scandal.

40 Following the suicide: The classic study of the Clinton impeachment is to be found in *Washington Post* reporter Peter Baker's *The Breach*. The Rudy-Scanlon discussion quoted here is from the end of chapter 1, the whole of which can be found online at www.nytimes.com/books/first /b/baker-breach.html. Hereinafter cited as *The Breach*.

40 But when Congress: Ibid.

40 President Clinton soon: Ibid.

40 By late 1998: Ibid.

41 As communications director: Feehery, "Hammered."

41 The two DeLay: Ibid.

41 By the fall: Ibid.

41 Rudy and Scanlon: *The Breach.*

42 Tom DeLay and: This and the next four paragraphs are all from "DeLay Aide Enriched."

43 Tom DeLay, Armey: *New York Times*, 1/7/06.

43 A senior policy adviser: Ibid.

43 Buckham hadn't forgotten: *Hammer Comes Down*, 128, 195–96.

43 As a newly: Ibid.

43 When Enron lost: From here to break, Ibid.

44 In his day: This and next three paragraphs, "DeLay Aide Enriched."

44 Between 2001 and: *New York Times*, 3/30/05; AP, 4/11/05; and *New York Times*, 4/7/05.

45 The DeLays weren't: "DeLay Aide Enriched."

45 And why not?: Ibid.

45 So who was: Ibid.

46 In any case: Ibid.

46 Wendy Buckham, though: Ibid.

46 As USFN began: Ibid.

46 What is that?: Ibid.

Chapter Four: Who's Your Daddy? Part I

47 In 1991, George: The convoluted story of George W. Bush's early forays into the business world has been told many times, nowhere better or more succinctly than in Craig Unger, *House of Bush, House of Saud: The Secret*

Relationship Between the World's Two Most Powerful Dynasties (New York: Scribner, 2004), hereinafter cited as *House of Bush, House of Saud,* 113–28. See also Bill Minutaglio, *First Son: George W. Bush and the Bush Family Dynasty* (New York: Three Rivers Press, 2001), hereinafter cited as *First Son,* 207–8, 212, 246–47, 251–52, 257. See also Molly Ivins and Lou Dubose, *Shrub: The Short but Happy Political Life of George W. Bush* (New York: Random House, 2000), hereinafter cited as *Shrub,* 14–42. See also Molly Ivins and Lou Dubose, *Bushwhacked: Life in George W. Bush's America* (New York: Random House, 2003), hereinafter cited as *Bushwhacked,* 3–30.

47   The younger Bush's: *House of Bush, House of Saud,* 119–23.

47   Spectrun 7 was: *Shrub,* 22.

48   As he would: Ibid., 22–23.

48   Arbusto, thinly capitalized: Ibid., 24–26.

48   Arbusto received a: Ibid.; and *Bushwhacked,* 7.

48   Molly Ivins and: *Bushwhacked,* 7.

49   Renamed Bush Exploration: *Shrub,* 26.

49   Renamed yet again: Ibid., 29, 31; and *House of Bush, House of Saud,* 121.

49   In exchange for: *Shrub,* 28; and *Bushwhacked,* 8–9.

49   Harken had problems: *Bushwhacked,* 9.

49   Fortunately, like so: Ibid., 11–12.

50   Almost exactly two: Ibid., 12–13; and *Shrub,* 32.

50   The circumstances were: *Shrub,* 12; and *Bushwhacked,* 11.

50   Undeterred, Bush sold: *Shrub,* 34–37; and *Bushwhacked,* 13.

51   As managing partner: *Shrub,* 34–42; and *First Son,* 231, 237–39, 239–40, 251.

51   The general counsel: *Bushwhacked,* 4–5, 6, 9–11, 13–14.

51   Doty's boss at: Ibid.

52   On August 21: *House of Bush, House of Saud,* 124; and *First Son,* 284.

52   A precursor firm: *"Keep Out of Politics!,"* 3–4, 338, 344, 346, 422. See also Griffin Smith Jr.'s "Empires of Paper," *Texas Monthly,* November 1973. The history of Baker Botts is told in Kenneth Lipartito and Joseph Pratt, *Baker & Botts in the Development of Modern Houston* (Austin: University of Texas Press, 1991). See also "Baker Botts," *Handbook of Texas Online,* www.tsha.utexas.edu/handbook/online/articles/BB, hereinafter cited as "Baker Botts."

52   As the *Handbook*: "Baker Botts."

52   One of the: "Empires of Paper."

53   Baker & Botts: Ibid.; and "Baker Botts."

53   Lawyer-writer Griffin: "Empires of Paper."

53   The man who: "Baker Botts."

53   It was Lovett: *"Keep Out of Politics!,"* 8; and "Baker Botts."

53 Setting a pattern: "Baker Botts."

54 His greatest public: Ibid.

54 "Captain" Baker—as: Ibid.

54 While Captain Baker: Ibid.

54 Lovett's hand could: Ibid.

54 In 1919, at: Jonathan Foster Fanton's "Robert A. Lovett: The War Years" (Yale University Ph.D. dissertation, 1978) contains sections on Lovett's early career; and Mickey Herskowitz, *Duty, Honor, Country: The Life and Legacy of Prescott Bush* (New York: Rutledge Hill Press, 2003).

55 "Young Bob," though: Fanton, "Robert A. Lovett."

55 Robert A. Lovett: Official Department of Defense biography; Walter Isaacson and Evan Thomas, *The Wise Men* (New York: Simon & Schuster, 1986); and Townsend Hoopes and Douglas Brinkley, *Driven Patriot: The Life and Times of James Forrestal* (New York: Knopf, 1992), 40.

55 For his part: The rise of the Bush family and the interwoven web of its connections with the likes of the Harrimans, the Walkers, the Rockefellers, and their banking relatives, the Stillmans, is skillfully dealt with in Kevin Phillips's *American Dynasty: Aristocracy, Fortune, and the Politics of Deceit in the House of Bush* (New York: Viking, 2004), hereinafter cited as *American Dynasty.* Of particular interest is the "The Not-Quite Royal Family," 15–50, and the two intriguing appendices on pages 335–48.

56 Davis, a former: "Edmund J. Davis" entry in *Handbook of Texas.*

56 After the war: Ibid.

56 Not surprisingly, the: Ibid.

57 To these traditional: Bill Minutaglio, *The President's Counselor: The Rise to Power of Alberto Gonzales* (New York: Rayo, 2006), hereinafter cited as *President's Counselor,* 102–3; and Ben Barnes, *Barn Burning, Barn Building: Tales of a Political Life, from LBJ to George W. Bush and Beyond* (Albany, Tex.: Bright Sky Press, 2006), hereinafter cited as *Barn Burning,* 109–11. See also *Architect,* 230–31. See also Jim Moore, "Bush, Miers, the Guard, and the Texas Lottery: A Reprise," www.huffington-post.com, hereinafter cited as "Bush, Miers."

57 Described by *Newsweek: Newsweek,* 7/20/2000.

57 With the lottery: *Newsweek,* 7/17/2000; and "Bush, Miers." A partisan but nevertheless suggestive account is by Bob Fertik, "Bush Aides Possibly Altered National Guard Records to Conceal Grounding and Missed Duty," 11/4/2000, http://archive.democrats.com, hereinafter cited as "Bush Aides Possibly Altered." The best, nonpartisan account is Ralph Blumenthal, "Court in Transition: The Record," *New York Times,* 10/7/2005, hereinafter cited as "Court in Transition."

58 Miers's choice to: "Court in Transition."

58 All this made: *Barn Burning,* 109–11.

58 With the threat: Ibid.

58 The story, as: Ibid.

58 But with pressure: See "Bush, Miers" and "Court in Transition."

59 In his lawsuit: Ibid.

59 After a federal: Ibid.

59 That did not: Ibid.; and "Bush Aides Possibly Altered."

60 Governor George W.: *Boy Genius,* 23–25, 66–67.

60 Temperamentally, Laney was: Ibid., 81–83.

61 The war began: Mimi Swartz, "Hurt, Injured Need A Lawyer? Too Bad!" (*Texas Monthly,* November 2005).

61 According to its: Ibid.

61 Back in 1994: Anonymous, conversation with the author.

62 As ably recounted: *Boy Genius,* 96–99, 99–105.

62 The endgame was: Ibid., 103–4.

63 Rove's cat's-paw in: From here to end of the chapter, ibid., 104.

Chapter Five: Casino Jack

64 Scanlon had, moreover: "End of the Affair."

64 In late 1999: Ibid.

65 But it wasn't: Matthew Continetti, "Money, Mobsters, Murder: The Sordid Tale of a GOP Lobbyist's Casino Deal Gone Bad," *Weekly Standard,* 11/28/05, hereinafter cited as "Money, Mobsters."

65 While Abramoff affected: Ibid.; and "Rise and Fall."

65 A 1989 Brooklyn: "Money, Mobsters."

65 What brought Adam: Ibid.; and "Rise and Fall."

65 SunCruz Casinos operated: "Rise and Fall"; and "Money, Mobsters."

66 But on August: Ibid.

66 Boulis turned to: Ibid.

66 Now that the: Ibid.

66 The original plan: *Newsday,* 12/27/05.

67 Only days after: Ibid.

67 Encouraged by Abramoff: "Money, Mobsters."

67 The onslaught continued: Ibid.

68 Yet, this was: Ibid.

68 Busy as he: This section, to the next text break, is largely based on the most important—and most revealing—dissection of how Abramoff operated, Susan Schmidt and James V. Grimaldi's "How a Lobbyist Stacked the Deck: Abramoff Used DeLay Aide, Attacks on Allies to Defeat Anti-Gambling Bill," *Washington Post,* 10/16/05, hereinafter cited as "Stacked the Deck."

68 On July 17: *New York Times,* 1/09/06.
72 Jack Abramoff, it: "Money, Mobsters"; and "Rise and Fall."
72 That night, Abramoff: "Money, Mobsters."
73 Abramoff's courtship of: Ibid.; and "Rise and Fall."
73 There was just: "Rise and Fall"; and "Money, Mobsters."
73 R. Alexander Acosta: *Washington Post,* 8/12/05.
73 Among Jack Abramoff's: "Money, Mobsters"; and *New York Times,* 1/10/06.

Chapter Six: Who's Your Daddy? Part II

75 The veteran journalists: *Architect,* 103–4.
75 Rove, they note: Ibid.
77 And to a: *Bush's Brain,* 16; and *Boy Genius,* 128–31, 169.
77 Taking his cue: *Boy Genius,* 117–25.
77 George W. Bush: Ibid., 124.
78 Meanwhile, Karl Rove: Ibid., 125.
78 Meanwhile, the money: Ibid., 122–23.
78 When McCain threatened: Ibid., 140–50.
79 By October the: Ibid., 120.
80 The story of: Jeffrey Toobin, *Too Close to Call: The Thirty-Six-Day Battle to Decide the 2000 Election* (New York: Random House, 2001), hereinafter cited as *Battle.*
80 Begin in Texas: Ibid., 17–18.
80 Democrats had had: Ibid.
80 Thus it was: Ibid., 18.
80 By ten o'clock: Ibid.
81 Two hours later: Ibid., 19–20.
81 An eternity too: Ibid., 21–22.
81 Over the next: Ibid.
81 "We've got a": Ibid., 24–25.
81 Gore himself now: Ibid.
81 "Are you saying": Ibid.
81 Gore snapped back: Here to break, ibid., 24–25.
82 Baker had begun: James A. Baker III offers his own version of the Florida recount in *"Keep Out of Politics!,"* 361–90. *Battle,* 40–42.
82 They were old: *Battle,* 40–42.
83 Just why George: Lou Dubose and Jake Bernstein, *Vice: Dick Cheney and the Hijacking of the American Presidency* (New York: Random House, 2006), hereinafter cited as *Vice,* 139–44.
83 Dick Cheney, who: Ibid.

83 Now, as the: From here to break, *Battle,* 42.

84 The vote, as: Ibid., 29.

84 Of the three: Ibid., 33.

85 Bush, as the: Ibid., 54.

85 Gore's two closest: Ibid., 38, 82.

85 When his "client": Ibid., 36, 52.

86 If, as Toobin: Ibid., 45–47.

86 The Gore team: Ibid., 63.

86 Skilled lawyer that: Ibid., 66.

86 Once arrived: Ibid., 52, 94–95.

87 The local: Ibid., 95.

87 Barry Richard and: Ibid., 95–96, 184, 273.

87 A dozen: Ibid., 210–22. See individual profiles for Terrell, Bristow, and Cooper at the Baker Botts Web site, www.bakerbotts.com.

88 Jeffrey Toobin—himself: *Battle,* 97.

88 The armada set: Ibid., 257–58.

88 Jim Baker made: Ibid., 136–37.

89 Nor had Baker: Ibid., 156.

89 The Gore legal: Ibid., 184.

90 Some in the: Ibid.

90 The former clerks: Ibid.

90 And in this: Ibid., 192–95.

91 Clinton knew whereof: Ibid., 248–49.

Chapter Seven: The Price of Friendship

95 Hisa's account is: "Tribal lobbying."

95 For the previous: On the issue of unpaid oil royalties to the federal government, see any of the many excellent pieces done by Edmund L. Andrews, among them, *New York Times,* 1/10/07, 1/13/07, 1/16/07, 1/17/07, 1/19/07, 1/21/07, and 1/24/07.

95 The importance of: Rosenbaum, "$500 an Hour."

95 The move to: "Rise and Fall"; and *Washington Post,* 12/29/05.

96 Greenberg's lobbying fees: Rosenbaum, "$500 an Hour."

96 All Washington took: Ibid.

96 Rosenbaum added that: Ibid.

96 Abramoff went on: Ibid.

96 Different though the: Ibid.

96 For his $32: "Tribal Lobbying."

97 Take Super Bowl: This section from here to the break is based on Susan Schmidt and James V. Grimaldi, "Untangling a Lobbyist's Stake in a

Casino Fleet," *Washington Post,* 5/1/05, hereinafter cited as "Untangling Stake," along with "Money, Mobsters," as well as "Rise and Fall."

98 Jack Abramoff, pressed: "Tribal Lobbying."

98 Needless to say: www.alabama-coushatta.com.

99 Their prosperity would: The story of the Tiguas is told in detail in the pages of *"Gimme Five,"* 140–82.

99 The 1,250-member: Ibid.

99 At the time: An excellent account of the Tigua shakedown is to be found in Lou Dubose, "No Picnic at Speaking Rock," *Texas Observer,* 12/17/04. Other useful accounts are to be found in the *Boston Globe,* 6/3/05, and *New York Times,* 6/13/05. The Bush quote is from the *Times* account.

100 In March 2001: Ibid.

100 By the time: Ibid. On March 15, 2001, for example, Abramoff e-mailed Reed to warn him, "We're spending $ at a pretty high burn rate." Cited in Senate Indian Affairs Committee, "Oversight Hearings on In RE Tribal Lobbying Matters, et al.," http//indian.senate.gov.

100 In a suit: *New York Times,* 7/13/06; *Fort Worth Star-Telegram,* 7/13/06; and *Austin American-Statesman,* 7/13/06.

101 For another, as: "Tribal Lobbying."

101 Suzi Paynter, a: Andrew Wheat, "Thin Reed: Will Abramoff's Deep Throat Swallow God's Mouthpiece?" *Texas Observer,* 1/27/06, hereinafter cited as "Thin Reed."

101 Paynter was right: Ibid.; and "Tribal Lobbying."

101 Scanlon was worried: "Tribal Lobbying."

102 Reed was also: Ibid.

102 Jack Abramoff would: Ibid.

102 The question, under: "Thin Reed."

102 Appropriately enough for: www.rclub.org; "Thin Reed"; and "Tribal Lobbying."

102 After the bill: "Thin Reed"; and "Tribal Lobbying."

103 Not everyone on: "Tribal Lobbying."

103 The boss clearly: Ibid.

103 The by now: Ibid.

103 One day later: "Untangling Stake."

104 Among the more: "Rise and Fall."

104 In early 2001: "Tribal Lobbying."

104 Why, after all: Ibid.

104 That's where Scanlon: Ibid.

104 The American International: Ibid.

105 Still, in the: Ibid.

105 Now, in the: Ibid.

105 Scanlon and Abramoff: Ibid.

105 He continued, "Here": Ibid.

105 And split up: Ibid.

105 How the scheme: Ibid.

106 The Senate Indian: *"Gimme Five."*

106 Entities owned or: Ibid.

106 Why sell for: Ibid.

106 More opportunities beckoned: "Tribal Lobbying."

106 Pastor Young: See www.second.org and www.winningwalk.org.

106 In the nearly: www.second.org.

107 In June 1992: www.sbc.net.

107 With five separate: www.second.org.

107 Years later, in: AP dispatch, 5/08/06.

107 Reed reported: "Tribal Lobbying."

107 Not only was: Ibid.

107 "So let me": Ibid.

107 Seriously, Scanlon told: Ibid.

108 After 9/11, America: Ibid.; and *Time,* 10/22/05.

108 Four months later: *Time,* 10/22/05.

108 As the report: House Government Reform Committee, *The Abramoff Investigation,* 9/29/06, hereinafter cited as *Abramoff Investigation.*

109 Texas attorney general: *"Gimme Five."*

109 On September 27: Ibid.

109 A month and: "Tribal Lobbying."

109 "Look out!" Scanlon: Ibid.

109 Cornyn was expected: Ibid.

109 A few weeks: Ibid.

109 Reed added, "We": Ibid.

109 Cornyn would later: AP dispatch, 11/12/05.

109 If anyone really: *El Paso Times,* 12/4/01; and "Tribal Lobbying."

110 In 1998 and: *El Paso Times,* 12/4/01.

110 Influential Austin lobbyist: Ibid.; www.hillcopartners.com; and Texans for Public Justice, www.tpj.org.

110 Cornyn, of course: "Tribal Lobbying."

110 A few days: Ibid.

111 While Abramoff was: "End of the Affair."

111 In a December: AP dispatch, 1/10/06.

111 The cost of: Ibid.

112 When Willie Tan: *Time,* 10/23/05; and *Abramoff Investigation.*

112 The reply—from: *Time,* 10/23/05; and *Abramoff Investigation.*

112 "You win :)": *Abramoff Investigation.*

112 When, in December: *Time,* 10/23/05.
112 Normally, the appointment: Ibid.
112 If this Republican: Ibid.
113 Needless to say: Ibid.

Chapter Eight: High Energy

114 Pragmatic, moderate, questioning: Ron Suskind, *The Price of Loyalty: George W. Bush, the White House, and the Education of Paul O'Neill* (New York: Simon & Schuster, 2004), hereinafter cited as *Price of Loyalty,* 263.
115 Eventually, O'Neill was: Ibid., 309.
115 For one thing: Ibid., 96.
115 The coming war: Ibid.
115 O'Neill thought he: Ibid., 144, 157.
116 By the time: Ibid., 78, 157.
116 In stark contrast: Ibid., 130, 88, 97, 126–27.
116 Under the influence: Ibid., 98–102, 127, 129–30.
117 Cabinet meetings, O'Neill: Ibid., 73, 147–48.
117 So it was: Ibid., 153, 145–46.
117 A dead giveaway: Andrew Lundquist profile at Web site of Lundquist Nethercutt & Griles, www.lngassociates.com.
117 The work of: *Price of Loyalty,* 146.
118 As the old: Ibid.
118 The truth, O'Neill: Ibid., 149.
118 Bush might have: Ibid., 45–49.
119 Only when discussion: Ibid., 46.
120 Freed now of: From here to end of paragraph beginning "Under Chairman Tauzin" is based on Thomas B. Edsall and Justin Blum, "Rep. Barton Faces Energy Challenge," *Washington Post,* 4/14/05, hereinafter cited as "Rep. Barton."
120 As the spring: The Westar section is drawn from findings of the internal investigation by the law firm Debevoise & Plimpton on behalf of the special committee of the board of directors of Westar Energy. The report, which relied on 450 boxes of documents and 200 interviews with 150 people, ran 368 pages. Westar Energy, Inc., "Report to the Special Committee to the Board of Directors," April 29, 2003, hereinafter cited as "Debevoise Report." The report is available online at www.concernedshareholders.com/CCS_WestarEnergy%20ReportExc.pdf.
125 The real Enron: See, for example, Kurt Eichenwald, *Conspiracy of Fools.*
126 When O'Neill brought: *Price of Loyalty,* 205–6.

126 In the wake: Author's interviews and notes.

128 By the summer: This entire section based on "Debevoise Report."

Chapter Nine: What's the Matter with Texas? Part I

135 "Government preparing to": AP dispatch, 2/26/01.

135 Once the detailed: The data actually arrived a few days early, on March 12. AP dispatch, 3/12/01.

135 State Representative Delwin: Ibid.

136 The thirty-two seats: Ibid.

136 When reporter Hector: *Los Angeles Times,* 3/13/01.

136 The big news: Ibid.

136 The New Texas: Ibid.

136 A perfect example: Ibid.

137 But another Texas: Ibid.

137 Republicans were almost: AP dispatch, 3/14/01; and Charlie Cook, "Off to the Races," 5/22/01, www.cookpolitical.com.

138 Republican Party officials: AP dispatch, 4/26/01.

138 That became a: *Austin American-Statesman,* 5/26/01.

139 Meanwhile, it would: Ibid.

139 Reporter Copelin also: Ibid.

140 House Redistricting Committee: *Austin American-Statesman,* 5/27/01.

141 By the end: AP dispatch, 6/30/01.

141 Once again, the: Ibid.

141 As yet there: *Amarillo Globe-News,* 7/02/01.

141 That, of course: *Roll Call,* 7/9/01.

142 The LRB voted: *Washington Times,* 7/30/01.

143 Meanwhile, the fine: *Austin American-Statesman,* 8/1/01.

143 On July 3: Ibid.

143 The timing and: Ibid.

143 Republican lawyer Andy Taylor: Bernstein and Mann, "The Rise of the Machine," *Texas Observer,* 8/29/03.

143 A Baker Botts: Ibid.

143 Speaking for Attorney: *Austin American-Statesman,* 8/01/01.

143 Taylor later joined: Bernstein and Mann, "The Rise of the Machine," *Texas Observer,* 8/29/03.

143 Speaking for himself: *Amarillo Globe-News,* 7/22/01.

144 What was clear: *San Antonio Express-News,* 8/22/01.

144 On September 12: *San Antonio Express-News,* 9/13/01.

144 Following a two-week: *Dallas Morning News,* 10/4/01.

145 Privately, Frost was: *Washington Post,* 10/4/01, 10/5/01.

145 A week later: *Washington Post,* 10/12/01.

145 One week later: *Amarillo Globe-News,* 10/20/01.

147 Final arguments in: *San Antonio Express-News,* 11/2/01.

147 Alford was an: Ibid.

148 Not surprisingly, lawyer: Ibid.

148 However carefully the: *Roll,* 11/15/01; *New York Times,* 11/15/01; *Houston Chronicle,* 11/15/01; *Washington Times,* 11/15/01; *Fort Worth Star-Telegram,* 11/15/01; *Washington Post,* 11/15/01; *Dallas Morning News,* 11/15/01; and *Austin American-Statesman,* 11/15/01.

148 But in a: *Dallas Morning News,* 11/29/01.

Chapter Ten: What's the Matter with Texas? Part II

150 Came the November: From here to end of the paragraph that begins "Charles Hurwitz of" is all drawn from Jake Bernstein and Dave Mann, "The Rise of the Machine," *Texas Observer,* 8/29/03, hereinafter cited as "Rise of the Machine."

158 Now it was: The tale of the so-called Killer-D's is told in *Hammer Comes Down,* 209–21, as well as in a long, contemporary account in the *New York Times,* 5/15/03.

158 This time, it: *Austin American-Statesman,* 6/25/03, 6/27/03.

158 "has gotten an arm-twisting": *Austin American-Statesman,* 6/25/03.

158 Eventually, desperate Senate: *Hammer Comes Down,* 218–22.

159 The *Washington Post's*: *Washington Post,* 12/10/05.

159 The panel voted: The decision, along with countless other legal documents concerning the various Texas redistricting cases, is available online at the Web site of Chicago-based law firm Jenner & Block (www.jenner.com), conveniently assembled as the "Texas Redistricting U.S. Supreme Court Cases Resources Center." Another extremely helpful online source of media accounts of the Texas redistricting drama is to be found at www.fairvote.org, under the rubric "Public Interest Guide to Redistricting."

160 In Washington, a: *Dallas Morning News,* 6/9/05.

Chapter Eleven: The Heart of the Matter

161 Down in Texas: "Tribal Lobbying."

161 To further tighten: Ibid.

161 Not to worry: Ibid.

161 After all, as: Ibid.

162 Republican State Comptroller: Fox Butterfield, "For a Tribe in Texas, an

Era of Prosperity Undone by Politics," *New York Times*, 6/13/05, hereinafter cited as "Tribe in Texas."

162 No matter the: "Tribal Lobbying."

162 A twenty-four-hour-a-day operation: "Tribe in Texas."

162 Abramoff e-mailed Scanlon: "Tribal Lobbying."

162 In an e-mail: Ibid.

162 The next day: Ibid.

163 In an e-mail: Ibid.

163 By February 18: Ibid.

163 Abramoff's reply to: Ibid.

163 When a few: Ibid.

163 Abramoff was still: Ibid.

164 Not to worry: Ibid.

164 The plan, as: Ibid.

164 In the end: Ibid.; and *"Gimme Five."*

164 And in their: *"Gimme Five"*; and "Tribal Lobbying."

164 Another prominent recipient: *"Gimme Five."*

165 In total, Burns: Lou Dubose, "Senatorial Courtesy: Will John McCain Let Republican Perps Walk?" *Texas Observer*, 9/24/04, hereinafter cited as "Senatorial Courtesy"; *Washington Post*, 12/17/05; and *"Gimme Five."*

165 Still, it did: *"Gimme Five."*

165 Nor was Vasell: *"Gimme Five"*; "Tribal Lobbying"; and *Missoulian*, 1/18/06. It should be pointed out that some excellent daily reporting on the Abramoff scandal was done from afar, by the *Billings Gazette* and the *Missoulian*, both of Montana.

165 Other recipients of: *"Gimme Five"*; and "Tribal Lobbying."

165 On March 20: Ibid.

165 Six days later: Ibid.

166 That same month: "End of the Affair."

166 Scanlon's behavior grew: Ibid.

166 Mike Scanlon wasn't: Glen Justice, "For Lobbyist, a Seat of Power Came with a Plate," *New York Times*, 7/06/05, hereinafter cited as "Seat of Power."

166 At the head: Ibid.

166 From his personal: Ibid.

166 A few years: "Tribal Lobbying."

166 No, replied Tigua: From here to break, ibid.

167 And if Washington's: Ibid.

167 So passed the: Ibid.

167 "Did you get": "Tribal Lobbying."

167 Rudy's job was: Ibid.

168 Rudy, a few: Ibid.

168 Boulanger replied, "I'm": Ibid.

168 Rudy wrote back: Ibid.

168 But then Leadership: Ibid.; and *New York Times,* 12/15/05.

168 Abramoff's assistant Holly: "Tribal Lobbying."

168 The President's Dinner: *New York Times,* 12/15/05.

168 If Jack Abramoff: "Tribal Lobbying."

168 The Tiguas did: Ibid.; and *"Gimme Five."*

168 Jack Abramoff didn't: *"Gimme Five"*; and "Tribal Lobbying."

169 In the end: *"Gimme Five"*; and "Tribe in Texas."

169 Ney would later: Chuck Neubauer and Walter F. Roche Jr., "Golf, and Playing by the Rules," *Los Angeles Times,* 3/9/05, hereinafter cited as "Golf"; and *Washington Post,* 11/5/05.

169 In August, recently: *"Gimme Five."*

169 There was just: Ibid.; and "Tribal Lobbying."

170 Without Dodd, the: *"Gimme Five."*

170 According to news: *New York Times,* 5/13/05.

170 When it didn't: "Tribal Lobbying."

170 In an e-mail: Ibid.

170 Years later, interviewed: Michael Crowley, "A Lobbyist in Full," *New York Times,* 5/01/05.

170 It even reached: "Tribal Lobbying."

170 Abramoff replied, "We'z": Ibid.

171 A week later: Ibid.

171 The e-mail exchange: "Tribal Lobbying."

171 The wheels on: From here to the break is based on reporting in *Los Angeles Times,* 5/06/05, and particularly on Walter F. Roche Jr.'s seminal piece "Bush Removal Ended Guam Investigation," *Los Angeles Times,* 8/08/05, hereinafter cited as "Guam Investigation."

172 Meanwhile, the wedding: "End of the Affair."

173 In November, the: Ibid.

173 Shortly afterward, Miller: Ibid.

173 Mike Scanlon's salary: Ibid.

173 Jack Abramoff, who: *"Gimme Five"*; and *Washington Post,* 8/12/05.

173 During the first: *"Gimme Five."*

174 Whatever the exact: "Tribal Lobbying."

174 The question again: *"Gimme Five."*

174 The same bank: Ibid.

174 "You are a": Here to chapter end, "Tribal Lobbying."

Chapter Twelve: Master of the House

176 That did not: Details on benefits provided by the act can be found at the U.S. Department of Health and Human Services Web site, www.medicare .gov/MPDPF.

177 On the one: "Notes to Consolidated Financial Statements," *2005 Annual Report*, IBM, 95.

177 After representing south: *Los Angeles Times*, 2/09/04.

178 The day-to-day legislative: See Anna Palmer and Emma Schwartz, "How Much Does Lobbyist Susan Hirschmann Know About Her Former Boss's Business?" *Legal Times*, 4/24/06, hereinafter cited as "Hirschmann."

178 And when the: *New York Times*, 6/28/03; *Washington Post*, 6/28/03; *Los Angeles Times*, 6/28/03; and *Wall Street Journal*, 6/28/03.

179 After the Senate: *New York Times*, 11/23/03; *Washington Post*, 11/23/03; *Los Angeles Times*, 11/23/03; and *Wall Street Journal*, 11/23/03.

179 Even Republicans were: *60 Minutes*, 4/1/07.

179 At 5:50 a.m.: Ibid.

180 The value of: *Hammer Comes Down*.

181 Or consider this: Jeffrey H. Birnbaum, "The Road to Riches Is Called K Street," *Washington Post*, 6/22/05, hereinafter cited as "Road to Riches."

181 Of this, a: "Road to Riches."

181 The *Washington Post*'s: Ibid.

181 The cost of: *Washington Post*, 4/9/07.

181 Robert L. Livingston: "Road to Riches."

182 As newly crowned: "Rep. Barton."

182 The energy bill: Ibid.

182 The *Post* found: Ibid.

182 Not surprisingly, the: Ibid.

182 Like DeLay, Barton: Ibid.

183 A framed motto: Ibid.

Chapter Thirteen: Schiavo Spring

184 On September 21: *Austin American-Statesman*, 9/22/04.

184 The three men: Ibid.

184 A little more: *New York Times*, 10/01/04; and *Washington Post*, 10/01/04.

185 As outlined by: Ibid.

185 Just one week: *New York Times*, 10/7/04; and *Washington Post*, 10/07/04.

185 With rumors of: *New York Times*, 11/18/04; and *Washington Post*, 11/18/04.

185 Nor did the: *Austin American-Statesman*, 3/1/05.

186 The suit had: From here to the break is largely based on Jake Bernstein, "Roadmap to a Scandal: The First TRMPAC-Related Trial Set the Stage for the Criminal Process to Come," *Texas Observer*, 8/26/05, hereinafter cited as "Roadmap to a Scandal."

187 The *New York*: *New York Times*, 3/13/05.

187 There were also: Ibid.

188 Embattled though he: *Washington Post*, 3/16/05.

188 At the same: Ibid.; and *New York Times*, 3/16/05.

189 The Senate hastily: *New York Times*, 3/20/05, 3/21/05.

190 Less than a: *Los Angeles Times*, 3/27/05.

190 By month's end: *Wall Street Journal*, 3/28/05.

191 And still they: *Washington Post*, 3/31/05.

191 On April 10: *Washington Post*, 4/10/05.

191 GOP sources told: Ibid.

191 Even in defeat: *New York Times*, 4/6/05.

192 Even Bill Frist: Ibid.

192 DeLay's hometown newspaper: *Houston Chronicle*, 4/7/05.

192 Craddick, of course: Ibid.

192 Not, it turned: Ibid.

193 The Christian right: Ibid.

193 The *Houston Chronicle*: Ibid.

193 By early April: *New York Times*, 4/8/05; and *Houston Chronicle*, 4/7/05.

193 While the Christian: *Dallas Morning News*, 4/7/05.

194 Meanwhile, TRMPAC's woes: AP dispatch, 4/11/05.

194 This, however, was: *Newsweek*, 4/18/05.

194 On April 12: *Washington Post*, 4/13/05.

194 Jack Abramoff, facing: *Houston Chronicle*, 4/13/05; and "Untangling Stake."

194 Jack has made: *Houston Chronicle*, 4/13/05.

195 Meanwhile the hue: *New York Times*, 4/15/05.

195 That same day: Ibid.

195 Meanwhile, the money: AP dispatch, 4/16/05.

196 It was a: *Washington Post*, 4/19/05.

196 Seriously bad news: *New York Times*, 4/28/05.

196 A story in: Ibid.

197 Less than a: *New York Times*, 5/05/05.

197 Writing in the: *Washington Post*, 5/05/05.

197 A day later: *Washington Post*, 5/6/05.

197 DeLay received a: *New York Times*, 5/06/05.

197 The opening prayer: *Washington Post*, 5/6/05.

197 The $2,000-a-plate evening: *New York Times*, 5/13/05.

197 Among the few: Ibid.

198 Among the other: Ibid.

198 "The message tonight": AP dispatch, 5/13/05; and Lou Dubose, "Follow the Leader: The Right and Its Big Night for Tom DeLay," *Texas Observer,* 5/27/05.

198 Writing in the: Ibid.

198 Bob Perry flew: Ibid.

198 Back in Texas: *Washington Post,* 5/27/05.

198 The news in: *New York Times,* 6/08/05.

Chapter Fourteen: Bush Justice

201 More than six: Joshua Micah Marshall, "Talking Points Memo," www.talkingpointsmemo.com, 2/04/07.

203 The onus for: *New York Times,* 12/06/02; and *Washington Post,* 12/06/02.

204 Small fry with: Sensenbrenner was an heir to the Kimberly-Clark fortune (makers of Kleenex and Kotex, among other products), with an estimated net worth of about $10 million. As luck would have it, Chairman Sensenbrenner won $250,000 in late December 1997 on a lottery ticket purchased at Congressional Liquors on Capitol Hill. See T. R. Goldman, "The Man with the Iron Gavel," *Legal Times,* 5/2/05.

205 Widely loathed and: *New York Times,* 7/11/06.

208 Behind the scenes: *President's Counselor,* 109–10.

209 The principal beneficiary: My discussion of the background and rise of Alberto Gonzales is largely based on Minutaglio's *President's Counselor.*

209 Seeking a way: Ibid., 41, 46, 49–51.

210 With thoughts of: Ibid., 50–51.

210 Quiet and reserved: Ibid., 54–60. The author, while an undergraduate at Rice, took classes with Professor Cuthbertson.

211 When the time: Ibid., 60.

211 Far older than: Ibid., 72–74.

211 Pablo Gonzales's son: Ibid., 75–76.

211 Known almost universally: Ibid.; and *Handbook of Texas.*

212 The client list: *President's Counselor,* 76, 83–84.

213 By the time: Ibid., 92.

213 "Empires of Paper": "Empires of Paper."

213 At V&E, Gonzales: *President's Counselor,* 77.

213 He had also: Ibid., 95, 102–3.

213 The two made: Ibid., 103.

214 It would thus: Ibid.

214 For Miers, the: Ibid., 106, 111.

214 Taking the job: Ibid., 114.

214 Gonzales proved as: Ibid., 132, 152.

215 Gonzales had also: The testimony can be found in *President's Counselor*, 138–39.

215 Under Texas law: *President's Counselor*, 143–44.

215 The particulars were: *First Son*, 99, 102. See also, "Bush Admits Being Caught with Wreath in '66 Prank," *Dallas Morning News*, 9/6/98.

215 A year later: *First Son*, 113; and *President's Counselor*, 144.

216 What made the: *President's Counselor*, 144. See also "Bush Silent on DUI When He Got 1996 Jury Summons," *Atlanta Constitution*, 11/4/00.

216 As Harriet Miers: *President's Counselor*, 145–46.

216 On inauguration eve: Ibid., 190–91.

216 Bowen aside, the: Ibid., 192–94.

217 The team player: Ibid., 242.

217 In the wake: Ibid., 230–31, 237.

218 And because no: Ibid., 234–35, 297–98.

218 John Yoo, the: John Yoo, *War by Other Means: An Insider's Account of the War on Terror* (New York: Atlantic Monthly Press, 2006), 30–31.

219 Called upon to: Frederick Lewis Allen, *Only Yesterday: An Informal History of the 1920's* (New York: Harper & Brothers, 1931), 102.

219 But under: *Theodore Rex*, 90.

Chapter Fifteen: Trouble in Texas

221 Down in Georgia: AP dispatch, 6/18/05.

221 And there was: *New York Times*, 6/21/05.

221 When the Senate: *"Gimme Five"*; and "Tribal Lobbying."

222 Coushatta tribal leaders: "Tribal Lobbying."

222 Among the charges: Ibid.; and *"Gimme Five."*

222 One tribal leader: AP dispatch, 6/22/05.

222 The news out: AP dispatch, 7/07/05.

223 One week later: *Washington Post*, 7/13/05.

223 In reality, Colyandro: *Austin American-Statesman*, 9/08/05.

223 The same day: Ibid. Some of the best reporting on the Ronnie Earle investigations was done by *Austin American-Statesman* reporter Laylan Copelin. See also Jake Bernstein's seminal reporting "Roadmap to a Scandal."

224 The corker, though: Texas Association of Business (TAB), "E-Mail on Indictment," 9/09/05.

225 His task, as: AP dispatch, 9/28/05.

225 When, on September: Ibid.

225 The most blatantly: Ibid.

225 The exact language: Ibid.

225 To hear Congressman: Ibid.

226 The latest Austin: Ibid., and *New York Times*, 9/29/05.

226 Word of this: *New York Times*, 9/29/05.

226 What all this: Ibid.

226 DeLay, Democratic lawyer: Ibid.

227 Conservative senior: Ibid.

227 Ever since *l'affaire*: Ibid.

227 Low profile, but: Ibid.

228 Elected to the: Ibid.

228 As the Associated: AP dispatch, 10/6/05.

228 All you had: Ibid.

228 Well in advance: Ibid.

229 On May 24: Ibid.

229 Nor did the: Ibid.

229 In the words: Ibid.

229 In a September: *New York Times*, 9/29/05.

230 "Even though DeLay": Ibid.

230 The latest *New*: Ibid.

230 "But in the glass": Ibid.

230 Where a couple: *Los Angeles Times*, 9/30/05.

230 Within the DeLay: *New York Times*, 10/2/05.

231 Down in Texas: Ibid.

231 In part this: Ibid.

231 A forceful reminder: *Washington Post*, 10/3/05.

231 In a way: Ibid.

232 Some members of: Ibid.

232 As the authors: Ibid.

233 Six days after: *Washington Post*, 10/05/05.

233 DeLay's lawyers claimed: Ibid.

233 Earle countered, saying: Ibid.

233 And, indeed, based: *Washington Post*, 10/07/05.

233 The *Post* article: Ibid.

233 According to other: Ibid.

234 Back in Washington: *New York Times*, 10/08/05.

234 As the "no": Ibid.

235 This time the: Ibid.

235 But the measure: Ibid.

235 Henry Waxman the: Ibid.

235 The title of: *New York Times*, 10/12/05.

235 DeLay, a senior: Ibid.

235 It was one: AP dispatch, 10/13/05.

235 One week later: *Washington Post,* 10/18/05.

235 DeLay's laywers were: *Washington Post,* 10/22/05.

235 DeLay's attorneys: *Washington Post,* 10/22/05.

236 The same October: Ibid.

236 It was all: *Washington Post,* 11/4/05.

236 Ultimately, the torch: *New York Times,* 11/8/05.

237 If DeLay couldn't: *Washington Post,* 11/6/05.

237 In Washington, DeLay: Ibid.

237 It was at: Ibid.

237 Approached by DeLay's: Ibid.

238 What everyone knew: Ibid.

238 The impasse in: Bloomberg News dispatch, 11/18/05.

238 The event was: Ibid.

238 "Tom DeLay's bid": Reuters dispatch, 1/05/06.

239 Now too, individual: Ibid.

239 Others felt the: Ibid.

239 The handful of: Ibid.

239 The worst news: Ibid.

239 With Blunt and: *Washington Post,* 1/7/05.

240 Besides Blunt and Boehner: Ibid.

240 Eventually, even the: AP dispatch, 1/7/05.

240 In his letter: Ibid.

240 In closing, the: Ibid.

241 The former leader: *Boston Globe,* 2/17/06.

241 Critics had long: Ibid.

241 Language for the: Ibid.

241 "I'm like a": *Houston Chronicle,* 3/5/06.

241 It must have: Ibid.

242 Well, every dime: Ibid.

242 To no one's: *New York Times* and *Washington Post,* both 4/1/06.

242 It was now: *New York Times, Washington Post,* and *Houston Chronicle,* 4/4/06.

242 Though DeLay told: *New York Times,* 4/05/06.

Chapter Sixteen: Casino Jack Sinks

244 On September 21: Julia Robb, "Millions Misspent," *Town Talk,* 9/21/03.

244 Greenberg lawyers representing: "Rise and Fall."

244 The dam burst: Susan Schmidt, "A Jackpot from Indian Gaming Tribes," *Washington Post,* 2/22/04, hereinafter cited as "Jackpot." See also *"Gimme Five."*

245 A week later: Ibid.; and "Rise and Fall."

245 "The committee," Dorgan: *"Gimme Five"*; and "Tribal Lobbying."

245 An AP account: Ibid.

245 Yet even as: "Lobbyist in Full."

245 On August 11: *New York Times* and *Washington Post,* 8/12/05.

246 Anthony Moscatiello, sixty-seven: "Money, Mobsters."

246 Moscatiello, whom authorities: Ibid.

246 Adam Kidan was: Ibid.

246 Abramoff was clearly: *Los Angeles Times,* 9/21/05.

246 In that story: Ibid.

246 As we have: Ibid.

247 Tyco lobbyist Ayoob: Ibid.

247 Flanigan, in a: Ibid.

247 It was a: Anne E. Kornblut, "Name of Rove's Aide Appears in Two Washington Inquiries," *New York Times,* 10/27/05, hereinafter cited as "Rove's Aide."

247 A Filipino-American born: Ibid.

248 Though "published rumors": Ibid.

248 Colleagues, in fact: Ibid.

248 Kornblut asked Grover: Ibid.

248 Come the release: *Abramoff Investigation.*

248 Among the high-ranking: Ibid.

248 From her initial: "Rove's Aide."

249 Needless to say: *Los Angeles Times,* 9/21/05.

249 Himself now under: *New York Times, Washington Post,* and *Los Angeles Times,* 10/09/05.

249 Citing Flanigan's role: Ibid.; and "ACLU Letter to the Senate Judiciary Committee Regarding the Nomination of Timothy Flanigan for Deputy Attorney General," 7/26/05.

249 Among the "torture": "ACLU letter."

250 In doing so: James B. Comey, Acting Attorney General, to Patrick J. Fitzgerald, 12/30/03, available online at U.S. Department of Justice, Office of Special Counsel, www.usdoj.gov/usao.

250 On November 21: *New York Times, Los Angeles Times,* and *Washington Post,* 11/22/05.

250 The headline in: *New York Times,* 11/20/05.

251 For the first: Ibid.; and *Wall Street Journal,* 11/25/05.

251 Writing in the: *New York Times,* 12/02/05.

252 Kornblut carried the: Ibid.

252 Six weeks later: *Washington Post, New York Times,* and *Los Angeles Times,* 1/04/06; and *Newsday,* 12/27/05.

252 A day later: *New York Times,* 1/05/06; and "End of the Affair."

253 On March 29: *New York Times, Los Angeles Times, Washington Post,* and *Miami Herald,* 3/30/06.

253 Two days later: *Washington Post* and *New York Times,* 4/01/06.

253 Later, David Safavian: *New York Times* and *Washington Post,* 9/20/05.

253 The charges stemmed: *Legal Times,* 5/15/06.

254 By the spring: *"Gimme Five."*

254 Unfortunately for the: *"Gimme Five"*; and "Tribal Lobbying."

254 Abramoff had often: "Tribal Lobbying."

254 The story of: *"Gimme Five."*

255 With such as: Susan Schmidt, "Abramoff Cited Aid of Interior Official," *Washington Post,* 8/28/05, hereinafter cited as "Interior Official."

255 Needless to say: "Tribal Lobbying."

255 A monument to: Ibid.

256 Senator McCain put: Ibid.

256 McCain also observed: Ibid.

256 Unbelievable too was: Ibid.

256 In his best: Ibid.

256 But there was: Ibid.

256 DORGAN: "It almost": Ibid.

256 MS. FEDERICI: "But": Ibid.

256 Even from behind: Ibid.

257 On December 2: Ibid.

257 Federici's response: "I'll": Ibid.

257 Not trusting Italia: Ibid.

257 Chris Petras having: Ibid.

257 Griles was by: *"Gimme Five"*; and "Tribal Lobbying."

258 Whether or not: "Tribal Lobbying."

258 Federici's reply: "I": Ibid.

260 "The meeting with": Ibid.

260 Mike Scanlon thought: Ibid.

260 In the Tigua: Ibid.

260 At an open: Ibid.

261 Seated next to: Ibid.

261 To quote from: *Washington Post,* 8/8/06.

261 Alas, it was: *New York Times,* 9/16/06; and *Washington Post,* 9/16/06.

262 Ney also admitted: *Washington Post,* 9/16/06.

262 Less than a: From here to end of bullets, AP dispatch, 9/20/06; and *New York Times* and *Washington Post,* 9/21/06.

263 To read the: *Abramoff Investigation.*

263 The report was: *Washington Post,* 9/29/06.

263 Based on some: Ibid.

263 Most of Team: From here to the end of the chapter, ibid., and *New York Times,* 9/29/06.

Epilogue: Day of Reckoning

265 In Texas, Tom: *New York Times,* 8/7/06.

265 Alas, a slew: Ibid.

266 DeLay's legacy, meanwhile: Ari Berman, "All DeLay's Children," *Nation,* 6/19/06.

266 Among these were: Ibid.

267 Nor did it: *Abramoff Investigation.*

275 And that meant: On Griffin, see Jane Mayer's "Wind on Capitol Hill: Bullets," *New Yorker,* 3/27/07.

277 Alas it did: *Boy Genius,* 39–41, 46–47.

INDEX